LONGSTREET HIGHROAD GUIDE
TO THE
ARIZONA MOUNTAINS & GRAND CANYON

BY STEWART AITCHISON

FOREWORD BY
THE GRAND CANYON TRUST

LONGSTREET
ATLANTA, GEORGIA

Published by
LONGSTREET PRESS, INC.
2140 Newmarket Parkway
Suite 122
Marietta, Georgia 30067

Great efforts have been made to make the information in this book as accurate as possible. However, over time trails are rerouted and signs and landmarks may change. If you find a change has occurred to a trail in the book, please let us know so we can correct future editions. *A word of caution:* Outdoor recreation by its nature is potentially hazardous. All participants in such activities must assume all responsibility for their own actions and safety. The scope of this book does not cover all potential hazards and risks involved in outdoor recreation activities.

Printed by RR Donnelley & Sons, Harrisonburg, VA

1st printing 2000

Library of Congress Catalog Number 00-104188

ISBN: 1-56352-592-5

Book editing, design, and cartography by Lenz Design & Communications, Inc., Decatur, Georgia. www.lenzdesign.org. Online version: www.sherpaguides.com

Composite cover illustration from works by Harry Fenn and Thomas Moran, *Picturesque America,* 1872

Cover design by Richard J. Lenz, Decatur, Georgia

Illustrations by Danny Woodard, Loganville, Georgia

Photographs by Stewart Aitchison

May all your trails be crooked, winding, lonesome, dangerous,
leading to the most amazing view…where something strange
and more beautiful and more full of wonder
than your deepest dreams waits for you.

—Edward Abbey, *Desert Solitaire*, 1968

Contents

Arizona

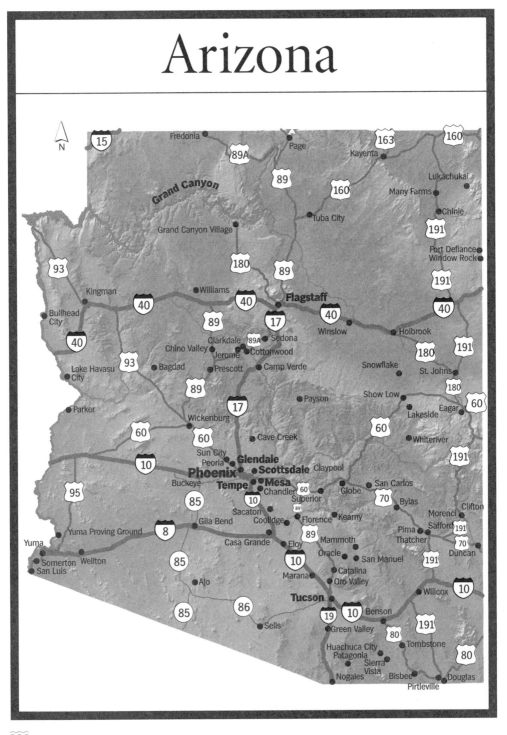

Legend

Amphitheater		Wheelchair Accessible		Special Areas	
Parking		First Aid Station		Town or City	
Telephone		Picnic Shelter		Physiographic Region/ Misc. Boundary	
Information		Horse Trail		Arizona Trail	
Picnicking		Horse Stable		Regular Trail	
Dumping Station		Shower		State Boundary	
Swimming		Biking		70 Interstate	
Fishing		Comfort/Rest Station		522 U.S. Route	
Interpretive Trail		Cross-Country Ski Trail		643 State Highway	
Camping		Snowmobile Trail		SR2010 State Route	
Bathroom		Park Boundary		FR470 Forest Service Road	

How Your Highroad Guide is Organized

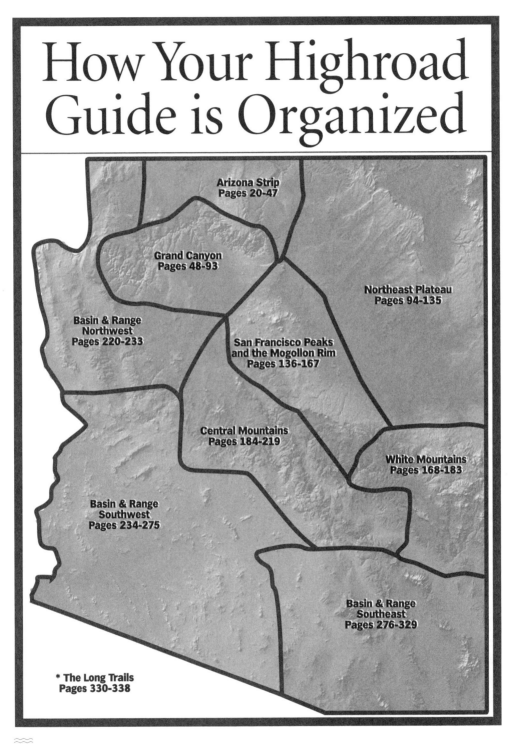

Arizona Strip
Pages 20-47

Grand Canyon
Pages 48-93

Northeast Plateau
Pages 94-135

Basin & Range
Northwest
Pages 220-233

San Francisco Peaks
and the Mogollon Rim
Pages 136-167

Central Mountains
Pages 184-219

White Mountains
Pages 168-183

Basin & Range
Southwest
Pages 234-275

Basin & Range
Southeast
Pages 276-329

* The Long Trails
Pages 330-338

How To Use Your Longstreet Highroad Guide

T he *Longstreet Highroad Guide to Arizona Mountains and Grand Canyon* includes a wealth of detailed information about the best of what Arizona's mountains have to offer, including hiking, camping, scenic driving, biking, and horseback riding. The Longstreet Highroad Guide also presents information on the natural history of Arizona, plus interesting facts about flora and fauna, giving the reader a starting point to learn more about what makes the mountains and deserts so special.

The book is divided into nine major sections based on geographic regions. There are two additional chapters: One at the beginning on the state's natural history, and one at the end on the Arizona Trail, Route 66, and Other Historic Trails.

The maps in the book are keyed by figure numbers and referenced in the text. These maps are intended to help orient both casual and expert mountain enthusiasts. On page VII is a legend to explain symbols used on the maps. Remember that hiking trails frequently change as they fall into disuse or new trails are created. Serious hikers may want to purchase additional maps from the U.S. Geological Service before they set out on a long hike. Sources are listed on the maps.

WARNINGS ABOUT MOUNTAIN AND DESERT TRAVEL

Traveling in the mountains and deserts of Arizona can be hazardous. Extreme temperatures, lack of water, flash floods, and dangerous animals can cause injury or death. Backcountry travelers should be well versed in first aid, carry all necessary supplies (including adequate supplies of water and clothing), and let someone know of your proposed route and return.

Weather conditions can change rapidly and dramatically. During the summer, desert temperatures can exceed 120 degrees Fahrenheit in the shade. In this kind of heat, a person will require about a gallon of water per day while just resting! Obviously, summer hiking should be limited to the higher, cooler elevations. Conversely, wintertime mountain temperatures may dip well below zero. Combined with wind, the chill factor can be extreme. Dress in layers, take plenty of high-energy food, and keep well hydrated.

Ironically, flash floods in the "dry" Arizona deserts are a leading cause of injury and death. Rocky ground, narrow canyons, and sudden cloudbursts can produce frightening and deadly floods. Also, be aware of lightning. Often you are the highest object in the open desert or along a mountain ridge.

For the most part, Arizona's wildlife and plants won't harm the alert traveler. The

Brittlebush (Encelia *sp.) and prickly pear cactus* (Opuntia *sp.) along the Clear Creek Trail in the Grand Canyon National Park.*

larger animals, such as bears, coyotes, and lions, tend to avoid human contact. However, it is still a good idea to practice "clean" camping to prevent attracting animals with food odors. Two animals that can be bothersome, especially in heavily camped areas, are rock squirrels and deer mice. During the day, rock squirrels like to rifle through your food and at night, the mice take over. If you leave food unattended, place it in an animal-proof container and/or hang it out of animals' reach. Always watch where you place your hands and feet and unpleasant encounters with snakes or scorpions are unlikely. Other than cacti and other plants with spines or thorns, there are few species to worry about. Poison ivy does sometimes occur near streams or springs, but usually can be easily avoided.

People recreating in Arizona must assume responsibility for their own actions and safety. The scope of this book does not allow for disclosure of all the potential hazards and risks. Learn as much as possible about the outdoor activities in which you are participating, be prepared for the unexpected, and be cautious. However, should you need to obtain help, call 911 or the local sheriff's office. Using a cell phone for a real emergency is fine, but using one for a minor inconvenience is not looked upon favorably by law enforcement personnel or search and research teams. Remember that carrying a cell phone is no excuse for going into the wilds unprepared. Besides, there are many places in Arizona where a cell phone will not work.

LEAVE NO TRACE

Help keep backcountry areas in their wild state by practicing a Leave No Trace ethic. Here are some suggestions: Travel in small groups; use a camp stove instead of building a fire; pack out all trash; stay on trails or select rocky ground when traveling cross-country; don't cut across switch-backs; to lessen impact, camp at least 200 feet from lakes, streams, meadows, and trails; if possible, use existing campsites; wash away from any water source; and bury human waste in the top 6 to 8 inches of organic soil and carry out used toilet paper. As a backcountry courtesy to others, please keep the noise level down, wear colors that blend in with the environment, give uphill hikers the right-of-way, and keep pets under control.

The collared lizard (Crotaphytus collaris) *frequently basks on boulders and feeds on insects and other lizards.*

For more information, contact The National Leave No Trace Program, phone (800) 332-4100.

Users of Off-Highway Vehicles need to tread lightly and drive responsibly. For more OHV information, contact the OHV Program Coordinator, Arizona State Parks, 1300 West Washington, Phoenix, AZ 85007. Phone (602) 542-4174 or (800) 285-3703. Web site www.pr.state.az.us.

Foreword

This year I spent nearly 30 nights rafting and hiking below the rim of the Grand Canyon. Each time something new was revealed—a shy coral pink rattlesnake on the North Kaibab Trail, Deer Creek flash flooding during a summer monsoon storm, or the full moon rising over the canyon walls.

From the rim, the Grand Canyon often seems unreal and unapproachable. But below the rim, the canyon comes alive. Close up, you can see rocks shifted by unimaginable forces, the river constantly changing its path through sandbars and rock, the impact of wind and sun. When the effects of light and shadow are added, the inner Grand Canyon becomes a teacher.

I think of conservation in this region much in the same way. From a distance, Arizona seems a remote and untouched landscape. Visitors unacquainted with the area sometimes ask what our worry is about. Spend some time here, though, and you will see close up the impacts of human society—air and noise pollution, overgrazed lands, unhealthy forests, trampled stream banks, rivers tamed and diverted. Live here, and you live with the impacts of growth—more traffic jams in our towns and national parks, more noise everywhere, more lights in our nighttime skies.

But these impacts are not inevitable. The Grand Canyon Trust's efforts over the years have proven that we can change the course of our future. With good science, dedication, hard work, and a dash of hope, we have shown that a small group of people, backed by many caring individuals, can bring about lasting conservation solutions. Some of our accomplishments include cleaning up power plants that pollute the air around the Grand Canyon, restricting overflights in our beloved national park, and restoring the ponderosa pine forests around Arizona.

When I am out and about hiking anywhere in Arizona, I like to think of Terry Tempest Williams's poetic line, "The eyes of the future are looking back at us and they are praying for us to see beyond our own time." This is also the Grand Canyon Trust's goal for Arizona—to see beyond our own time and to work for a different future. As we do, we see a land that is still wild and remote with flowing streams and healthy forests, a balance between human and natural communities, and people who live and visit here acting as willing and enthusiastic stewards of this magnificent place. Aitchison's book will guide you to some of Arizona's unique and special landscapes and introduce you to their rich natural and cultural history.

—Geoffrey S. Barnard, President, Grand Canyon Trust, Flagstaff

Preface

I have spent more than 40 wonderful years exploring and learning about Arizona, but writing the *Longstreet Highroad Guide to Arizona & Grand Canyon* has allowed me the luxury of consolidating some of that accumulated knowledge into a single reference work. If I didn't realize it before, I certainly understand now just how vast, diverse, and beautiful my home state is. Forty years' worth of journeys have only scratched the surface of what Arizona has to offer.

This guidebook gives the reader only a taste of Arizona's amazing natural areas and parks. No single volume could possibly include all the trails, all the routes, and all the things to do in the more than 113,909 square miles of Arizona, the sixth largest state in the Union. Things change over time, too. As this book was going to press, President Bill Clinton signed a proclamation creating a new national monument in Arizona, the Ironwood National Monument located about 35 miles northwest of Tucson.

When you explore, please tread lightly on the land. The deserts, woodlands, and forests can be challenging, sometimes-harsh environments, but remember that they are fragile resources and demand our utmost stewardship. Enjoy, but be careful not to destroy. Let these wild places renew your spirit. See you on the trail.

—Stewart Aitchison

A hiker rests on Plateau Point off Bright Angel Trail in Grand Canyon National Park.

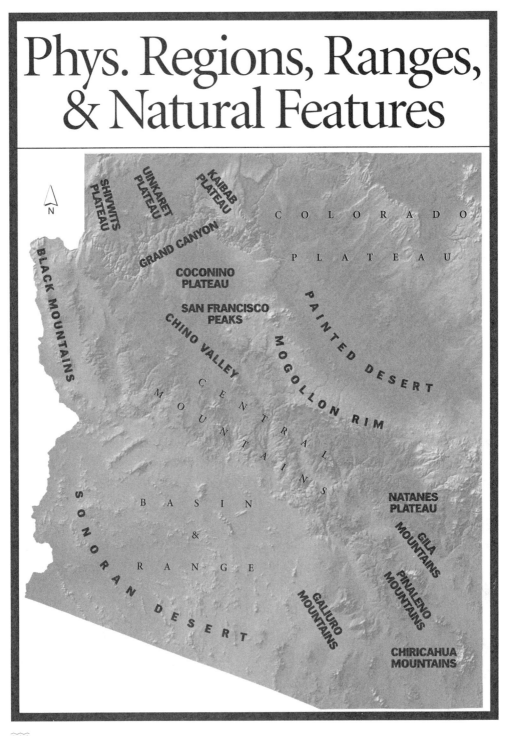

Phys. Regions, Ranges, & Natural Features

Acknowledgments

A reference book like this one is the product of many generous people. Many thanks to Susan Lamb, who was kind enough to bring me to the attention of Marge McDonald, project director for the Highroad Guides series. Pam Holliday, Richard Lenz, and Kara Wiergacz had the onerous task of shaping my manuscript into a readable and useful book. Mapmaker Chip Evans and illustrator Danny Woodard both did a great job. The rest of the folks at Longstreet Press and Lenz Design & Communications deserve the credit for putting all the pieces together. To all of you, my sincerest thanks.

Many government employees gave unselfishly of their time and expertise about the natural areas of Arizona. A few of them are listed here: Tessy Shirakawa, Chief of Interpretation, Petrified Forest National Park; Joyce H. Wright, Business Manager, Arizona Strip Interpretive Association; Rick Best, Chief Interpreter, Navajo National Monument; Joseph Spehar, Apache-Sitgreaves National Forests; Conny J. Frisch, Forest Supervisor, Kaibab National Forest; Charlotte Minor, Kaibab National Forest; John Neeling, Wilderness Ranger, Kaibab National Forest; John Nelson, Recreation Officer, Coconino National Forest; Peter Pilles, Archaeologist, Coconino National Forest; James R. Novy, Fisheries Program Manager, Arizona Game and Fish Department; Devin J. Wanner, Public Affairs Specialist, Prescott National Forest; Dan Merritt, Receptionist, Tonto National Forest; Larry Widner, District Ranger, Globe Ranger District, Tonto National Forest; Tom Bonomo, District Ranger, Verde Ranger District, Prescott National Forest; Frank Holmes, Permit Sales Clerk, San Carlos Apache Tribe; Beverly Blair, Globe Ranger District, Tonto National Forest; David Weir, Information Receptionist, Coronado National Forest; Ron Morfin, Yuma Field Office, BLM; Bruce Asbjorn, Outdoor Recreation Planner, Kingman Field Office, BLM; Michael Ferguson, Deputy State Director, Resources Division, BLM; Ken Mahoney, Arizona BLM Wilderness Program Coordinator; and Jackie Price, Park Ranger, Cibola National Wildlife Refuge. Other kind folks who have given me new insights to Arizona's natural and cultural history include the following: James E. Babbitt, Bill Breed, Wallace Covington, Rose Houk, Margaret Moore, Peter Price, Wayne Ranney, Christa Sadler, Scott Thybony, and Tom Whitham. Thank you to the librarians at the Northern Arizona University Cline Library, the Flagstaff Public Library, and the Museum of Northern Arizona Research Library for their tireless efforts in helping me locate books and references.

And finally, hugs and kisses go to my wife Ann for giving me the freedom and encouragement to write and to my daughter Kate, who is a naturalist-in-training and often shares with me her unique 11-year-old perspective on life.

If there are any remaining factual errors in the text, they are mine alone.

—Stewart Aitchison

Federal & Indian Lands of Arizona

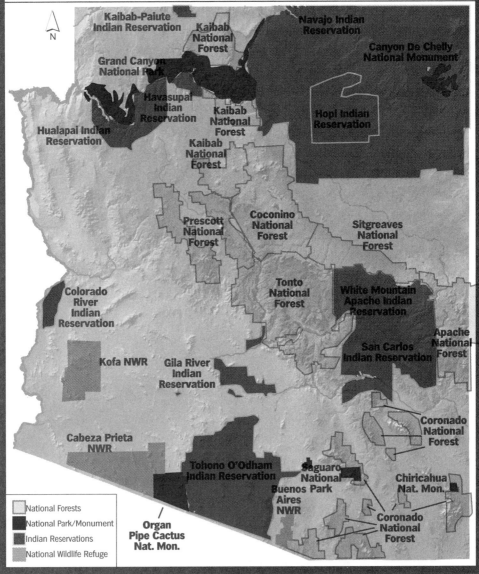

The Natural History of Arizona

The earth's history reaches back about 4.5 billion years. Over a third of that mind-boggling time span is recorded and exposed in the rocks of Arizona. The origin of Arizona's oldest rocks is clouded by the tremendous amount of time that has passed and by changes to the rocks themselves.

Most of the Precambrian rocks started off as igneous or sedimentary layers that through the process of mountain building were metamorphosed into new types. For example, the igneous rock basalt was often changed into the metamorphic rock schist. The sedimentary rock sandstone was sometimes transformed into the metamorphic rock quartzite. During Precambrian time, Arizona's rock layers were pushed and contorted into a huge mountain range, which was then worn down to a broad, flat, sea-level peneplain, except for a few scattered islands. Then thousands of feet of sediments were deposited on top of this surface only to be later broken apart by great

[*Above:* The Chinle Formation is popularly called the Painted Desert]

Geologic Time Scale

Era	System & Period	Series & Epoch	Some Distinctive Features	Years Before Present
CENOZOIC	Quaternary	Recent	Modern man.	11,000
		Pleistocene	Early man; northern glaciation.	1/2 to 2 million
	Tertiary	Pliocene	Large carnivores.	13 + 1 million
		Miocene	First abundant grazing mammals.	25 + 1 million
		Oligocene	Large running mammals.	36 + 2 million
		Eocene	Many modern types of mammals.	58 + 2 million
		Paleocene	First placental mammals.	63 + 2 million
MESOZOIC	Cretaceous		First flowering plants; climax of dinosaurs and ammonites, followed by Cretaceous-Tertiary extinction.	135 + 5 million
	Jurassic		First birds, first mammals dinosaurs and ammonites abundant.	181 + 5 million
	Triassic		First dinosaurs. Abundant cycads and conifers.	230 + 10 million
PALEOZOIC	Permian		Extinction of most kinds of marine animals, including trilobites. Southern glaciation.	280 + 10 million
	Carboniferous	Pennsylvanian	Great coal forests, conifers. First reptiles.	310 + 10 million
		Mississippian	Sharks and amphibians abundant. Large and numerous scale trees and seed ferns.	345 + 10 million
	Devonian		First amphibians; ammonites; fishes abundant.	405 + 10 million
	Silurian		First terrestrial plants and animals.	425 + 10 million
	Ordovician		First fishes; invertebrates dominant.	500 + 10 million
	Cambrian		First abundant record of marine life; trilobites dominant.	600 + 50 million
	Precambrian		Fossils extremely rare, consisting of primitive aquatic plants. Evidence of glaciation. Oldest dated algae, over 2,600 million years; oldest dated meteorites 4,500 million years.	

faulting and tilting to create a second mountain range, which, too, was beveled off by erosion.

The remaining Precambrian rocks, such as schists, gneisses, and granites, are now exposed at the bottom of the Grand Canyon and in many of the canyons and mountains found along a band running northwest-southeast from Lake Mead to the Pinaleño Mountains. One striking Precambrian-aged rock (Mazatzal Quartzite) exposure in central Arizona is Four Peaks at the southern end of the Mazatzal Mountains. Not far to the southeast of Four Peaks, some of Arizona's oldest fossils, blue-green algae called stromatolites, are found in the Precambrian Mescal Limestone, which makes up the canyon walls along the Salt River near Roosevelt Dam. In fact, the dam itself was constructed in part of blocks of this fossiliferous limestone.

During Paleozoic time, from approximately 600 to 240 million years ago, most of Arizona was covered by a series of shallow seas. Again, thousands of vertical feet of sandstone, shale, and limestone accumulated. Marine life was abundant and many organisms were preserved as fossils. At the close of the Paleozoic Era, there was a great extinction of many of these marine creatures that had been so successful for a third of a billion years. Trilobites and most species of brachiopods bid their farewell.

What followed was the rise of the "terrible lizards," the dinosaurs. During the Mesozoic, from 230 to 70 million years ago, Arizona was mostly above sea level. Central and southern Arizona was uplifted into the Mogollon Highlands. Sluggish rivers flowed out of these mountains carrying mud and sand, which were deposited on coastal plains to the northwest and southwest. Dinosaurs and their ancestors lived in this warm, sometimes wet environment. Under the right conditions, their bodies were buried before decomposing and their bones were slowly petrified only to be revealed millions of years later in the Painted Desert. Later, northern Arizona became buried under a series of sandy deserts. The sand dunes would eventually become the sandstones so predominant in the cliffs of present-day northeastern Arizona.

Near the end of the Mesozoic Era and the dramatic extinction of the dinosaurs, another great period of mountain building began. This was the Laramide orogeny, an extensive period of mountain building in western North America, which lasted well into the Cenozoic Era.

The Laramide orogeny in Arizona consisted mostly of major uplifting in southern Arizona followed by extensive eruptions of volcanic rocks. This period of volcanism was followed by intense compression, as a result of tectonic plate movements, directed in a northeast-southwest direction. This compression caused tremendous folding and thrust faulting of the rocks. Then large masses of granitic magma invaded the rocks of southern Arizona. Some of the intrusions are now exposed as the cliffs high on Kitt Peak and in the Santa Catalina Mountains. These Laramide intrusions also were responsible for emplacement of many of Arizona's copper deposits.

As Cenozoic time progressed, the southern Arizona mountains were eroded down and their sediments carried by rivers and streams northward to lakes in Utah and

Merriam's Life Zones

Merriam's life zone concept is an important tool in explaining the geographic distribution of plant and animal communities.

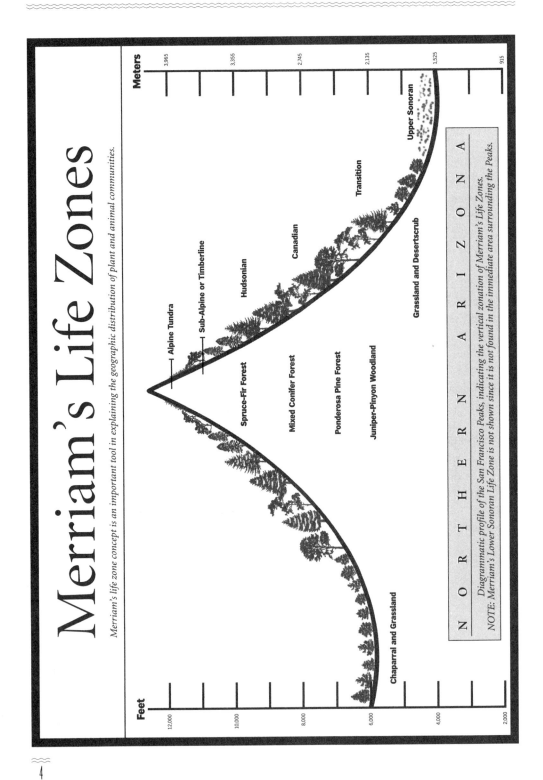

Meters

3,965

3,355

2,745

2,135

1,525

915

Feet

12,000

10,000

8,000

6,000

4,000

2,000

Alpine Tundra

Sub-Alpine or Timberline

Hudsonian

Canadian

Transition

Upper Sonoran

Spruce-Fir Forest

Mixed Conifer Forest

Ponderosa Pine Forest

Juniper-Pinyon Woodland

Grassland and Desertscrub

Chaparral and Grassland

N O R T H E R N   A R I Z O N A

Diagrammatic profile of the San Francisco Peaks, indicating the vertical zonation of Merriam's Life Zones.
NOTE: Merriam's Lower Sonoran Life Zone is not shown since it is not found in the immediate area surrounding the Peaks.

Colorado. In the late Oligocene, intense tectonism began again. Explosive outpourings of ash formed thick beds of tuff, which would eventually make up mountain ranges such as the Chiricahua, Galiuro, and Superstitions.

While all of this activity was going on in central and southern Arizona, the northern part of the state was relatively quiet. The horizontal layers of Paleozoic and Mesozoic sedimentary rock were slowly being uplifted as a unit to become the southern part of the Colorado Plateau. The Colorado River and various tributaries were cutting down into this layer-cake of deposits to create numerous canyons including the Grand Canyon.

Merriam And Life Zones

In 1889, government biologist C. Hart Merriam, his wife, and several scientist friends arrived in Flagstaff ostensibly to study the "scientific...and economic importance...of a region comprehending a diversity of physical and climatic conditions." After spending the summer hiking to the top of the San Francisco Peaks, descending to the bottom of the Grand Canyon, and nearly dying of thirst while crossing the Painted Desert, Merriam returned home to Washington, DC and conceived his Life Zone Theory. Merriam noted that seven distinct plant and animal communities were arranged in horizontal bands, his life zones, according to elevation in northern Arizona. This idea became an important tool in explaining the geographic distribution of plants and animals. He further proposed that temperature was the leading factor in determining which plant or animal could live in a particular life zone.

Although Merriam's Life Zone idea was a gross oversimplification of the real world, and many other environmental factors besides temperature play a role in plant and animal distribution, he is still credited with being one of the first ecologists in North America.

Stretching of the earth's crust to the south and west of the Colorado Plateau resulted in many parallel faults. The blocks of land in between these faults rotated, which formed small mountain ranges with typically one steep side and one less steep. Thus the Basin and Range Country was developing. And between the Colorado Plateau and the Basin and Range Country was an intermediate area of mountains, canyons, and mesas that geologists call the Central Highlands.

Evolution of Arizona's Landscape

As we have seen, Arizona's landscape has not always been as it is today. A myriad of oceans, deserts, swamps, and other environments have come and gone over the millennia. At the same time that Arizona's three major physiographic provinces—the Colorado Plateau, Central Highlands, and Basin and Range Country— were forming,

Microbiotic Crust

A fragile surface crust composed of cyanobacteria (blue-green algae), green algae, diatoms, lichens, fungi, and bacteria covers many desert soils. Mosses and liverworts may also be present. This microbiotic crust, sometimes called cryptogamic (which means hidden) crust, provides a home for protozoa, nematodes, and tiny arthropods. The crust helps bind the friable desert soil together, thus slowing erosion. Since the cyanobacteria are nitrogen fixers, the crust increases the nitrogen supply in the soil. This makes the soil more hospitable to other plants.

Unfortunately, microbiotic crusts are highly vulnerable to crushing by hoofed animals, vehicles, and human trampling. The crushing, even from a single footprint or tire passage, can markedly reduce nitrogen fixation and also open the soil to increased erosion. Recovery may take over 250 years! This is a good reason for staying on established trails and roads.

plant and animal communities were evolving in response to these topographic and environmental changes.

Beginning about 2 million years ago and lasting until about 10,000 years ago, there were ice ages, some major and others minor, separated by periods of warmer temperatures and lesser precipitation. This span of time is called the Pleistocene or Ice Age.

During the Pleistocene, raging rivers and slow-moving mountain glaciers were putting the finishing touches on Arizona's canyons, mesas, and peaks. Large mammals ruled the Southwest. Mammoths, shrub oxen, camels, Harrington's goat, Shasta ground sloth, tapir, and other strange beasts of the Ice Age were dominant. Much of the land was cloaked in forest, woodland, or grassland. Deserts were to come in the future.

Some scientists believe that the ice ages have ended, whereas others argue that we are just experiencing another interglacial period and the glaciers will return again.

Be that as it may, the last 10,000 years or so have witnessed a gradual warming and drying of the American Southwest (although there have been brief fits and starts). As certain plants attempted to retreat to cooler and wetter locations (often mountaintops or shady canyon bottoms), other species could not adapt or move and died out. A few plants were able to adjust to the new conditions and essentially stayed *in situ*. Species that were adapted to arid conditions migrated northward from Mexico into Arizona and deserts were born.

Also about this time, ponderosa pine, today's most common forest tree in Arizona, appears in the American Southwest for the first time. Prior to about 10,000 years ago, Arizona woodlands of pinyon pine and juniper blended into Douglas fir and spruce forest as one climbed to higher elevations. But somehow ponderosa pine began to invade the area, probably from the mountains of northern Mexico, and managed to carve out an ecological niche for itself between the woodland and the other forest communities. Exactly how this happened is still being unraveled by biologists.

As the plant communities evolved so did their resident animal communities. Many of the larger grazing and browsing Ice Age mammals died out because of the changing climate and along with that, the disappearance of some of their plant foods. Once these herds of herbivores began to dwindle so did many of the populations of predators. The demise of these animals may also have been hastened by a new, very efficient hunter on the scene—man. Certain plants and animals became restricted to the banks of the few remaining perennial streams and rivers. In a sense then, Southwestern riparian zones are relictual ice age habitats.

Arizona's Biological Diversity

Arizona's animal and plant life is not abundant, a consequence of the general lack of water. But Arizona does display a remarkable diversity of life—desert to alpine habitats, drifting sand to boggy cienegas, cactus to spruce. This remarkable land supports a surprisingly wide array of fauna and flora. The major habitats—desert, grassland, chaparral, woodland, forest, and tundra—are closely related to elevation (*see* sidebar on Merriam and Life Zones, page 5). For every 1,000 feet in elevation gained there is a corresponding decrease in temperature of 3 to 5 degrees Fahrenheit. Likewise, going up in elevation generally results in greater amounts of precipitation.

The enormity and ruggedness of some of Arizona's topographic features, such as the Grand Canyon, may act as a physical barrier to certain species. For example, rock pocket mice (*Perognathus intermedius*) are found almost exclusively on the south side of the canyon, while their relatives, long-tailed pocket mice (*Perognathus formosus*) are only found on the north side.

Some habitats act as refugia, often harboring plants and animals that are endemic (restricted) to that location. For instance, isolated hanging gardens (formed when a spring issues from a cliff in the desert) may shelter endemic monkeyflowers (*Mimulus* sp.), ferns, or snails. The isolated coniferous forests capping the mountaintops of southeastern Arizona are another example of refugium and a likely place for plants and animals to evolve into endemics. Arizona has more plant endemics than any other state in the U.S.

More than 3,000 species of vascular plants occur in Arizona. Of these, about 68 species belong to the cactus family. Arizona is well known for its giant saguaro (*Carnegiea gigantea*) that may grow to be more than 50 feet tall. Arizona also has far more kinds of cholla (*Opuntia* sp.) than any other state.

Arizona is also home to a staggering multitude of invertebrate species ranging from almost microscopic jumping plant lice (*Psylla* sp.) to lumbering, 4-inch-long, black and orange wasps known as tarantula hawks (*Pepsis* sp.). There is insect endemism here, too: Three kinds of butterflies are found only in the Grand Canyon—pegala satyr (*Cercyonis pegala damei*), Grand Canyon ringlet (*Coenonympha ochracea furcae*), and

Collecting Rocks And Minerals

With so many fascinating rock layers exposed in Arizona, it's easy to become a rock collector. However, there are some rules that must be observed. There is no rock collecting allowed within any national parks or national monuments or on Indian reservations. On national forest and Bureau of Land Management (BLM) land some restricted collecting can be done. Invertebrate fossils, such as clams, snails, ammonites, trilobites, and corals, and plant fossils can be gathered in small amounts for personal use. Vertebrate fossils, including sharks, fish, dinosaurs, turtles, and mammals, may be collected only by scientists and then only after obtaining a permit from the appropriate government agency. The BLM has set aside several areas in Arizona specifically for mineral collectors. Of course, collecting on private land or on mining claims is only allowed with the landowner's permission.

For more information: BLM Arizona State Office, 222 North Central Avenue, Phoenix, AZ 85004. Phone (602) 417-9200.

Grand Canyon swallowtail (*Papilio indra kaibabensis*).

Prior to 1900, there were about 25 kinds of native freshwater fishes inhabiting Arizona's waterways. Today, there are more than four times as many species of fish, mostly as a result of accidental and often intentional introductions. Several of the native species are now extinct because of competition with exotic species, overfishing, and/or loss of appropriate habitat.

Although there is a general paucity of aquatic habitats, Arizona is home to 22 species of amphibians. One is the Sonoran desert toad (*Bufo alvarius*), which is one of the world's largest toads, growing up to 7.5 inches in length. The toad's parotid glands, oval wartlike glands posterior to the eyes, secrete a hallucinogenic substance similar to LSD. The state also boasts 94 species of reptiles, including the striking western banded gecko (*Coleonyx variegatus*). This lizard's pale pink-and-brown-banded smooth skin is translucent, and it is the only Arizona reptile with a voice—a soft squeak.

Only Texas and California surpass Arizona's 434 species of birds. The avifauna of Arizona is a blend of typical Rocky Mountain, Southwest desert, and northern Mexico species. Occasionally eastern North American migrants pass through the southeastern corner of the state. Arizona is also an important wintering area for many birds, such as eagles and hawks, and especially waterfowl, waders, and shorebirds, who spend time along the lower Colorado River valley.

There are more than 135 species of mammals native to Arizona, ranging from the majestic elk (*Cervus elaphus*) to the diminutive water shrew (*Sorex palustris*). Those natives, whose ranges lie totally within Arizona or nearly so, include the gray-collared chipmunk (*Eutamias cinereicollis*), Arizona gray squirrel (*Sciurus arizonensis*), Arizona pocket mouse (*Perognathus amplus*), Arizona cotton rat (*Sigmodon arizonae*), and Stephen's wood rat (*Neotoma stephensi*).

With such faunal diversity it's easy to understand why biologists, birders, and other wildlife enthusiasts are drawn to Arizona.

🌵 DESERTS

The common denominator to all deserts is low precipitation (usually less than 10 inches annually) accompanied by high evaporation. Biologists recognize four major deserts in North America, the Great Basin, Sonoran, Mohave, and Chihuahuan. Arizona contains portions of all four.

ARIZONA GRAY SQUIRREL
(*Sciurus arizonensis*)

The Great Basin desert extends from southeastern Oregon and southern Idaho down through most of Nevada and western Utah and covers much of northern Arizona. It is characterized by fairly high elevation (averaging about 1 mile above sea level), hot summers, very cold winters, and precipitation that falls mostly in the winter. These environmental factors, along with poor soils, result in a habitat consisting mostly of small, hardy shrubs, such as big sagebrush (*Artemesia tridentata*), blackbrush (*Colegyne ramosissima*), four-wing saltbush (*Atriplex canescens*), Mormon tea (*Ephedra* sp.), and snakeweed (*Gutierrezia* sp.). The Great Basin desert is a very tough place for a plant or animal to "make a living."

The Sonoran desert takes in nearly all of Baja California and northwestern Mexico and then extends north into southeastern California and southern and western Arizona. Elevations in this desert range from sea level to about 3,000 feet. Summers are deathly hot, and there is rarely frost in the winter. Precipitation tends to come at two different times of the year: In summer (usually July and August) there are localized, violent thunderstorms, and in winter (roughly November through March) come widespread, gentle rains. Although the total annual amounts are scanty, certain plants are adapted to utilizing moisture from one rainy period or the other. This apparently reduces competition for the small amount of rain and allows more species of plants to exist in this desert than one might expect. Also, the mild winter temperatures allow giant cacti, like the saguaro (*Carnegiea gigantea*), to flourish. In colder climes, the water in the stems of the cacti freezes, expands and breaks the cellular walls, and the plant dies. Thus the Sonoran desert boasts 300 species of cacti. Another group of plants that sets this desert apart from the others is the legume trees. Here you will find mesquite (*Prosopis* sp.), catclaw acacia (*Acacia greggii*), palo verde (*Cercidium* sp.), smoke tree (*Dalea spinosa*), ironwood (*Olneya tesota*), and others.

Centered around the southern tip of Nevada, the Mohave desert extends to the

Ravens In The Sun

The common raven (*Corvus corax*) is one of the most ubiquitous birds in Arizona. But considering their color and the color of most of the larger birds in the desert, doesn't it seem more reasonable that birds out in the hot sun should be light in color, ideally white? Yet ravens are black, turkey vultures (*Cathartes aura*) are dark brown, and most of the desert hawks are dark, too. The answer to this seemingly contradictory situation is that the dark feathers absorb the radiant energy, but the underlying downy feathers insulate the body so that the heat is not transferred to the skin. Conversely in arctic climes, animals are often white, which allows heat to pass more easily to their skin surface, which is usually dark.

west into California and places like Death Valley and to the east into the northeastern corner of Arizona and a little ways up the Grand Canyon. Like the Great Basin desert, the Mohave can experience hard freezes and winter rains. Mostly low shrubs, like creosotebush (*Larrea tridentata*) and saltbush live here although stunning annuals may carpet the ground in wet years. The only common tree is the Joshua tree (*Yucca brevifolia*), a type of yucca.

The Chihuahuan desert lies primarily in north central Mexico with extensions into Texas and New Mexico, but some typical species of this desert, such as creosotebush (*Larrea divaricata*), tarbush (*Flourensia cernua*), and Chihuahuan white thorn (*Acacia constrictor*), also appear in southeastern Arizona. Although the Chihuahuan desert is at about the same latitude as the Sonoran, the Chihuahuan is much colder in the winter because it is at a higher elevation (mostly above 3,500 feet) and not protected from arctic air masses by any barrier. Most of the rain falls in the summer. Vegetation is mostly low shrubs, leaf succulents, and small cacti. Trees are rare.

GRASSLAND

Grasslands were once more extensive in northern and southeastern Arizona. However, by the early 1900s, a combination of overgrazing by livestock, controlling of wildfires, and shifting rainfall patterns ruined the health of many of these grassland areas. Woody, unpalatable species, such as snakeweed, rabbitbrush (*Chrysothamnus* sp.), blackbrush, and sagebrush (*Artemesia* sp.), and introduced grasses, like cheatgrass brome (*Bromus tectorum*), began to replace the tasty native grasses.

Unlikely as it may seem, some of Arizona's grasslands harbor an amphibian, Hammond's spadefoot toad (*Scaphiopus hammondi*). Once the summer rains begin, these toads appear from their underground burrows to find a mate and lay eggs in the temporary rain pools. After breeding and spending some time eating, the adults retreat underground to resume their solitary vigil for the next summer season.

Many species of reptiles can be found in the grasslands including greater earless lizard (*Cophosaurus texanus*), Clark's spiny lizard (*Sceloporus clarki*), Eastern fence lizard (*Sceloporus undulatus*), side-blotched lizard (*Uta stansburiana*), and tree lizard (*Urosaurus ornatus*). While snakes are not very common, there are many different species. Some to be expected are striped whipsnake (*Masticophis taeniatus*), western patchnosed snake (*Salvadora hexalepis*), gopher snake (*Pituophis melanoleucus*), night snake (*Hypsiglena torquata*), western diamondback rattlesnake (*Crotalus atrox*), and blacktail rattlesnake (*Crotalus molossus*).

Because of the lack of trees, most birds only forage in the grasslands and nest elsewhere; only a few are ground nesters. Of the former, the turkey vulture (*Cathartes aura*), red-tailed hawk (*Buteo jamaicensis*), golden eagle (*Aquila chrysaetos*), and common raven (*Corvus corax*) are representative. Ground nesters include Gambel's quail (*Callipepla gambelii*), greater roadrunner (*Geococcyx californianus*), common and lesser nighthawks (*Chordeiles minor* and *C. acutipennis*), and horned lark (*Eremophila alpestris*).

Mammals seen during the day might include antelope jackrabbits (*Lepus alleni*), desert cottontails (*Sylvilagus audubonii*), antelope squirrels (*Ammospermophilus* sp.), and pronghorn (*Antilocarpa americana*). Typical nocturnal grassland species are desert shrews (*Notiosorex crawfordi*), deer mice (*Peromyscus* sp.), coyotes (*Canis latrans*), gray fox (*Urocyon cinereoargenteus*), and spotted skunks (*Spilogale gracilis*).

CHAPARRAL

On steep, rocky slopes of moderate elevation one can often find a mix of fairly large, evergreen shrubs, such as scrub oak (*Quercus turbinella*), silk-tassel bush (*Garrya* sp.), manzanita (*Arctostaphylos* sp.), and mountain mahogany (*Cercocarpus* sp.). Collectively, these shrubs make up a type of habitat called chaparral.

There are no amphibians, reptiles, or mammals that are considered to be restricted or characteristic of the chaparral in Arizona. However, reptile populations can be quite high. The same can be also said about small mammal populations. Rock squirrels (*Spermophilus variegatus*), woodrats (*Neotoma* sp.), and cliff chipmunks (*Eutamias dorsalis*) are common species. The relatively large number of rodents makes for good hunting for predators like the rattlesnake (*Crotalus* sp.). Perhaps surprisingly, the highest densities of black bear (*Ursus americanus*) in the state, as many as one per square mile, occur in the chaparral habitat. The bears prefer these areas because of the dense foliage in which to hide, plus many of the chaparral plants bear edible fruit, nuts, or berries.

A few species of birds show a preference for chaparral. Look for the orange-

COMMON
RAVEN
(*Corvus corax*)

crowned warbler (*Vermivora celata*), MacGillivray's warbler (*Oporornis tolmiei*), Lazuli bunting (*Passerina amoena*), and spotted towhee (*Pipilo maculatus*).

🌿 WOODLANDS

Arizona has a variety of woodlands. Woodlands away from streams and rivers tend to be composed of short-statured, evergreen trees whereas those woodlands along watercourses tend to have considerably taller, mostly deciduous species. In northern Arizona, pinyon pine (*Pinus edulis* and *P. monophylla*) and juniper (*Juniperus* sp.) woodlands cover broad areas and mix at lower elevations with various desert elements. At higher elevations, the pinyon and juniper may intermingle with ponderosa and other forest species.

More than a dozen species of evergreen or live oak grow in Arizona, especially in the southeastern part of the state. The exact number is not definitive since oaks often hybridize, confusing the species nomenclature. Oak woodlands often appear at the edge of or mix with riparian habitats, particularly those found in canyon bottoms. An oak and pine woodland is usually composed of the lone deciduous oak in Arizona, the Gambel oak (*Quercus gambelii*) and ponderosa pine. Other trees may include alligator-bark juniper (*Juniperus deppeana*), Rocky Mountain juniper (*Juniperus scopulorum*), and maple (*Acer* sp.).

Animal life in these dry woodlands is not highly distinctive. Much of the wildlife is species that are also found in adjacent plant communities. Typical birds include band-tailed pigeon (*Columba fasciata*), acorn woodpecker (*Melanerpes formicivorus*), Lewis's woodpecker (*Melanerpes lewis*), ash-throated flycatcher (*Myiarchus cinerascens*), gray flycatcher (*Empidonax wrightii*), western scrub jay (*Aphelocoma californica*), pinyon jay (*Gymnorhinus cyanocephalus*), Scott's oriole (*Icterus parisorum*), juniper titmouse (*Baeolophus griseus*), bushtit (*Psaltriparus minimus*), blue-gray gnatcatcher (*Polioptila caerulea*), and black-throated gray warbler (*Dendroica nigrescens*). Although deer, rock squirrels, chipmunks, and wood rats may be common, the only characteristic mammal of the dry woodland is probably the pinyon mouse (*Peromyscus truei*).

Deciduous woodlands are found along the relatively few stream and rivers in Arizona. These riparian zones occur at various elevations and within the other major habitat types, from low desert to alpine forest. Back 10,000 or more years, when the Southwest was wetter and cooler, the trees, shrubs, and other plants of today's riparian zone were not restricted to the banks of rivers and streams.

Some of the riparian species include cottonwood (*Populus* sp.), willow (*Salix* sp.), Arizona black walnut (*Juglans major*), Arizona sycamore (*Platanus wrightii*), and velvet ash (*Fraxinus velutina*).

In terms of wildlife, riparian areas are probably the most important habitats in the Southwest. Biologists estimate that at least 80 percent of all the animals use riparian areas at some stage of their lives. Animals come to the riparian habitat to feed, to mate, to nest, or to simply take a drink. Riparian zones also act as migratory corridors for many birds and some mammals.

As you might expect, most of Arizona's amphibians, along with a few reptiles, are restricted to riparian areas. Some of them are Woodhouse's toad (*Bufo woodhousei*), southwestern toad (*Bufo microscaphus*), tiger salamander (*Ambystoma tigrinum*), canyon treefrog (*Hyla arenicolor*), and leopard frog (*Rana* sp.). The Sonoran mud turtle (*Kinosternon sonoriense*), western garter snake (*Thamnophis elegans*), and narrow-headed garter snake (*Thamnophis rufipunctatus*) also occur near water.

Breeding bird populations along streams may be 10 times or more larger than populations in the adjacent, nonriparian areas. A number of bird species are considered to be riparian obligates. This means that these particular species place more than 90 percent of their nests in riparian vegetation. In Arizona, some of these obligates include yellow warbler (*Dendroica petechia*), Lucy's warbler (*Vermivora luciae*), southwestern willow flycatcher (*Empidonax traillii extimus*), yellow-breasted chat (*Icteria virens*), song sparrow (*Melospiza melodia*), Bell's vireo (*Vireo bellii*), warbling vireo (*Vireo gilvus*), violet-crowned hummingbird (*Amazilia violiceps*), common black-hawk (*Buteogallus anthracinus*), Swainson's thrush (*Catharus ustulatus*), summer tanager (*Piranga rubra*), and Bullock's oriole (*Icterus bullockii*).

Birds that place between 60 and 90 percent of their nests in the riparian areas are designated dependent species. Some of these riparian dependents include Bewick's wren (*Thryomanes bewickii*), elf owl (*Micrathene whitneyi*), ferruginous pygmy-owl (*Glaucidium brasilianum*), Harris's hawk (*Parabuteo unicinctus*), phainopepla (*Phainopepla nitens*), red-faced warbler (*Cardellina rubrifrons*), and white-eared hummingbird (*Hylocharis leucotis*).

The gray fox, striped skunk (*Mephitis mephitis*), raccoon (*Procyon lotor*), coatimundi (*Nasua nasua*), and ringtail (*Bassariscus astutus*) prefer riparian habitats.

BEAVER
(Castor canadensis)

Beaver (*Castor canadensis*) and muskrat (*Ondatra zibethicus*), obviously, are restricted to creeks and rivers. The Arizona gray squirrel (*Sciurus arizonensis*) feeds primarily on the nuts of the Arizona black walnut and the cones of the Arizona cypress (*Cupressus* sp.), two trees pretty much confined to riparian areas. Many species of bats roost nearby and feed on insects hovering above streams.

These critical riparian habitats make up less than 2 percent of the land in the state. Sadly, many of the riparian areas have been severely impacted by livestock grazing, cutting of the native vegetation, dams, and water diversion projects.

⬛ FORESTS

The forests of Arizona can be divided into the relatively dry, open ponderosa pine (*Pinus ponderosa*) forest and the relatively wet, dense montane forest composed of Douglas fir (*Pseudotsuga menziesii*), limber pine (*Pinus flexilis*), spruce (*Picea* sp.), bristlecone pine (*Pinus aristata*), alpine fir (*Abies lasiocarpa*), and aspen (*Populus tremuloides*). Much of Arizona's ponderosa forest is no longer as open as it once was because of the control of wildfires over the last century. In presettlement days (before the 1880s), the ponderosa pine density was about 20 to 150 trees per acre. Today, there are commonly 850 trees per acre and in some places more than 1,200 trees per acre. These dense "dog-hair thickets" are low in wildlife value because the trees are too close together and/or too small for some nesting animals. Additionally, the accumulation of dead pine needles and branches on the forest floor allows wildfires to be hotter and bigger and more damaging to the forest than in the past. In fact, it was frequent, small fires, usually caused by lightning, that had created the open, parklike forests the first pioneers encountered.

The ponderosa pine forest of northern Arizona tends to be almost exclusively

WESTERN TANAGER

(Piranga ludoviciana)
Male western tanagers are bright yellow, with a red head and black on the upper back, wings, and tail. Females are greenish above and yellowish below.

composed of the single tree species. There may be small stands of Gambel oak or an occasional Rocky Mountain juniper or alligator-bark juniper. Moving south in the state, the ponderosa pine forests begin to include more species of trees, such as silver leaf oak (*Quercus hypoleucoides*), madroño (*Arbutus arizonica*), white pine (*Pinus ayacahuite*), and Chihuahua pine (*Pinus chihuahuana*) as well as more shrubs.

ELK
(*Cervus elaphus*)

On the higher, and typically wetter and cooler mountain slopes, Douglas fir, blue and Engelmann spruce (*Picea pungens* and *P. engelmannii*), limber pine, corkbark fir (*Abies lasiocarpa arizonica*), and aspen grow in dense stands. In the highest forests, those approaching timberline, occur alpine fir, bristlecone pine, and dwarf juniper (*Juniperus communis*).

There is one amphibian that could be considered characteristic of Arizona's forests. This is the Arizona treefrog (*Hyla wrightorum*), the official state amphibian. This tiny frog emerges from underground to breed in shallow rainpools that collect after the summer rains begin. After breeding and while the tadpoles are transforming into frogs, the adults climb into the pine trees and feed on insects for a few weeks. Then all the adult frogs, old and new, retreat underground for a long wait until the next summer season.

No reptile is representative of the forests, although Eastern fence lizards (*Sceloporus occidentalis*), short-horned lizards (*Phrynosoma douglassi*), and gopher snakes (*Pituophis melanoleucus*) may be common. However, a number of birds are typical, including the flammulated owl (*Otus flammeolus*), broad-tailed hummingbird (*Selasphorus platycercus*), Williamson's sapsucker (*Sphyrapicus thyroideus*), olive-sided flycatcher (*Contopus cooperi*), Steller's jay (*Cyanocitta stelleri*), mountain chickadee (*Poecile gambelii*), pygmy nuthatch (*Sitta pygmaea*), brown creeper (*Certhia americana*), mountain bluebird (*Siala currucoides*), Townsend's solitaire (*Myadestes townsendi*), yellow-rumped warbler (*Dendroica coronata*), western tanager (*Piranga ludoviciana*), evening grosbeak (*Coccothraustes vespertinus*), pine siskin (*Carduelis pinus*), red crossbill (*Loxia curvirostre*), and dark-eyed junco (*Junco hyemalis*).

The mammals that are somewhat restricted to forest habitats are Merriam's shrew (*Sorex merriami*), golden-mantled ground squirrel (*Spermophilus lateralis*), gray-collared chipmunk (*Eutamias cinereicollis*), Abert's and Kaibab squirrels (*Sciurus aberti aberti* and *S. a. kaibabensis*), red squirrel (*Tamiascirus hudsonicus*), and elk (*Cervus elaphus*).

ALPINE TUNDRA

True alpine tundra exists only on the highest summits of the San Francisco Peaks. In this life zone, the growing season is short, usually lasting only from June to September. About 80 species of alpine tundra plants, including avens (*Geum turbinatum*), sandwort (*Arenaria* sp.), moss campion (*Silene acaulis*), Jacob's ladder (*Polemonium viscosum*), mountain timothy (*Phleum alpinum*), and bladder fern (*Crystopteris fragilis*), are found on the Peaks amid the broken rocks. About a quarter of these species can also be found in the arctic tundra. One plant endemic to the alpine tundra is the San Francisco Peaks groundsel (*Senecio franciscanus*). The water pipit (*Anthus spinoletta*), dwarf shrew (*Sorex nanus*), and deer mouse (*Peromyscus maniculatus*) are the only vertebrates known to breed in the alpine tundra on the Peaks.

The Ancient Ones

Eleven thousand years ago in the remote northeast corner of the Grand Canyon, a Paleo-Indian hunter in search of camels, Harrington's goats, shrub oxen or Shasta ground sloths lost his spear with its diagnostic fluted stone point. At the southeastern end of Arizona, another band of Paleo-Indian hunters had killed a 12-foot-tall mammoth and was butchering it with sharp stone tools along the banks of the San Pedro River. These hunters had also used spears to bring down this large beast. But as hunters, they could not afford to stay long in one place. Their life consisted of constantly searching for game. Archaeologists have discovered only a few of these ancient spear points and stone tools in Arizona and little else to shed light on the lives of the Paleo-Indians.

By 8,000 years ago, as the climate changed, the last of the Pleistocene megafauna were disappearing from Arizona, and the Paleo-Indian culture was evolving into what archaeologists term the Archaic culture. A larger version of the modern bison still roamed the area and apparently was a favorite prey item for these Archaic hunters,

Rock Art And Desert Varnish

The Indians carved or pecked numerous enigmatic petroglyphs into the dark desert varnish that coats some rocks and cliffs. The varnish is a thin, usually less than a millimeter, layer of clay minerals containing oxides of manganese, iron, and trace amounts of more than 30 minor compounds, such as copper and zinc oxides. Amazingly, in some cases the varnish is produced by specialized bacteria, called mixotrophs, that live on the rock surface and derive some of their energy from inorganic manganese. After a rain, the wet rock surface stimulates the proliferation of bacteria, which then secrete an enzyme that helps oxidize manganese and iron from dust that has blown onto the rocks.

who used the atlatl, a spear-throwing device. But other game animals, such as deer, bighorn sheep, squirrels, and rabbits, were also taken. Fishing may have been practiced, too. Additionally, these people were experimenting with various wild plant foods. Grasses, berries, nuts, and roots were harvested.

Antiquities

Remember that local, state, and federal laws protect all historical and archaeological buildings, ruins, artifacts, and other materials. Enjoy these precious resources but take only memories.

One very important plant was the agave or century plant (*Agave* sp.) and its relatives. For years, an agave builds up a store of rich carbohydrates in its base. Then one spring, the plant sends up a tall stalk tipped with flowers. An animal pollinator, either a bird, insect, or bat, carries pollen from one plant to another (fruits containing seeds form) and then the entire plant dies. The people gathered agaves prior to their growing the stalk. The basal leaves were chopped off, leaving the "heart" which resembles a pineapple in size and shape. The hearts would be placed in a stone-lined pit in which a fire had been burning to heat up the rocks. The pit would be filled in with dirt and left for a day or so. The baked hearts would be exhumed and a feast would commence. Any leftovers were smeared on flat rocks and left to dry into something like fruit leather.

About 3,000 years ago, corn arrived in the American Southwest through trade with Indians from Mexico. At first, corn was just a minor supplement to the Archaic culture's diet of wild foods; yet, these hunter-gatherers were slowly becoming farmers.

As farmers, the people spent more time in a particular locale so it made sense to construct some sort of dwelling. The first homes were pit houses and understandably were usually placed near permanent water sources. A hole, one to several feet deep and several yards across, was dug. Poles were planted around the perimeter of the hole to support a roof. The roof and walls were typically made out of more branches and brush and perhaps coated with a plaster of mud and clay. Entrance was gained either through a side opening or through the roof's smoke hole.

Eventually more items were introduced through trade that had profound impacts on their society. The timing of these introductions varied from place to place, but the results were the same. Beans, in the varieties of pinto, lima, and tepary, were added to their corn diet providing a complete array of amino acids for making protein. Pottery making began. This was particularly handy for cooking things like beans. About the same time, the bow and arrow came along. The atlatl was good for large targets but not very efficient when hunting small game. The easily portable bow and arrow was a boon to hunting.

Better foods, more game in the larder, and new ways to prepare them apparently helped in the survival of more people because the prehistoric population began to rapidly increase. By A.D. 600, more and more people were gathering into larger communities. Aboveground stone and mud rooms were built side by side and sometimes stacked on top of each other to form pueblos or villages. Pit houses were used less as living quarters and often for religious purposes. The pit was dug deeper so that the roof would be flush with the ground surface, and a ladder led down through an opening in the roof. Raised platforms, ball courts, and other specialized architectural features appeared as life became more complicated and society more complex.

Life was good in the thirteenth century. Men lived to the ripe old age of 40; women maybe survived to 35 years. These life-spans are short by today's standard but longer than the average life-span in Western Europe at the same time period.

Archaeologists classify the various major farming groups as the Anasazi, Cohonino, Sinagua, Fremont, Mogollon, Salado, and Hohokam. In many ways, they were basically the same people and probably had the same language, with any cultural and material differences being the result of adapting to locale environmental conditions. For example, on the Colorado Plateau most practiced dry-farming, that is, waiting and praying for nature to rain on their fields. In central Arizona, the farmers dug elaborate canals to carry water from the Salt and Gila rivers to irrigate their crops. Some of the modern agricultural canals follow the prehistoric ones.

But the agricultural lifestyle was not going to last. Various factors, among them drought, disease, overuse of the natural resources, and perhaps warfare, combined to force the people to leave or dramatically change their way of life. Some moved east into New Mexico along the Rio Grande and its tributaries; others reverted to a wandering, hunting, and gathering lifestyle. By A.D. 1450, many of these distinctive cultures—the Anasazi, Cohonino, Sinagua, Fremont, Mogollon, Salado, and Hohokam—had vanished from Arizona.

About this same time, and perhaps earlier, other Native Americans invaded the Southwest. Ute, Paiute, Apache, and Navajo people appeared from the north. Today, 25 different Indian tribes are officially recognized in Arizona.

Arizona's historic period begins in 1539 with Estévan, a Moorish slave, who was with the Spaniard Fray Marcos de Niza exploring north toward the American Southwest. Estévan had gone ahead of the padre, perhaps traversing part of Arizona, and sent back word of the discovery of "seven very great cities." Unfortunately, the cities' residents killed Estévan. Upon learning of this tragedy, Niza retreated back to Mexico. Niza's report of cities containing unbelievable riches spurred Francisco Vásquez de Coronado to mount an expedition the next year to find and conquer the Seven Cities of Cíbola. The expedition traveled through eastern Arizona and then into New Mexico.

The Spaniards were disappointed to discover that legendary Cíbola was in reality the stone and mud pueblos of Zuni (in New Mexico). However, some of Coronado's men, led by García López de Cárdenas, are credited with being the first Europeans to see the Grand Canyon. Not long after this foray came Spanish padres seeking Indian souls instead of gold. Some Native Americans fared better than others under the Spanish invasion, but all Indians suffered from the introduction of European diseases. The Spanish occupation of Arizona was sporadic and ended in 1821, when the land came under Mexico's rule.

By the 1820s, American fur trappers such as James Ohio Pattie, Jedediah Smith,

Bill Williams, Pauline Weaver, and Kit Carson were exploring along Arizona's streams and rivers even though the land was not yet part of the United States. Arizona was of little importance in the Mexican War of 1847-48, which was ignited by American desire for Texas and California. The Treaty of Guadalupe Hidalgo ceded to the United States not only those two states, but everything in between and north of the Gila River. Almost immediately, prospectors, ranchers, and settlers were arriving in the Southwest in record numbers and displacing the original residents—the Native Americans. The land south of the Gila was added by the $10 million Gadsden Purchase of 1853. Arizona was granted separate territorial status from New Mexico in 1863, and the next year Prescott was selected as its capital.

Control of the Indians, especially the Apache and Navajo, was the new territory's most pressing problem. Creation of Arizona's 20 reservations proceeded sporadically and haphazardly over 119 years. The first was the Gila River Reservation, established in 1859. The last was the Pascua Yaqui Reservation, established in 1978. The reservations range in size from the enormous Navajo Nation, which covers nearly 16 million acres and is the largest in the United States, to the tiny Tonto Apache Reservation, which occupies about 85 acres south of Payson.

Also in the late 1800s, copper, gold, and silver were discovered. Farmers were attracted to river valleys, such as the Salt, Gila, and San Pedro. Ranchers brought in livestock by the thousands. Loggers cut trees with abandon in the high forests. With the surrender of the great Apache war leader Geronimo in 1886, settlement of the territory surged forward. Three years later, the growing farming community of Phoenix wrested the capital from Prescott.

The natural resources of Arizona were being threatened by unbridled development. To help control some of this overuse, the first forest reserve was created on the North Rim of the Grand Canyon in 1893. The San Francisco, Black Mesa, and Prescott reserves followed it five years later. Theodore Roosevelt issued presidential proclamations setting aside numerous other stretches of timber in central and southern Arizona. In 1908 those reserves were consolidated into national forests encompassing more than 13 million acres.

Roosevelt also established several of Arizona's national monuments, including Petrified Forest (1906), Montezuma Castle (1906), Tonto (1907), Grand Canyon (1908), and Tumacacori (1908). In contrast to the national forests, most of the early monuments were designed to protect cultural resources, particularly archaeological sites. That process began in 1892, when Congress allocated 480 acres for the preservation of the ruins of Casa Grande.

On Valentine's Day, 1912, President William Taft signed a bill making Arizona the nation's 48th state. Today, 44 percent of the state is still under federal jurisdiction, about 27 percent is Indian reservation land, about 13.5 percent is state land, and only 15.5 percent is in private ownership. The struggle over management of Arizona's remaining wild areas and natural resources continues.

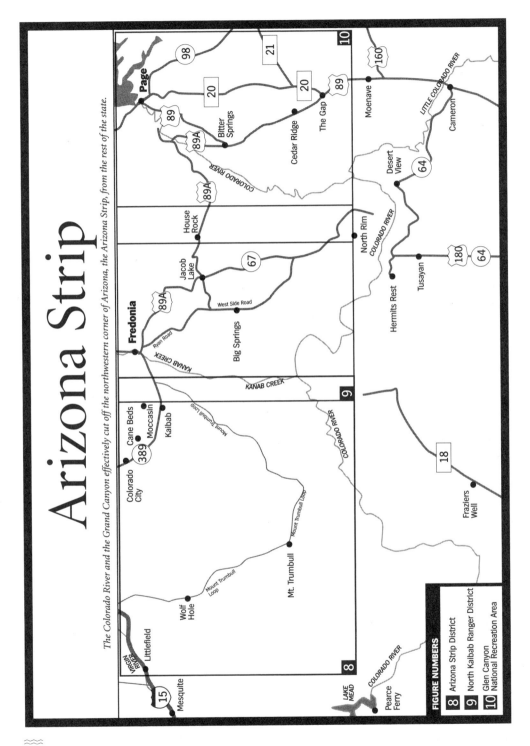

Arizona Strip

The Colorado River and the Grand Canyon effectively cut off the northwestern corner of Arizona, the Arizona Strip, from the rest of the state.

FIGURE NUMBERS

8 Arizona Strip District
9 North Kalbab Ranger District
10 Glen Canyon National Recreation Area

Arizona Strip

The Colorado River and the Grand Canyon effectively cut off the northwest corner of Arizona from the rest of the state. This is the Arizona Strip country, an area politically connected to Arizona but geographically and historically more a part of Utah. Back in 1911 when Utah was trying to acquire the Strip, poet, travel writer, and Arizona historian Sharlot Hall, along with Flagstaff guide Allen Doyle, set out on a daring (for a woman of that time) two-month journey to explore the Strip, record its natural resources, talk to its residents, and chronicle its history. Upon her return, Hall wrote a series of articles asserting the importance of retaining the Strip as an attribute of Arizona.

The Arizona Strip can be broken into six major subdivisions—the Marble Platform, the Kaibab, Kanab, Uinkaret, and Shivwits plateaus along with some Basin and Range country. Going east to west, the relatively flat desert of the Marble Platform

[*Above:* Glen Canyon Dam spans the Colorado River and is 710 feet high]

Arizona Strip District

Only a few small towns and scattered ranches exist on the vast, 11,000-square-mile Arizona Strip, an area about the size of Massachusetts.

Ref: DeLorme Arizona
Atlas and Gazetteer

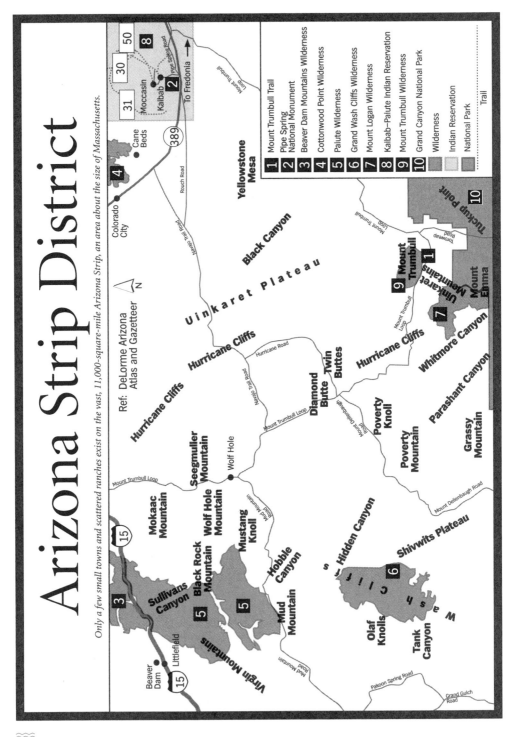

1 Mount Trumbull Trail
2 Pipe Spring National Monument
3 Beaver Dam Mountains Wilderness
4 Cottonwood Point Wilderness
5 Palute Wilderness
6 Grand Wash Cliffs Wilderness
7 Mount Logan Wilderness
8 Kaibab–Paiute Indian Reservation
9 Mount Trumbull Wilderness
10 Grand Canyon National Park

Wilderness
Indian Reservation
National Park

Trail

rises like a cresting wave to become the high, forested Kaibab Plateau. Continuing west, the land drops back into arid country in a series of dramatic steps to form the Kanab, Uinkaret, and Shivwits plateaus. The west side of the Shivwits, the Grand Wash Cliffs, marks the edge of the physiographic Colorado Plateau and gives way to the lower deserts and corrugated mountains of the Basin and Range country. The sedimentary rocks making up these plateaus and mountains are basically the same ones exposed in the walls of the Grand Canyon. Capping some of these rocks are thick layers of volcanic basalt (*see* Natural History, page 1, for more about the geology).

Only a few small towns and scattered ranches exist on the vast, 11,000-square-mile Arizona Strip, an area about the size of Massachusetts. Colorado City, famous or perhaps notorious, as a community of polygamists; Moccasin and Kaibab on the Kaibab Paiute Reservation; Fredonia, a quiet, friendly ranching outpost and, with about 1,300 residents, the largest town on the Strip; and Littlefield, a farming community along I-15. Marble Canyon, Lees Ferry Lodge, Cliff Dwellers Lodge, and Jacob Lake are all too small to qualify as villages but do offer lodging, meals, fishing supplies, and a few basic services in incredibly scenic surroundings. Colorado City has recently become more tourist-oriented, especially since archaeologists have an ongoing excavation of a prehistoric site in the middle of town; call the town office at (520) 875-2646 for information.

The Virgin River Canyon, the Virgin Mountains, and the Beaver Dam Mountains along I-15 are all outstanding features of the Arizona Strip but are geologically part of the Basin and Range country and dealt with in the Basin and Range Northwest chapter.

Arizona Strip District

[Fig. 8] With the exception of the Kaibab Plateau, the Bureau of Land Management (BLM) manages most of the Arizona Strip. Many of the outstanding natural areas were designated wilderness areas in 1984. On January 11, 2000, President Bill Clinton signed a proclamation protecting over 1 million acres of the wild and scenic Shivwits Plateau as the Grand Canyon-Parashant National Monument. This new monument is adjacent to the northwest boundary of Grand Canyon National Park and incorporates the Mount Trumbull, Mount Logan, and Grand Wash Cliffs wilderness areas as well as a portion of the Paiute Wilderness (*see* page 23). Exploring most of the Arizona Strip requires a high-clearance vehicle, preferably four-wheel-drive, with plenty of fuel and a complete camping outfit including water, food, tools, and first aid kit. Leave an itinerary and date of return with someone reliable. Some of the roads on the Strip can be difficult at best to very hazardous and perhaps totally impassible to any kind of vehicle. Please leave gates as you find them, and keep motorized vehicles (including all-terrain vehicles [ATVs] and motorcycles) on existing roads.

For more information: Bureau of Land Management, Interagency Information Office, 345 E. Riverside Drive, St. George, UT 84790. Phone (435) 688-3246. Web site www.azstrip.az.blm.gov or www.az.blm.gov/parashant.

COTTONWOOD POINT WILDERNESS

[Fig. 8(4)] The Cottonwood Point Wilderness consists of 6,860 acres of thousand-foot-high multicolored sandstone cliffs, pinyon (*Pinus edulis*)-juniper (*Juniperus* sp.) woodland, and a canyon containing a hidden oasis of Fremont cottonwood (*Populus fremontii*), willow (*Salix* sp.), and oak (*Quercus* sp.) trees. The cliffs are composed mostly of Navajo Sandstone and are part of the Vermilion Cliffs that cut across northern Arizona. This wilderness area is an extension of the Canaan Mountain Wilderness Study Area in southern Utah.

There are no established trails, but experienced hikers may enjoy hiking along the base of the cliffs into Cottonwood Canyon. The easiest access is from Colorado City. Start at the town cemetery and walk east along an old road for about 0.25 mile to reach the cliffs. Be sure to carry plenty of water. Keep an eye out for mule deer (*Odocoileus hemionus*), coyotes (*Canis latrans*), and mountain lion (*Felis concolor*) tracks. Catching thermals along the cliffs may be golden eagles (*Aquila chrysaetos*) and other raptors.

Directions: This trailless wilderness is located immediately east of Colorado City.
Activities: Hiking, horseback riding, camping, nature study, hunting.
Facilities: None.
Dates: Open year-round.

COYOTE
(*Canis latrans*)

Fees: None.

Closest town: Colorado City.

For more information: Bureau of Land Management, Interagency Information Office, 345 E. Riverside Drive, St. George, UT 84790. Phone (435) 688-3246.

MOUNT TRUMBULL WILDERNESS

[Fig. 8(9)] Because of its remoteness, the 7,880-acre Mount Trumbull Wilderness, now part of the new Grand Canyon-Parashant National Monument, is rarely visited except by a few deer or turkey hunters. But a hike to the top of Mount Trumbull, at 8,028 feet, the highest peak of the Uinkarets (Paiute for "place of the pines"), rewards one with amazing 100-mile vistas in all directions.

The Uinkarets is a small range of geologically young (no older than 5 million years) volcanic mountains that form the western edge of the Toroweap Valley. Trumbull is a shield volcano, a broad, low, shield-shaped igneous feature built up from a series of basaltic lava flows.

On the higher slopes, pinyon-juniper woodland is replaced by ponderosa pine (*Pinus ponderosa*), scattered Gambel oak (*Quercus gambelii*), and a few small stands of quaking aspens (*Populus tremuloides*). The few shrubs are manzanita (*Arctostaphylos* sp.), mountain mahogany (*Cercocarpus* sp.), and cliffrose (*Cowania mexicana*). In the 1970s, the Arizona Game and Fish Department released 25 rare Kaibab squirrels (*Sciurus aberti kaibabensis*) near Nixon Spring. Today both Trumbull and Mount Logan have populations of these tassel-eared squirrels. Turkeys (*Meleagris gallopavo*) have also been introduced. Native mammals include mule deer (*Odocoileus hemionus*), coyotes (*Canis latrans*), and black-tailed jackrabbits (*Lepus californicus*).

Nineteenth century explorer and geologist John Wesley Powell named Mount Trumbull for a Connecticut senator. Powell, who was the first to successfully boat the Colorado River through the Grand Canyon in 1869, often named geographic features after influential friends and potential political allies.

At the base of the mountain is the site of a steam-powered sawmill built by Mormons in 1870. The mill provided pine timbers for the construction of the Mormon Temple in St. George, Utah. Wagons pulled by oxen carried the timbers over 80 miles of rough road. The wagon wheel ruts are still visible in places, and the wagon road, the Temple Trail, is marked with BLM signs.

Directions: Drive west from Fredonia on AZ 389 approximately 8 miles and turn left (south) onto the gravel Mount Trumbull Road, County Road 109. Follow it about 46 miles then turn right onto CR 5 and go another 7 miles to the BLM Nixon Guard Station (a work station and crew quarters) opposite the signed Mount Trumbull trailhead, the only trail within the wilderness.

Activities: Hiking, horseback riding, camping, nature study, hunting.

Facilities: None.

Dates: Open year-round although wet weather can make the gravel road impassable.

Fees: None.

Closest town: Fredonia, about 60 miles.

For more information: Bureau of Land Management, Interagency Information Office, 345 E. Riverside Drive, St. George, UT 84790. Phone (435) 688-3246.

MOUNT TRUMBULL TRAIL

[Fig. 8(1)] The trail climbs through ponderosa pine forest to the summit and impressive vistas of the Arizona Strip country, the western Grand Canyon, and beyond.

Trail: 2.7 miles one-way; last mile is cross-country but well marked with rock cairns.

Degree of difficulty: Moderate.

Elevation: 6,500 to 8,028 feet.

Surface: Rocky.

MOUNT LOGAN WILDERNESS

[Fig. 8(7)] Mount Logan is another peak of the Uinkaret range and probably receives less hiker visitation than even Mount Trumbull. Like Mount Trumbull, Powell named Logan for an eastern senator. The wilderness, now within the Grand Canyon-Parashant National Monument, covers 14,650 acres of extremely rugged volcanic country dotted with small stands of pine.

Depending on the type of vehicle being driven, the trail to the summit can be as short as 0.5 mile. A poor dirt road goes south from Mount Trumbull for several miles and then skirts the eastern edge of the Mount Logan Wilderness area almost to the top of the mountain. The view from the 7,866-foot summit ridge down into the fiery red amphitheater called Hells Hole is breathtaking. The colorful rocks are mostly the Moenkopi and Chinle formations, Mesozoic sedimentary layers that underlie the younger volcanic rocks.

TIGER SALAMANDER (Ambystoma tigrinum)

Directions: Drive west from Fredonia on AZ 389 approximately 8 miles and turn left (south) onto the gravel Mount Trumbull Road, County Road 109. Follow it about 46 miles then turn right onto CR 5 and go another 7 miles to the Nixon Guard Station. Turn left (south) onto BLM Road 1044 and drive about 4 miles to a major fork. The right fork skirts the wilderness area.

Activities: Hiking, horseback

riding, camping, nature study, hunting.

Facilities: None.

Dates: Open year-round but road may be impassable during wet weather.

Fees: None.

Closest town: Fredonia, about 65 miles.

For more information: Bureau of Land Management, Interagency Information Office, 345 E. Riverside Drive, St. George, UT 84790. Phone (435) 688-3246.

GRAND WASH CLIFFS WILDERNESS AND THE SHIVWITS PLATEAU

[Fig. 8(6)] The 36,300-acre Grand Wash Cliffs Wilderness, now part of the Grand Canyon-Parashant National Monument, encompasses a 12-mile section of the Grand Wash Cliffs. The cliffs are part of the western edge of the Colorado Plateau and extend from almost the Utah/Arizona state line south across the Colorado River (where they form the "mouth" of the Grand Canyon) toward old historic Route 66. The Paleozoic sedimentary cliffs are in two sets, an upper and lower escarpment, separated by the relatively flat Grand Gulch Bench. The lower cliffs drop 1,600 feet to the Mohave Desert floor dotted with Joshua trees (*Yucca brevifolia*) and are dissected by deep, narrow canyons. Here desert bighorn sheep (*Ovis canadensis*), desert tortoise (*Gopherus agassizi*), and the Gila monster (*Heloderma suspectum*) live. The upper cliffs soar 1,800 above Grand Gulch Bench and support pinyon-juniper woodland where mule deer and coyotes roam.

Directions: In a high clearance, preferably four-wheel-drive, vehicle go from St. George, UT on Bureau of Land Management Road (BLM) 1069 south to Wolf Hole then take BLM 1004 west to County Road (CR) 101 and travel south for about 15 miles to BLM 1007. Travel south on BLM 1007 to BLM 1003. Take BLM 1003 east about 6 miles until a faint track to the right is seen. Follow this track about 0.5 mile to where a cable blocks further driving. It's possible to walk along old road for about

Neotenic Salamanders

Arizona's only species of salamander is the tiger (*Ambystoma tigrinum*). It has a remarkably wide distribution, ranging from desert to boreal forest. Like other amphibians, it normally lays eggs in a pool of water, and they hatch into swimming larvae. Gradually the larvae transform into adult salamanders. However, in and around the small ponds located on the Kaibab Plateau, few adult tiger salamanders can be found. Yet, there are plenty of immature larval forms (neotenic) swimming in the water. Where did they come from? At high elevations, where temperatures are low and the growing season short, the tiger salamanders rarely change into the true adult form. Miraculously, the neotenics may retain gills and other juvenile characteristics yet can become breeders and lay eggs.

There is one other odd fact about these salamanders: Some are born as broad-headed cannibals and the rest are narrow-headed herbivores. Biologists are still trying to figure out this strange phenomenon.

12 miles to the southern boundary of the wilderness. Experienced, adventurous hikers can explore cross-country. Carry plenty of water and a copy of the BLM's Arizona Strip District Visitor Map.

Activities: Hiking, camping, nature study, and hunting.

Facilities: None.

Dates: Open year-round.

Fees: None.

Closest town: St. George, UT about 50 miles.

For more information: Bureau of Land Management, Interagency Information Office, 345 E. Riverside Drive, St. George, UT 84790. Phone (435) 688-3246.

PARIA CANYON-VERMILION CLIFFS WILDERNESS

[Fig. 9(13)] The 110,000-acre Paria Canyon-Vermilion Cliffs Wilderness straddles the Arizona/Utah state line. The wilderness area consists of two parts—Paria Canyon, which is a popular, 38-mile backpacking trip, and the Vermilion Cliffs, which are easily viewed from Highway 89A and are now home to reintroduced California condors (*Gymnogyps californianus*). The BLM is recommending that the Paria River be designated as a National Wild and Scenic River. Additionally, the confluence of the Paria and Colorado rivers is critical habitat for the endangered razorback sucker (*Xyrauchen texanus*) and humpback chub (*Gila cypha*). Now that the Colorado River below Glen Canyon Dam is cold and clear, the eggs of these two native species need the relatively warmer waters of the Paria River to develop.

Directions: To reach the head of the Paria Canyon drive either 40 miles east from Kanab, UT on US 89 or 30 miles west of Page on US 89.

Activities: Hiking, camping, and nature study.

Facilities: White House Campground, information center.

Dates: Open year-round, however canyon bottoms are susceptible to flash flooding.

Fees: Hiking fee.

Closest town: Page, about 30 miles.

For more information: Bureau of Land Management, Kanab Field Office, 318 North 100 East, Kanab, UT 84741. Phone (435) 644-2672. Web site paria.az.blm.gov.

PARIA CANYON BACKPACK

One of the premier canyon hikes in the entire Southwest is the four- to six-day backpack through Paria Canyon. Only downstream hiking is permitted to make sure hikers are through the narrowest part of the canyon (i.e., the section most susceptible to flash flooding) before the weather can change. Reservations and permits are required for overnight hiking.

Paria Canyon was visited at least 700 years ago when Pueblo Indians used the canyon as an access route between southern Utah and northern Arizona. Crops of corn, beans, and squash were planted in the lower end of the canyon. The Indians hunted the plentiful mule deer and desert bighorn sheep. At the mouth of Wrather

Canyon is a small rock overhang, which contains evidence that it was used as an ancient campsite. Petroglyphs are scattered throughout the canyon.

In November 1776, Franciscan padres named Atanasio Domínguez and Silvestre Vélez de Escalante were struggling to return to Santa Fe, New Mexico, after an aborted attempt to reach Monterey, California. They became the first whites to encounter the mouth of Paria Canyon as they threaded their way along the base of the Vermilion Cliffs to the Colorado River at the head of the Grand Canyon (Lees Ferry). After having two men swim across the icy river and back, they decided it was too dangerous for the entire party to cross there. Surrounded by the high Vermilion Cliffs, the padres appropriately named their camp *Salsipuedes*—"get out if you can!" After a week of exploration, a treacherous route up and over the cliffs was found in Paria Canyon. While traveling north, they survived on cactus pads, berries, and horse meat until they found an old Indian trail that took them back down to the Colorado. The route led between Tower and Boundary buttes, where the river was wide and shallow and negotiable on horseback. This ford became known as the Crossing of the Fathers but is now under the waters of Lake Powell. The padres' ordeal is compellingly told in their own words in *The Domínguez-Escalante Journal: Their Expedition through Colorado, Utah, Arizona and New Mexico in 1776*, edited by Ted Warner.

Almost 100 years later, canyon explorer John Wesley Powell floated past the mouth of the Paria River while on his first descent of the Colorado River. The next year, 1870, Mormon missionary Jacob Hamblin, on his way to the Hopi Mesas, crossed the Colorado near the mouth of the Paria River and noted that this might be a good ferry location. Two years later John D. Lee started his ferry service here.

Since the 1950s discovery of Wrather Arch, one of the Southwest's largest natural stone arches in a side canyon to the Paria Canyon, there has been a steady increase in recreational use of the area. In 1969 Paria Canyon Primitive Area was established and 15 years later, Congress designated it wilderness. The popularity of this hike has forced the BLM to initiate a reservation system. The best detailed hiking guide is Michael Kelsey's *Hiking and Exploring the Paria River*.

The massive sandstone walls of Paria Canyon were deposited from 200 to 60 million years ago when dinosaurs ruled the earth. The region alternated between sea, lake, and desert conditions. About 40 million years ago, the area began to rise; and slow, meandering streams drained the uplands. As the stream gradient increased so did downward cutting; the streams became entrenched in deep, narrow canyons.

From the trailhead to just below Wrather Canyon, the walls are composed mostly of Navajo Sandstone, a wind-blown dune deposit. Over the next 5 miles or so, the Kayenta Formation, a series of thin-bedded sandstones, shales, and limestones, and the underlying Moenave Sandstone appear. Nearing the mouth of the Paria, the colorful clays and shales of the Chinle Formation emerge. Uranium is found in the Chinle, and several claims were staked in this area during the 1950s.

The longest and most spectacular tributary to the Paria is Buckskin Gulch. This twisting labyrinth cut into the Navajo Sandstone is less than 2 feet wide in places, yet undulating, sensuous walls rise hundreds of feet. Logs and debris carried by flash floods are wedged between the walls 20, 30, or more feet above the canyon floor. July, August, and September have high flash flood danger due to thunderstorms. However, floods can occur any time of the year. Paria Narrows and Buckskin Gulch are the most dangerous areas. Get a long-range forecast before entering the canyons.

Raccoon (*Procyon lotor*), gray fox (*Urocyon cinereoargenteus*), bobcat (*Felis rufus*), and mule deer call the canyon home. If the number of desert bighorn sheep petroglyphs is any indication, sheep must have been plentiful in prehistoric times. During the late nineteenth century, with the introduction of domestic sheep and over hunting, the native sheep disappeared. Fortunately, in the 1980s bighorn were successfully reintroduced.

Speckled dace (*Rhinichthys osculus*) are the native fish well adapted to living in the silty waters of the Paria River and are of absolutely no interest to the sport fisherman.

Directions: White House is the main trailhead and is reached by going 30 miles northwest of Page on US 89 to the BLM Paria Information Station near milepost 21, just east of the Paria River. From here a dirt road leads south 2 miles to an old homestead where there is a parking and camping area with pit toilets and picnic tables. If the road is chained off to entry, then the canyon is unsafe to hike because of flood danger.

For more information: To view available hiking dates, secure a reservation, and pay fees, contact the Paria Canyon Project Web site paria.az.blm.gov. Or call the Kanab Field Office at (435) 644-2672. Since the trail ends at Lees Ferry, some sort of car shuttle will be necessary. For a list of private shuttle services, contact Bureau of Land Management, Kanab Field Office, 318 North 100 East, Kanab, UT 84741. Phone (435) 644-2672.

Trail: 38 miles one-way; can only be done as a one-way trip.

Degree of difficulty: Moderate.

Elevation: 4,280 feet at White House trailhead to 3,100 feet at Lees Ferry.

Surface: Varies between rocky, sandy, and wading the Paria River.

CONDOR VIEWING AREA

[Fig. 9(1)] Just before US 89A begins to climb out of House Rock Valley onto the Kaibab Plateau and where the Vermilion Cliffs turn to the north, a dirt road takes off to the north. About 2 miles down the dirt road, you come to an interpretive sign and a chance to see condors. This area is one of the focal points of the amazing story of recovery of the California condor (*Gymnogyps californianus*) from the brink of extinction. The endangered California condor is a member of the Cathartidae or New World vulture family. Like other vultures, condors only eat carrion, and their feet lack the strength for grasping or attacking live prey. An adult condor may weigh as much as 22 pounds and have a wingspan of 9.5 feet.

There are only two historic records of the California condor being seen the Grand Canyon region, and one of the two was shot by prospectors at Pierce Ferry near the mouth of the Canyon in March 1881. During late Pleistocene times, condors must have been fairly common as suggested by the large number of bones that have been discovered in caves within the Grand Canyon. But by the early twentieth century, condors were gone from Arizona and barely surviving in California and Baja California.

Unfortunately by 1986, there was only one breeding pair left in the wild anywhere. The birds' demise had been due to the loss of habitat, collecting of eggs, wanton shooting, poisoning, and collisions with power lines. A bold plan was launched to capture the remaining condors and breed them in captivity. Five years later, the first captive-bred condors were released in California's Sespe Condor Refuge. And in 1996 a half dozen birds were released here at the Vermilion Cliffs. This recovery effort is a cooperative project between the U.S. Fish and Wildlife Service, the Arizona Game and Fish Department, the Bureau of Land Management, and The Peregrine Fund. The condors are being raised at the Los Angeles Zoo, the San Diego Wild Animal Park, and The Peregrine Fund's World Center for Birds of Prey in Boise, Idaho.

In November 1998, eight California condors were released in the Hurricane Cliffs area of the Arizona Strip, southeast of St. George, Utah.

About 20 condors now live in northern Arizona and southern Utah. They tend to return to their respective release sites but occasionally fly as far south as the South Rim of the Grand Canyon and have been reported near Grand Junction, Colorado. Researchers hope that breeding in the wild will take place in the next couple of years.

Directions: Drive about 18 miles east of Jacob Lake on US 89A. Turn left (north) onto dirt House Rock Valley Road and continue about 2 miles to signs.

Activities: Hiking, nature study.

Facilities: Interpretive sign.

Dates: Open year-round.

Fees: None.

Closest town: Fredonia, 48 miles.

For more information: Web site www.peregrinefund.org. or www.gf.state.az.us.

HOUSE ROCK BUFFALO RANCH

[Fig. 9(2)] By the end of the nineteenth century, the American bison (popularly called buffalo) was nearing extinction. One person who became concerned was an ex-buffalo hunter by the name of Charles Jesse "Buffalo" Jones. In earlier days, he had taken advantage of the booming market for buffalo hides and meat, but eventually he became angered by the merciless waste and put away his rifle. Jones turned to roping buffalo calves and breeding them in hopes of perpetuating the species. He also had a dream of crossing bison bulls with black Scottish Galloway cows to produce a hybrid with the virtues of each parent, namely silky hair, delicious meat, the capacity to eat tough scrubby range plants, and the ability to cope with harsh weather. In 1906, he

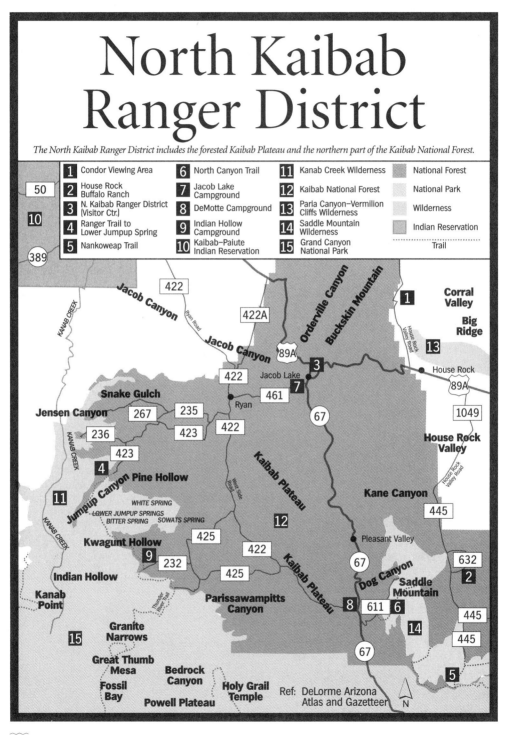

North Kaibab Ranger District

The North Kaibab Ranger District includes the forested Kaibab Plateau and the northern part of the Kaibab National Forest.

1 Condor Viewing Area
2 House Rock Buffalo Ranch
3 N. Kaibab Ranger District (Visitor Ctr.)
4 Ranger Trail to Lower Jumpup Spring
5 Nankoweap Trail
6 North Canyon Trail
7 Jacob Lake Campground
8 DeMotte Campground
9 Indian Hollow Campground
10 Kaibab–Paiute Indian Reservation
11 Kanab Creek Wilderness
12 Kaibab National Forest
13 Paria Canyon–Vermilion Cliffs Wilderness
14 Saddle Mountain Wilderness
15 Grand Canyon National Park

National Forest
National Park
Wilderness
Indian Reservation
Trail

Ref: DeLorme Arizona Atlas and Gazetteer

was granted permission from the federal government to try his experimental breeding within the Grand Canyon Forest Reservation (which later became the Kaibab National Forest).

Problems arose. Only sterile male calves were produced. The persistence of the bison's characteristic large shoulder hump in the fetus made birth difficult or impossible without human assistance. The "cattalo experiments" were deemed a financial failure. The buffalo were eventually sold to the Arizona Game and Fish Department and moved down into House Rock Valley.

The herd is kept at about 100 animals with an annual harvest of 24 to 30 animals. Hunts are held once a year on a lottery basis. One buffalo is allowed per hunter's lifetime. It's considered one of the toughest hunts in the state because of the difficulty in locating the animals. The buffalo range over 60,000 acres of sagebrush and grassland so spotting one is a challenge; you are more likely to see pronghorn and jackrabbits. Only a few poor dirt roads cross the area so cross-country travel is mostly on foot.

Directions: Turn south onto the dirt FS 445 off of US 89A about 20 miles east of Jacob Lake. Go about 19 miles then turn left onto FS 632. The ranch is 2 miles away.

Activities: Nature study and hunting.

Facilities: None.

Dates: Open year-round, but road may be impassable when wet.

Fees: None.

Closest town: Page, about 80 miles.

For more information: Arizona Game and Fish Department, Flagstaff Region II Office, 3500 S. Lake Mary Road, Flagstaff, AZ 86001. Phone (520) 774-5045.

North Kaibab Ranger District (U.S. Forest Service)

[Fig. 9] The North Kaibab Ranger District, which is the northern part of the Kaibab National Forest, includes the forested Kaibab Plateau (*Kaibab* is Paiute for "mountains lying down," which refers to the lack of distinct peaks on this plateau) except for a strip of Park Service land running along part of the north rim of the Grand Canyon. The drive south from Jacob Lake to Grand Canyon National Park, AZ 67, is one of the loveliest national forest drives in the Southwest and has been designated as a National Scenic Byway. The highway winds through old-growth ponderosa pine (*Pinus ponderosa*), past stands of quaking aspens (*Populus tremuloides*), and through mountain meadows sprinkled with wildflowers during the summer and herds of mule deer at dawn and dusk. The record size and numbers of the North Kaibab deer are well known to hunters. Douglas fir (*Pseudotsuga menziesii*), blue

Pothole Life

After a summer rain has filled depressions, or potholes, and the desert sun has heated the water, a myriad of life may appear—spadefoot toads, boatmen beetles, and incongruously, freshwater shrimp. Sometimes there are three species of shrimp—fairy (*Branchinecta* sp.), clam (*Cyzicus* sp.), and tadpole (*Triops* sp.). Amazingly, the eggs of these creatures can endure hot, dry conditions for as long as 25 years, and then if the moisture and temperature conditions become optimal, they hatch. Males are uncommon, and parthenogenesis (cloning) is the more usual mode of reproduction. If all goes well, new eggs are produced before the tiny desert pool evaporates, and the adults desiccate, die, and blow away in the wind.

spruce (*Picea pungens*), and Engelmann spruce (*Picea engelmannii*) crowd the road along its higher reaches. The highway is usually closed by snow from November to mid-May. During the long winter, only snowmobilers and adventuresome cross-country skiers explore the Kaibab.

A segment of the Arizona Trail traverses the length of the Kaibab Plateau and national forest. Details can be found in the chapter on the Arizona Trail.

For more information: North Kaibab Visitor Center, US 89/AZ 67, Jacob Lake, AZ 86022. Phone (520) 643-7298. The center is open only from May through October and has books, maps, postcards, and other items about the area. An excellent resource book available there is the *Recreational Opportunity Guide: North Kaibab Ranger District*. The main office for the North Kaibab Ranger District can be contacted at PO Box 248, Fredonia, AZ 86022. Phone (520) 643-7395. Web site www.fs.fed.us/r3/kai.

KANAB CREEK WILDERNESSES

[Fig. 9(11)] Kanab Canyon is the largest tributary canyon flowing into the Grand Canyon from the north. The lower 10 miles of Kanab are included within Grand Canyon National Park, but many more miles of Kanab and its own tributary canyon system are included in two adjacent wilderness areas. On the west side of Kanab Creek is the BLM-administered Kanab Wilderness (which has only one remote trailhead at Hack Canyon), and on the east side is the U.S. Forest Service-administered Kanab Wilderness (which has six trailheads). The combined wildernesses cover about 68,600 acres.

Kanab Creek and its tributaries have cut a network of deep, vertical-walled gorges into the Kanab and Kaibab plateaus. Within these walls lies a maze of water and wind sculptured fins, knobs, potholes, and other fantastic geologic features. Elevations range from about 2,000 feet to 6,000 feet. The upper reaches serve as a winter range for the Kaibab mule deer herd. The wilderness is also home for nearly the entire state population of chukar (*Alectoris chukar*), an introduced partridge that is native to Turkey and India. Vegetation is varied but sparse except for riparian growth in the creek bottoms where the endangered willow flycatcher (*Empidonax traillii*) may be breeding. This is a splendid area to explore but don't under estimate the difficulty of the terrain. There is very little dependable water and summer temperatures often exceed 100 degrees Fahrenheit. There are numerous trails but many are poorly marked and infrequently maintained. One to try is the Ranger Trail. Also, the Grand Canyon Field Institute offers llama-supported, naturalist-led trips into this wilderness.

Hikers on the Ranger Trail inside Kanab Creek Wilderness.

Directions: To access the eastern side of the wilderness, drive south from Fredonia or west from Jacob Lake to reach FS 422 (Ryan Road; also shown on some maps as FS 22). Depending upon what part of the wilderness you want to access, take the appropriate Forest Service road leading west. High clearance, four-wheel-drive vehicles are recommended.

Activities: Hiking, horseback riding, camping, nature study, deer and chukar hunting.

Facilities: None.

Dates: Open year-round, weather permitting.

Fees: None.

Closest town: Fredonia, 30 miles.

For more information: Bureau of Land Management, Interagency Information Office, 345 E. Riverside Drive, St. George, UT 84790. Phone (435) 688-3246. Or the USFS Visitor Center, US 89/AZ 67, Jacob Lake, AZ 86022. Phone (520) 643-7298. Or the North Kaibab Ranger District, PO Box 248, Fredonia, AZ 86022. Phone (520) 643-7395. Grand Canyon Field Institute at PO Box 399, Grand Canyon, AZ 86023; phone: (520) 638-2485. E-mail gcfi@grandcanyon.org. or visit their Web site www.thecanyon.com/fieldinstitute.

RANGER TRAIL TO LOWER JUMPUP SPRING

[Fig. 9(4)] The trail drops in a couple of short switchbacks to the floor of Jumpup Canyon, where you find Upper Jumpup Spring, which is piped into a stock trough. From the spring, the trail basically follows the canyon bottom. With each bend in the canyon, the view becomes more spectacular. Eventually the upper canyon walls sweep back to reveal the expanse known as the Esplanade, a relatively flat bench of red

Supai Sandstone that extends for miles within the Grand Canyon. Trails branch off to the east and west allowing exploration of the Esplanade and beyond. The trail to Lower Jumpup Spring continues straight ahead another 0.25 mile along the canyon floor, dropping a little below the Esplanade into a grove of Fremont cottonwoods (*Populus fremontii*). The exact location of Lower Jumpup Spring, bubbling out of the gravelly bed, shifts several hundred yards up- and downstream depending upon the rainfall of that particular year.

Directions: From the North Kaibab Visitor Center at Jacob Lake, drive south 0.25 mile on AZ 67 then turn west on FR 461. Continue on FR 461 and FR 462 for about 9 miles to FR 422. Turn right and go 2 miles to FR 423. Follow FR 423 for 3.3 miles to FR 235. Continue on FR 235 for about 7 miles until it becomes FR 423 again. Follow FR 423 about 8 miles to the end of the road at Jumpup Cabin and the beginning of the trail. The last 8 miles are suitable only for high-clearance vehicles in dry weather.

Trail: 4 miles, one-way.

Degree of difficulty: Moderate.

Elevation: 5,400 feet at trailhead to 4,000 feet at Lower Jumpup Spring.

Surface and blaze: Rocky, cairned.

▨ SADDLE MOUNTAIN WILDERNESS

[Fig. 9(14)] The 40,600-acre Saddle Mountain Wilderness is located in the extreme southeastern corner of the North Kaibab Ranger District. Elevations vary from 6,000 feet on the Marble Canyon rim to over 8,000 feet on Saddle Mountain. The name Saddle Mountain originates from the profile of a prominent ridge that appears from the distance like a saddle, horn and all. Geologically, Saddle Mountain is part of the Kaibab Monocline, a huge fold in the earth's crust that forms the east side of the Kaibab Plateau.

The terrain is very steep and rocky, and the wilderness is bounded on three sides by precipitous canyons. A lightning-caused fire in 1960 consumed about 8,000 acres of forest and allowed New Mexican locust (*Robinia neomexicana*), oak (*Quercus* sp.), aspen (*Populus tremuloides*), elderberry (*Sambucus* sp.), and other plants to invade and establish prime deer habitat.

The only perennial flowing stream on the North Kaibab Ranger District is found in North Canyon within this wilderness area. The rare Apache trout (*Oncorhynchus apache*) has been introduced here and has done well enough to allow fishermen to try their luck (*see* page 176 for more about Apache trout).

Directions: Saddle Mountain Wilderness is located in the extreme southeastern corner of the national forest. During the summer and early fall, access is possible from AZ 67. Year-round access is usually feasible from the Buffalo Ranch Road (FR 445), which takes off of US 89A about 20 miles east of Jacob Lake.

Activities: Hiking, horseback riding, camping, nature study, hunting, fishing.

Facilities: None.

Dates: Open year-round, weather permitting.

Fees: None.

Closest town: Page, about 90 miles.

For more information: North Kaibab Visitor Center, US 89/AZ 67, Jacob Lake, AZ 86022. Phone (520) 643-7298. Or the North Kaibab Ranger District, PO Box 248, Fredonia, AZ 86022. Phone (520) 643-7395.

NANKOWEAP TRAIL

[Fig. 9(5)] The Nankoweap Trail parallels the north rim of Nankoweap Canyon and offers a sense of great open spaces, with spectacular views of the Grand Canyon, Marble Canyon, Cocks Comb, House Rock Valley, and the Vermilion Cliffs. One end of the trail can be accessed from the Kaibab Plateau (FR 610) but is heavily over-grown with New Mexican locust. A better choice is starting at the trailhead in House Rock Valley.

Note that this Forest Service Nankoweap Trail is the only way to reach the Park Service's Nankoweap Trail within the Grand Canyon National Park (*see* page 80).

Directions: Turn off US 89A about 20 miles east of Jacob Lake. Head south 27 miles on the House Rock Valley/Buffalo Ranch Road (FR 445) to the wilderness boundary and trailhead.

Trail: About 0.5 mile in there is a major fork. The left fork is the Saddle Mountain Trail that goes east contouring about 5 miles to the edge of Marble Canyon and a terrific view down to the Colorado River. The right fork is the Nankoweap Trail. It takes about 1.5 hours to climb the 3 miles to the rim overlooking Nankoweap Canyon. This is a good turn-around point. Do not attempt to descend into Nankoweap Canyon unless you have a great deal of experience hiking in the Grand Canyon and a Park Service permit for any overnight camping within the park.

Degree of difficulty: Moderate.

Elevation: 6,560 feet at trailhead to 7,520 feet to the rim.

Surface and blaze: Rocky, cairned, some old blazes on trees.

NORTH CANYON TRAIL

[Fig. 9(6)] This trail offers panoramic views off the Kaibab Plateau toward House Rock Valley, the Vermilion Cliffs, and Marble Canyon and then drops into a lush canyon verdant with spruce, fir, and maple. The stream provides fishermen with their only opportunity in the Grand Canyon region to fish for the rare Apache trout.

Directions: From the DeMotte Campground (*see* page 38) go 0.7 mile south on AZ 67 and turn left onto FR 611. Follow FR 611 about 4.4 miles to the East Rim Viewpoint and the trailhead.

Trail: 2 miles one-way to stream.

Degree of difficulty: Moderate.

Elevation: 8,811 feet at the trailhead to about 7,200 feet at stream.

Surface: Rocky.

NATIONAL FOREST CAMPGROUNDS

Although at-large camping is possible throughout most of the national forest, for those campers looking for a few amenities, the North Kaibab Ranger District has three developed campgrounds.

JACOB LAKE CAMPGROUND

[Fig. 9(7)] Jacob Lake Campground makes a good base for exploring the surrounding area. Grand Canyon National Park is less than an hour's drive away. The many Forest Service roads in the area offer scenic drives to various overlooks and endless challenges for mountain bikers.

Directions: From the intersection of US 89A and AZ 67 at Jacob Lake, go south on AZ 67 about 0.5 mile and turn right onto FS 461. The campground is about 1 mile down on the left.

Activities: Camping, hiking, wildlife viewing, naturalist programs, horseback riding, scenic driving, and mountain biking.

Facilities: 54 camping sites, drinking water, picnic sites, restrooms, and trailer sites.

Dates: Open May 15 to Nov. 1 (depending on snowfall).

Fees: There is a camping fee.

Closest town: Fredonia, 32 miles.

For more information: USFS Visitor Center, US 89/AZ 67, Jacob Lake, AZ 86022. Phone (520) 643-7298. Or the North Kaibab Ranger District, PO Box 248, Fredonia, AZ 86022. Phone (520) 643-7395.

DEMOTTE CAMPGROUND

[Fig. 9(8)] Like Jacob Lake, DeMotte Campground also makes a good base to explore the surrounding area. Grand Canyon National Park is only a few miles away. Forest Service roads lead to viewpoints along the eastern side of the Kaibab Plateau. This part of the forest is a particularly good area for spotting mule deer and turkey.

Directions: From the intersection of US 89A and AZ 67 at Jacob Lake, go south on AZ 67 about 25 miles to campground on the right.

Activities: Camping, hiking, wildlife viewing, horseback riding, scenic driving, and mountain biking.

Facilities: 23 camping sites, drinking water, picnic sites, restrooms, and trailer sites.

Dates: Open June 1 to Nov. 1 (depending on snowfall).

Fees: There is a camping fee.

Closest town: Fredonia, 57 miles.

For more information: USFS Visitor Center, US 89/AZ 67, Jacob Lake, AZ 86022. Phone (520) 643-7298. Or the North Kaibab Ranger District, PO Box 248, Fredonia, AZ 86022. Phone (520) 643-7395.

INDIAN HOLLOW CAMPGROUND

[Fig. 9(9)] Hikers who are going to go down the Thunder River Trail (*see* page 84) often use this remote campground. It's also one of the few places accessible by vehicle where you can camp on the very rim of the Grand Canyon without a permit.

Directions: From Fredonia take FS 422 to FS 425 then FS 232 to campground at end of road. High-clearance vehicles are advisable. This is also the trailhead for the Thunder River Trail.

Activities: Camping, hiking, and wildlife viewing.

Facilities: Several cooking grills and pit toilets; otherwise undeveloped.

Dates: Open May 1 to late Nov. (depending on snowfall).

Fees: None.

Closest town: Fredonia, about 50 miles.

For more information: USFS Visitor Center, US 89/AZ 67, Jacob Lake, AZ 86022. Phone (520) 643-7298. Or the North Kaibab Ranger District, PO Box 248, Fredonia, AZ 86022. Phone (520) 643-7395.

Pipe Spring National Monument

[Fig. 8(2)] Pipe Spring National Monument offers visitors an opportunity to tour an intact historic fort, complete with kitchen, telegraph room, cheese room, parlor, bedrooms, blacksmith shop, harness room, various cabins, and gardens and orchard.

On the vast, thirsty Arizona Strip, the free-flowing Pipe Spring has been a welcomed oasis for centuries. Prehistoric Basketmaker and Pueblo Indians lived near the spring over a thousand years ago. Later the Southern Paiutes, nomadic people of the Great Basin, camped at the spring during annual migrations. From here, they hunted rabbit and deer and gathered pinyon nuts, grass seeds, and prickly pear cactus (*Opuntia* sp.) for food. The first known white men to enter the area were the Spanish padres Francisco Domínguez and Silvestre Vélez de Escalante who passed within 8 miles of the spring in 1776. In October 1858, the spring was "discovered" by Mormon missionaries en route to the Hopi Pueblos to the southeast.

Pipe Spring and the lush native grasses in nearby Pipe Valley were soon put to use by the Mormons. In 1863 Dr. James M. Whitmore, a Mormon convert and cattleman from Texas, began ranching at Pipe Spring. Whitmore and his herder, Robert McIntyre, built a temporary shelter and added ponds, grapevines, and fences. On January 11, 1866, Navajo raiders (these were Navajos who had escaped capture by Kit Carson, *see* Canyon de Chelly history, page 115) crossed the Colorado River to steal stock and killed both men. The Navajos, with their lightning-quick attacks, drove settlers from Kanab, Utah, and other communities east of the Virgin River. In 1868 the Utah Militia settled at Pipe Spring to keep the marauders south of the Colorado.

Although the Navajos had signed a peace treaty with the United States in 1868, they did not consider the Mormons to be U.S. citizens and so continued to raid them. Peace between the Navajos and the Mormons returned in 1870 when missionary Jacob Hamblin and the western explorer Major John Wesley Powell signed a treaty with the Navajos at Fort Defiance, Arizona.

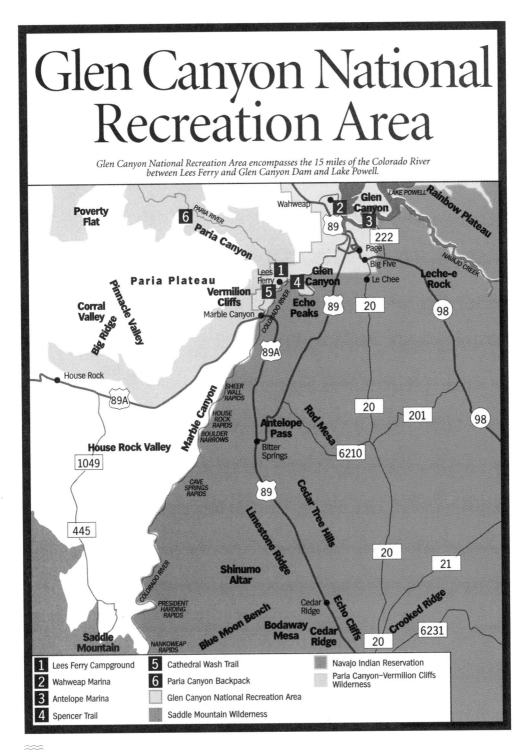

Glen Canyon National Recreation Area

Glen Canyon National Recreation Area encompasses the 15 miles of the Colorado River between Lees Ferry and Glen Canyon Dam and Lake Powell.

Poverty Flat

PARIA RIVER

6

Paria Canyon

LAKE POWELL

Wahweap

2

Glen Canyon

89

3

Rainbow Plateau

222

Page

Big Five

Le Chee

Leche-e Rock

NAVAJO CREEK

Paria Plateau

Pinnacle Valley

Corral Valley

Big Ridge

Lees Ferry

1

5

Vermilion Cliffs

Marble Canyon

COLORADO RIVER

4

Glen Canyon

Echo Peaks

89

20

98

89A

House Rock

89A

Marble Canyon

SHEER WALL RAPIDS

HOUSE ROCK RAPIDS

BOULDER NARROWS

Red Mesa

20

201

98

House Rock Valley

1049

Antelope Pass

Bitter Springs

6210

Cedar Tree Hills

CAVE SPRINGS RAPIDS

89

445

Limestone Ridge

20

21

COLORADO RIVER

Shinumo Altar

PRESIDENT HARDING RAPIDS

Blue Moon Bench

Cedar Ridge

Echo Cliffs

Crooked Ridge

6231

Saddle Mountain

NANKOWEAP RAPIDS

Bodaway Mesa

Cedar Ridge

20

1	Lees Ferry Campground	5	Cathedral Wash Trail		Navajo Indian Reservation
2	Wahweap Marina	6	Paria Canyon Backpack		Paria Canyon–Vermilion Cliffs Wilderness
3	Antelope Marina		Glen Canyon National Recreation Area		
4	Spencer Trail		Saddle Mountain Wilderness		

Brigham Young, president of the Mormon Church, became interested in Pipe Spring as a location for the church's southern Utah tithing herd, the cattle contributed by Mormon families as a tithe to the church. By chance, Young, Hamblin, and Powell met at Pipe Spring on September 12, 1870. Young made plans to build a fort to protect the valuable water supply, the grazing grounds, and those "called" by the church to serve there.

Building began in late 1870. Joseph W. Young, president of the Stake of Zion at St. George, Utah, was initially in charge of construction. Anson Perry Winsor was soon appointed superintendent of the ranch and diligently attended to the construction of the fort that was to bear his name. Winsor Castle consisted of two rectangular, two-story houses with walls connecting their ends to form a courtyard. Building stone was quarried from the red sandstone cliffs west of the fort, and lumber was hauled from a nearby sawmill.

Pipe Spring declined in importance in the 1880s, but continued to be an active church ranch for most of the decade. It was a popular stopover along the trail between the Virgin River towns and the Colorado River. The trail by the fort became known as the Honeymoon Trail because so many young couples traveled it returning home to Arizona after being married in the St. George Temple. The route of the Honeymoon Trail continues across the Colorado River at Lees Ferry then southeasterly along the base of the Echo Cliffs. Near Tuba City, the trail then roughly follows the Little Colorado River upstream to the numerous Mormon-founded towns of eastern Arizona. Today highways US 89 and 89A follow much the same path.

The fort changed hands several times and eventually was abandoned. In 1923, President Warren G. Harding proclaimed Pipe Spring a national monument to be a memorial of western pioneer life.

Directions: Located 14 miles southwest of Fredonia just off AZ 389.

Activities: Self-guided and occasionally ranger-led tours; seasonal special activities related to pioneer life.

Facilities: Visitor center, bookstore, gift shop, small cafe, restrooms.

Dates: Open year-round except Christmas, New Year's Day, and Thanksgiving. Hours vary seasonally.

Fees: There is a charge to enter the monument.

Closest town: Fredonia, 14 miles.

For more information: Superintendent, Pipe Spring National Monument, HC65 Box 5, Fredonia, AZ 86022. Phone (520) 643-7105. Web site www.nps.gov/pisp.

Glen Canyon National Recreation Area

[Fig. 10] Long before there was a Glen Canyon, long before there were the Colorado and San Juan rivers, the various rocks of the region were laid down. During Paleozoic times, 310 to 280 million years ago, limestones, gypsum beds, and shale were deposited in shallow seas. There then followed the Mesozoic Era and 200 million years of vast, dry, sandy deserts occasionally interrupted by wetter periods. Massive layers of sandstone separated by shale accumulated. Then for a few million years, volcanoes added colorful beds of volcanic ash that buried trees and dinosaurs, eventually petrifying the wood and bones.

Within the last few million years, the Colorado and San Juan rivers were born and began to carve down into these sedimentary rocks to form a series of spectacular desert canyons including one that would be named Glen. Spectacular Glen Canyon, only known to a few Indians, explorers, prospectors, and river runners, began to be drowned by a reservoir in 1963.

Glen Canyon National Recreation Area encompasses the 15 miles of the Colorado River between Lees Ferry and Glen Canyon Dam and one of the largest man-made reservoirs in North America—Lake Powell. The lake is named after explorer John Wesley Powell who, along with nine men in the summer of 1869, became the first to successfully boat the Colorado River through Utah and the Grand Canyon. On July 28, they entered Glen Canyon in southern Utah and found its waters relatively calm compared with the wild rapids upstream.

Nearly a century earlier, in 1776, two Spanish priests began an expedition that provided the first written record of Glen Canyon. Father Domínguez, Father Escalante, and their party set out from Santa Fe, New Mexico, in July to pioneer an overland route to a military garrison on the California Coast at Monterey. After three months, having skirted much of the canyon country by going north and then west, the party reached the edge of the Great Basin in western Utah, where they decided to turn back before the onset of winter. They traveled south, then east. On October 26, the party reached the Colorado River at the mouth of the Paria River. When crossing there

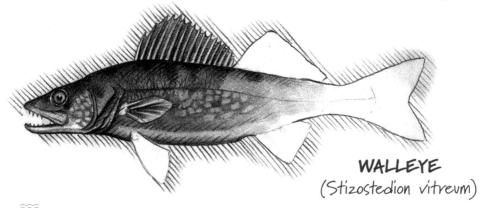

WALLEYE
(Stizostedion vitreum)

BROWN TROUT
(Salmo trutta)

RAINBOW TROUT
(Oncorhynchus mykiss)

BROOK TROUT
(Salvelinus fontinalis)

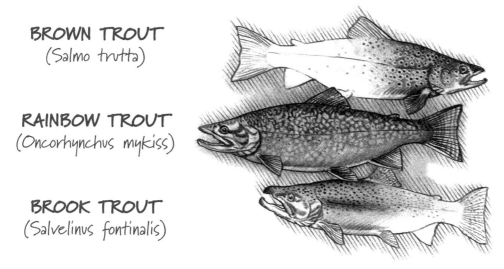

proved nearly disastrous, the explorers climbed out of the river bottom and made camp near today's Wahweap Marina. They spent four more days searching for a way across the river. Finally, on November 7, they chopped steps in the sandstone wall at Padre Creek and safely led their pack stock to the banks of the Colorado. Here the crossing was wide but shallow. Unfortunately, the Crossing of the Fathers is now under Lake Powell's waters.

In 1956, President Dwight Eisenhower inaugurated the construction of Glen Canyon Dam. The 710-foot-high dam required 5,370,000 cubic yards of concrete, the last bucket of which was poured on September 13, 1963. Construction cost $155 million and 18 lives. The dam's electrical generators can produce 1.3 million kilowatts, enough power for a city of 1 million. When at full capacity, the lake surface is 3,700 feet above sea level and covers an area of 161,390 acres, making it second in size only to Lake Mead at the western end of the Grand Canyon. The lake is 186 miles long, 560 feet deep, backs into 96 major side canyons, and contains 26,214,861 acre-feet of water, enough to cover the entire state of Utah with 6 inches of water. Only a relatively small portion of the lake and national recreation area lies within Arizona. Most of the nearly 200-mile-long lake is in Utah.

The Arizona part of the recreation area consists of two distinct districts—the lake area behind the dam and the river below the dam. The lake area is primarily accessible via Wahweap Marina, a few miles northwest of Page, and the Lone Rock Road, several more miles to the west.

Boating, swimming, and water skiing are very popular on Lake Powell. Anglers try their luck, too. The primary game species include largemouth bass (*Micropterus salmoides*), striped bass (*Morone saxatilis*), black crappie (*Pomoxis nigromaculatus*), channel catfish (*Ictalurus punctatus*), bluegill sunfish (*Lepomis macrochirus*), brown trout (*Salmo trutta*), and walleye (*Stizostedion vitreum*). For the latest fishing information check out this Web site www.nr.state.ut.us/dwr/lpfish.htm. Or call (800) ASK-FISH.

The Carl Hayden Visitor Center, adjacent to Glen Canyon Dam, contains a remarkably detailed giant relief map of the region. Take a few minutes to study this map to get an eagle's eye appreciation of the intricate, maze-like topography of this part of the Colorado Plateau.

A very scenic, 15-mile flat-water float trip from the base of the dam to Lees Ferry through the last remnant of Glen Canyon is offered by Wilderness River Adventures, phone (602) 645-3279.

The clear, cold water emerging from Glen Canyon Dam makes excellent trophy trout habitat. Anglers frequently catch very large rainbow trout (*Oncorhynchus mykiss*), sometimes in excess of 10 pounds. Brown (*Salmo trutta*) and brook trout (*Salvelinus fontinalis*) have also been introduced. Guided fishing trips are available through Lees Ferry Lodge (520-355-2231) or Lees Ferry Anglers (520-355-2261 or 800-962-9755). A current fishing report and other information can be found at this Web site www.leesferry.com.

Unfortunately the cold river water makes it difficult if not impossible for the native fish to reproduce. Their eggs do not develop properly. Of the eight species of native Colorado River fish, four have been extirpated including the Colorado squaw-fish (*Ptychocheilus lucius*), the largest minnow in North America, which attained lengths of 6 feet and weighed 100 pounds.

Below the dam, the main access is via the Lees Ferry Road. The ferry site lies in the break between Glen, Marble, and Paria canyons. A natural corridor between Utah and Arizona, Lees Ferry was named for and settled by Mormon John D. Lee, who established the first ferry service at this site. (Note: For arcane reasons of the U.S. Board of Geographic Names, Lees Ferry does not have an apostrophe.) Hoping to protect one of their own from the law, Mormon church leaders instructed Elder Lee, who had been implicated in the 1857 Mountain Meadow Massacre, the tragic killing of over 100 pioneers from Missouri while on their way to California, to start a ferry in the remote Vermilion Cliffs area. Upon seeing her new home, polygamist Lee's 17th wife Emma is said to have cried, "Oh, what a lonely dell."

Just days after arriving, in January 1872, Lee took his first customers, a band of 15 Navajos, across the Colorado. His makeshift ferryboat was the flat-bottomed scow *Cañon Maid*, which John Wesley Powell and his Mormon guide, Jacob Hamblin, had built and used to cross the river in 1870. Two years later, Lee was arrested in Panguitch, Utah, while visiting one of his wives. After two trials, Lee was convicted and shot by firing squad at the site of the massacre near St. George, Utah.

From 1873 to 1896, Warren Johnson and his son ran the ferry. A stone fort, built in 1874 as a result of unrest between area Navajos and settlers, later became a trading post. The fort and another post constructed around 1913 still stand. The dangerous ferry crossing was replaced by Navajo Bridge across Marble Canyon (the head of Grand Canyon) in 1929. Interpretive trails through the fort, along the Colorado River, and at the Lonely Dell Ranch in the adjacent Paria River valley offer glimpses of early Mormon pioneer and subsequent mining lifestyles. A very thorough history of this area has been written by P.T. Reilly and is called *Lee's Ferry: From Mormon Crossing to National Park.*

Today's Lees Ferry offers a ranger station, campground, launch ramp, courtesy dock, fish-cleaning station, and access to 15 miles of the Colorado River (upriver to the dam only). Located on US 89A approximately 6 miles from Lees Ferry are the Navajo Bridge Interpretive Center, a restaurant, a service station, a post office, and a store. Whitewater river trips through the Grand Canyon begin at Lees Ferry but reservations and permits are required. For river trip information, call Grand Canyon National Park at (520) 638-7888.

Directions: Glen Canyon Dam and the Carl Hayden Visitor Center are about 2 miles northwest of Page on US 89. Lees Ferry is located southwest of Page and reached by taking US 89 south 25 miles and then driving US 89A approximately 15 miles to the Lees Ferry Road. It's another 6 miles down to the ferry site.

Activities: Boating, camping, hiking, fishing, river float trips, whitewater river trips, and free dam tours.

Facilities: Visitor center, marina, boat rentals, lodging, campgrounds, laundry, showers, restaurants, service station.

Dates: Open year-round; Carl Hayden Visitor Center closed Thanksgiving, Christmas, and New Year's Day.

Fees: There are entrance and recreation use fees.

Closest town: Page is about 2 miles from the dam and 46 miles from Lees Ferry.

For more information: Glen Canyon National Recreation Area, PO Box 1507, Page, AZ 86040-1507. Phone (520) 608-6404. Web site www.nps.gov/glca. Lees Ferry, phone (520) 355-2234. For information about boat rentals, lodging, and tours, contact Lake Powell Resorts & Marinas, PO Box 56909, Phoenix, AZ 85079. Phone (800) 799-6951. Web site www.visitlakepowell.com. For services and facilities in nearby Page, contact the Page-Lake Powell Chamber of Commerce, PO Box 727, Page, AZ 86040.

LEES FERRY CAMPGROUND

[Fig. 10(1)] Lees Ferry Campground is a good base from which to explore the Lees Ferry area and Marble Canyon, which is the beginning of the Grand Canyon.

Directions: The campground is about 4 miles in from US 89A on the Lees Ferry Road.

Activities: Camping, hiking, fishing, and motor boating (upstream to the dam only).

Facilities: Nearby ranger station, launch ramp, courtesy dock, and fish-cleaning station.

Dates: Open year-round.

Fees: There is a camping fee.

Closest town: Page, 46 miles.

For more information: Glen Canyon National Recreation Area, PO Box 1507, Page, AZ 86040-1507. Phone (520) 608-6404. Lees Ferry, phone (520) 355-2234 or 608-6404.

Grasshopper Mouse

Living in desert grasslands is a little mouse that has been described as "howling like a wolf and attacking like a lion." That might be a bit of an exaggeration for the diminutive grasshopper mouse (*Onychomys leucogaster*) that only measures 5 or 6 inches from nose to tip of tail, but it does behave quite differently than most mice. Commonly, these mice rear up on their hind legs, use their tail for balance, point their head upwards, and emit a tiny squeak, the so-called howl. They also make ultrasonic calls. Then they're off searching for food, not seeds and vegetation like other mice, but invertebrates, reptiles, and even the occasional rodent up to three times their size. Cannibalism is not uncommon. The actions of these aggressive and combative mice have been likened to those of shrews. Thus the phrase "Be a man or be a mouse" takes on new meaning.

WAHWEAP MARINA

[Fig. 10(2)] Wahweap Marina is the largest marina and lodging facility in Glen Canyon National Recreation Area.

Directions: 5.5 miles from the Carl Hayden Visitor Center along Lakeshore Drive.

Activities: RV and tent camping, hiking, fishing, boating, swimming, water skiing, diving, and snorkeling.

Facilities: Lodging, food services, gift shops, 2 campgrounds (one with hook-ups), picnic area, laundry, showers, fish-cleaning station, service station, and full marina services including slips, buoys, boat rentals, tours, repairs, dry storage, and fueling.

Dates: Open year-round.

Fees: There are entrance, camping, and launching fees.

Closest town: Page, 7 miles.

For more information: Glen Canyon National Recreation Area, PO Box 1507, Page, AZ 86040-1507. Phone (520) 608-6404. Wahweap Campground, phone (520) 645-1059.

ANTELOPE MARINA

[Fig. 10(3)] Most of the southeast shore of Lake Powell is Navajo Reservation land. The Navajo Tribe is currently constructing Antelope Marina on Antelope Point a few miles northeast of Page.

Directions: The site can be reached by taking AZ 98 east out of Page about 6 miles and then turning left (north) onto Navajo Route N22B. Go about 5 miles to the lakeshore.

For more information: Glen Canyon National Recreation Area, PO Box 1507, Page, AZ 86040-1507. Phone (520) 608-6404.

HIKING IN THE LEES FERRY AREA
SPENCER TRAIL

[Fig. 10(4)] The Spencer Trail climbs to the top the steep Vermilion Cliffs. Even if you do not go all the way, you are treated to great views looking down the Colorado

River toward Marble Canyon, the beginning of the Grand Canyon. From the cliff top, you can see Lake Powell and the high plateaus of southern Utah.

Charles Spencer, one of the more colorful prospectors and entrepreneurs to come to the canyon country, built this trail in 1910. He planned to transport coal from Warm Creek, located some 28 miles to the north, to Lees Ferry. The coal was going to be used to power pumps and sluices to aid in his search for gold. After trail construction was completed, it was decided that mule trains could not carry enough coal, so another more elaborate scheme was devised.

Spencer had a dismantled 92-foot-long paddle wheel steamboat hauled in by wagon and reconstructed at the mouth of Warm Creek. The boat, christened the Charles H. Spencer, was loaded with coal and set off for Lees Ferry. Upon arrival at the ferry, it was determined that all the coal the boat could carry would be needed just to make the round trip! Also by this time, further tests showed that the amount of gold in the Chinle shales at the base of the Vermilion Cliffs was too small to be profitable. The Charles H. Spencer was moored and eventually sank.

Directions: Begins about 0.5 mile upstream from the Lees Ferry parking lot. Follow the path that parallels the river. The Spencer Trail begins about opposite the wreckage of the ship the Charles H. Spencer. (There may also be a trailhead sign on the river path.)

Trail: 1.5 miles one-way.

Degree of difficulty: Strenuous.

Elevation: 3,180 to 4,680 feet.

Surface and blaze: Rocky, some cairns.

CATHEDRAL WASH TRAIL

[Fig. 10(5)] Cathedral Wash is a popular way for fishermen to reach the Colorado River. The wash takes its name from the dark chocolate brown monolith Cathedral Rock, which is next to the Lees Ferry Road. The rock is composed of Moenkopi shales capped by resistant Shinarump Conglomerate. These rock layers date from Mesozoic time and once covered the entire Grand Canyon region.

Directions: Park at the second pullout, overlooking the wash, on the Lees Ferry Road; about 1.4 miles from US 89A.

Trail: 1.25 miles one-way, follows a narrow canyon to a small, sandy beach and Cathedral Rapid on the Colorado.

Degree of difficulty: Easy except for one short moderate section.

Elevation: 3,440 feet at trailhead to 3,100 feet.

Surface: Rocky and sandy.

GRASSHOPPER MOUSE
(Onychomys leucogaster)

Grand Canyon Country

The Grand Canyon is ½ to 18 miles wide, up to 1 mile deep, and 277 miles long, with ⅓ of the earth's geologic history exposed in its walls.

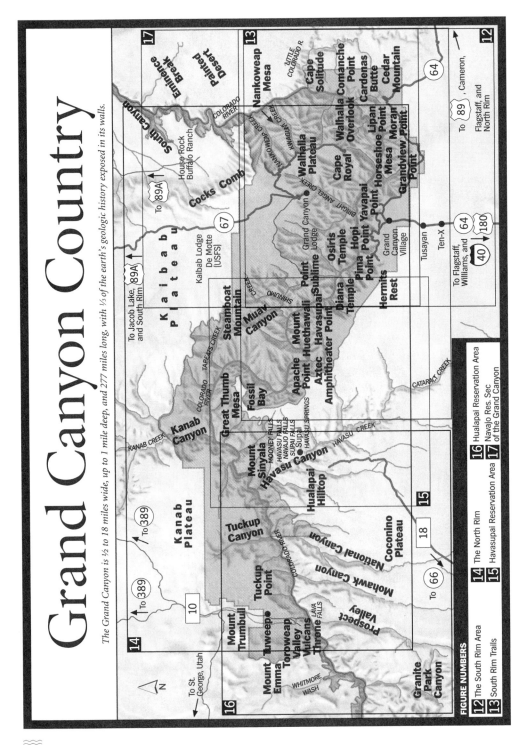

FIGURE NUMBERS

12 The South Rim Area
13 South Rim Trails
14 The North Rim
15 Havasupai Reservation Area
16 Hualapai Reservation Area
17 Navajo Res. Sec of the Grand Canyon

Grand Canyon Country

The Grand Canyon as a topographic feature extends from Lees Ferry to the Grand Wash Cliffs and is located in the southern portion of the larger physiographic province known as the Colorado Plateau. The Colorado Plateau covers northwestern New Mexico, western Colorado, much of eastern and southern Utah, and northern Arizona. This region is composed mostly of sedimentary rocks deposited in horizontal layers, which have been uplifted an average of 1 mile above sea level. These rock layers have been carved by the Colorado River and its myriad tributaries into a maze of canyons. There is no other place on earth quite like the geologic wonderland of the Colorado Plateau, and the Grand Canyon epitomizes the plateau country.

The statistics—0.5 to 18 miles wide, up to 1 mile deep, and 277 miles long as the

[*Above:* A view of the Grand Canyon from the South Rim at Yaki Point]

John Wesley Powell

In 1861 an intense, largely self-taught, 27-year-old public school principal from Illinois joined the Union Army to fight against slavery. The next spring at Shiloh as John Wesley Powell raised his right arm to signal the charge, a Confederate minié ball shattered the bone in his arm, requiring amputation. Undaunted, Powell continued to serve until the end of the Civil War. He then taught courses in botany, zoology, anatomy, entomology, and geology at Illinois Wesleyan University.

The summers of 1867 and 1868 were spent out in the Rockies with his wife, Emma, and a small crew of students and relatives exploring and studying the upper reaches of the Colorado River. Powell hoped to "shed light on the central forces that formed the continent." This goal eventually led to a plan to explore a large blank area on the best maps of the time. He would descend the Green River to its junction with the Grand River and continue down the Colorado. He would flesh out the terra incognito.

The nation's first transcontinental railroad had recently been completed, and Powell took advantage of the train to have four wooden boats of his design shipped out to Green River Station, Wyoming Territory. On May 24, 1869, Powell and his nine-man crew of volunteers pushed off into the unknown. Rapids quickly extracted their toll. A boat was lost and one man left near Vernal, Utah. On August 10, they arrived at the mouth of the Little Colorado and the beginning of the "Great Unknown." Little did they realize how difficult the rapids ahead would be. Endless days dragged on as the men toiled with the heavy boats, navigating what rapids they could, often lining (standing on shore while hanging onto the boat with ropes and letting the current take the boat through the rapid) or carrying the boats around unrunnable cascades. Food was running short and what they had left was moldy.

After three months on the river, they came upon yet another horrendous rapid—this time with no way to walk around. Three men had had enough of the river and of Powell's arrogant, aloof leadership. They hiked out what is now called Separation Canyon and were never seen again.

As it turned out, this was about the last bad rapid. The next day, August 30, Powell and the remaining five men emerged from the Canyon.

Powell's exploits made him a national hero. He would return to the river in 1871-72 better funded and with the previous trip's experience. Powell went on to become a powerful bureaucrat in Washington, DC, eventually founding and heading the U.S. Geological Survey and the Smithsonian's Bureau of American Ethnology. He was also a founding member of the National Geographic Society.

Colorado River flows—hardly begin to convey the awesome spectacle that is the Grand Canyon. A third of the earth's geologic history is exposed in its walls and slopes that stair step from boreal forests on the North Rim to Sonoran-like desert at its bottom. And while geologists have unraveled many of the intricacies of each individual layer of rock, the details of the formation of the great Canyon are still being worked out. Likewise, biologists have recorded and studied the diversity of plants and animals within its walls but have barely begun to understand the interrelationships of the Canyon's dynamic and complex ecosystems.

Although the Grand Canyon is one, albeit large, physical entity, it is not an ecological island. Events beyond the rims often impact the Canyon's well-being. A diverse group of agencies, each with its own agenda and often composed of departments with differing goals, manages the Canyon and its bordering lands. Various sections of the Canyon fall under the jurisdiction of the National Park Service, including Glen Canyon National Recreation Area, Grand Canyon National Park, and Lake Mead National Recreation Area. Three Indian reservations (Navajo, Havasupai, and Hualapai), the U.S. Forest Service, the Bureau of Land Management, as well as state and local governments, also manage parts of the Canyon.

Perhaps President Theodore Roosevelt proclaimed the ultimate management directive for the Canyon nearly a century ago: "What you can do is keep it for your children, your children's children, and for all who come after you." Obviously, the challenges of protecting the Grand Canyon are daunting. The Grand Canyon Trust, a conservation group based in Flagstaff, Arizona is attempting to raise awareness of the fragility of what they term the Greater Grand Canyon area. The Trust's goals for the region include protecting its wildness; maintaining and restoring the health of the ecosystems; creating and promoting environmentally sustainable human use and development; and building a strong constituency for conservation. No small task, indeed. The Grand Canyon Trust can be contacted at 2601 N. Fort Valley Road, Flagstaff, AZ 86001. Phone (520) 774-7488. Or look at their Web site www.grandcanyontrust.org.

Grand Canyon National Park

Grand Canyon National Park protects most of but not the entire Canyon. The park can be divided into four main areas—Marble Canyon, the South Rim, the North Rim, and Toroweap. Each area has its own personality. Steep-walled Marble Canyon, which makes up the first 50 or so miles, is fairly isolated with only dirt roads reaching the rim and no tourist facilities. The 7,000-foot-high South Rim is very accessible, by road, plane, and train, and receives the bulk of the annual 5,000,000 visitors. Their first look is usually from Mather Point, but the Colorado River is hidden from view in a dark inner gorge 3 miles distant and 1 mile down. The North Rim is about a thousand feet higher than the South Rim and much quieter since it lies farther from any major highway. And the Toroweap area is quite a ways off the usual tourist beat and has few tourist amenities.

🌸 GEOLOGY

The rocks of the Grand Canyon have attracted people for thousands of years. Native people collected red and yellow ocher for paint and medicine and gathered sacred salt from caves. The Spanish came in search of gold but left empty-handed. The lure of valuable minerals brought American prospectors, but the limited deposits of copper, asbestos, and uranium proved too difficult to extract and too costly to ship to market.

In 1869, geologist John Wesley Powell's successful trip down the Colorado River and subsequent report and popular articles revealed the geologic wonder of the region to the general populace. People learned that the Canyon walls held more than mineral wealth.

Each colorful layer of rock exposed in the walls of the Canyon is a window back to a different time and environment. The oldest layers (Proterozoic Era), those exposed at the very bottom, date back 1.7 billion years, an incomprehensibly long time ago. Sedimentary and igneous rocks were subjected to intense heat and folding to become high mountains of metamorphic schists, gneisses, and granites (the Vishnu Group). After a half billion years, erosion had worn these mountains down to a nearly level plain. The land subsided allowing an ocean to invade. In this sea, sands and limy muds accumulated for another 300 million years to a thickness of 12,000 feet; these are collectively called the Grand Canyon Supergroup. About 900 million years ago, these sediments were lifted upward, faulted into blocks, and tilted to create mountains and intervening valleys. After another 330 million years, this uplifted terrain was eroded into a lowland of small hills and broad valleys. The blocks that were faulted downward were protected from erosion and are still visible as tilted layers along the river in the eastern Grand Canyon and also near the foot of the South Kaibab Trail.

Above these very ancient rocks are a series of horizontal beds. The contact where the first flat-lying strata (usually the Tapeats Sandstone) rests on the older schists, granites, or tilted strata represents a gap in time of up to 830 million years.

During this time, life on earth was making the giant leap from single-celled organisms to more complex creatures. By the time the next ocean covered the region, some 550 million years ago, there had been an explosion of new life forms. Within the Tapeats Sandstone, Bright Angel Shale, and Muav Limestone (all marine deposits) is an amazing fossil record of trilobites, marine worms, jellyfish, and a myriad of other sea animals.

The region slowly rose and the sea retreated. The top of the Muav Limestone was exposed to erosion, and streams and rivers meandered across its surface. The sediments deposited in the river channels became the Temple Butte Limestone.

Another long period of erosion was followed by the invasion of another shallow, warm sea where more marine limestone was deposited to form the massive Redwall Limestone. The purity of this limestone suggests that calcium carbonates from onshore were emptying into this sea. The calcium carbonate precipitated out on the ocean floor. Deposited along with the precipitates were the shells of billions of sea animals.

The next thousand feet of reddish rock above the Redwall Limestone are shale, siltstone, sandstone, and some limestone. The upper third is the relatively soft Hermit Shale, forming a slope. Fern leaf, raindrop, and insect wing impressions are common fossils in the Hermit Shale. The series of ledges, cliffs, and minor slopes between the Hermit Shale and Redwall Limestone is the Supai Group. Iron oxides leaching out of these red formations wash down and stain the surface of the Redwall Limestone, which is naturally gray.

The land rose again and prevailing winds from the north eventually covered the area with deep, golden sand dunes. The dunes are preserved as the massive Coconino Sandstone, marked with elegant patterns called crossbedding that hint at its wind-blown origins. Fossilized reptile tracks found in this formation always go up the bedding planes, almost never down. This mystery was solved by watching modern lizards walking on sand. Going uphill, the animals tend to leave distinct tracks; going down, the lizard's momentum produces blurred tracks.

Eventually the Coconino desert was submerged under a sea and more limestone, sandstone, and gypsum were deposited as the Toroweap Formation.

Next came a brief erosional period and the invasion of yet another ocean. This sea teemed with mollusks, sea lilies, sponges, trilobites, and brachiopods leaving behind the Kaibab Limestone. While all these sedimentary rocks, from the Tapeats through the Kaibab, were being laid down, evolution was leading to vascular plants and the first fish, amphibians, and reptiles. Then biological disaster. For reasons still not clear, at the end of the Paleozoic Era came a huge extinction of mainly marine creatures. The number of species that vanished then was actually larger than the number involved in the later extinction of the dinosaurs.

The next major geologic era, the Mesozoic, witnessed a series of sandy deserts and the coming of the terrible lizards—the dinosaurs. Probably 2,000 feet of sandstones and shales covered the Grand Canyon region, but most have been eroded away over the last 65 to 70 million years. Mesozoic rocks still exist north and east of the Canyon as the Vermilion Cliffs, as the Kaibito and Paria plateaus, and as small isolated remnants such as Shinumo Altar, Gold Hill, Cedar Mountain, and Red Butte.

The story of how the Grand Canyon came to be is one of weathering, erosion, and transport, but the details are still shrouded in mystery. John Wesley Powell believed that at one time an ancestral Colorado River flowed across a relatively flat plain. Part of the plain began to rise into a oblong highland—the Kaibab Plateau. The river's relentless downcutting was able to match the slow rising of the surrounding ground. The river's ancient course was maintained as the deep canyon was carved. Powell and other early geologists concluded that the Canyon must be extremely old, perhaps 50 million years or more. A beautiful, simple, elegant theory, but wrong.

Kaibab and Abert's Squirrels

A rare treat on the North Rim is to catch a glimpse of the Kaibab squirrel (*Sciurus aberti kaibabensis*), a unique form of the tassel-eared group of tree squirrels. The Kaibab squirrel has a dark charcoal head and body, a rust patch on its back, and a striking snow-white fluffy tail. This squirrel is found only on the Kaibab Plateau.

On the South Rim lives the Abert's squirrel (*Sciurus aberti aberti*). It has a gray body with white underparts and a gray tail fringed with white. Both tassel-eared squirrels occur only where there is ponderosa pine and depend almost exclusively upon that particular pine for food and nest building. (In the 1970s, the Arizona Game and Fish Department transplanted Kaibab squirrels to the limited pine forests of the Uinkaret Mountains on the Arizona Strip.)

The isolated population of uniquely colored Kaibab squirrels is an excellent example of what biologists call insular evolution. Islands, whether they are in the middle of the sea or a biologically isolated land habitat, often have species that are endemic (restricted) to them. In this case, the "island" is a ponderosa pine forest surrounded by desert.

How did the squirrels get to the Kaibab Plateau? One scenario suggests that before the Grand Canyon existed, the ancestors of these squirrels all lived in one huge intact pine forest. As the Colorado River carved the Grand Canyon, the forest and resident squirrels became separated from each other. Over eons of time, the isolated North Rim population began to exhibit the dark body fur and white tail genes.

The problem with this explanation is one of timing. Ponderosa pine probably did not migrate into northern Arizona (presumably from the south) until a mere 10,000 to 11,000 years ago. The Grand Canyon is at least several million years old. So, how did the pine make its way to the north side and how and when did the squirrel follow? Food for thought. Stay tuned for answers.

One thing known for certain is the important role these squirrels play in the health of the ponderosa forests. Interwoven around the roots of the pines are specialized fungi. The fungi absorb water and minerals from the soil and produce growth stimulants, all of which are absorbed by the tree. The pine photosynthesizes sugars for itself and the fungi, a beautiful symbiotic relationship. The fungi produce underground fruiting bodies called false truffles. But, how do its spores get spread around to new pine seedlings? That's where the squirrels fit in. Using their noses, they locate the false truffles (even under a foot of snow), dig them up, and eat with relish. The squirrels defecate on the run, spreading fungal spores through the forest.

Later geologists have determined that the Kaibab Plateau was uplifted first, and then the river carved the Canyon through it. Does this mean that the river had to flow uphill, to get over the Kaibab Plateau? No, but it does present a perplexing problem.

Maybe more than one river was involved. The Canyon seems to be relatively young, perhaps between 1.7 and 4.5 million years old. That's a mind-boggling amount of erosion in such a short geologic time. All that can be said for certain is that a river system is responsible for the downcutting. Other kinds of erosion, such as frost wedging, widen the Canyon. The stair step profile or cross-section of the Canyon is due to the varying hardness of each rock layer: softer ones form slopes, the harder layers tend to be cliffs.

Notice the striking asymmetrical profile of the Canyon. The South Rim is about 2 or 3 miles from the river, whereas the North Rim is 5 to 6 miles away. Both rims dip slightly to the south. Rain hitting the South Rim tends to run away from the Canyon. Precipitation landing on the North Rim tends to run into the Canyon, thus side canyons are longer and cut more deeply on the north side.

After the Canyon was carved nearly to the dimensions we see today, molten rock oozed out of cracks in the earth and poured over the western Grand Canyon landscape. At least 12 times, magma flowed into the Canyon and hissed and sizzled as it met the Colorado River, cooling and hardening into dams. The greatest of these occurred about 1.2 million years ago and created a lake 2,000 feet deep and backing upstream past Moab, Utah. Eventually these lakes overtopped the dams and wore them away.

To view the Grand Canyon is to peer through a geologic window of time. The scene is fraught with contradictions, inconsistencies, and unresolved questions. As conservationist John Muir wrote many years ago, "the whole cañon [sic] is a mine of fossils...forming a grand geological library." Geologists are still trying to read the whole story.

🔲 FLORA AND FAUNA

On a warm September day in 1889, government biologist Clinton Hart Merriam and his assistant Vernon Bailey started down a prospector's trail into the Grand Canyon. As they descended, they noted that the plant communities changed dramatically. On the South Rim they had found tall, stately ponderosa pines, and in cool, north-facing ravines a few Douglas fir (*Pseudostuga menziesii*) and white fir (*Abies concolor*) were growing.

ABERT'S SQUIRREL
(*Sciurus aberti aberti*)

A thousand feet below the rim, they passed through a woodland of pinyons and juniper. Another couple of thousand feet brought them into the stark, but not barren, desert scrub of the Tonto Platform. Blackbrush (*Coleogyne ramosissima*) was common. Merriam's legs gave out, but Bailey continued all the way to the Colorado River and reported more desert. This one included brittlebush (*Encelia farinosa*), honey mesquite (*Prosopis glandulosa*), and catclaw acacia (*Acacia greggii*). Biologically, their hike was like going from the forests of southern Canada to the Sonoran Desert of northern Mexico.

If they had visited the North Rim above 8,700 feet, they would have encountered a boreal forest of Engelmann spruce, alpine (*Abies lasiocarpa*) and white firs, and Douglas fir amid groves of quaking aspens.

What causes these changes? Merriam claimed temperature was one of the major forces. Dropping 1,000 vertical feet increases the temperature 3 to 5 degrees Fahrenheit. Further investigation showed that precipitation also changes with elevation, lower elevations receiving less. Which direction a slope faces makes a tremendous difference in the microclimate: South-facing slopes are hotter and drier than north-facing slopes. Soil type and available nutrients also determine what kinds of plants can grow in a particular location.

Merriam described the plants and animals as living in broad horizontal bands across the landscape, which he called "life zones." However, where Merriam saw distinct horizontal life zones, other biologists see a blending from one plant community to another. Like a rainbow, from a distance there seem to be distinct, individual colors; but close-up, the gradation from one color to the next becomes apparent. So it is with plant and animal distribution.

ENGELMANN SPRUCE
Picea engelmannii

The major terrestrial habitats in the Grand Canyon area include boreal forest, ponderosa pine forest, pinyon-juniper woodland, desert, and riparian (streamside) communities. It's interesting to note that three of North America's major deserts meet in the Grand Canyon. On the Tonto Platform grow typical Great Basin Desert shrubs. In the central part of the Canyon along the Colorado River grow Sonoran

Desert plants, and in the western Grand Canyon, species of the Mohave Desert enter.

With such a wide range of habitats, it should be no surprise that the Grand Canyon harbors over 1,500 species of plants, over 300 species of birds, 76 species of mammals, 35 species of reptiles, and 6 species of amphibians.

DOUGLAS FIR
(Pseudotsuga
menziesii)

▦ HISTORY

Nomadic hunters, known to archaeologists as Paleolithic hunters, wandered across western North America at the end of the last Ice Age, about 11,000 years ago, in search of big game— particularly mammoths but also camels, Harrington's mountain goats (*Oreamnos harringtoni*), shrub oxen, and Shasta ground sloths (*Nothrotheriops shastensis*). Bones and scat from these beasts have been discovered in the Grand Canyon or nearby, so it is likely that at least a few bands of these early people passed this way. The hunters used the atlatl, a spear-throwing device, to bring down the huge mammals. A thousand or so years later, the mammoths were extinct in the Southwest, and giant bison became the main prey item.

Over the next several thousand years, a warming and drying climatic trend led to dramatic changes in the Canyon's plant and animal communities. Many of the large Ice Age mammals went extinct. Remaining herds of big game drifted eastward onto the Great Plains, followed by the Paleolithic hunters. Then a different group of people moved into the area, possibly from the Great Basin.

Unlike their predecessors, this archaic culture depended more and more on wild plant foods while continuing to hunt deer, bighorn sheep, and smaller game. The people used grinding stones to pulverize grasses and other seeds into flour. They carefully crafted baskets, cordage, and nets of hair and vegetable fibers. And because they migrated frequently, they built only insubstantial brush huts. In the western Grand Canyon, an incredible panel of painted ghostlike beings is attributed to these people. They also left enigmatic figurines fashioned from split willow (*Salix* sp.) twigs in hard-to-reach caves.

By A.D. 200, several varieties of corn, introduced through trade with people from Mexico, were becoming an important part of their diet. These emerging farmers explored the Canyon for suitable home sites and for bighorn sheep and pinyon nuts. By A.D. 700, some built small cliff houses or occasionally larger pueblos along the rims or within the Canyon. Over the next several centuries, more people moved into the Canyon. They sowed beans, corn, and squash, perhaps a little cotton. The bow and arrow replaced the atlatl, exquisite pottery was made, and several styles of yucca-fiber sandals were crafted. The farmers living in the eastern portion of the Canyon are now referred to as the Anasazi. To the west were the Cohonina.

By A.D. 1130 these farmers had apparently abandoned the area probably because of overuse of the natural resources, overpopulation, and an extended drought. Greater precipitation 50 years later allowed some of these people to return and build settlements along the rim, such as Tusayan. But less than a century later, they were gone.

The beginning of the fourteenth century witnessed Cerbat Indians, possibly ancestors of the modern Hualapai and Havasupai, entering the Canyon region from the lower Colorado River valley. They spread as far east as the Little Colorado but stayed primarily on the south side of the Colorado River. The Cerbat lived in circular brush wickiups, and instead of yucca-fiber sandals, they wore leather moccasins.

During this time, Southern Paiutes made seasonal trips from the north to the Kaibab Plateau to hunt deer and gather plants. The Southern Paiutes would occasionally cross the Colorado and raid the Cerbats, who would sometimes retaliate. Today, the Southern Paiute Kaibab Band has a small reservation north of the Canyon and west of the town of Fredonia.

The Hualapai Reservation stretches along the South Rim in the western Grand Canyon, and most of the Havasupai people live in the village of Supai within the depths of Havasu (Cataract) Canyon.

The prehistoric period ended in 1540 when Spaniard Garcia López de Cárdenas and his soldiers spent three days looking for a way to the Colorado River below Desert View. They were led here by Hopi who, of course, knew of many ways into the Canyon but were not about to reveal this to the strangers. One old Hopi trail led to a cave where sacred salt was gathered and beyond to a strange spring that marked the *Sipapuni* or place of emergence from the Underworld into this world. Discouraged by the austere country and lack of gold, the Spaniards returned to Mexico.

MOUNTAIN LION
(*Felis concolor*)

Not until two centuries later did the next Europeans visit the Grand Canyon. In the meantime, the first Navajos probably came into the region. The Navajo Nation now abuts the eastern boundary of the park.

On June 20, 1776, Fray Francisco Tomás Garcés entered the *Río Jabesu* (Havasu) Canyon via a wooden ladder fastened to a cliff face. Here he met the Havasupai people who were growing crops along Havasu Creek.

Although still Mexican territory until 1848, the area was traversed by American trappers in their never-ending quest for more animal pelts. Few of these men left written accounts, but one who did was James Ohio Pattie. Unfortunately, his 1826 diary is so vague that his exact route in northern Arizona is impossible to trace. Pattie did write of the Canyon and river within as "these horrid mountains, which so cage it up, as to deprive all human beings of the ability to descend to its banks."

In 1869, geologist John Wesley Powell became the first to successfully descend the Colorado River through the Grand Canyon by boat. The following year Mormon missionary Jacob Hamblin and Paiute leader Chuarrumpeak located trails and springs in the Grand Canyon region to help in Powell's further scientific studies of the Colorado Plateau (and to aid Mormon settlement).

Zane Grey's Lions

In 1907 Pearl Grey, a young dentist from Ohio, came to the North Rim to learn more about Buffalo Jones's experiments in crossing bison bulls with black Galloway cows to produce a hybrid that would hopefully display the better qualities of each parent. Also, Buffalo Jones promised to take the dentist "ropin'" for lions."

Out on the Powell Plateau, Jones's hunting hounds would tree a mountain lion and, unbelievably, Jones would climb into the tree and lasso the angry cat. The incredulous young Ohioan took pictures and kept detailed notes. Later he rejected dentistry to write a novel based upon his summer adventure entitled, *The Last of the Plainsmen*. He signed his work with his middle name Zane instead of his first and launched a very successful career as author of Westerns.

After Powell became director of the U.S. Geological Survey, he sent other geologists to southern Utah and northern Arizona. Clarence Dutton's *Tertiary History of the Grand Cañon District* (1882) is considered the classic geologic report on the region.

As prospectors, engineers, scientists, and map makers explored the Canyon, they named many of its features. Powell and his crew christened Bright Angel Creek in contrast to the Dirty Devil River, Surprise Valley for obvious reasons, and Vasey's Paradise in honor of a botanist friend. Railroad surveyor Robert Brewster Stanton commemorated crew member Peter Hansbrough's drowning with Point Hansbrough. Geologist Clarence Dutton's love of architectural terms and Eastern religions led to Brahma, Buddha, and Shiva temples, Hindu Amphitheater, the Palisades, Vishnu Creek, and Zoroaster Canyon. Topographers François Matthes and Richard Evans bestowed mythical, classical, and religious names such as Apollo Temple, Krishna Shrine, Excalibur, Guinevere Castle, Lancelot Point, and Walhalla Plateau. Early resident and prospector William Wallace Bass thought of Copper Canyon, Garnet Canyon, and Serpentine Canyon.

The end of the nineteenth century saw ever-increasing exploitation of the Canyon's meager mineral and grazing resources. Tourists arrived at Farlee's Hotel near

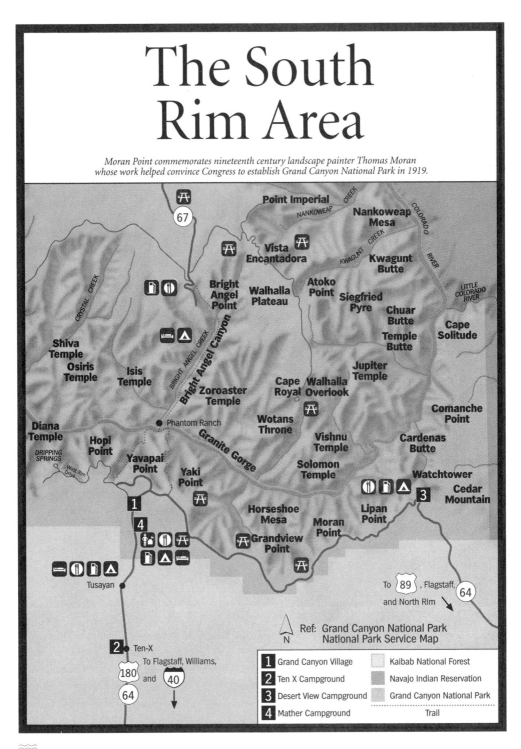

The South Rim Area

Moran Point commemorates nineteenth century landscape painter Thomas Moran whose work helped convince Congress to establish Grand Canyon National Park in 1919.

Point Imperial

Nankoweap Mesa

NANKOWEAP CREEK

COLORADO RIVER

67

Vista Encantadora

Kwagunt Butte

KWAGUNT CREEK

Bright Angel Point

Walhalla Plateau

Atoko Point

Siegfried Pyre

Chuar Butte

LITTLE COLORADO RIVER

CRYSTAL CREEK

Shiva Temple

Osiris Temple

Isis Temple

Temple Butte

Cape Solitude

Zoroaster Temple

BRIGHT ANGEL CREEK

Bright Angel Canyon

Jupiter Temple

Diana Temple

Cape Royal

Walhalla Overlook

Comanche Point

DRIPPING SPRINGS

Phantom Ranch

Wotans Throne

Hopi Point

West Rim Drive

Yavapai Point

Granite Gorge

Vishnu Temple

Cardenas Butte

Yaki Point

Solomon Temple

Watchtower

1

Horseshoe Mesa

Lipan Point

Cedar Mountain

4

3

Grandview Point

Moran Point

Tusayan

To 89, Flagstaff, and North Rim

64

Ref: Grand Canyon National Park
National Park Service Map

N

2 Ten-X

To Flagstaff, Williams,

180   and   40

64

1 Grand Canyon Village	Kaibab National Forest
2 Ten X Campground	Navajo Indian Reservation
3 Desert View Campground	Grand Canyon National Park
4 Mather Campground	Trail

Diamond Creek in the western Grand Canyon in 1883, and the next year, Mrs. Ayer from Flagstaff became the first (non-Native American) woman to descend into the central part of the Grand Canyon. Her guide was John Hance, who had come to the Canyon hoping to find gold and silver but discovering more money in the pockets of tourists. One of his guests wrote, "God made the cañon [sic], John Hance the trails. Without the other, neither would be complete."

President Theodore Roosevelt first visited the Canyon in May 1903. While standing on the South Rim, he instructed, "Leave it [the Grand Canyon] as it is. You cannot improve upon it. The ages have been at work on it, and man can only mar it." Five year later, Roosevelt made the Canyon a national monument. However because of opposition by miners and other developers, not until 1919 did Congress establish it as a national park.

The South Rim

[Fig. 12] Nearly 5 million people a year come through the two South Rim entrance stations and search for a parking space. Plans eventually call for a new parking area outside the park boundary and a light rail shuttle to whisk tourists to the rim. But until then, it may take a little patience to weather the crush of summer visitation.

Here's a hint: Park your car wherever you can find a space and take the free West Rim Shuttle or Village Loop Shuttle (refer to Park Service newspaper *The Guide* given to you at the entrance station or available around the park for information about parking areas and shuttle stops). Get off and stroll between the named viewpoints. You'll soon discover that many folks do not walk even a short distance from their cars. Find a comfortable boulder to sit on or lean against, not too close to the edge, and just soak in the scene. Listen for the "yank, yank, yank" of a white-breasted nuthatch (*Sitta carolinensis*), the "gronk" of a shiny black common raven (*Corvus corax*), the tripping-down-the-scale song of the canyon wren (*Catherpes mexicanus*), and the wind whispering secrets through the pines. And as of 1999, reintroduced California condors have been frequenting several of the viewpoints along the South Rim. Breathe in the vanilla scent of the ponderosa pine (*Pinus ponderosa*) and the pungent odor of sagebrush (*Artemisia tridentata*), and feel the strong desert sun on your back. (Remember sunscreen and hat.) Let your thoughts drift across the Canyon with the clouds. Contemplate the play of shadows across the distant cliffs and ledges.

PONDEROSA PINE
(Pinus ponderosa)

In late afternoon, return to the Grand Canyon Village (*see* page 63) and walk the short distance down the Bright Angel Trail (*see* page 73) to the tunnel cut through the limestone cliff. Just beyond the tunnel, look up to your left. Under a large overhang are a dozen or so dark red pictographs of antlered creatures, humanlike forms, and geometric shapes. Long before this was a hiking trail, a couple of hundred, maybe a couple of thousand years ago, a Havasupai or Anasazi Indian crawled up there to paint these figures. Their fine execution suggests they were meant to be more than just doodles.

Uplifting and faulting in this side canyon broke the sheer cliffs apart allowing Indians to climb down to the life-giving springs bubbling up on the Tonto Platform below. They planted small plots of corn and beans and squash here and continued to use the site even after prospectors improved the old Indian route into a mule trail. Ralph Cameron, his brother Niles, and Pete Berry came to the Canyon in 1890 and staked claims along the Indian trail, which gave them legal title to it. They charged tourists and others the exorbitant fee of a buck a head plus another dollar for each stock animal.

Although the Canyon was declared a national monument in 1908, Ralph Cameron and company managed to keep private control of the Bright Angel Trail. Also starting about 1900, the Santa Fe Railway and Fred Harvey Company began their joint effort to monopolize tourism at the South Rim.

Rivalry between the Santa Fe Railway and the Camerons for the tourist trade was intense. To prevent its customers from having to pay Cameron to use his trail, the railroad built the Hermit Road (West Rim Drive) in 1912 and constructed the Hermit Trail into the Canyon. By 1925 the National Park Service had completed the South Kaibab Trail to also avoid the Bright Angel and Cameron's toll; however, only three years later Cameron lost title to the Bright Angel, which then became a public route.

If you're still having trouble finding that parking space, just blame it on Teddy Roosevelt. Almost a hundred years ago, he implored, "Keep it [the Grand Canyon]...as the one great sight which every American...should see."

Directions: The South Rim of the Grand Canyon is reached from Williams via AZ 64 or from Flagstaff via US 180 and then AZ 64. It is also possible to enter the park from the east by taking AZ 64 from its junction with US 89 at Cameron.

Activities: Scenic drives, hiking, guided tours, mule rides, nature study, camping, and fishing.

Facilities: Lodging, campground, food services, general store, bank, post office.

Dates: Open year-round.

Fees: There are entrance and camping fees.

Closest town: Williams, 56 miles; Flagstaff, 80 miles. Tusayan, which is adjacent to the park boundary, while not a "town" does have tourist services including lodging and restaurants.

For more information: Grand Canyon National Park, Trip planner, PO Box 129, Grand Canyon, AZ 86023. Phone (520) 638-7888. Web site www.thecanyon.com/nps.

GRAND CANYON VILLAGE

[Fig. 12(1)] While the walls of the Grand Canyon record the long history of the earth, buildings record more recent pioneer history. The oldest standing building in Grand Canyon Village on the South Rim is Buckey O'Neill's Cabin. William Owen "Buckey" O'Neill was an author, miner, politician, sheriff, and judge. Like most Grand Canyon pioneers, O'Neill was drawn to the region by the possibility of discovering valuable minerals. In the 1890s he built this log cabin, which later became part of Bright Angel Lodge.

Engineer Robert Brewster Stanton dreamed of building a railroad along the Colorado River through the Grand Canyon. His river-level survey of 1889-90 proved that a rail line could be built to transport minerals to market, but no financial backers came forward.

Six years earlier, in 1883, the Atlantic & Pacific and Atchison, Topeka and Santa Fe Railway companies joined forces to complete a line across northern Arizona following the 35th parallel, a route originally surveyed for a wagon road in the 1850s. Just three months after the A&P work gangs reached Peach Springs, 20 miles south of the Colorado River, Julius and Cecilia Farlee were ready to ferry train passengers down a rough and dusty road to their newly built hotel along Diamond Creek, the first hotel in or at the Grand Canyon.

Entrepreneur Buckey O'Neill convinced a mining company to build a spur line from Williams to his copper mine at Anita, about 15 miles south of the Canyon. When the mines closed, the rail line went bankrupt, but the Santa Fe Railway bought it and finished laying tracks to the South Rim. Congress authorized Indian Gardens within the Canyon as the terminus, but this section was never constructed.

On September 17, 1901, all 22 Grand Canyon Village residents watched the first train pulled by Locomotive 282 roll to a stop at the rim. Now instead of a day or two of jostling in a rough stage for a fare of $15 to $20, one could ride the 60 miles from Williams to the Canyon in the relative comfort of the train in three hours for only $4.

Ironically and fatefully, the Santa Fe Railway sponsored the first auto adventure to the South Rim. While car travel would eventually lead to an abandoning of the railroad, this early experiment was not problem-free. On January 6, 1902, a steam-powered Toledo Locomobile was expected to make the trip from Flagstaff in less than four hours. But after breaking down 30 miles short of the goal and already two days late, it had to be towed by mules the rest of the way to Grandview Point.

Once the train tracks arrived at the South Rim, the Santa Fe Railway and Fred Harvey Company took to providing lodging for tourists. In 1904 Chicago architect Charles F. Whittlesey was commissioned to design a hotel on the rim. He combined the qualities of a "Swiss chalet with a Norway villa" in the stately El Tovar Hotel. The hotel, constructed of Oregon pine, was completed the following year. None of the 80 guest rooms had a private bath, but the hotel did boast electricity provided by a steam generator. At a cost of $250,000, the El Tovar was deemed "probably the most expensively constructed and appointed log house in America."

Also in 1904, the Fred Harvey Company hired Mary Jane Colter, one of the first female architects in the United States, to design an Indian house across from the hotel. Colter wanted a structure that represented the history of the area and decided to model this building after the ancient Hopi village of Oraibi. The Hopi House became living quarters for Hopi craftsmen and a store where the Harvey Company sold Indian-made arts and crafts and other souvenirs. Navajos lived in nearby hogans, their traditional log and mud houses.

In 1935, Colter redesigned the Bright Angel Lodge, which had started out as a collection of ramshackle cabins and tents along the rim shortly before the turn-of-the-century. The stones framing the 10-foot-high fireplace in the lodge's History Room are from various layers of rock within the Canyon, arranged in geologic order from top to bottom. Colter decorated the lobby with 25 hats from famous westerners, including one of Pancho Villa's sombreros.

The Kolb brothers, Ellsworth and Emery, were photographers who arrived at the South Rim shortly after the turn of the century. In 1904, they constructed a small building precariously perched on the rim. Over the next two decades, the Kolbs added on to their studio until a business and residence of several stories overlooked the head of the Bright Angel Trail. Each morning the descending mule train carrying tourists would pause for the Kolbs to take the riders' pictures. Prints would be ready upon their ascent.

After World War II, Americans began visiting the canyon in ever-increasing numbers; most drove in their own cars. Train passenger numbers dwindled, and in 1968 the last train left the Canyon with fewer than 200 passengers aboard. For two decades the abandoned tracks rusted, ties rotted, and trees and shrubs grew between the rails. Then Phoenix businessman Max Biegert decided to reopen the line. In 1989, 88 years to the date from the first train ride to the South Rim, thousands at the Grand Canyon Depot greeted a vintage steam engine pulling passenger cars. For information about taking the train from Williams to the Grand Canyon, call (800) THE-TRAIN.

The Grand Canyon Village is the main center for lodging, meals, and Canyon information. Along with the historic El Tovar Hotel and Bright Angel Lodge are the newer Kachina and Thunderbird lodges. The less expensive Maswik and Yavapai lodges and Mather Campground are located a little farther away in the pine forest. Eating establishments range from the simple, inexpensive Bright Angel Fountain to the elegant El Tovar Dining Room (no shorts, please). A general store carries groceries and camping equipment.

For general information, as well as books and displays about the park, a stop at the Visitor Center and a free copy of the Park Service newspaper *The Guide* is a must. (A free *Accessibility Guide* is also available at the Visitor Center for physically challenged visitors.) The nearby Yavapai Observation Station and the Kolb Studio offer more information and books.

Near Maswik Lodge is the Backcountry Information Center where permits for overnight backpacks into the Canyon can be obtained (*see* Hiking the Inverted Mountains, page 71).

From the village area a scenic 8-mile road called the Hermit Road (West Rim Drive) skirts the rim to the west (*see* below). Another road leading to the east—the Desert View Drive (State Highway 67)—eventually leads to Cameron and U.S. Highway 89 (*see* page 66).

One of the two maintained rim-to-river trails, the Bright Angel Trail (*see* page 73), begins next to Kolb Studio. The other trail, the South Kaibab (*see* page 75), is located off the Desert View Drive near Yaki Point. Both lead to the Bright Angel Campground and Phantom Ranch, the only developed tourist facilities at the bottom of the Canyon. At the river, a trail connects the South Kaibab to the Bright Angel.

During the busy summer months, free shuttle buses transport visitors around the village area and out on the Hermit Road (West Rim Drive). Scheduled for completion in the near future is the Canyon View Information Plaza. The plan calls for day-use visitors to travel by light rail from the gateway community of Tusayan to the plaza 6 miles north. At Mather point, an orientation center will help visitors find their way around the Canyon by bus, on foot, or by bicycle. Current information may be obtained at the Web site www.nps.gov/grca/greenway.

In addition, nine historic buildings in the village area are to be transformed into a visitor discovery and education complex, providing in-depth educational opportunities. Also planned is a new trail system to promote pedestrian and bicycle travel along the South Rim from Hermits Rest to Desert View.

HERMIT ROAD (WEST RIM DRIVE)

[Fig. 12] The Hermit Road (West Rim Drive) winds about 8 miles from Grand Canyon Village to Hermits Rest. Don't be confused by the name. There is no West Rim; the road simply goes west along the South Rim. During the summer, the road is closed to private vehicles, but a free shuttle bus service makes frequent stops at several points along the way.

From Trailview and Trailview II, look back to the south to see the village. Bright Angel Trail drops off the rim next to the old Kolb Studio and works its way to Indian Gardens Campground, recognizable by the large Fremont cottonwood (*Populus fremontii*) trees growing along Garden Creek.

On the way out to Maricopa Point, notice the fence blocking off an ecologically sensitive area. Unusual weathering of the exposed limestone has created small pockets of soil where the rare sentry milkvetch (*Astragalus cremnophylax*) and diminutive forms of evening primrose (*Oenothera* sp.) and mosslike rockmat (*Petrophytum caespitosum*) grow.

The Orphan Mine headframe is visible from Powell Point. Daniel Hogan discovered copper here in 1893, but a more valuable deposit of uranium was mined from 1954 until 1966. The Canyon's small deposits of copper, silver, and uranium are the result of a geologic feature known as a breccia pipe. These "pipes" formed when the roof of a cave in the Redwall Limestone collapsed. Pieces of rock (breccia) from the overlying formations tumbled into the cave. Groundwater carried down dissolved minerals, which precipitated out in the breccia.

About 5 miles directly across the canyon from Hopi Point is Shiva Temple, an isolated mesa that was once part of the North Rim. Today the mesa is joined to the North Rim by a narrow ridge. In 1937, the American Museum of Natural History mounted an expedition to look for unique species of small mammals that may have been isolated on Shiva Temple. The popular press had the biologists searching for dinosaurs. Although deer antlers and Pueblo artifacts were found, no unique mammals or large Jurassic Park reptiles were seen.

Mohave Point offers a view of three major rapids on the Colorado River—Hermit, Granite, and Salt Creek. If you are lucky, you might see a raft or kayak splashing through the whitewater.

The Abyss, at the head of Monument Creek, drops a breathtaking 3,000 feet to the Tonto Platform. Remnant stands of Douglas fir and white fir on the north-facing cliffs are a biological relics from the Pleistocene Epoch, some 11,000 years ago, when the climate here was wetter and cooler than today.

Looking down from Pima Point, parts of the Hermit Trail, constructed in 1911, can be seen winding down to the square outlines of cabin foundations and the corral of a guest ranch built by the Santa Fe Railway. The camp was abandoned in 1930 after the Bright Angel Trail became a free, public route.

The Hermit Road (West Rim Drive) ends at Hermits Rest, another rustic stone building designed by Mary Colter in 1914. This is also the trailhead for the unmaintained Hermit Trail (*see* page 74).

DESERT VIEW DRIVE

The Desert View Drive meanders along the South Rim about 25 miles from the village area to Desert View. All the major viewpoints are signed, but the unnamed overlooks and pullouts also offer outstanding vistas. So far, this drive is always open to private vehicles except for the short side road to Yaki Point, which is accessible only by walking or taking a shuttle bus.

At Yavapai Point is a small museum and bookstore. From here, it's possible to see Phantom Ranch, the only tourist lodge within the Canyon, nestled along Bright Angel Creek. This is where the mule riders stay. In the thick grove of cottonwoods a little farther downstream is the Bright Angel Campground. The Kaibab Suspension Bridge spanning the Colorado River is also visible. The bridge is 440 feet long and about 60 feet above the river. The bridge's 10, 1-ton cables were hand-carried into the Canyon by 42 Havasupai men in 1928.

Coming into the park through the South Entrance, the first official viewpoint encountered is Mather Point, named after Stephen Mather, first director of the

National Park Service. Short paths lead out to several dramatic overlooks. During the summer, Park Service rangers are often stationed here to answer visitors' questions.

Sections of the South Kaibab Trail (*see* page 73), which begins nearby, can be seen from Yaki Point. (In the summer, access to this point is limited to walkers and the free shuttle buses.) Across the Canyon and a little to the northeast, Clear Creek has cut a long gash into the North Rim. In the spring, a white spot appears in the Redwall Limestone cliff overlooking upper Clear Creek. This is Cheyava Falls, a seasonal waterfall, probably the tallest in the Grand Canyon. The falls burst from a cave and drop about 600 feet plus several hundred more of cascades.

In the late 1800s, copper was discovered on Horseshoe Mesa below Grandview Point. By 1892, miner Pete Berry and others had completed the Grandview Trail to bring the copper and other minerals to the rim. Even though some of the copper ore assayed at a rich 70 percent pure, the cost of transporting it out of the Canyon and to a smelter proved too expensive. Several years later, Berry built a hotel near the rim and began to take tourists down his trail, but after the railroad reached what would become the Grand Canyon Village, this business venture failed too.

Moran Point commemorates nineteenth century landscape painter Thomas Moran. His work helped convince Congress to establish Grand Canyon National Park in 1919.

Tusayan Ruin is an Anasazi site that was occupied during the twelfth century. A short interpretive walk around the excavated ruin and a small museum explain the site.

Lipan Point offers an exceptional view of the Colorado River. To the north, the river flows through an open valley, curves sharply past the delta of Unkar Creek where an Anasazi village once stood, and then crashes through Unkar Rapids, a 25-foot drop. To the west, the Colorado thunders over Hance Rapids and plunges into the dark Inner Gorge. To the south, the San Francisco Peaks, sacred mountains to the Hopi and Navajo, dominate the horizon.

Near Desert View is another old Indian route (*see* Tanner Trail, page 71). Seth Tanner, a Mormon pioneer and occasional prospector from Tuba City, decided in the 1880s to improve the route. There were rumors that infamous Mormon John D. Lee had buried Dutch ovens full of gold in the Canyon. Perhaps Tanner hoped to find this hidden treasure; instead, after a half dozen years of searching, he located copper and silver deposits in Palisades Creek. The path became known as the Tanner Trail.

To improve access, prospector Franklin French relocated the upper section of the trail to its present location near Lipan Point. According to French, "We called it a trail, but it was only a roughly marked out suggestion of where a trail ought to be." In attempting to get supplies to the river, he recounted, "Drunken men will often do things they dare not attempt when sober. I thought I would try it on the mules...when they drank, I dosed the water heavily with whiskey...The mules were as reckless as Jack Tars on a frolic. We got there all the same, but a sorrier looking set of remorseful, repentant mules than we had the next morning the eye of man never saw."

Desert View is the easternmost overlook on the South Rim. There is a park service information center, grocery store, curio shop, snack bar, service station, campground, and the distinctive Watchtower. The 70-foot-high stone tower was conceived by Mary Colter and built in 1932 with Hopi labor. The tower resembles those built by the Anasazi; inside are objects and paintings depicting Hopi legends.

CAMPGROUNDS
MATHER CAMPGROUND AND TRAILER VILLAGE
[Fig. 12(4)] **Directions:** Located in the Grand Canyon Village area.

Activities: Camping and hiking, occasional evening programs.

Facilities: 317 campsites, drinking water, tables, and restrooms. Showers, laundry, and hookups are available.

Dates: Open year-round. From Mar. through Oct. make reservations by calling Biospherics at (800) 365-2267.

Fees: There is a camping fee.

Closest town: Williams, 56 miles; Tusayan, 6 miles.

For more information: Grand Canyon National Park, PO Box 129, Grand Canyon, AZ 86023. Phone (520) 638-7888.

DESERT VIEW CAMPGROUND
[Fig. 12(3)] **Directions:** 25 miles east of Grand Canyon Village along the Desert View Drive.

Activities: Camping and hiking.

Facilities: 50 campsites, drinking water, tables, and restrooms.

Dates: Open May through Oct., sometimes longer. Make reservations by calling Biospherics at (800) 365-2267.

Fees: There is a camping fee.

Closest town: Cameron, 30 miles.

For more information: Grand Canyon National Park, PO Box 129, Grand Canyon, AZ 86023. Phone (520) 638-7888. To contact the campground directly, phone (520) 638-2372.

TEN X CAMPGROUND
[Fig. 12(2)] **Directions:** 2 miles south of Tusayan along AZ 64 in the Kaibab National Forest.

Activities: Camping and hiking.

Facilities: 70 campsites, drinking water, tables, and restrooms.

Dates: Open May through Oct.

Fees: There is a camping fee.

Closest town: Williams, 50 miles; Tusayan, 2 miles.

For more information: Tusayan Ranger District, Kaibab National Forest, PO Box 3088, Tusayan, AZ 86023. Phone (520) 638-2443.

Hiking the Inverted Mountains

Renowned Canyon hiker Harvey Butchart succinctly warns, "The Grand Canyon is not the place for one's first experience in hiking." Butchart came to Flagstaff in 1945 to begin a teaching career. He hiked in the Grand Canyon and soon set about, as a mathematician would, a systematic exploration of the world below the rim. For the next 50 years, the wiry, indefatigable Butchart hiked and climbed in nearly every corner of the Grand Canyon making many discoveries of historical or archaeological interest. He eventually logged more than 12,000 miles and bagged 83 of the Canyon's hundred or so major buttes and temples. Now in his 90s, he is no longer hiking in the Canyon, but has put some of his vast knowledge about Canyon routes in his book, *Grand Canyon Treks: 12,000 Miles Through the Grand Canyon.*

A Grand Canyon hike is like mountain climbing in reverse. The trailheads are at high elevations (6,000 feet or more) and the trails, of course, go down. Then when you are tired, blistered, and dusty, the hardest part of the trip, the climb out, is ahead of you. Safely assume that the uphill portion of your hike will take about twice as long as the descent.

Furthermore, except for the Bright Angel, North and South Kaibab, and a few short rim trails, none are maintained on a regular basis. Expect steep, sometimes treacherous footing, and lots of loose rocks that make it easy to sprain your ankle or worse.

During the summer, the inner Canyon literally becomes a life-threatening oven. Temperatures can soar to over 115 degrees Fahrenheit in the shade. Hikers must drink a gallon of water a day or risk heat exhaustion, sunstroke, or death. The Colorado River may look tempting for a refreshing swim, but it may be your last. The water is very cold and the currents deceptively strong. More hikers drown than expire any other way! In the winter, sudden blizzards can bury the upper reaches of the trails or cover them with ice. Hypothermia, the dangerous lowering of one's body core temperature, and frostbite are possible.

Weather-wise, spring and fall are the best times to hike in the Canyon. Even then, the importance of carrying adequate water cannot be overemphasized. Except for piped water in campgrounds, all water sources—springs, creeks, and the Colorado—should be treated.

Also, keep an eye on your food. During the day, aggressive rock squirrels can chew through packs to reach food. Hang your food at night to keep it safe from mice, wood rats, ringtails, and deer.

From the South Rim, two maintained trails lead to the river—the Bright Angel (9.3 miles to Bright Angel Campground) and South Kaibab (6.4 miles to the Bright Angel Campground). The Hermit Trail (9.5 miles to the river) and the Grandview Trail (3.0 miles to Horseshoe Mesa) are good introductions to the more primitive routes into the Canyon.

Only one maintained trail descends from the North Rim, the 14.5-mile North

South Rim Trails

During the summer, the inner canyon temperatures can soar to over 115 degrees Fahrenheit in the shade.

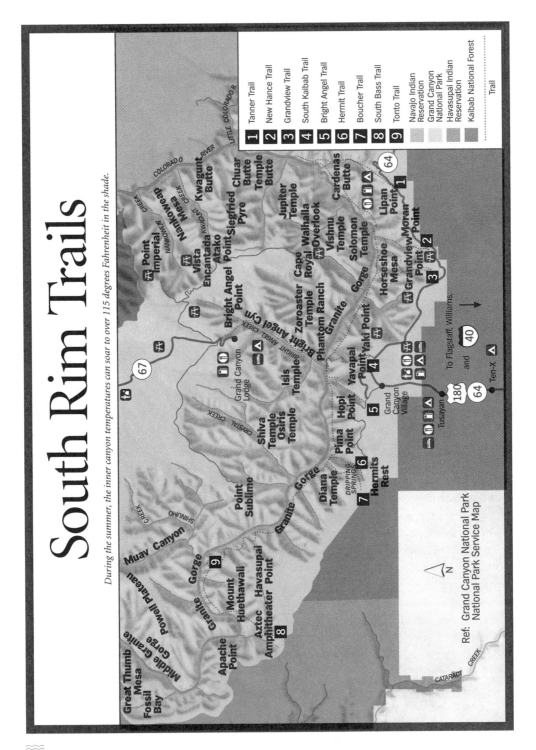

1 Tanner Trail
2 New Hance Trail
3 Grandview Trail
4 South Kaibab Trail
5 Bright Angel Trail
6 Hermit Trail
7 Boucher Trail
8 South Bass Trail
9 Tonto Trail

Navajo Indian Reservation
Grand Canyon National Park
Havasupai Indian Reservation
Kaibab National Forest
Trail

Ref: Grand Canyon National Park
National Park Service Map

Kaibab (*see* page 81). Combining this with the Bright Angel or South Kaibab trails allows a cross-canyon adventure.

One of the best hiking guides to the Canyon is the *Official Guide to Hiking the Grand Canyon* by Scott Thybony. Updates are available at the Web site www.grandcanyon.org.

A permit is required for all overnight backpacking whether in the park or on the reservation. Get a copy of the park's Backcountry Trip Planner by writing the Backcountry Information Center, Grand Canyon National Park, PO Box 129, Grand Canyon, AZ 86023 or calling (520) 638-7875 between 1 and 5 p.m. daily.

For a hassle-free hike, the Grand Canyon Field Institute offers educational, naturalist-led backpacking and llama-supported trips into the Canyon. Contact the Field Institute at P.O. Box 399, Grand Canyon, AZ 86023. Phone (520) 638-2485. E-mail gcfi@grandcanyon.org. Or visit their Web site www.the canyon.com/fieldinstitute.

SOUTH RIM TRAILS
TANNER TRAIL

[Fig. 13(1)] The trail drops in a series of steep switchbacks (some are washed out and require a little scrambling) through the Kaibab, Toroweap, and Coconino formations before leveling off just south of Escalante Butte. The Tanner Trail then contours around Escalante and Cardenas buttes while slowly descending through the Hermit and Supai formations. More steep, rocky switchbacks descend the Redwall Limestone cliff before the trail turns north to parallel Tanner Canyon. The trail angles downward toward the Colorado River.

Today the trail receives enough use that route finding is usually no problem for experienced canyon hikers. This wasn't the case back in 1959 when a man and two boys lost their way. The man fell to his death while trying to climb down a cliff. The boys found another way to the river, but one of them died of thirst before reaching water. The lone survivor decided to try to float down the river to Phantom Ranch by hanging on to a driftwood log, a nearly fatal mistake. A Park Service search party finally rescued him.

The Anasazi, and later the Hopi, used this route with some variations to reach homes within the canyon and sacred salt deposits. It was near Lipan Point that the first Europeans saw the Grand Canyon. Hopi guides led Garcia López de Cárdenas here in 1540, but they did not disclose to the Spaniards that they knew ways into the canyon.

During the 1880s, Seth Tanner prospected in the eastern Grand Canyon. He discovered a little copper and silver near the river. He and other miners relocated the upper trail to its present location in 1889.

Directions: The trailhead is located just east of the Lipan Point parking lot off the Desert View Drive.

Trail: About 10 miles one-way to the Colorado River.

Degree of difficulty: Very strenuous.

Elevation: 7,300 feet at trailhead to 2,700 feet at Colorado River.

Surface and blaze: Rocky; cairns in places; map reading essential.

NEW HANCE TRAIL

[Fig. 13(2)] This trail is very steep and hard to follow. Get the latest trail information from the Park Service Backcountry Information Center. The nineteenth century prospector John Hance built this trail, originally known as the Red Canyon Trail, after rockslides destroyed an earlier trail of his. He found some copper and a little asbestos. Hance soon realized that there was more gold in the pockets of tourists than the walls of the Grand Canyon, so he became a tour guide.

Hance also became the Grand Canyon's legendary storyteller. One favorite tale was about the time the Canyon was socked-in with clouds, and Hance decided to snowshoe across to the North Rim. He nearly died when the wind suddenly blew the fog away, and he was left stranded on a pinnacle. But even with all of his imaginative wit, Hance was stumped for an answer one day when, upon telling a crowd that he had dug the Grand Canyon, a small girl asked, "Where did you put all that dirt?" Legend has it that years later, on his deathbed, Hance's last words were, "I wonder what I could have done with all that dirt."

The red of Red Canyon is the Hakatai Shale, one of the layers of the Precambrian Grand Canyon Supergroup. The asbestos Hance and others discovered in the Grand Canyon occurs in the Bass Limestone, another member of the Supergroup. Asbestos is an alteration product of the mineral serpentine. The serpentine appears as green veins as much as 1 foot thick and contains bands of green to yellow fibrous asbestos.

Directions: Park at the signed Moran Point on the Desert View Drive and walk about 1 mile southwest along the rim to the signed trailhead.

Trail: 8 miles one-way to Colorado River.

Degree of difficulty: Very strenuous.

Elevation: 7,000 feet on rim to 2,600 feet at river.

Surface and blaze: Rocky; occasional cairns; map reading skills required.

GRANDVIEW TRAIL

[Fig. 13(3)] Growing on the Canyon rim at Grandview Point are pinyons and junipers. Shrubs include cliffrose (*Cowania mexicana*), Gambel oak (*Quercus gambelii*), mountain mahogany (*Cercocarpus* sp.), big sagebrush (*Artemisia tridentata*), and Mormon tea (*Ephedra viridis*). Just below the rim on the north-facing slopes are some white firs (Abies concolor) and Douglas firs. These quickly give way to pale hoptree (*Ptelea trifoliata*), false mock orange (*Fendlera rupicola*), single-leaf ash (*Fraxinus anomala*), Utah serviceberry (*Amelanchier utahensis*), skunk bush (*Rhus trilobata*), and fern bush (*Chamaebatiaria millifolium*). Nearing Horseshoe Mesa, the larger shrubs are replaced by blackbrush (*Coleogyne ramosissima*), broom snakeweed (*Gutierrezia* sp.), four-wing saltbush (*Atriplex canescens*), and rabbitbrush (*Chrysothamnus* sp.).

In prehistoric times, the Anasazi and other Indians gathered blue and green copper ore from Horseshoe Mesa to use as paint. By 1892 Pete Berry along with Ralph and

Niles Cameron were improving the old Indian trail so they could mine the copper, which proved to be high-grade. At the Columbian Exposition in Chicago, ore samples were awarded a prize for being over 70 percent pure. The Last Chance Mine was soon shipping out over 1 ton of ore per day. Several cabins and a mess hall were constructed on Horseshoe Mesa. Unfortunately for the miners, the cost of transportation and smelting was exceeded when the price of copper crashed in 1907. The mines closed.

During the mining period, more and more tourists arrived at Grandview Point having taken the stagecoach line from Flagstaff. The miners accommodated these visitors by building the Grandview Hotel on the rim. After the Santa Fe Railway completed their spur line to the South Rim near the Bright Angel Trail in 1901, most tourists abandoned the rough stage ride for the more easily accessible Fred Harvey hotels.

Directions: The trail begins right at Grandview Point on the Desert View Drive.

Trail: 3 miles one-way to Horseshoe Mesa. There are three routes off of Horseshoe Mesa to the Tonto Platform, but they are all quite difficult.

Degree of difficulty: Moderate to Horseshoe Mesa.

Elevation: 7,400 feet at trailhead to 4,800 feet on Horseshoe Mesa.

Surface and blaze: Rocky; cairned.

SOUTH KAIBAB TRAIL

[Fig. 13(4)] The South Kaibab and Bright Angel trails are the only two regularly maintained rim-to-river trails. The South Kaibab Trail is often combined with the Bright Angel to make a loop trip. The South Kaibab is steeper than the Bright Angel, has virtually no shade, and has no water, so it is usually the descent route. After overnighting at the bottom, either in the Bright Angel Campground or at Phantom Ranch, the ascent is made via the Bright Angel Trail.

At 1.5 miles down, the trail crosses Cedar Ridge. The cedars are actually junipers, the short scrubby trees with shredding bark and blue berry-like cones.

Directions: The trailhead is near Yaki Point on the Desert View Drive, and from Mar. through Oct. is accessible only by the free shuttle (check with the NPS Backcountry Information Center or Park Service newspaper *The Guide* to find out departure times and locations) or on foot.

Trail: 6.3 miles one-way to the Colorado River.

Degree of difficulty: Moderate.

Elevation: 7,260 feet at trailhead to 2,480 feet at the river.

Surface and blaze: Well-maintained dirt and rock surface.

BRIGHT ANGEL TRAIL

[Fig. 13(5)] The Bright Angel Trail is the best known and most used trail into the Grand Canyon. Hikers share the path with up to 100 or more mules per day. For at least a thousand years, people have traveled up and down this route made feasible by the Bright Angel Fault, which has offset and broken the cliffs. Prehistoric and historic Havasupai Indians climbed down to Garden Creek and raised crops of corn, beans, and squash.

By 1891, miners had improved the trail and were operating it as a toll road, charging $1 per person and stock animal. Not until 1928 did the National Park Service gain control of the trail and offer free access. During the summer, there is drinking water available 1.5, 3, and 4.5 miles below the rim. There are restrooms 1.5 and 4.5 miles below the rim. A good day hike for someone fit is to go down the 4.5 miles to Indian Gardens Campground, out 1.5 miles to Plateau Point, and return to the rim. This 12-mile hike should not be attempted in the heat of summer.

In spite of all the traffic on the Bright Angel, this is still an excellent area to see desert bighorn sheep and mule deer. Soaring and diving along the cliff faces are violet-green swallows (*Tachycineta thalassina*) and the similar white-throated swifts (*Aeronautes saxatalis*). Ravens (*Corvus corax*) and turkey vultures (*Cathartes aura*) are commonly seen riding the thermals. Grayish-brown rock squirrels (*Spermophilus variegatus*) and sometimes chipmunks (*Eutamias* sp.) will beg along the trail. Please do not feed them. It encourages aggressive behavior and causes unnatural concentrations of these rodents, which usually results in the outbreak of disease.

Directions: The trailhead is immediately west of the Kolb Studio in Grand Canyon Village.

Trail: 7.8 miles one-way to the Colorado River, another 1.5 miles to junction with the base of the South Kaibab Trail.

Degree of difficulty: Moderate.

Elevation: 6,860 feet at trailhead to 2,400 feet at river.

Surface and blaze: Well-maintained dirt and rock surface.

HERMIT TRAIL

[Fig. 13(6)] To avoid having their guests pay toll fees to use the Bright Angel Trail, the Santa Fe Railway built its own mule trail into the Canyon. First a road from the railroad station to Hermit's Rest was constructed, and then a trail into Hermit Canyon was engineered. From 1912 to 1930, the railroad operated a tourist camp on the Tonto Plateau. To supply the camp, a 3,000-foot-long cable was strung between Pima Point and Hermit Camp. Even a Model T Ford was lowered into the canyon and driven around the camp area. Once the Bright Angel Trail was open to free travel, Hermit Camp was abandoned.

Hermit Creek supports a lush riparian community of coyote willow (*Salix exigua*), desert broom (*Baccharis* sp.), arrowweed (*Tessaria sericea*), and the non-native tamarisk (*Tamarix chinensis*). Mesquite (*Prosopis glandulosa*), catclaw acacia (*Acacia greggii*), and prickly pear cacti (*Opuntia* sp.) are also common.

Directions: The signed trailhead is at the end of the short dirt road behind the Hermit's Rest parking area, 8 miles west of Grand Canyon Village on the Hermit Road (West Rim Drive). Note that from Mar. through Oct., Hermit's Rest is accessible only by free shuttle, which leaves from just west of the Bright Angel Lodge, or on foot.

Trail: 7.8 miles one-way to Hermit Creek; another 1.7 miles to the Colorado River.

Degree of difficulty: Strenuous.

Elevation: 6,640 feet at the trailhead to 2,380 feet at the river.
Surface and blaze: Rocky to hard-packed soil, a few washouts; cairned in places.
BOUCHER TRAIL
[Fig. 13(7)] The Boucher Trail is another rim-to-river route, one that some hikers call "sporting" because of its tendency to skirt very narrow ledges. There are great views down into Hermit Canyon and the observant hiker will notice beautiful fern fossils in the red Hermit Shale.

Louis Boucher came to the Grand Canyon about 1891 to seek his fortune. He had a camp at Dripping Springs where he kept goldfish in a trough. He built a trail from the springs along the west side of Hermit Canyon and then contouring under Columbus Point into Travertine Canyon. His trail then dropped down through the Supai Formation to a break in the Redwall Limestone that gave access to Long (now called Boucher) Canyon. He named the trail Silver Bell, perhaps after the bell that hung from his white mule's neck. At Boucher Creek, he planted orange, fig, peach, pear, apricot, apple, nectarine, and pomegranate trees, none of which seem to exist today. He also raised tomatoes, chilies, cucumbers, melons, and grapes. Ruins of his stone cabin and one of his abandoned mining adits can be seen along the creek. He never struck it rich, so in 1909 he moved on to Utah.

Directions: Generally reached by taking the upper part of the Hermit Trail to Hermit Basin, then following the signed Dripping Springs Trail to its signed junction with the Boucher.
Trail: 10.5 miles one-way from Hermit trailhead to the Colorado River.
Degree of difficulty: Very strenuous.
Elevation: 6,640 feet at the trailhead to 2,320 feet at the river.
Surface and blaze: Rocky; faint to nonexistent in places; steep; cairned in places.
SOUTH BASS TRAIL
[Fig. 13(8)] The South Bass Trail takes you into one of the more remote parts of the Grand Canyon. It is here, too, that the Esplanade, a broad, relatively flat platform, begins and runs to the west. The trail crosses the Esplanade and passes by Mt. Huethawali, a small butte, before plunging steeply through the Supai and Redwall formations to the floor of Bass Canyon. The trail continues along the dry streambed until almost reaching the Colorado River. Bass Canyon ends as an unclimbable cliff overlooking the river. To reach the river, look for a faint trail leading up and out of the streambed to the west. After about 0.3 mile, a rock cairn marks a short but steep break in the cliffs that leads down to Bass Rapids.

William Bass learned about this route into Trail (now called Bass) Canyon from the Havasupai Indians. Bass had come West in 1883 for his health at the age of 34. Doctors were certain that he did not have long to live, but the dry climate of the Southwest might help. Bass was so impressed with the Grand Canyon that he started a tourist business on the rim. Visitors went down to the Colorado River and crossed to the north side, initially using a small boat and then later in a cage suspended from

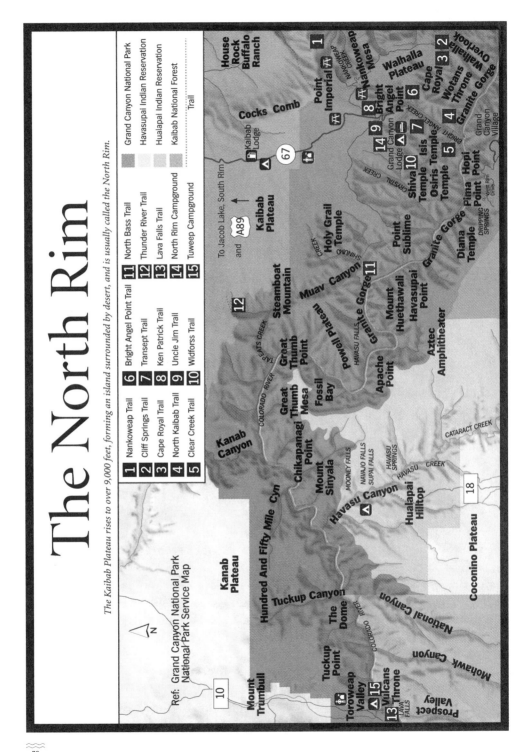

The North Rim

The Kaibab Plateau rises to over 9,000 feet, forming an island surrounded by desert, and is usually called the North Rim.

Ref: Grand Canyon National Park
National Park Service Map

Legend:

Grand Canyon National Park
Havasupai Indian Reservation
Hualapai Indian Reservation
Kaibab National Forest
·········· Trail

1. Nankoweap Trail
2. Cliff Springs Trail
3. Cape Royal Trail
4. North Kaibab Trail
5. Clear Creek Trail
6. Bright Angel Point Trail
7. Transept Trail
8. Ken Patrick Trail
9. Uncle Jim Trail
10. Widforss Trail
11. North Bass Trail
12. Thunder River Trail
13. Lava Falls Trail
14. North Rim Campground
15. Tuweep Campground

a cable. (There is no river crossing today.) On the north side along Shinumo Creek, Bass built a camp and kept a garden. Eventually he improved an old trail from the North Rim down to the creek, which allowed him to take hunting parties to the Kaibab Plateau.

In 1895, Bass married one of the visiting tourists, Ada Diefendorf, a music teacher from New York. Life at their home at the trailhead lacked most luxuries including running water. To do laundry, Ada would pack the dirty clothes down to Shinumo Creek, a three-day round trip. But the hard life apparently agreed with Mr. Bass for he lived to be 84 and so did Mrs. Bass.

Directions: The trailhead is located about 31 miles west of the Grand Canyon Village via rough, sometimes impassable dirt roads. Also, one road crosses a corner of the Havasupai Reservation and a permit may be required. Check with the Backcountry Information Center for the latest permit information and which roads are open.

Trail: 7.8 miles one-way from the trailhead to the Colorado River.

Degree of difficulty: Very strenuous.

Elevation: 6,650 feet at trailhead to 2,250 feet at the river.

Surface and blaze: Rocky, washed out in places; cairned; map reading skills required.

TONTO TRAIL

[Fig. 13(9)] The Tonto Trail follows the Tonto Plateau almost 100 miles from Red Canyon to Garnet Canyon. It allows hikers to interconnect most of the rim-to-river trials and thus complete loop trips. The trail is not nearly as level or distinct as it may appear when peering down at it from the South Rim. The Tonto Trail may wander and contour endlessly to go 1 mile in a straight line. Maybe that's how it received its name, which is Spanish for "foolish." There is little reliable water and no shade. Good route finding skills are necessary. Most of the time the trail traverses over the greenish Bright Angel Shale or brown Tapeats Sandstone. Occasionally it dips into the Precambrian rocks.

Directions: Can only be reached by taking one of the South Rim-to-river trails.

Trail: About 95 miles long one-way, but rarely hiked from end to end.

Degree of difficulty: Moderate.

Elevation: Averages around 3,600 feet.

Surface and blaze: Rocky to packed soil; route-finding skills required.

The North Rim

[Fig. 14] Within the Arizona Strip, the Kaibab Plateau rises abruptly to over 9,000 feet, forming a biological island surrounded by a sea of desert, and is the area usually called the North Rim. Unlike the South Rim where entrepreneurs, prospectors, schemers, and dreamers arrived early, exploration was longer in coming on the North Rim. The high country is buried under deep snows half the year, and the lower deserts are crossed by only a few meager, mostly unpaved roads.

One way to reach the North Rim is to take US 89 and US 89A north from Flag-staff. Sections of the highway follow the old Mormon Honeymoon Trail wagon road, which traces an even earlier Indian path. There is no hint of a canyon until US 89A bridges the Colorado near the head of the Grand Canyon.

The highway swings around the base of the Vermilion Cliffs, cuts across the Marble Platform, and then begins the steep climb up the wavelike crustal fold called the Kaibab Monocline. On top of the Kaibab Plateau, turn south on AZ 67 at Jacob Lake for the 45-mile journey through lovely ponderosa, fir, spruce, and aspen forest broken by verdant meadows to the North Rim, which in this case is the southern tip of the Kaibab Plateau. Here you will find the rustic Grand Canyon Lodge, the Park Service visitor center, and other tourist amenities.

But don't hurry along the road. Stop often and listen for the eerie, liquid, flutelike phrases of a hidden hermit thrush drifting by; look for a cautious bobcat creeping down to Harvey Pond for a drink; admire the mule deer browsing at the edge of DeMotte Park ("park" being an old cowboy term for meadows); laugh at the wild turkeys gobbling across the road. And be alert for the flash of a snowy white tail on the south end of a northbound Kaibab squirrel.

In the evening make the short walk from the Grand Canyon Lodge to Bright Angel Point. The light is softer now; the Canyon's colors are richer. Listen for the rush of water far below at Roaring Springs. This large spring is the source of drinking water for both the North and South rims. The inner secret parts of the Canyon are already in deep shadow. Brahma and Zoroaster temples glow in the waning light, and far to the south, the San Francisco Peaks oversee a phalanx of lesser volcanoes. It is only 10 miles as the raven flies to Grand Canyon Village on the South Rim. By trail the distance is 22, but by road, it is more than 200 miles away.

The road from Jacob Lake to the North Rim, across the Kaibab Plateau, is usually open only from mid-May to early November. Tourist facilities on the North Rim such as the Grand Canyon Lodge, campground, Park Service visitor center, and stores, are open only from mid-May to mid-October.

A paved Park Service road leads east and then south to spectacular views at Point Imperial, Vista Encantada, Roosevelt Point (surprisingly, Teddy Roosevelt, staunch supporter of making the Canyon a national park, did not have any feature named for him until July 3, 1996, when Roosevelt Point was designated on the North Rim), Walhalla Overlook, and Cape Royal.

For those prepared with the proper vehicle, supplies including water and a good map, and patience, a 63-mile dirt road leaves State Highway 389 about 9 miles west of Fredonia and travels to the awesome, vertigo-inducing Toroweap Overlook, where the Park Service operates Tuweep Campground (see page 79). Here the Canyon walls drop nearly 3,000 vertical feet to the Colorado River. Lava Falls, one of the biggest of the river's rapids, can be seen downstream.

Directions: The main part of the North Rim is 45 miles south of Jacob Lake at the end of AZ 67.

Activities: Scenic drives, hiking, and mule rides.

Facilities: Lodging, food services, gift shops, visitor center, general store, campground, showers, and laundry.

Dates: Open May 15 to Oct. 15; the North Rim remains open for day use only after Oct. 15 until snow closes highway AZ 67 from Jacob Lake.

Fees: There is an entrance fee.

Closest town: Fredonia, about 75 miles.

For more information: Grand Canyon National Park, PO Box 129, Grand Canyon, AZ 86023. Phone (520) 638-7888. For lodging in the park, call AmFac (303) 297-2757. For mule ride information, call (520) 638-9875 in season or (435) 679-8665 during the winter.

NORTH RIM CAMPGROUND

[Fig. 14(14)] **Directions:** From Jacob Lake, take AZ 67 south about 48 miles to campground on right.

Activities: Camping, hiking, wildlife viewing, naturalist programs, and horseback riding.

Facilities: 82 camping sites, drinking water, picnic sites, restrooms, handicap access, and trailer sites.

Dates: Open May 15 to Oct. 15 (dates may vary depending on snowfall).

Fees: There is a camping fee.

Closest town: Fredonia, about 75 miles.

For more information: Grand Canyon National Park, PO Box 129, Grand Canyon, AZ 86023. Phone (520) 638-7888. For camping reservations, which can be made up to five months in advance, call DESTINET at (800) 365-2267.

TUWEEP CAMPGROUND

[Fig. 14(15)] **Directions:** From Fredonia go west on AZ 389 about 9 miles then turn left (south) onto a dirt road, County Road 109. There are several forks, which are usually signed, but continue south about 63 miles to Toroweap Overlook and the Tuweep Campground.

Activities: Camping and hiking.

Facilities: 10 campsites, restrooms, and picnic tables; otherwise primitive.

Dates: Open year-round but wet weather may make the dirt road impassable.

Fees: None.

Closest town: Fredonia, about 72 miles.

For more information: National Park Service, PO Box 129, Grand Canyon, AZ 86023. Phone (520) 638-7888.

🔲 NORTH RIM TRAILS
NANKOWEAP TRAIL

[Fig. 14(1)] The Nankoweap Trail is one of the most difficult and challenging Grand Canyon trails. However since prehistoric times, the Nankoweap area has attracted people. In 1993 a stone spear point, of the type crafted by the Folsom culture, was discovered in Nankoweap Canyon, proving that Paleolithic hunters were in the Grand Canyon at least 10,000 years ago. By A.D. 200 the Anasazi were planting corn and squash on terraces above Nankoweap Creek and the Colorado River. Today native plants such as honey mesquite (*Prosopis glandulosa*), catclaw acacia (*Acacia greggii*), blackbrush (*Coleogyne ramosissima*), and prickly pear cactus (*Opuntia* sp.) have reclaimed the farm plots.

Later bands of Southern Paiute hunters roamed the area. Possibly the Paiute name *Nankoweap*, which translates as "people killed here," refers to an Apache and Paiute battle that supposedly took place near the head of the Nankoweap Canyon.

In 1882, John Wesley Powell, then director of the U.S. Geological Survey, supervised the construction of a horse trail into Nankoweap so that geologist Charles Doolittle Walcott could study the ancient, tilted Precambrian rock layers. Several years later, horse thieves connected this trail with the Tanner Trail to take stolen stock across the Grand Canyon. Not only was the trail arduous, but also swimming the Colorado could be fatal for man and beast. During the Prohibition Era of the 1920s, illegal moonshiners also utilized this remote trail. As recently as 1937, horses were used on the Nankoweap Trail, although one was lost over a cliff. Today it is hard to imagine that this trail was ever good enough for horse travel. There are a couple sections where hikers may need a belay for safety.

During the winter months, bald eagles are sometimes observed fishing for rainbow trout that are spawning in Nankoweap Creek.

Directions: The trailhead can be accessed from the west via Forest Service Road 610, or from the north through House Rock Valley via FS 445. FS 445 is a lower elevation access road and is more reliable year-round. Note that both trailheads are called Nankoweap/Saddle Mountain Trail and both are numbered FS Trail 57 (*see* Saddle Mountain Wilderness, page 36, for more information).

Trail: From the end of FS 445 to the National Park Service (NPS) trailhead is 3 miles on FS Trail 57, and then it is another 11 miles one-way from the NPS trailhead to Colorado River.

Degree of difficulty: Extremely strenuous and dangerous.

Elevation: 7,520 feet at NPS trailhead to 2,760 at the river.

Surface and blaze: Rocky, packed dirt, loose scree; cairned in places; routefinding skills very important.

CLIFF SPRINGS TRAIL

[Fig. 14(2)] This short trail leads to a spring on the Walhalla Plateau that was once an important campsite for Indians and early tourists to the North Rim.

Directions: About 3 miles north of the Grand Canyon Lodge, turn off AZ 67 onto the Point Imperial/Cape Royal Road. At the next junction, turn right onto the Cape Royal Road. Follow it to Angels Window Overlook. The trail begins across the road from the overlook and descends a ravine past a small prehistoric ruin to a cliff-sheltered spring.

Trail: 1 mile one-way.

Degree of difficulty: Easy.

Elevation: 7,600 feet.

Surface: Rocks and dirt.

CAPE ROYAL TRAIL

[Fig. 14(3)] This trail leads hikers past Angels Window, a natural limestone arch, to the very tip of Walhalla Plateau and a terrific, almost 360-degree canyon view.

Directions: About 3 miles north of the Grand Canyon Lodge, turn off AZ 67 onto the Point Imperial/Cape Royal Road. At the next junction, turn right onto the Cape Royal Road. Follow it to its end. The signed trailhead is at the parking area.

Trail: 0.6-mile loop.

Degree of difficulty: Easy.

Elevation: 7,865 feet.

Surface: Paved.

NORTH KAIBAB TRAIL

[Fig. 14(4)] The first 5 miles of the North Kaibab Trail quickly descends into Roaring Springs Canyon to meet Bright Angel Creek. Roaring Springs, as the name suggests, can be heard long before it is seen. Water gushes out of a cave in the Redwall Limestone and cascades down to Bright Angel Creek. Water from the springs is pumped to both the North and South rims to serve tourists and residents.

About 2 miles down the creek is Cottonwood Campground. Fremont cottonwood (*Populus fremontii*), box elders (*Acer negundo*), pale hoptree (*Ptelea trifoliata*), Knowlton hop hornbeam (*Ostrya knowltoni*), and coyote willows (*Salix exigua*) line the creek banks. American dippers (*Cinclus mexicanus*) may be seen doing their "kneebends" on boulders in the stream or "flying" underwater in search of aquatic invertebrates to eat.

About 1.5 miles downstream from the campground is a short side trip to Ribbon Falls. The waters of Ribbon Creek are highly mineralized with calcium carbonate derived from the limestone formations above. As the mineral slowly precipitates out of the creek water, an apron of calcium carbonate or travertine is formed behind the falls. Moss, maidenhair ferns (*Adiantum capillus-veneris*), yellow columbines (*Aquilegia triternata*), and scarlet monkeyflowers (*Mimulus cardinalis*) thrive in the spray from the falls.

Back on the main trail, travel another 3 miles to reach the entrance of The Box, where vertical walls of black Precambrian schist tower 1,000 feet above the creek. After 3 miles more, you reach Phantom Ranch, built in 1922 and the only lodge within the Grand Canyon. Mail can be sent out from the ranch, and it will be post-marked "Mailed from the bottom of the Canyon." The delightful booklet *Recollections of Phantom Ranch,* written by Elizabeth Simpson delves into the fascinating history of this isolated guest ranch.

The Bright Angel Campground and the Colorado River are 1 mile beyond Phantom Ranch.

Directions: This trail begins at the North Kaibab trailhead parking lot, 2 miles north of the Grand Canyon Lodge.

Trail: 14.5 miles one-way from trailhead to the Colorado River.

Degree of difficulty: Moderate.

Elevation: 8,250 feet at the trailhead to 2,480 at the river.

Surface and blaze: Well maintained.

CLEAR CREEK TRAIL

[Fig. 14(5)] This trail begins 0.5 mile north of Phantom Ranch, climbs up to the Tonto platform, and then contours about 9 miles east to Clear Creek, where good campsites along the creek can be found. A moderate 4-mile bushwhack upstream brings one to the foot of Cheyava Falls.

In the late spring of 1903, William Beeson, a Cameron Hotel tour guide, was driving a buggy along the South Rim. While pointing out the buttes and temples, he was astonished to see what looked like a sheet of ice on the wall up Clear Creek Canyon on the far side. The Kolb brothers, early South Rim residents, looked at it through their telescope and determined that it was not ice but a huge waterfall coming out of the Redwall Limestone cliff and cascading down nearly 1,000 feet. By summer, the falls had dried up. Five years later, Ellsworth Kolb and a friend hiked to Bright Angel Creek at the bottom of the Grand Canyon and spent the next day working their way to Clear Creek. They returned with the first photographs of what would become known as Cheyava Falls (*Cheyava* is a Hopi word meaning "intermittent"), the highest in the Grand Canyon.

Directions: This trail branches off the North Kaibab Trail about 0.5 mile north of Phantom Ranch and contours easterly to Clear Creek.

Trail: 8.7 miles one-way from junction with the North Kaibab Trail to Clear Creek. Cheyava Falls is a moderate bushwhack 4 miles upstream.

Degree of difficulty: Moderate.

Elevation: 2,640 feet at trailhead to 4,160 feet on the Tonto Plateau to 3,600 feet at Clear Creek.

Surface and blaze: Rocky to packed dirt; a few rock cairns.

BRIGHT ANGEL POINT TRAIL

[Fig. 14(6)] This scenic trail runs along a knife-edge ridge separating Roaring Springs Canyon and The Transept.

Directions: Starts at Grand Canyon Lodge.

Trail: 0.5 mile one-way to viewpoint.

Degree of difficulty: Easy.

Elevation: 8,100 feet.

Surface: Paved.

TRANSEPT TRAIL

[Fig. 14(7)] This trail follows the rim along The Transept, one of the longest tributary drainages to Bright Angel Canyon.

Directions: Starts at Grand Canyon Lodge.

Trail: 1.5 miles one-way to the North Rim Campground.

Degree of difficulty: Easy.

Elevation: 8,200 feet.

Surface: Rock and dirt.

KEN PATRICK TRAIL

[Fig. 14(8)] After the first 3 miles or so, this trail has been described as "more of an intense introduction to orienteering than a stroll through the forest." Yet for someone looking for an adventurous rim hike, this is it. At its end, the trail breaks out of the forest for terrific vistas from Point Imperial.

Directions: This trailhead is located at the eastern end of the North Kaibab trailhead parking lot.

Trail: 10 miles one-way from trailhead to Point Imperial.

Degree of difficulty: Moderate, but parts are brushy.

Elevation: 8,250 feet at trailhead to 8,803 at Point Imperial.

Surface and blaze: Forest floor and dirt; portions are obscure.

UNCLE JIM TRAIL

[Fig. 14(9)] James T. "Uncle Jim" Owens worked as a game warden on the North Rim in the early 1900s. He guided Western novelist Zane Grey and president Teddy Roosevelt on mountain lion (*Felis concolor*) hunts. Owens claimed to have killed more than 1,200 mountain lions though others estimate the number closer to 500. Marguerite Henry immortalized him in the classic children's novel *Brighty of the Grand Canyon*. This trail starts out as the Ken Patrick Trail, which skirts the rim of Roaring Springs Canyon. After 1 mile, the Uncle Jim Trail turns right (south) and goes out to some very nice vistas on Uncle Jim Point.

Directions: The trailhead is the same as for the Ken Patrick Trail.

Trail: 2.5 miles one-way.

Degree of difficulty: Easy.

Elevation: About 8,250 feet.

Surface and blaze: Well-marked forest path.

WIDFORSS TRAIL

[Fig. 14(01)] This trail leads to Widforss Point, which honors Swedish artist Gunnar Widforss who painted many watercolors of the Grand Canyon during the 1920s and 30s. Once you arrive at the point, you will see the fantastic views that inspired this artist.

Directions: Drive about 1 mile on the gravel road across from the North Kaibab trailhead parking lot to reach the trailhead.

Trail: 5 miles one-way from trailhead to Widforss Point.

Degree of difficulty: Easy.

Elevation: 8,100 feet at trailhead to 7,900 feet at Widforss Point.

Surface and blaze: Well-marked forest path.

NORTH BASS TRAIL

[Fig. 14(11)] This is the north extension of the cross-canyon route pioneered by William Bass (*see* South Bass Trail description, page 75). The trail is very rugged but scenic as it follows the perennial but intermittent White Creek which feeds into Shinumo Creek. Shinumo is a permanent trout stream and also home to American dippers (*Cinclus mexicanus*) who "fly" underwater to catch invertebrates. About 1 mile from the Colorado River, the trail crosses a fairly open terrace. It is here that nineteenth century engineers thought a switchyard for a railroad through the Grand Canyon could be built. Fortunately this never happened in this lovely wilderness. Hikers should plan at least 3 to 4 days to complete a round-trip from rim to river and return.

Directions: From AZ 67 head west on FS 422, an all-weather road. At the top of the ridge take FS 270, then turn right onto FS 223. Turn left on FS 268 and bear left on FS 268B. Turn right (west) at the intersection with the Swamp Point Road. Road conditions deteriorate on the last 10 miles from the park boundary to Swamp Point and the marked trailhead. High clearance, four-wheel-drive vehicles are recommended. Roads may not be free of snow until early June.

Trail: About 14 miles from trailhead to the Colorado River.

Degree of difficulty: Very strenuous; requires considerable route-finding skill.

Elevation: 7,500 feet at trailhead to 2,200 feet at river.

Surface and blaze: Rocky, steep, loose scree; few cairns.

THUNDER RIVER TRAIL

[Fig. 14(12)] Rumors of placer gold attracted miners into the area in the 1870s. They constructed the upper portion of the trail, which was then used by geologist Clarence Dutton several years later.

The trail descends through the upper cliffs to the broad Esplanade terrace. After about 5 miles, the trail switchbacks into Surprise Valley. Although the trail has just dropped through the Supai and Redwall formations, the bottom of the "valley" is once again Supai. Over 1 cubic mile of rock has slumped downward. The route continues easterly, crossing several washes and rolling hills. Then steep switchbacks lead past Thunder River, plunging down a 100-foot cliff. The river flows only 0.5 mile before entering Tapeats Creek. The trail continues downstream to the Colorado River.

Directions: There are two trailheads. The several miles longer and less steep route is reached by turning west off of AZ 67 onto FS road 422 toward Dry Park. Then take

FS 425 to FS 232 to its end at Indian Hollow and the signed trailhead. The other trail, sometimes called the Bill Hall Route, is reached by taking FS 425 to FS 292 and continuing west along the rim on FS 292A until it ends at the trailhead. All these roads may be closed by snow until June.

Trail: About 15 miles from Indian Hollow trailhead to the Colorado River. The Bill Hall Route is about 3 miles shorter.

Degree of difficulty: Moderate but long.

Elevation: 6,400 feet at Indian Hollow to 2,000 feet at Colorado River.

Surface and blaze: Rock and packed dirt.

LAVA FALLS TRAIL

[Fig. 14(13)] This route leads down to the Colorado River and Lava Falls, one of the most feared of the river's 150 major rapids.

Directions: The trailhead is located on the southwestern side of Vulcan's Throne about 2.5 miles from the Toroweap Valley Road. About 3.5 miles south of the Toroweap Ranger Station turn right (west) onto the dirt road bearing toward Vulcan's Throne, an extinct cinder cone. The road goes through Toroweap Lake, which is usually dry. If not dry, do not attempt to cross it. Park and walk around the lake.

Trail: About 1.5 miles one-way; do not let the short distance deceive you.

Degree of difficulty: Very strenuous.

Elevation: 4,000 feet at trailhead to 1,675 at the Colorado River.

Surface and blaze: Loose rock; cairned.

MULE RIDES

South Rim—Mule rides from the South Rim are booked up to a year in advance. For information about one- and two-day trips into the Canyon including overnight stays at Phantom Ranch, the only lodge within the Canyon, call the Grand Canyon National Park Lodges at (303) 297-2757 or write to them at South Rim, Grand Canyon, AZ 86023.

North Rim—It is often easier to book a one-day mule ride into the Canyon from the North Rim on short notice. Check at Grand Canyon Lodge or call (520) 638-9875 in season or (435) 679-8665 during the winter.

THE COLORADO RIVER

Birthed in the glaciers and snow pack on the Rocky Mountain continental spine and draining an area the size of Texas, the Colorado River writhes 1,450 miles to the sea. Well, almost to the sea. Today the river is usually dry a few miles south of the U.S./Mexico border. Dammed, diverted, evaporated—it is all used up.

A hundred years ago, the free-flowing waters of the Green River and the Grand River flowed together to form the Colorado deep in the heart of what is now Canyonlands National Park in east-central Utah. Then in 1921, the state of Colorado convinced Congress to officially change the name of the Grand River to the Colorado

River. The older name still lingers as Grand Lake, Grand Junction, and Grand Mesa, all in Colorado. At 730 miles the Green River is the longer tributary and contributes about two-thirds of the Colorado's volume; so hydrologically the Green probably should have earned the name Colorado. But politics overshadowed science and logic.

Large-scale regulation of the river began with the 1922 Colorado River Compact, which divided seven western states—Wyoming, Utah, Colorado, New Mexico, Arizona, Nevada, and California—into upper and lower basins. The compact allocated 7.5 million acre-feet of water annually to each basin (1 acre-foot is the amount of water that covers 1 acre to 1 foot in depth). A 1944 treaty also guaranteed Mexico 1.5 million acre-feet each year. However, since 1930 the Colorado's annual flow has only averaged 14 million acre-feet. Evaporation from reservoirs removes another 2 million acre-feet, resulting in a shortfall of 4.5 million acre-feet. Today, various Indian tribes that were not included in the 1922 compact are seeking to acquire their "fair share" of the Colorado, too.

There simply is not enough water to go around. Explorer and geologist John Wesley Powell understood this. He called for organized development of the Southwest that was based upon the location of the limited amount of water. But few listened.

The first large dam placed on the Colorado was Hoover, completed in 1935. Its reservoir, Lake Mead, at times backs nearly 40 miles into the lower Grand Canyon. The last major dam was Glen Canyon, just 15 river miles upstream of the Grand Canyon and completed in 1963. The Colorado may be the world's most legislated, litigated, and debated river.

The Colorado River within the Grand Canyon drops 2,000 feet through 160 major rapids and is considered one of the premier whitewater adventures in North America. Flash floods and debris flows have dumped tons of boulders from steep side canyons into the main stream. The Colorado can't always remove boulders, and thus a rapid is born. These obstructions cause the river to pool upstream creating not only a serene, calm respite but also upstream currents that often require the boatman to row the raft right to the brink of the rapid, all the while anxiously glancing over his shoulder at the maelstrom.

Following John Wesley Powell's successful 1869 journey down the Colorado River through the Grand Canyon, only a few brave men and women would challenge the rapids over the next 100 years. Two of these people were honeymooners, Glen and Bessie Hyde. In 1928 they plied the river in their homemade scow, got at least as far as 232 Mile Rapid in the western Grand Canyon, then vanished. Their boat was found upright still containing their gear, including Bessie's vague diary. It contained only dates with terse notations, despite the Hydes' plans to write a book about their adventure.

The first women to survive a river trip were two botanists, Elzada Clover and Lois Jotter, who accompanied Norman Nevills on his 1938 run. Nevills would eventually be the first to offer commercial trips through the Canyon. Beginning in the 1950s,

Georgie Clark White revolutionized river running by building huge rafts out of army surplus bridge pontoons. Her motorized G-rigs made the trip safer and more appealing to novices. And Georgie's leopard-print bathing suits became legendary.

Yet up until 1964, fewer than 1,000 people had gone down the river. Astonishingly, by 1972 more than 16,000 were enjoying the adventure each year. This sudden dramatic increase in river runners alarmed the Park Service. Studies were begun to examine the possible ecological impacts and ways to mitigate those problems. Not far into their study, scientists realized that Glen Canyon Dam, completed in 1963 upstream of the Grand Canyon, was also playing havoc with the river's ecosystem and its banks.

The river that was named for its reddish-brown color and was once, "too thick to drink, but to thin to plow" was turned into a clear, cold stream. The millions of tons of mud and silt carried by the Colorado now settle in the quiet waters of Lake Powell. The annual spring floods that laid in new sandy beaches and scoured away riverside vegetation within the Grand Canyon no longer occur because of the dam's regulation of water flow. Native fish adapted to warm, sediment-laden water are being replaced by exotic rainbow trout for anglers. Plants, some native, some not, invade the riverbanks, establishing a new riparian habitat that allows certain indigenous animals to flourish and changes the migratory behavior of others. The threatened willow flycatcher (*Empidonax traillii*) nests in the exotic salt cedar along with the formerly uncommon Bell's vireo (*Vireo bellii*). Paradoxically, the yellow-billed cuckoo (*Coccyzus americanus),* another riparian-dependent bird, has not been seen since 1971. Dozens of bald eagles now overwinter by feeding on the introduced trout. All these changes and more are the direct or indirect result of the construction of Glen Canyon Dam.

Today more than 24,000 people a year enjoy river trips through the Canyon. All trash and human waste is carried out. In 1992, Congress passed the Grand Canyon Protection Act, which mandates that Glen Canyon Dam be operated to minimize any detrimental impacts to native plants and animals. In spite of these new rules, more and more people are discussing the possibility of draining Lake Powell to allow the Colorado River to flow more naturally through the Grand Canyon. For information about this novel idea, contact the Glen Canyon Institute, PO Box 1925, Flagstaff, AZ 86002. Phone (520) 556-9311. Web site www.glencanyon.org.

Seventeen river companies offer whitewater trips lasting anywhere from three days to three weeks. Most trips embark from Lees Ferry between April and October. A few partial trips start or end at Phantom Ranch, which can only be reached by a hike or mule ride. Note that trips are often booked up to a year in advance. Private river running trips require a permit from the River Permits Office. The current waiting list for private permits is six to eight years long!

For more information: National Park Service, PO Box 129, Grand Canyon, AZ 86023. Phone (520) 638-7888. For a private permit, contact the River Permits Office at the same address.

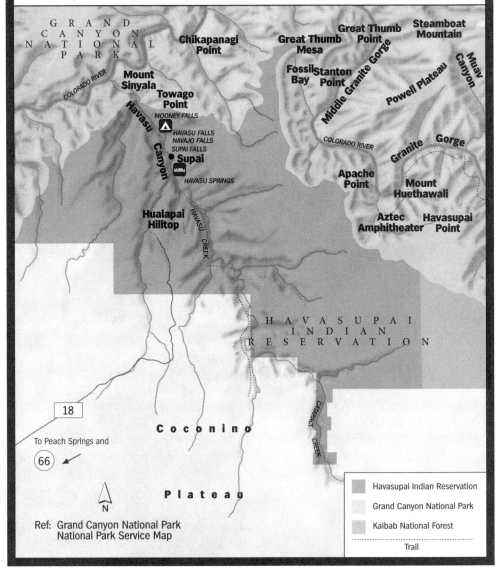

Havasupai Reservation Area

Havasupai means "people of the blue-green water," a name that comes from the aqua color of Havasu Creek.

GRAND CANYON NATIONAL PARK

Chikapanagi Point

Great Thumb Mesa

Great Thumb Point

Steamboat Mountain

Mount Sinyala

COLORADO RIVER

Towago Point

Fossil Bay

Stanton Point

Middle Granite Gorge

Muav Canyon

Powell Plateau

Havasu

MOONEY FALLS

HAVASU FALLS
NAVAJO FALLS
SUPAI FALLS

Supai

Canyon

COLORADO RIVER

Granite Gorge

HAVASU SPRINGS

Apache Point

Mount Huethawali

Hualapai Hilltop

HAVASU CREEK

Aztec Amphitheater

Havasupai Point

H A V A S U P A I
I N D I A N
R E S E R V A T I O N

18

To Peach Springs and

66

C o c o n i n o

CATARACT CREEK

N

P l a t e a u

Ref: Grand Canyon National Park
National Park Service Map

Havasupai Indian Reservation

Grand Canyon National Park

Kaibab National Forest

Trail

Havasupai Reservation Section of the Grand Canyon

[Fig. 15] The *Havasupai* ("people of the blue-green water") have lived in the Grand Canyon area for centuries. Traditionally, they would spend the summers growing corn, beans, and squash along streams within the Grand Canyon. They would also harvest wild agaves, or century plants, to roast and eat like squash. During the winter, the people migrated to the Canyon rims and hunted mule deer, rabbits, and squirrels. Pinyon nuts and other wild plant foods were gathered, along with plenty of firewood to keep warm.

This seasonal migration came to an abrupt halt in the summer of 1880 when the federal government established a reservation for the Havasupai in the bottom of Havasu Canyon. The original reservation was a tract of land about 5 miles wide and 12 miles long where about 200 people lived and farmed. The government made no provision for the annual migration to the rim country. Nor did the Havasupai immediately understand their predicament. For nearly a century, the Havasupai battled in the courts to regain some of their traditional land. Finally, in 1975, the reservation was enlarged to incorporate some of the highlands. The poignant story of this struggle is told in Stephen Hirst's *Life in a Narrow Place*.

The best time to visit the Havasupai in their village, Supai, is between late spring and early fall, before the weather turns cold and blankets the plateau with snow. On Labor Day weekend the tribe holds its annual Peach Festival, which attracts many visitors including members of other tribes. A rodeo is also held. It's a splendid time to learn a little about this ancient culture, buy exquisitely made baskets, and take in the exceptional beauty of the Indians' isolated canyon home.

The Havasupai Reservation includes Havasu Creek, which is arguably the prettiest stream in Arizona. The only ways to reach the creek and Supai Village are by trail or by helicopter; there is no road into the canyon or to the village. The Hualapai Hilltop Hiking and Horse Trail descends into Hualapai Canyon in a series of steep switchbacks. Eventually the trail drops into a dry, rocky stream bed that finds its way into a shady, narrowing gorge. Shortly after passing the junction of Havasu Creek, you cross Havasu Creek.

The creek begins innocently enough as a series of springs a few miles above Supai Village. It flows quietly through the village and then drops over Navajo Falls where a magical transformation takes place. The creek water turns aqua blue. What is happening is a chemical reaction as more air, hence oxygen, gets dissolved in the water. The oxygen combines with dissolved carbonate minerals to form travertine (a form of calcium carbonate). The travertine begins to precipitate out but suspended particles refract the sunlight in such a way that the water appears turquoise to the eye. Hold a glass of it up so that light can shine through, and it is clear. But don't drink it. While safe to swim in, the water's calcium carbonate makes a great natural laxative, plus the village is upstream. The high concentration

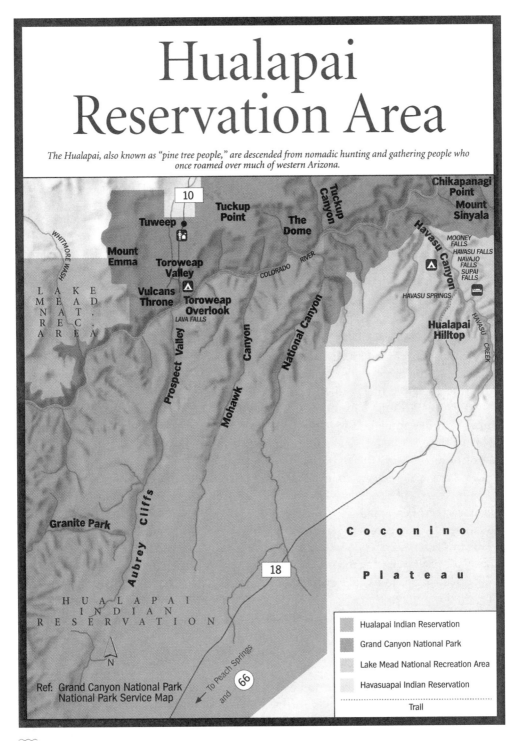

Hualapai Reservation Area

The Hualapai, also known as "pine tree people," are descended from nomadic hunting and gathering people who once roamed over much of western Arizona.

10

Tuckup Point

Tuweep

The Dome

Tuckup Canyon

Chikapanagi Point

Mount Sinyala

Mount Emma

Toroweap Valley

COLORADO RIVER

Havasu Canyon

MOONEY FALLS
HAVASU FALLS
NAVAJO FALLS
SUPAI FALLS

Vulcans Throne

Toroweap Overlook

LAVA FALLS

WHITMORE WASH

L A K E   E
M E A D .
N A T C
R E C A
A   R E A

HAVASU SPRINGS

Hualapai Hilltop

National Canyon

Prospect Valley

Mohawk Canyon

HAVASU CREEK

Granite Park

Aubrey Cliffs

C o c o n i n o

P l a t e a u

18

H U A L A P A I
I N D I A N
R E S E R V A T I O N

N

To Peach Springs and

66

Ref: Grand Canyon National Park
National Park Service Map

Hualapai Indian Reservation

Grand Canyon National Park

Lake Mead National Recreation Area

Havasuapai Indian Reservation

Trail

of minerals also precludes the survival of any fish of interest to anglers. A little farther down the trail, the creek plunges over the 100-foot Havasu Falls into a deep turquoise pool. The trail and stream pass through a campground. Just beyond is yet another falls, Mooney, which is the highest at 190 feet. To reach the base of the Mooney Falls and to continue downcanyon, the trail goes through two tunnels cut into the travertine cliffs by miners back in the 1880s. Continuing downstream the canyon becomes wilder and the trail less developed, but a determined hiker can make it the dozen miles to the Colorado River.

Directions: Turn north off AZ 66 (Old Historic Route 66) about 7 miles east of Peach Springs onto the Hualapai Hilltop Road. It is about 60 miles to the Havasupai Reservation, the parking area, and the trailhead. If you have previously arranged with the Havasupai Tourist Enterprise for a horse or helicopter, this is where you will be met.

Activities: Hiking or horseback riding or helicoptering to Supai Village and Havasu Creek.

Facilities: Supai has a lodge and cafe; a campground with tables, drinking water, and pit toilets.

Dates: Open year-round.

Fees: There are separate fees for hiking, camping, horse and helicopter rides.

Closest town: Peach Springs, about 67 miles.

For more information: Havasupai Tourist Enterprise, Supai, AZ 86435. Phone (520) 448-2121 or 2141. For lodging, contact: Havasupai Lodges, Supai, AZ 86435. Phone (520) 448-2111.

Trail: About 8 miles one-way to Supai Village, another 2 miles to the campground.

Degree of difficulty: Moderate.

Elevation: 5,200 feet at trailhead to 3,200 feet at Supai Village.

Surface: Rocky to sandy but easy to follow.

Hualapai Reservation Section of the Grand Canyon

[Fig. 16] The Hualapai Reservation takes in part of the western Grand Canyon along the South Rim. The *Hualapai* ("pine tree people") are descended from nomadic hunting and gathering people who once roamed over much of western Arizona. They are closely related to the Havasupai and Yavapai. The only town on their reservation is Peach Springs located on old historic Route 66. A 21-mile dirt road travels north to the Colorado River at Diamond Creek. This is the only road that goes to the bottom of the Grand Canyon. A permit is required to use the road and can be obtained at the River Runners Office where the Diamond Creek Road begins out of town. Be extremely wary of flash floods especially during the summer rainy season. More than one vehicle has gone on an unplanned river trip.

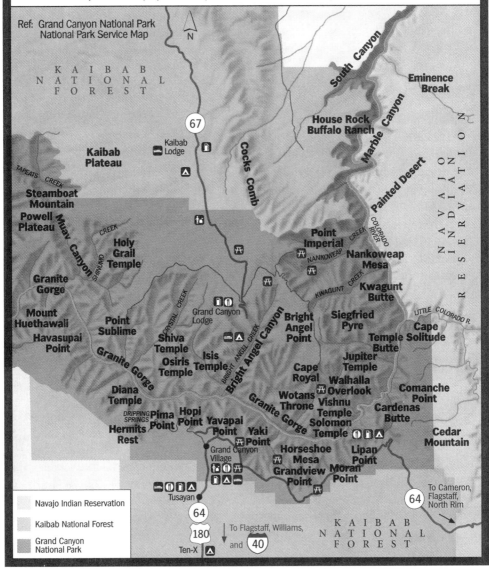

Navajo Res. Area of the Grand Canyon

The eastern side of the Grand Canyon from Lees Ferry down to the Little Colorado River is part of the Navajo Indian Reservation.

Ref: Grand Canyon National Park
National Park Service Map

N

KAIBAB NATIONAL FOREST

67

South Canyon

Eminence Break

Marble Canyon

House Rock
Buffalo Ranch

Kaibab Lodge

Kaibab Plateau

Cocks Comb

Painted Desert

NAVAJO INDIAN RESERVATION

TAPEATS CREEK

Steamboat Mountain

Powell Plateau

Muav Canyon

CREEK

SHINUMO

Holy Grail Temple

COLORADO RIVER

Point Imperial

NANKOWEAP CREEK

Nankoweap Mesa

Granite Gorge

CRYSTAL CREEK

KWAGUNT CREEK

Kwagunt Butte

Mount Huethawali

Point Sublime

Grand Canyon Lodge

Bright Angel Point

Siegfried Pyre

LITTLE COLORADO R.

Cape Solitude

Havasupai Point

Granite Gorge

Shiva Temple

Isis Temple

BRIGHT ANGEL CREEK

Bright Angel Canyon

Temple Butte

Jupiter Temple

Osiris Temple

Cape Royal

Walhalla Overlook

Comanche Point

Diana Temple

Granite Gorge

Wotans Throne

Vishnu Temple

Cardenas Butte

DRIPPING SPRINGS

Pima Point

Hopi Point

Yavapai Point

Solomon Temple

Cedar Mountain

Hermits Rest

Yaki Point

Horseshoe Mesa

Lipan Point

Grand Canyon Village

Grandview Point

Moran Point

Tusayan

64

To Cameron, Flagstaff, North Rim

64

Navajo Indian Reservation

Kaibab National Forest

Grand Canyon National Park

180

Ten-X

To Flagstaff, Williams, and 40

KAIBAB NATIONAL FOREST

For experienced Grand Canyon hikers, there are many possibilities for cross-country wilderness hikes, but a permit is required from the tribe. Contact Hwal'Bay Ba:j Enterprises for permits, PO Box 359, Peach Springs, AZ 86434. Phone (520) 769-2419 or (800) 622-4409. For the novice, a better option is the exciting boat trip on the Colorado River through the western Grand Canyon from Diamond Creek to Lake Mead. The Hualapai offer half-day, one-day, and two-day trips. Call Hualapai River Runners at (888) 255-9550. Tribal members lead guided wilderness hunts for desert bighorn sheep, elk, mule deer, turkey, and other game. Contact the Wildlife Conservation Office at (520) 769-2227.

Directions: Peach Springs is located 54 miles northeast of Kingman on AZ 66 (Old Route 66).

Activities: Hiking, horseback riding, camping, nature study, hunting, and rafting.

Facilities: Lodging, cafe, general store and service station in Peach Springs.

Dates: Open year-round; some activities are seasonal.

Fees: There is a permit fee and fees for various activities.

Closest town: Peach Springs.

For more information: Contact Hwal'Bay Ba:j Enterprises, PO Box 359, Peach Springs, AZ 86434. Phone: (520) 769-2419 or (800) 622-4409. For lodging information, phone (888) 255-9550.

Navajo Reservation Section of the Grand Canyon

[Fig. 17] The eastern side of the Grand Canyon from Lees Ferry down to the confluence of the Colorado and Little Colorado rivers is part of the Navajo Reservation. There are no marked trails, but several of the tributary canyons are passable to the river to the careful, experienced hiker. Any hiking or camping in this area requires a permit from the Navajo Tribe. Fishing in this section requires a license from the Arizona Game and Fish Department, not the Navajo tribe.

Directions: Lies west of US 89 from Cameron north to Navajo Bridge.

Activities: Hiking, camping, nature study, and fishing.

Facilities: None.

Dates: Open year-round.

Fees: There are fees for hiking, camping, and fishing.

Closest town: Page is about 35 miles from the northern part; Cameron is about 20 miles from the southern portion.

For more information: For a hiking or camping permit, contact Cameron Visitor Center, PO Box 549, Cameron, AZ 86020. Phone (520) 679-2330. Or Navajo Nation Parks and Recreation Department, PO Box 9000, Window Rock, AZ 86515. Phone (520) 871-6647. For a fishing license, contact Arizona Fish and Game Department, 2221 W. Greenway Road, Phoenix, AZ 85023. Phone (602) 942-3000.

Northeast Plateau

This corner of Arizona is primarily desert scrub and grasslands interspersed with pinyon-juniper woodlands.

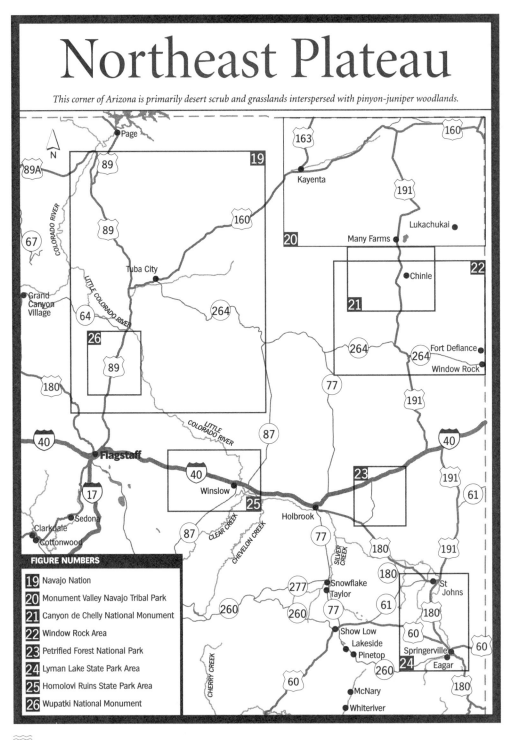

FIGURE NUMBERS

19 Navajo Nation
20 Monument Valley Navajo Tribal Park
21 Canyon de Chelly National Monument
22 Window Rock Area
23 Petrified Forest National Park
24 Lyman Lake State Park Area
25 Homolovi Ruins State Park Area
26 Wupatki National Monument

Northeast Plateau Country

L ike most of the Arizona Strip and the Grand Canyon area, the northeastern portion of Arizona is also part of the physiographic province known as the Colorado Plateau. And typical of the Colorado Plateau, it is a land primarily composed of mostly flat-lying Paleozoic and Mesozoic sedimentary rock layers that have been uplifted and then dissected by the downcutting of streams and weathered into canyons, mesas, and buttes. Biologically, this corner of Arizona is primarily desert scrub and grassland interspersed with pinyon-juniper woodlands. The several higher mountains and mesas have ponderosa pine forest and small stands of Douglas fir and even aspen.

[*Above:* Monument Valley Navajo Tribal Park is renowned for its red sandstone buttes, mesas, and pinnacles]

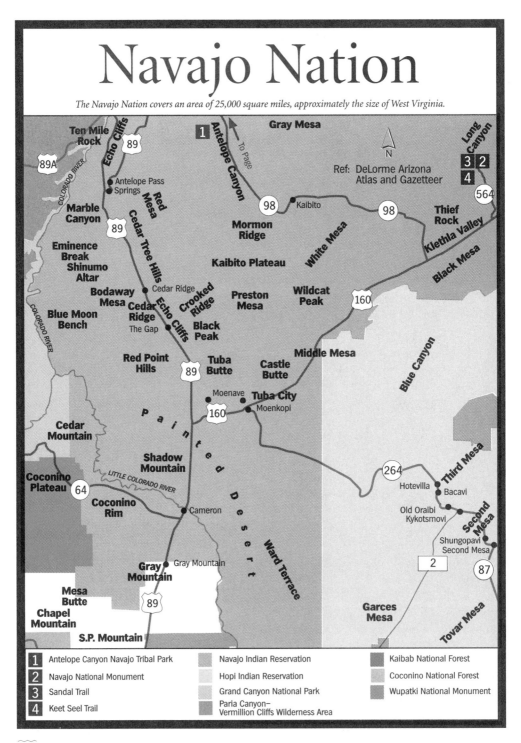

Navajo Nation

The Navajo Nation covers an area of 25,000 square miles, approximately the size of West Virginia.

Ten Mile Rock
Gray Mesa
Long Canyon
Echo Cliffs
89
89A
1
Antelope Canyon
To Page
N
Ref: DeLorme Arizona Atlas and Gazetteer
3 2
4
564
Colorado River
Antelope Pass Springs
Red Mesa
98
Kaibito
98
Thief Rock
Marble Canyon
89
Mormon Ridge
White Mesa
Klethla Valley
Eminence Break
Shinumo Altar
Cedar Tree Hills
Kaibito Plateau
Black Mesa
Bodaway Mesa
Cedar Ridge
Crooked Ridge
Preston Mesa
Wildcat Peak
160
Blue Moon Bench
Cedar Ridge
Echo Cliffs
The Gap
Black Peak
Colorado River
Red Point Hills
89
Tuba Butte
Castle Butte
Middle Mesa
Blue Canyon
Moenave
Tuba City
Moenkopi
160
Cedar Mountain
P a i n t e d
Shadow Mountain
264
Hotevilla
Bacavi
Third Mesa
Coconino Plateau
64
Little Colorado River
Coconino Rim
Cameron
Old Oraibi
Kykotsmovi
Second Mesa
D e s e r t
Shungopavi
Second Mesa
Gray Mountain
Gray Mountain
Ward Terrace
2
87
Mesa Butte
89
Chapel Mountain
Garces Mesa
Tovar Mesa
S.P. Mountain

1 Antelope Canyon Navajo Tribal Park
2 Navajo National Monument
3 Sandal Trail
4 Keet Seel Trail

Navajo Indian Reservation
Hopi Indian Reservation
Grand Canyon National Park
Paria Canyon–Vermillion Cliffs Wilderness Area

Kaibab National Forest
Coconino National Forest
Wupatki National Monument

Native American Reservations

NAVAJO NATION

[Fig. 19] Most of northeastern Arizona is Navajo Reservation or as some prefer, Navajo Nation. The reservation spills over into New Mexico and a little into Utah to cover an area of over 25,000 square miles or approximately the size of West Virginia. Much of the land is high desert and woodland. To many outsiders, it may seem bleak and lonely, but over 250,000 people are spread out across that land mostly living in isolated family groups. To the Navajo, it is their traditional home between the four sacred mountains—Hesperus and Blanco peaks in Colorado, Mount Taylor in New Mexico, and the San Francisco Peaks in Arizona.

Scientists claim that the Navajo language is of Athapascan origin, thus these people probably have come from the north (i.e., Canada). One scenario has the Navajo arriving in the Four Corners area in the early sixteenth century. Many Navajos dispute this, saying that their ancestors were contemporaneous with the Anasazi.

Many Navajo families still live in camps, a term leftover from the days when the people were semi-nomadic and their homes were seasonal camps. Today, a Navajo camp generally consists of a hogan, a traditional, dome-shaped, log house covered with clay and having a single door that faces east and a smoke hole. Next to the hogan is usually a modern house or trailer; a ramada or summer shade, a structure with a ceiling often made of tree branches with the leaves still attached but no walls; and not too far away, an outhouse.

The hogan is a warm, cozy place in the winter and is frequently used during traditional ceremonies. The summer shade is the ideal place to work or sleep during the hot summer months.

For over a century, the Navajo country has been subjected to intense livestock grazing. This, along with perhaps some natural climatic changes, has caused dramatic changes to the local environment and the native plant communities. Erosion seems to have increased beginning around the turn of the last century. Many of the deep arroyos or washes incised into the soft, sandy sediments that crisscross the reservation are no more than 100 years old. As grazing animals removed the

Navajo Time

From the first week of April until the last week of October, the Navajo Nation, including Navajo National Monument, Monument Valley, and Canyon de Chelly, is on Mountain Daylight Savings Time. The rest of Arizona plus the Hopi Reservation remains on Mountain Standard Time the entire year. Thus during the spring, summer, and fall, the Navajo Nation is one hour ahead of the rest of Arizona. By changing to Mountain Daylight Savings Time, the Navajos in Arizona conform with sections of their reservation in Utah and New Mexico.

Lizard Sex

Of the dozen species of lizards that live on the high desert plateau of northern Arizona, one has a most unusual way of procreating. The plateau striped whiptail (*Cnemidophorus velox*) only comes in the female gender. There are no males. During the breeding season, two females approach each other. One takes on the role of a male lizard—doing push up displays, head bobbing, etc. If that impresses the other lizard, she allows the male-acting one to mount her. It's all show; however, that action seems to stimulate the submissive female's body into producing hormones that cause her unfertilized eggs to begin to grow into baby lizards. She lays three to five eggs in late June or early July, and they hatch several weeks later. The young are genetic clones of their mother. This method of reproduction is called parthenogenesis and, while rare in vertebrates, is not uncommon in invertebrates.

sparse desert vegetation, flash flooding and wind erosion increased, and arroyos were cut. As the arroyo deepened, springs were destroyed, and what had been a permanent stream became intermittent or completely dried up.

The sheep, horses, and cattle ate what they liked and left other plants, usually woody shrubs like sagebrush (*Artemisia* sp.), rabbitbrush (*Chrysothamnus* sp.), and saltbush (*Atriplex* sp.), or poisonous wildflowers like locoweed (*Astragalus* sp.) and jimson weed (*Datura mete-loides*), which became more common. Nutritious native grasses were replaced with inedible exotic ones like cheatgrass (*Bromus tectorum*). Introduced weeds, such as tumbleweed (*Salsola kali*), became prevalent.

Grazing pressure, loss of water sources, and uncontrolled hunting have greatly reduced the number of the larger native animals such as deer and bighorn sheep. The very adaptable coyote is extant as well as many of the smaller mammals like ground squirrels and mice. Huge colonies of Gunnison's prairie dogs (*Cynomys gunnisoni*) were poisoned in the early 1900s in a misguided attempt to improve the range for livestock. Black-footed ferrets (*Mustela nigripes*) that preyed on the "dogs" are now gone from the reservation.

Bird life is also scarce. Ravens are common partly because they have such catholic tastes when it comes to food. Small flocks of horned larks (*Eremophlia alpestris*) dart out in front of your vehicle when you're driving down a dirt road. Pinyon and scrub jays haunt the woodlands. A northern harrier (*Circus cyaneus*) is occasionally seen cruising a few feet above the desert scrub. But the casual birder will probably be disappointed. The best place to see birds on the reservation is where there is water, and the best times are spring and summer.

While traveling on Navajo land, please respect their privacy and their customs. Enter tribal lands, off paved highways, with permits only. Do not disturb or remove animals, plants, rocks, or artifacts. The use of and possession of alcohol, drugs, and firearms are prohibited. Rock climbing and defacing canyon walls are not allowed.

Hiking and camping is allowed only in designated areas with a permit, which can be obtained from the Navajo Nation Parks and Recreation Department, PO Box 9000, Window Rock, AZ 86515. Phone (520) 871-6647. Limited hunting and fishing can be done on Navajo lands. Contact the Navajo Nation Department of Fish and Game, PO Box 1480, Window Rock, AZ 86515, phone (520) 871-6451. Photography for personal use is allowed. However, permission is required to photograph Navajo people or their property and a small gratuity is expected.

The Navajos are not the only Native Americans in the area. Several bands of Southern Paiutes live on the Navajo Reservation and only recently have received legal recognition. Northwest of St. Johns and not far south of Navajo land is a tiny Zuni Reservation. And close to the middle of the Navajo Nation is the Hopi Reservation.

For more information: Navajo Nation Parks and Recreation Department, PO Box 9000, Window Rock, AZ 86515. Phone (520) 871-6647. Web site www.navajoland.com. An excellent detailed traveler's guide to the Navajo reservation lands is *Native Roads* by Fran Kosik. Also, in Kayenta on US 160 is a visitor center that offers travel information including a listing of tour guides and bed and breakfast operators. The visitor center can be contacted at PO Box 545, Kayenta, AZ 96033. Phone (520) 697-3572.

HOPI RESERVATION

[Fig. 19] The Hopi, who only number about 10,000, live primarily in a dozen villages scattered over three mesas plus two additional villages near Tuba City. Anthropologists and archaeologists believe the Hopi are descendants of the prehistoric Anasazi and therefore have lived at least several thousands of years in the American Southwest. (Note that the term Anasazi is a corruption of a Navajo word that means roughly "ancestors of our enemies" and was applied by Navajo and archaeologist, alike, to describe the ancient people of the Four Corners area. Many Hopi would like their term for their ancestors used, *Hisatsinom*—people of the ancient times, but this term annoys some other Puebloan people.)

The Hopi Reservation encompasses over 1.5 million acres of land surrounded by the Navajo Reservation. Each village is self-governing and members of the tribe identify themselves

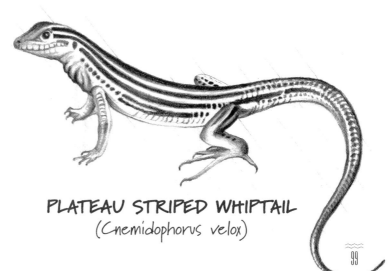

PLATEAU STRIPED WHIPTAIL
(Cnemidophorus velox)

with their village and clan. Seeking refuge from possible Spanish retaliation after the Pueblo Revolt of 1680, Tewa people from New Mexico founded one village, Hano, on First Mesa. Hopi and Tewa society are matrilineal in tradition.

Unlike their Navajo neighbors, the Hopi typically live in flat-roofed, stone- and clay-walled apartment complexes called pueblos. The pueblos or villages are usually laid out so that they enclose a central plaza area.

The Hopi continue to conduct centuries-old religious ceremonies throughout the year and understandably value their privacy. Absolutely no photography, sketching, or recording of religious ceremonies is permitted. Visitors are requested to honor each village's rules on visitation. Several villages have closed their religious Katsina dances to non-Indians; however, most social dances remain open. (Katsinas, also spelled Kachinas, are the supernatural beings that bring rain and good fortune to the Hopi people.) Snake dances and Flute ceremonies are also closed. Try the Hopi Tribal Office of Public Relations, (520) 734-2441, to find out which ceremonies may be open to the general public. Visitors may travel freely along primary highway corridors, near the Hopi Cultural Center on Second Mesa, and businesses along the highways. Off-road travel is prohibited.

The villages of First Mesa—Hano, Sichomovi, and Walpi—are recognized for their fine pottery, Katsina dolls, and weaving. Dramatically situated Walpi and the other villages of First Mesa can be visited with guides. These guided walking tours take about 45 minutes and give visitors an opportunity to learn about Hopi history, culture, and traditions. There are usually opportunities to see craftspeople at work and to buy items directly from their makers. Tours are arranged at Punsi Hall Visitor Center in Sichomovi year-round, seven days a week. There is a nominal fee. Call (520) 737-2262 for more information.

The Hopi Cultural Center at the "center of the universe," on Second Mesa, houses the Hopi Museum, arts and crafts shops, and a restaurant and inn. The restaurant is a good place to try traditional Hopi foods including the tissue-paper thin *piki* bread and *nok qui vi*, a corn and lamb stew with baked green chilis. The villages of Second Mesa—Shungopavi, Sipaulavi, and Mishongnovi—are famous for coiled baskets and Katsina dolls. The Hopi Cultural Center can be reached at PO Box 67, Second Mesa, AZ 86043. Phone (520) 734-2401.

Old Oraibi on Third Mesa is considered one of the oldest continuously inhabited villages in North America. Some of the houses date from at least the mid-twelfth century. Artisans here are noted for their wicker style of basket making, Katsina dolls, fine textile weavings, and silver overlay jewelry. The village of Kykotsmovi just below Third Mesa is the location of the Hopi Tribal Offices.

For more information: Hopi Cultural Center, PO Box 67, Second Mesa, AZ 86043. Phone (520) 734-2401. Web site www.nau.edu/~hcpop. An excellent detailed traveler's guide to the Hopi reservation is *Native Roads* by Fran Kosik.

ANTELOPE CANYON NAVAJO TRIBAL PARK

[Fig. 19(1)] Antelope Canyon is an exceptionally narrow slot-like canyon cut into the Navajo Sandstone. In places, a person can touch both sides with outstretched arms though the walls rise up for over 100 feet. The vertical walls twist and turn and almost double back on themselves. Its sensuously curving walls and ethereal light have attracted photographers, movie makers, and tourists. The canyon drains from the south into Lake Powell (once the Colorado River) and is the result of eons of floods wearing away at the soft sandstone. **Do not enter this canyon if there is any threat of a storm**. In 1997, 11 hikers drowned in a flash flood.

To the older Navajos, entering a place like Antelope Canyon is like entering a cathedral. They would pause before going in, to be in the right frame of mind and to prepare for protection from evil spirits and to show respect. They leave uplifted and with a better understanding of what Mother Nature has to offer. They are in harmony with something greater then themselves. It is a spiritual experience. The Navajos ask that visitors also enter quietly and respectfully, admire the changing light and the endlessly differing forms and images, and do not harm the desert plants and animals.

Directions: The entrance for upper Antelope Canyon is about 6 miles east of Page on AZ 98. Turn right just past milepost 299. To reach the entrance for the lower part of Antelope Canyon, stay on AZ 98 for another 0.25 mile beyond milepost 299 and turn left on Navajo Route N22B (Antelope Point Road). Go about 0.5 mile to entrance and parking.

Activities: Hiking with a guide and photography.

Facilities: None.

Dates: Open May through Oct.

Fees: There are fees for entry and the required guide and shuttle.

Closest town: Page.

For more information: Antelope Canyon Navajo Tribal Park, PO Box 4803, Page, AZ 86040. Phone (520) 698-3347.

Navajo National Monument

[Fig. 19(2)] Navajo National Monument preserves three of the best and largest prehistoric cliff houses in Arizona—Betatakin, Keet Seel, and Inscription House. These dwellings were built about 700 years ago by a culture archaeologists refer to as the Anasazi Puebloans (Anasazi).

Of the three, *Betatakin* (Navajo for "ledge house") is the most accessible. The 135-room ruin is perched in an alcove 452 feet high, 370 feet across, and 135 feet deep. Betatakin was built, occupied, and abandoned all in the last half of the thirteenth century. The easy Sandal Trail leads to an overlook of the cliff house (*see* page 102). A much more difficult, ranger-led hike to the ruin itself requires a free ticket issued the day of the hike. The Park Service does not take advanced reservations for this hike.

Keet Seel (Navajo for "broken pottery"), the largest cliff house in Arizona, is a 17-mile round-trip hike on the Keet Seel Trail (*see* below). It is remarkably well preserved and contains 160 rooms and perhaps six kivas (ceremonial rooms). Only 20 people per day are allowed to visit the site. Visitors must make reservations at least one day in advance, but not more than two months in advance.

Because of its fragile nature, Inscription House is currently closed to public visitation.

The monument's visitor center has exhibits on the prehistoric Anasazi and modern Navajo. A 25-minute video about the Anasazi or a 20-minute Betatakin tour video can be watched. Behind the center is an old-style Navajo forked-stick hogan and sweat lodge. A gift shop offers Navajo crafts and Hopi, Navajo, and Zuni jewelry.

Directions: Take US 160 about 20 miles southwest of Kayenta then turn right (north) onto AZ 564. The monument entrance is 9 miles away.

Activities: Viewing ruins, camping, and hiking.

Facilities: Campground, picnic area, water, restrooms; food and gas available 9 miles south at Black Mesa.

Dates: Open daily except Thanksgiving, Christmas, and New Year's Day.

Fees: There is an entrance fee.

Closest town: Kayenta, 29 miles.

For more information: Navajo National Monument, H.C. 71, Box 3, Tonalea, AZ 86044- 9704. Phone (520) 672-2366 or 2367. Web site www.nps.gov/nava.

SANDAL TRAIL

[Fig. 19(3)] From May through September, rangers lead groups (limited to 25) into Betatakin (2.5 miles one-way; 700-foot elevation change starting at 7,300 feet!). Call or write for exact length of season and tour times. But the Sandal Trail is a self-led, easy trail out to a viewpoint that looks into the canyon where Betatakin is located. Some of the native plants are identified along the way. Binoculars are helpful in seeing the details of the cliff house.

Directions: The Sandal Trail begins at the visitor center.

Trail: 0.5-mile trail winds through pinyon-juniper woodland to the rim of the canyon overlooking Betatakin.

Degree of difficulty: Easy.

Elevation: 7,300 feet to 7,140 feet.

Surface: Paved.

KEET SEEL TRAIL

[Fig. 19(4)] The remarkable preservation of Keet Seel makes it hard to believe that it has been abandoned for seven centuries. Its residents could just be out in their fields tending the crops of corn and beans or maybe off to visit their neighbors at

Betatakin. They left pottery, sandals, grinding stones, and other artifacts behind, never to return.

Call for the days the trail will be open. Only 20 people per day are allowed to visit the site. Visitors must make reservations at least one day in advance, but not more than two months ahead of time. A ranger stationed at the site accompanies visitors into the ruin. Backpackers can spend one night in a primitive campground near Keet Seel. Pit toilets are available. No wood fires are permitted.

The first 1.5 miles follows a dirt road to Tsegi Point, overlooking Tsegi Canyon. Then the trail descends 1,000 feet over rocky switchbacks and sand dunes to the canyon bottom and travels downstream a short distance before heading upstream into Keet Seel Canyon. Wading may be necessary. The Park Service recommends that **all** drinking water be carried in.

Directions: Directions to trailhead given with permit.
Trail: 8.5 miles one-way.
Degree of difficulty: Strenuous.
Elevation: 7,300 feet to 6,300 feet.
Surface and blaze: Sandy to rocky; cairned.

Monument Valley Navajo Tribal Park

[Fig. 20] Through numerous western movies and, more recently, a multitude of commercials and advertisements, millions of people from around the world readily recognize the monoliths of Monument Valley. To many, the valley's red sandstone buttes, mesas, and pinnacles are the quintessential images of the American Southwest.

Straddling the Utah/Arizona border, Monument Valley Navajo Tribal Park captures the imagination of those enamored with the mystique and legends of the Southwest. Visitors come from all over the world to immerse themselves in this timeless setting and absorb a little of the Navajo culture. Most visitors tour the park either in their own vehicles (the dirt tourist road, which is a 17-mile loop, can vary in negotiability depending upon the weather; check at visitor center) or with a guide in a variety of vehicles, ranging from open-air jeeps to air-conditioned buses. To really experience the valley, sign up for a multiday horseback trip. Each spring and fall, Don Donnelly's Horseback Vacations offers weeklong luxury horse riding trips that are unforgettable. Write them at 6010 S. Kings Ranch Road, Gold Canyon, AZ 85219 or call (800) 346-4403 or (480) 982-7822; Web site www.dondonnelly.com.

▓ GEOLOGY

There must be three conditions fulfilled in order for a "monument valley" to form. First, there must be a massive layer of hard rock overlying a massive layer of

Mon. Valley Navajo Tribal Park

One old Navajo name for Monument Valley translates into "a treeless place amid the rocks."

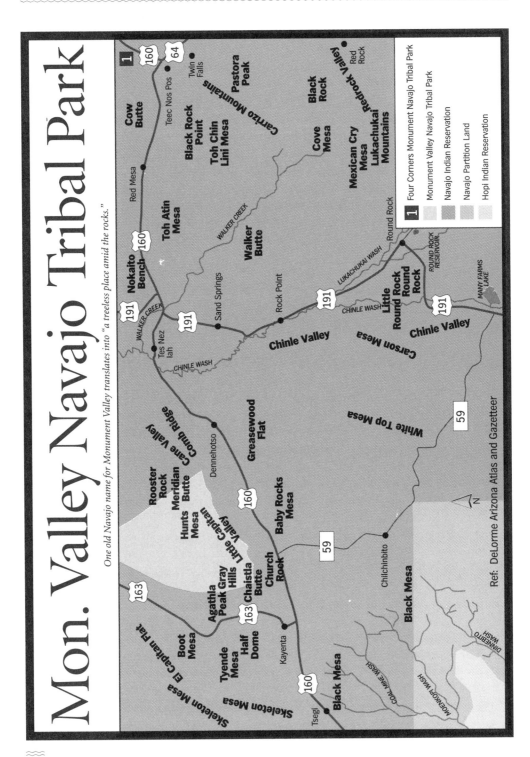

Ref: DeLorme Arizona Atlas and Gazetteer

1 Four Corners Monument Navajo Tribal Park
Monument Valley Navajo Tribal Park
Navajo Indian Reservation
Navajo Partition Land
Hopi Indian Reservation

softer rock. In Monument Valley the thick, relatively hard DeChelly Sandstone (when referring to the geologic formation, it is spelled DeChelly, but the canyon name is spelled de Chelly) sits on top of the softer claystone known as the Organ Rock Tongue. Second, these two layers must be in a relatively horizontal attitude. To the east and south of the valley, the DeChelly Sandstone and Organ Rock Tongue (along with several other sedimentary layers) are tilted and form the striking escarpment of Comb Ridge instead of the classic monuments. Third, these rock units must be in a dry climate. Put these same rocks in a humid, temperate zone, and they would be rounded off and quickly (geologically speaking) covered with soil and plants.

Once these three prerequisites are met, all that is needed is time—incomprehensible amounts of time. But nature has all she needs. Rains come and, at random, flow across the almost flat surface of the DeChelly Sandstone. Some of the water follows incipient cracks in the rock surface—cracks perhaps caused by stress related to the uplift of the region as well as an additional uplift within Monument Valley that has been going on for the last 65 million years. These cracks or joints are essentially vertical planes of weakness and

Navajo Weaving

In the late nineteenth century and earlier, Navajo weavers produced wearing blankets and other garments. However by the turn of the century, demand for blankets declined. Traders suggested to the weavers that they should make rugs for a growing market in the East. Particular designs, influenced by what the traders would purchase, became associated with specific trading posts, such as Crystal, Two Gray Hills, Ganado, Teec Nos Pos, but many weavers continued to create rugs with their own unique designs. Certain styles and colors have come and gone over the years, but Navajo weaving is still alive and well on the reservation. Current demand for older, historic rugs is high, plus many of today's weavers are producing true works of art. Buy from a reputable dealer who will certify the authenticity and quality including the absence of cotton warp and acrylic yarn. Some dealers include a photo of the weaver and at least one trader, Bruce Burnham of the R.B. Burnham and Company Trading Post, is encouraging weavers to weave in a distinctive hallmark.

are widened by water erosion. As the process continues, the vast, horizontal bed of sandstone is divided into smaller pieces with vertical sides. The hardness of the rock tends to preserve the precipitous nature of the sides of the forming mesa.

Once the downward-cutting channels encounter the softer Organ Rock Tongue Claystone, undercutting can take place and slabs of unsupported DeChelly Sandstone spall off along additional preexisting joints. These broken blocks of sandstone, along with the claystone, form the aprons or slopes that encircle the base of the monument. Through time the larger mesas are reduced in size to buttes, all the while continuing to display the classic profile of a monument. All the stages of monument development are wonderfully displayed in Monument Valley, which is not a valley at all in the usual sense.

The origin of today's landscape has been told, but what about the origin of the rock layers? The oldest rock unit exposed in Monument Valley is the Cedar Mesa Sandstone, which was laid down as sand in a shallow marine environment in early Permian time. The tourist road crosses the top of the Cedar Mesa Sandstone just after descending the hill from the visitor center. Careful observation reveals a joint system in the Cedar Mesa Sandstone.

As time passed, the area became more of a wet tidal flat with streams and rivers flowing westerly and southwesterly from a large mountain range, the Uncompahgre Mountains, several hundred miles to the northeast. The rivers carried heavy sediment loads of granitic and gneissic material and deposited them on the coastal lowlands. The boulders and larger pebbles settled out first, close to the mountains; the finer sand, clay, and silt were carried farther by the sluggish rivers and deposited as red beds 600 to 700 feet thick, from the vicinity of Canyonlands National Park (Utah) south through Monument Valley and west toward the Grand Canyon region.

At this time primitive amphibians and reptiles roamed the lowlands, and plant fossils indicate that the environment was arid. Geologists have named these red deposits the Organ Rock Tongue after an erosional feature that resembles a pipe organ west of Monument Valley.

By mid-Permian time, the sea attempted to encroach from the west but reached only a little east of where the Grand Canyon would one day form. From the shoreline eastward, desert winds piled quartz sand into mountainous dunes hundreds of feet high, patterned with ripples. The individual fine sand grains became coated with iron oxide, giving them a reddish orange cast. As more and more sediment was added to the deposit, the buried sand was slowly cemented together with silica and calcium carbonate "glue" carried by ground water into the 300- to 600-foot-thick DeChelly Sandstone.

Until the end of the Permian Period, the Monument Valley area remained a desert coastal lowland that was either gently eroding or with little or no additional sedimentation taking place. The Uncompahgre Mountains were nearly leveled, and the few remaining meandering streams were virtually clear of sediment.

Through the Triassic, Jurassic, and Cretaceous periods (about 245 to 65 million years ago), as the region fluctuated between coastal mud flats, swamps, and deserts, other deposits of sedimentary rocks were added to the geologic layer cake. However, in Monument Valley, most of these thousands of vertical feet of younger rock layers have been stripped away over the last 65 million years, as the Colorado Plateau has been uplifted 1 mile or more above sea level. A few of the mesas and monuments are still capped with remnants of younger geologic layers including a uranium-bearing deposit.

To the north and south of the tribal park along US 163 are several "monuments" that are not the typical erosional remnants of buff and red sedimentary rock, but rather are solitary towers of black rock that, according to Navajo lore, help hold up the sky. Alhambra Rock to the north and Agathla to the south are volcanic necks composed of basalt, the solidified magma that once filled a vent that possibly led to a now long-gone volcano. Some of these igneous features were created by the explosive energy of gas-charged magma drilling through the enclosing sedimentary layers.

FLORA AND FAUNA

One old Navajo name for Monument Valley translates into "a treeless place amid the rocks." Looking out across the valley from the high vantage point of the visitor center, the towering rocks and endless, azure sky overwhelm the visitor. It's easy not to notice the desert plant life.

On the dry, rocky valley floor, the predominate blackbrush (*Coleogyne ramosissima*) is interspersed with a few other hardy shrubs such as Mormon tea (*Ephedra torreyanna*), four-wing saltbush (*Atriplex canescens*), and shadscale (*Atriplex confertifolia*). Where the soil is sandier and more likely to absorb the scant winter and summer rains, there is a much greater diversity of perennials and lovely annual wildflowers. Some of the spring and summer flowering species include evening primrose (*Oenothera albicaulis*), indigo-bush (*Dalea* sp.), dwarf lupine (*Lupinus* sp.), crown-beard (*Vanclevia stylosa*), cryptantha (*Cryptantha* sp.), prickly poppy (*Argemone* sp.), fleabane daisy (*Erigeron* sp.), globemallow (*Sphaeralcea* sp.), phacelia (*Phacelia crenulata*), desert marigold (*Baileya multiradiata*), scarlet penstemon (*Penstemon eatonii*), western dock (*Rumex hymenosepalus*), desert peppergrass (*Lepidium fremontii*), sand verbena (*Abronia elliptica*), Gray's biscuit root (*Lomatium grayi*), sand gilia (*Gilia subnuda*), milk vetch (*Astragalus* sp.), Indian rice grass (*Oryzopsis* sp.), and galleta grass (*Hilaria jamesii*).

In late summer, rabbitbrush (*Chrysothamnus nauseosus*), broom snakeweed (*Gutierrezia sarothrae*), and sulphurflower (*Eriogonum* sp.) are ablaze with golden blossoms. A few purple sage (*Poliomintha incana*) plants may still fill the air with their strong, minty, volatile terpene oils. A new crop of tumbleweed (*Salsola kali*), an introduced weed from the steppes of Russia, is drying out and turning brown, soon to be ready for the winds to blow it and its seeds hither and yon.

Along the edges of washes grow plants that require a bit more moisture—cliffrose (*Cowania mexicana*), skunkbush (*Rhus trilobata*), desert ash (*Fraxinus anomala*), and the wispy tamarisk (*Tamarix pentandra*), an exotic species native to Arabian and Mideastern deserts that came to the American Southwest via transplants to California. In the shade of a cliff grow netleaf hackberry (*Celtis reticulata*), Utah serviceberry (*Amelanchier utahensis*), and mountain privet (*Forestiera neomexicana*), also known as desert olive.

Many of these plants are indicative of overgrazing. Sheep, cattle, and horses eat what they like and the "less desirable" species flourish. This grazing pressure, domestic animal diseases, and hunting have eliminated most of the larger native mammals like mule deer and desert bighorn sheep (*Ovis canadensis*) from Monument Valley.

Occasionally a wily coyote (*Canis latrans*) is seen skulking among the dunes. Typical birds include common raven (*Corvus corax*), black-throated sparrow (*Amphisiza bilineata*), Say's phoebe (*Sayornis saya*), canyon wren (*Catherpes mexicanus*), rock wren (*Salpinctes obsoletus*), house finch (*Carpodacus mexicanus*), and scrub jay (*Aphelocoma coerulescens*). The rare burrowing owl (*Athene cunicularia*), a small ground dwelling, diurnal bird, also lives in the valley and probably preys upon the common white-tailed antelope ground squirrels (*Ammospermophilus leucurus*).

▓ HISTORY

Navajo tradition relates that The People emerged into this world from the Underworld between the Four Sacred Mountains: the San Francisco Peaks near Flagstaff, Mount Taylor in New Mexico, and Hesperus and Blanco peaks in Colorado. The Diné wandered in the four cardinal directions to observe and learn about the surrounding world, which they found to be in terrible disarray and inhabited with horrible beasts. Eventually the Earth-Surface World was changed from monster-filled chaos into the well-ordered world of today's Diné.

While anthropologists would have us believe that the first Navajos didn't enter Monument Valley until the mid-1800s, at least some of the valley's residents claim a more ancient tie to the area. Some Navajo believe that their ancestors were contemporaneous with the Anasazi a millennium or more ago.

While Monument Valley's history prior to the 1850s is still largely a matter of conjecture, we do know that the outside world was crowding in on the Navajos. With the signing of the Treaty of Guadalupe Hidalgo in 1848, the rights of sovereignty of the Southwest passed from Mexico to the United States. To the Navajos and other Southwestern Indians, this historic event had little immediate impact, but over the course of the following decades the natives' lives would be irrevocably changed.

Although several treaties between the Navajos and the United States were drawn up, agreed to, and signed during the mid-1800s in an attempt to end conflicts, both sides failed to honor the terms. Finally in 1863, the U.S. government set on a course of all-out war against the Diné to, as stated in a directive to the army, "subdue them for all time or to annihilate them."

Using a scorched earth policy of killing livestock, devastating cornfields and orchards, and burning hogans, Colonel Kit Carson and the army were able to force the surrender of about 8,000 Navajos. Many died from starvation, disease, or exposure during their forced march in 1864 to an internment camp at Bosque Redondo near Fort Sumner, New Mexico.

One Navajo group that was able to escape Carson's men was led by *Hoskininni* ("Angry Warrior"). He and about 16 family members and neighbors fled Monument Valley toward Navajo Mountain. While in pursuit, Carson noted the imposing dark monolith of Agathla and named it El Capitan because of its commanding position at the southern entrance to the valley.

After four heart-breaking years, the Navajos at Bosque Redondo negotiated a treaty with the U.S. and were allowed to return to their homeland. Hoskininni and his people came out of hiding and returned to Monument Valley. The next dozen years were fairly peaceful, but then a new type of invader entered the valley.

On New Year's Eve 1880, James Merrick and Ernest Mitchell, two prospectors from Colorado, forded the San Juan River and headed south into Monument Valley. Merrick told others that he knew where the Navajos had a smelter and were handling ore that assayed 90 percent silver. He and Mitchell were going to look for the Indian mine.

Since returning to their homeland in 1868, the Navajos' production of silver buckles, buttons, clasps, and other items led to rumors of secret silver mines. After several weeks passed and the two prospectors did not return, an armed search party went out in February to look for them. The party discovered the bodies of Merrick and Mitchell, scalped and covered with rocks and brush, near the buttes that now bear their names. Local Navajos said that Paiutes had committed the murders, but the Paiutes pleaded innocence. The search party reported finding specimens of "very rich quartz ores" near the bodies. "Obviously" the men had discovered the mine and had been killed on their way out.

All the components of a good lost mine legend were present: hazy rumors that early Spanish explorers had known of the silver mine; the alleged discovery of the mine and subsequent killing of Merrick and Mitchell; and rugged, wild country guarded by Indians

The early twentieth century saw the arrival of the first tourists in Monument Valley. Western writer Zane Grey visited the valley with John Wetherill in 1913. Grey recounts the following in his autobiographical *Tales of Lonely Trails*: "My first sight of Monument Valley came with a dazzling flash of lightning. It revealed a vast valley, a strange world of colossal shafts and buttes of rock, magnificently sculptured, standing isolated and aloof, dark, weird, and lonely. When the sheet lightning flared across the sky showing the monuments silhouetted black against that strange horizon, the effect was marvelously beautiful. I watched until the storm died away."

On a hot summer day in 1921, a young sheepherder from Colorado, Harry Goulding, crested Comb Ridge and caught sight of Monument Valley for the first time. He knew instantly that this wild country was where he must live. Two years later Harry and his wife Mike (her given name was Leone, but Harry claimed that he couldn't learn how to spell it so he just called her Mike) arrived at the base of Tsay-Kizzi Mesa ready to homestead a section of state land. Harry had driven a truck while Mike negotiated the deep sand in a 1922 soft-topped Buick outfitted with oversize tires.

To the Navajos, Harry became known a Dibé Nineez, the tall man with sheep. Life was hard for the Gouldings, but the view from their "bedroom" couldn't be beat. At first they lived in a tent. Water was so scarce that Mike would claim, "We used the

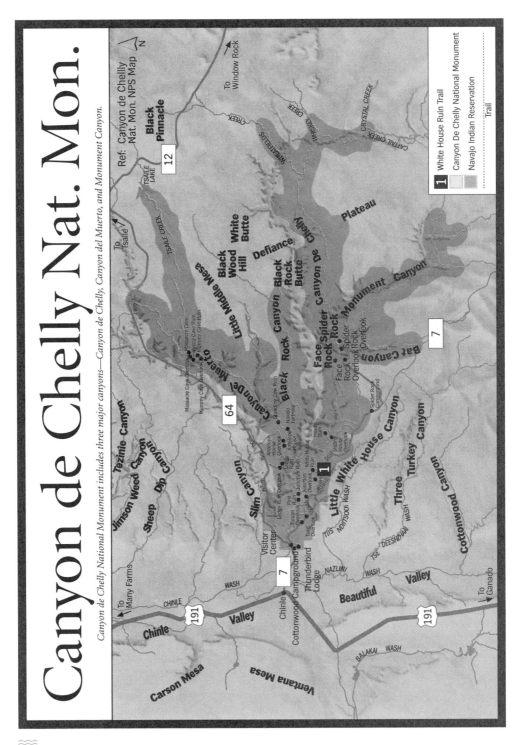

Canyon de Chelly Nat. Mon.

Canyon de Chelly National Monument includes three major canyons—Canyon de Chelly; Canyon del Muerto, and Monument Canyon.

Ref: Canyon de Chelly Nat. Mon. NPS Map

White House Ruin Trail

Canyon De Chelly National Monument

Navajo Indian Reservation

Trail

water twice to wash the dishes, mopped the floor with it, and then poured it on a little tree we were trying to grow." The Gouldings' two-story trading post, which still stands, was built in 1927-28. The few tourists that wandered out this way had Harry as their personal valley guide.

During the Great Depression, the economy affected even the isolated Navajos who had a difficult time selling their sheep, rugs, or jewelry. Harry Goulding believed that if Hollywood would film a western in the valley, much-needed cash would flow into the area. Goulding traveled to California armed with an album of photographs taken by the famous landscape photographer Josef Muench.

The photo album crossed the desk of film director John Ford at United Artists, and, as they say, the rest is history. Ford's first Monument Valley western, *Stagecoach*, starring an unknown actor by the name of Marion Morrison (today, better known as John Wayne), was released in 1939 and has become a classic. Ford made many other movies with the valley as the backdrop, including *My Darling Clementine* (1946), *Fort Apache* (1948), *She Wore A Yellow Ribbon* (1949), *Rio Grande* (1950), *The Searchers* (1956), and *Cheyenne Autumn* (1964).

As tourism increased, the Navajos decided in 1958 to establish 30,000 acres of Monument Valley as their first tribal park.

Directions: Located on the Arizona/Utah border about 26 miles north of Kayenta on US 163.

Activities: Self-guided or led tours; guided hiking, horseback riding, and vehicle tours.

Facilities: Visitor center, campground, restaurant, gift shop, and restrooms.

Dates: Open year-round except Christmas, New Year's Day, and Thanksgiving.

Fees: There is an entrance fee and additional fees for guided tours and camping.

Closest town: Kayenta, about 26 miles.

For more information: Monument Valley Navajo Tribal Park, PO Box 360289, Monument Valley, UT 84536. Phone (435) 727-3353 or 3287.

Four Corners Monument Navajo Tribal Park

[Fig. 20(1)] This is the only place in the United States where four states—Arizona, New Mexico, Colorado, and Utah—meet at a common point, now within the Navajo Reservation. The exact spot was first officially marked by a cement pad in 1912 although the area had been surveyed as early as 1868. The pad has since been re-placed with a monument made of granite, bronze discs, and colored concrete with the great seal of each state and the inscription "Four States Here Meet In Freedom Under God."

A favorite visitor activity is to have one's picture taken while standing in all four states at the same time.

Directions: The monument is located 0.25 mile west of US 160, 6 miles north of Teec Nos Pos, AZ, and 40 miles southwest of Cortez, CO.

Activities: Photography, buying of Indian arts and crafts.

Facilities: Visitor center, Navajo traditional foods, picnic tables, restrooms, no water.

Dates: Open year-round.

Fees: There is an entry fee.

Closest town: Cortez, CO, about 40 miles.

For more information: Navajo Parks and Recreation Department, PO Box 9000, Window Rock, AZ 86515. Phone (520) 871-6647.

Canyon de Chelly National Monument

[Fig. 21] Canyon de Chelly (pronounced d'SHAY) National Monument, established in 1931, protects not only one of the Southwest's most magnificent canyon systems, but also preserves spectacular prehistoric cliff houses, petroglyphs, and historic Navajo sites. The name is derived from the Anglo-American corruption of a Spanish corruption of the Navajo word *tsegi*, which roughly means "rock canyon." The monument is also unique in that Navajo families still live and farm within the canyons and along their rims. Therefore, it is important to remember that most of the land is private. Hiking or driving off established roads is not permitted. Watch out for livestock on roads; this is open range country. Always ask for permission before photographing or drawing any people or their homes; a fee is usually expected.

The monument encompasses three major canyons—Canyon de Chelly, Canyon del Muerto, and Monument Canyon—that all eventually coalesce and then abruptly end just east of the community of Chinle. At the mouth of the Canyon de Chelly the rock walls are only 30 feet high. Going up canyon, the walls rise until they are more than 1,000 feet above the floor. It has taken about 2 million years for the uplifted sandstone and igneous rocks of the Defiance Plateau to be broken by weathering and carved by streams to form the canyon complex. In a sense, Canyon de Chelly is the topographic opposite of Monument Valley. Whereas Monument Valley consists of mostly a featureless plain dotted with occasional remnants of DeChelly Sandstone left as mesas, buttes, and pinnacles, Canyon de Chelly is a deeply incised canyon complex in the margin of an uplifted plateau composed primarily of DeChelly Sandstone.

Both the North Rim and South Rim drives begin near the visitor center. The North Rim Drive is a 34-mile round-trip along the rim of Canyon del Muerto. Signed overlooks provide views of Anasazi ruins within the canyon. A free Park Service brochure and map helps guide you. At the first overlook along the North Rim Drive, Ledge Ruin, you can see living and storage structures and kivas built more than 900 years ago.

Antelope House Ruin Overlook is named for paintings of antelope attributed to

Navajo artist Dibé Yazhi (Little Sheep) who lived here in the early 1800s. The ruin, however, dates from the twelfth century and contains an unusual circular plaza.

At Mummy Cave Ruin Overlook, one of the largest ancient Puebloan villages can be seen. The cave was occupied for centuries and then abandoned by 1300. The east and west alcoves are comprised of living and ceremonial rooms. The central tower complex was built in the 1280s by people who migrated from Mesa Verde in southwestern Colorado.

Nearby Massacre Cave Overlook is named after the Navajo who were killed here in the winter of 1805 by a Spanish military expedition led by Antonio Narbona. About 115 Navajo took shelter on the ledge above the canyon floor but were discovered by Narbona's men. A fight ensued, and shots fired from the rim killed all the people on the ledge.

The 37-mile round-trip South Rim Drive offers panoramic views of the canyons. At Tsegi Overlook, Navajo farms dot the canyon floor. Horse and sheep graze, and crops such as corn, squash, peaches, and apples are raised. Most Navajo families abandon the canyon during the winter months and move to the rim, where it is warmer (more direct winter sunlight) and where there is plenty of firewood. Also, children can get to school more easily.

The confluence of Canyon del Muerto and Canyon de Chelly can be seen from Junction Overlook. There are also several Puebloan cliff houses on the far canyon wall. The one to the left is called First Ruin and was studied by archaeologist Cosmos Mindeleff in 1882. This dwelling contains 10 rooms and two kivas (ceremonial rooms) and was occupied between the late 1000s and late 1200s. Straight ahead is "Junction Ruin" which has 15 rooms and one kiva. Almost all of the cliff houses are on the north side of the canyon where they can receive more sunlight for warmth during the winter months.

White House Ruin Overlook reveals a lovely cliff house perched in a cave under a sweeping sandstone wall. Tree-ring dates from roof logs indicate the first building activity was around A.D. 1060, with some final additions about A.D. 1275. The people who lived here tilled the soil in the canyon bottom and planted corn, beans, and squash. They hunted venison and rabbit with bow and arrow and gathered wild plants for food, fiber, and medicine. A 2.5-mile (round-trip) trail descends from near the overlook into the canyon to the ruin (*see* White House Ruin Trail, page 116). This is the only trail in the monument that does not require a local guide. Be sure to take plenty of drinking water.

The dramatic 800-foot spire known as Spider Rock rises from the canyon floor at the junction of Canyon de Chelly and Monument Canyon and can be viewed from the Spider Rock Overlook. On the far side of Canyon de Chelly is Speaking Rock. According to a Navajo story told to naughty children, Speaking Rock reports the names of bad boys and girls to Spider Woman who lives atop Spider Rock, whereupon she descends and carries the offending child up to her lair. The white rocks at the top of Spider Rock are said to be the bleached bones of boys and girls who did not listen to their parents.

Using binoculars, a number of cliff houses can be seen from Spider Rock Overlook. In the distance is the volcanic plug or neck called Black Rock, and the Chuska Mountains, sometimes referred to as the Navajo Alps, are on the eastern horizon.

HISTORY

Archaeological evidence shows that people have lived in these canyons for nearly 5,000 years. The first residents built no permanent homes and the scant remains of their campsites and enigmatic images etched or painted on the canyon walls reveal little about their lives. These Archaic people embarked on daily hunting and gathering expeditions.

By 200 B.C., the people began to experiment with a new plant imported from the south called corn. These early farmers, who archaeologists term Basketmakers because of their exquisitely crafted baskets, built household compounds, storage facilities, and social and ceremonial complexes high on ledges in the walls of the canyons. They lived in small groups, hunted game, grew corn, and later, beans, and created paintings on the walls that surrounded them.

Eventually, beginning about A.D. 750, the dispersed hamlets of the Basketmakers gave way to a new settlement pattern—the village or pueblo. These Puebloan people perhaps banded together because of conflict or possibly for more cooperation in their agricultural pursuits. While villages offered opportunities for social interaction, trade, and ceremony, they also provided a breeding ground for disease, internal conflict, and overuse of intensely farmed fields.

After another five centuries, prolonged drought, disease, conflict, and possibly the allure of new religious ideas from the south led most of the Puebloans to abandon the canyons. Some of the people who left the canyons settled along the Little Colorado River and at the southern tip of Black Mesa. Today these people are known as the Hopi. Despite the trauma of dislocation, the Hopi describe these events as a part of a migratory cycle rather than abandonment. Between 1300 and 1600, some Hopi would occasionally spend the summers hunting and farming in Canyon de Chelly. And some took refuge here after the Pueblo Revolt of 1680 against the Spanish.

About 1700, the Navajo entered the area, probably by coming down through the Great Plains and then moving southwesterly. There was some intermarriage of Hopi and Navajo and definitely the exchange of many ideas. Like those before them, the Navajo used both the canyons and the upland plateau to support a diversified way of life.

Canyon de Chelly became known throughout the region for its fine fields of corn and orchards of delectable peaches. Small settlements of 3 to 10 hogans set in open clearings gave the landscape a tranquil, perhaps idyllic, quality.

This tranquility was shattered in the late 1780s when lengthy warfare erupted between the Navajo, other American Indians, and the Spanish colonists of the Rio

Grande valley. Characterized by quick raids and certain reprisal, they fought over land and the animals grazing upon it.

As a result, the Navajo used Canyon de Chelly as a refuge, a fortress hidden in the mysterious serpentine canyons. The Navajos fortified trails with stone walls, found hiding places in the high rock shelters, and stockpiled food and water at critical points throughout the canyon. Despite all of these precautions, Spanish, Ute, and U.S. military parties penetrated the defenses leaving death and uncertainty in their wake. The testimony of these times can be found in the traditional histories of the Navajo people, in the archaeological remnants of the canyon's fortified places, and in rock paintings that graphically narrate the endurance of the Navajo.

The years of Spanish and later Mexican control of what is now Arizona and New Mexico came to an end in 1846. During a remarkably short campaign, a U.S. military force under the command of Stephen Watts Kearny subdued Mexican forces and claimed the territory for the United States. Soon, Kearny offered the Navajo qualified peace and friendship in order to end decades of mutual raiding. For the next 17 years this agreement was tested by continued conflict, broken promises, and numerous expeditions into the Navajo territory.

In 1863, Colonel Kit Carson, under orders from the territorial commander, began a brutal campaign against the Navajo. In the winter of 1863-64, using information gained during earlier reconnaissance expeditions, Carson's force entered Canyon de Chelly's eastern end and pushed the Navajo toward the canyon mouth. All resistance proved futile and most of the Navajo were killed or captured. Later that spring, Carson's troops returned to Canyon de Chelly and completed their campaign of devastation by destroying the remaining hogans, orchards, and sheep.

A bitter, humiliating trial awaited the Navajo who survived the ordeal. About 8,000 men, women, and children were forced to march more than 300 miles—called the Long Walk—to Bosque Redondo near Fort Sumner, in New Mexico territory. Scores perished from thirst, hunger, and fatigue. Years of internment at Fort Sumner were no kinder. Poor soil, inadequate shelter, disease, and the unending sense of being lost in a foreign place brutalized the survivors. Finally, after four years of senseless incarceration, the Navajo were allowed to return home in 1868 to begin the process of rebuilding their lives and their spirit.

The Navajo faced starvation after they returned from Fort Sumner. Food distribution centers, such as the one established by the federal government at Fort Defiance, helped solve this problem. These centers and practices taken from Spanish and Mexican traders provided a model for the trading posts in Navajo country. Trading posts became a focal point for Navajo communities. Four trading posts were established near Canyon de Chelly. Two were built by John Lorenzo Hubbell in 1886 and 1900 but neither lasted long. Fragments of Camille Garcia's early-1900s post survive as sections of the modern Holiday Inn. Sam Day's trading post, built in 1902 at the mouth of Canyon de Chelly, was a log structure more than 60 feet long. It has been incorporated more or less intact as part of the Thunderbird Lodge's cafeteria.

Directions: About 3 miles east of Chinle on Indian Reservation Route 7.

Activities: Self-guided auto tours along the north and south rims, guided vehicle and hiking tours into the canyon, and horse trips into the canyon.

Facilities: Visitor center, two campgrounds (one maintained by the Park Service, the other is privately owned), nearby motels, and restaurants.

Dates: Open year-round; visitor center closed Christmas.

Fees: There is a fee for tours.

Closest town: Chinle.

For more information: Canyon de Chelly National Monument, PO Box 588, Chinle, AZ 86503-0588. Phone (520) 674-5500. Web site www.nps.gov/cach.

WHITE HOUSE RUIN TRAIL

[Fig. 21(1)] The trail winds down to the canyon floor. Cross Chinle Wash to view cliff dwellings. The wash may contain water during the spring snowmelt or rainy periods. Pit toilets are available at the bottom. There is no drinking water so carry plenty. Temperatures are cold in the winter and extremely hot in the summer. Stay on the trail. Please respect the privacy of the Navajo people. Do not enter dwellings or disturb historical or natural features.

Directions: The trailhead is at the White House Overlook on South Rim Drive.

Trail: 1.25 miles one-way.

Degree of difficulty: Easy.

Elevation: 6,000 to 5,500 feet.

Surface: Smooth sandstone to loose sand.

Hubbell Trading Post National Historic Site

[Fig. 22(1)] The Hubbell Trading Post is one of the oldest trading posts on the Navajo Reservation. Although the post was declared a national historic site in 1967, it is still managed as an active trading center and is eagerly sought out by visitors interested in Indian arts and crafts. During trader John Lorenzo Hubbell's half century on the reservation, he was known for his honesty in business dealings, for his hospitality to travelers, and for his wise counsel to his friends the Navajos.

The trading post's rug room contains stacks of varicolored blankets and rugs displaying the skill of the Navajo women weavers. From the large beams across the ceilings hang baskets made by many Southwestern tribes, saddles and saddle bags, bridles, and Indian water jugs. On the walls are small framed paintings of Navajo rugs by E.A. Burbank and other artists, who stayed with Hubbell. Hubbell had these designs made as examples for the weavers, and he would pay more for rugs woven in these styles. Eventually the rugs made with bold red, black, gray, and white geometric motifs became known as Ganado Reds. Today, Navajos still spend hours studying the silver earrings, bracelets, and necklaces in the jewelry case, for they appreciate the craftsmanship of their fellow artisans. Silver pieces with turquoise settings are their favorites.

Nearly everyone of note who passed through northeast Arizona stopped at the Hubbell Trading Post—presidents, generals, writers, archaeologists and other scientists, and artists. Theodore Roosevelt, Nelson A. Miles, Lew Wallace, and Mary Roberts Rinehart were among the distinguished visitors. Artist E.A. Burbank spent several months in the Hubbell home at various times; many of his paintings and drawings are displayed in Hubbell's house, which is adjacent to the post and open to ranger-led tours.

The Hubbell home portrays vividly the Navajo and the Southwest. Bookcases overflow with rare and invaluable collections of Americana. Indian rugs lie everywhere. Priceless reminders of a courageous pioneer family, the era they helped to shape, and their remarkable customers and guests fill the rooms.

Hubbell was born in 1853 at Pajarito, New Mexico, the son of a Connecticut Yankee who had gone West as a soldier and married into a family of Spanish descent. Mostly self-educated, he became familiar with the life, ways, and language of the Navajos while traveling about the Southwest as a young man and while serving as a clerk and as a Spanish interpreter.

Hubbell began trading in Ganado in 1876. From the beginning, Hubbell was not only a merchant to the Navajo but also their guide and teacher in understanding the ways of the white man. He was the trusted friend who translated and wrote letters, settled family quarrels, explained government policy, and helped the sick.

Hubbell had an enduring influence on Navajo rug weaving and silversmithing, for he consistently demanded and promoted excellence in craftsmanship. He built a trading empire that included stage and freight lines as well as several trading posts. At various times, he and his two sons, together or separately, owned 24 trading posts, a wholesale house in Winslow, and other business and ranch properties.

Hubbell's career as a trader spanned critical years for the Navajos. He came to the reservation when they were struggling to adjust to reservation life, with the ordeal of the Long Walk, including confinement at Fort Sumner, New Mexico, fresh in their minds. More than any other white man, he helped them make that adjustment. He was often their spokesman and contact with the outside world. Though Roman Catholic, Hubbell persuaded the Presbyterian Board of Foreign Missions to choose nearby Ganado for a mission site and, while the mission was being built, took the first missionaries into his home for a year.

He died on November 12, 1930, and was buried on Hubbell Hill, overlooking the trading post, next to his wife, Lina Rubi, and his closest Navajo friend, Many Horses.

One old man expressed the sadness of his fellow Navajos when he said the following:

You wear out your shoes, you buy another pair;

When the food is all gone, you buy more;

You gather melons, and more will grow on the vine;

You grind your corn and make bread which you eat;

And next year you have plenty more corn.

But my friend Don Lorenzo is gone, and none to take his place.

To the Navajos the trading post was a place of social life as well as business. To reach the post, they traveled many miles by horse and wagon or by foot over trails, which were usually dry and dusty, but in wet weather were slick with mud. The post was a place to sell their colorful handwoven rugs and beautiful turquoise and silver jewelry, but it was also a gathering place to meet old friends and relatives. Trading was a slow process and no effort was made to hurry it. The store was a center for news, gossip, and endless talk.

Hubbell Trading Post is typical of these stores. Inside its long, low stone walls is a rectangular iron stove. During winter it was always stocked with pinyon and juniper wood, and the Navajos, talking and laughing, lingered in the warmth. Behind the massive counters are shelves filled with coffee, flour, sugar, candy, Pendleton blankets, tobacco, calico, pocketknives, and canned goods. Hardware and harnesses hang from the ceiling. The post also boasted a blacksmith shop, a bakery, a farm, and a one-room school.

Competition between traders was sometimes quite keen. They sponsored rodeos or chicken pulls and at times helped sponsor native ceremonies to attract customers to their area. Some traders would pay more for wool and other products made by the Navajos who came from great distances. While their flour, coffee, and calico might be the least expensive brands, they spared no effort in attempting to handle the best in native goods such as buckskins and turquoise.

There was little legal tender, so much of the business was carried on by exchange of Navajo products for the trader's goods or the use of trade tokens that each trading post had made from brass, aluminum, or other metals according to its own specifications. The trader was dependent on the Navajos' toleration of a stranger in their midst as the Indians were on a sympathetic white man when they needed to deal with the outside world. The trader had to learn the Navajo language, acquire some understanding of the social structure and economic resources of the community, and respect their way of life. Failure to gain acceptance by the Navajo community might mean that the trader's nearest competitor, perhaps a full day's ride away, would buy the wool and lambs that were the ultimate source of the trader's own credit with the wholesale house.

Besides introducing many new products to the Navajos, the traders functioned as vital intermediaries between the Navajos and the white community. The traders' support of government programs—such as ones for education, livestock improvement, and modern medical care—was essential to their success. Some traders, such as Hubbell, helped Navajos obtain government aid in building dams and irrigation projects. Traders' wives often taught the Navajos canning or how to use the sewing machine. The Hubbells not only hired many Navajos but also recruited them for off-reservation jobs that were of educational as well as economic value.

And it was through the traders and their families that the U.S. was able to gain much of its knowledge of Indian ways, for most early writers relied upon traders rather than on the Indians themselves for information. In recent years, social scientists who have made serious studies of Indian culture also have found the traders helpful.

Shortly after World War II, trading posts on the Navajo Reservation began to decline. The impact of changing times lessened the Indians' dependence on the reservation trader. Many Navajos had served in the military forces and had returned from the war with a greater knowledge of the outside world.

During this period, large-scale exploitation of oil, gas, and uranium deposits brought big business to the Navajo country. With it came additional income for the Navajos, resulting in the replacement of the horse and wagon by the pickup truck as basic transportation for most Navajo families. The supermarkets and department stores with their wide variety of goods are now within easy traveling distances.

To compete with the modern conveniences of the chain stores, the trading posts, too, have become self-service. But Hubbell Trading Post, one of the oldest continuously operated trading posts on the Navajo Reservation, has changed little since its beginning over a century ago. Business is still done in the traditional way. As it did for today's Navajos' great-grandparents, the post serves as a bridge between cultures.

Other trading posts on the Navajo reservation of historic interest include these: Cameron Trading Post and Gallery (established 1916), Tuba Trading Post (1870), Dilkon Trading Post (1919), R.B. Burnham and Company Trading Post (though the building only dates from 1974, Bruce Burnham is a fourth-generation trader whose great-grandfather traded from a wagon), Round Rock Trading Post (1887), and Rough Rock Trading Post (1897). Of course, there are many other shops and galleries selling Indian arts and crafts. One very good resource book is the *Trading Post Guidebook* written by Patrick Eddington and Susan Makov.

Directions: 1 mile west of Ganado on AZ 264.

Activities: Self-guided and ranger-led tours of historic trading post and Hubbell's home.

Facilities: Active trading post and general store, visitor center, restrooms, picnic tables.

Dates: Open daily except Thanksgiving, Christmas, and New Year's Day.

Fees: None.

Closest town: Ganado.

For more information: Hubbell Trading Post National Historic Site, National Park Service, Box 150, Ganado, AZ 86505. Web site www.nps.gov/hutr.

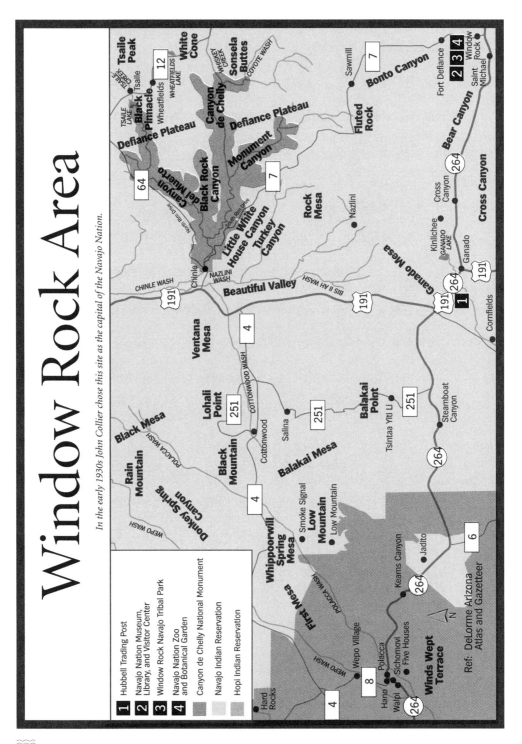

Window Rock Area

In the early 1930s John Collier chose this site as the capital of the Navajo Nation.

1 Hubbell Trading Post
2 Navajo Nation Museum, Library, and Visitor Center
3 Window Rock Navajo Tribal Park
4 Navajo Nation Zoo and Botanical Garden
◼ Canyon de Chelly National Monument
◼ Navajo Indian Reservation
◼ Hopi Indian Reservation

Ref: DeLorme Arizona Atlas and Gazetteer

Window Rock

[Fig. 22] In the shadow of the Chuska Mountains is Window Rock, the capital of the Navajo Nation. In the early 1930s, Commissioner of Indian Affairs John Collier chose this site for a Navajo administration center. Collier understood the importance of including the Navajo people in the decisions that would affect their children's education and health care. He implemented changes such as starting day schools to replace the boarding school system that isolated children from their parents and was culturally destructive. An octagonal hogan-shaped building was constructed for the Council House. Inside murals depict Navajo history and legends.

Fans of Tony Hillerman's mystery novels set on the Navajo Reservation will recognize Window Rock as the home of one of Hillerman's main characters—Lt. Joe Leaphorn.

The small but rapidly growing community hosts the world's largest American Indian fair, usually held the first weekend after Labor Day. Attractions include a parade, singing and dancing, crafts, agricultural shows, traditional foods, a rodeo, and the crowning of Miss Navajo.

For more information: Navajo Fair Office, PO Box 2370, Window Rock, AZ 86515. Phone (520) 871-6478 or 6702. Web site www.navajoland.com. There are no developed RV parks or campgrounds but there is lodging at the Navajo Nation Inn. Phone (520) 871-4108 or (800) 662-6189.

NAVAJO NATION MUSEUM, LIBRARY, AND VISITOR CENTER

[Fig. 22(2)] The Navajo Nation Museum, Library, and Visitor Center opened its doors August 1998, and houses a library, a children's museum, exhibit areas, an auditorium, an outdoor amphitheater, classrooms, and the office for Miss Navajo Nation. The center also serves as a repository for thousands of artifacts waiting for repatriation from museums and other collections from around the country.

Directions: It is located on AZ 264 in Window Rock.

Dates: Open Monday through Friday except holidays.

For more information: Navajo Nation Museum, Library, and Visitor Center, Window Rock, AZ 86515. Phone (520) 871-6436 or -7371.

WINDOW ROCK NAVAJO TRIBAL PARK

[Fig. 22(3)] Near the Navajo Council House is "the rock with a hole in it" or Window Rock. The natural Cow Springs Sandstone arch is nearly 50 feet in diameter. Loose rocks just below the arch mark the location of a prehistoric pueblo, probably built by the Anasazi. Please do not climb up to the hole.

Directions: Turn east off Indian Route 12 about 0.5 mile north of AZ 264.

Activities: Short trail through oddly eroded sandstone hills.

Facilities: Picnic tables, drinking water, and restrooms.

Petrified Forest National Park

A 27-mile scenic road leads visitors to colorful petrified wood within what is popularly called the Painted Desert.

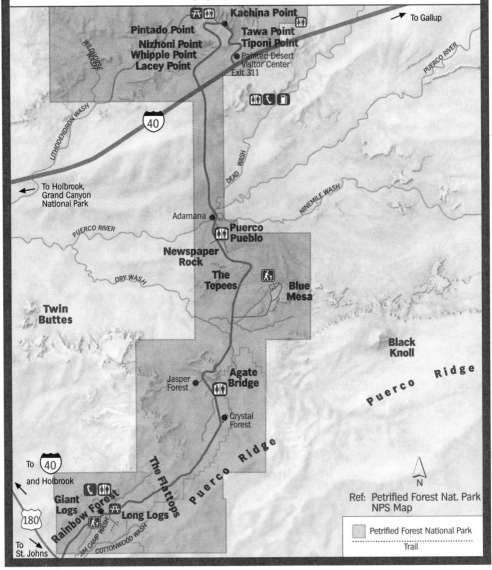

Dates: Open year-round, day-use only.

Fees: None.

Closest town: Window Rock.

For more information: Navajo Nation Museum, Library, and Visitor Center, Window Rock, AZ 86515. Phone (520) 871-6436 or -7371.

NAVAJO NATION ZOO AND BOTANICAL PARK

[Fig. 22(4)] Set beneath the towering sandstone pinnacles known as The Haystacks, the Navajo Nation Zoo and Botanical Park displays species native to the region and domestic animals culturally important to the Navajo. Domestic breeds include the famous Churro sheep that was introduced to the Southwest by the Spanish. These sheep have "double fleece," long silky wool prized for spinning, and they often have four horns.

Directions: The zoo is located north of AZ 264 about 0.5 mile east of the Window Rock Shopping Center.

Activities: Viewing native and domestic animals found in the region.

Facilities: Picnic tables, drinking water, and restrooms.

Dates: Open year-round (Monday-Friday, 8-5) except Christmas and New Year's Day.

Fees: None.

For more information: Navajo Nation Zoo and Botanical Park, PO Box 9000, Window Rock, AZ 86515; phone (520) 871-6573 or 6574.

Petrified Forest National Park

[Fig. 23] Cutting across the northeastern quarter of Arizona in a broad swath is the Chinle Formation. This is the rock unit responsible for the muted pastel, stark landscape popularly called the Painted Desert. Part of this vast desert landscape has been preserved as Petrified Forest National Park. The strange, unearthly scenery attracts photographers, fossil enthusiasts, and hikers. Most visitors tour the area via the 27-mile scenic road that traverses the length of the park. Visitors traveling west on I-40 access the north end of the park road from interstate Exit 311. Eastbound travelers can save time and gas by exiting I-40 in Holbrook and taking US 180 to the south entrance of the park.

For visitors entering the park from the interstate, the first stop is the Painted Desert Visitor Center, where a short film is shown on how wood is petrified and exhibits further explain the area's geology. Two wilderness areas within the park offer cross-country hiking and backpacking. Ask about hiking, wilderness camping permits, and maps at the visitor center. Remember to carry plenty of water.

The scenic road leaves the visitor center and goes north following the edge of a

Petrification vs. Permineralization

Several types of petrification have occurred in the Petrified Forest National Park. In one type all, or practically all, of the organic matter has been replaced by minerals. The resulting fossil has the external form of the object but little or none of the internal structure. Most of the petrified logs in Petrified Forest National Park are of this type. In the second kind of petrification, called permineralization, the cells and other spaces in the potential fossil are filled with mineral matter and much of the original organic parts remain unchanged. Much of the cellular detail in the fossil can be observed under a hand lens or microscope. Some of the logs exhibit both types of petrification.

plateau overlooking the Painted Desert. Eight overlooks along the rim provide sweeping panoramas. The Painted Desert Inn at Kachina Point was built in the 1920s and was rebuilt by the Civilian Conservation Corps in the late 1930s. In 1987, it was designated as a National Historic Landmark and now contains historical and rotating cultural exhibits and a bookstore. Access to the Painted Desert Wilderness is behind the inn; wilderness camping begins beyond the washes.

Chinde Point picnic area has water and restrooms in warmer months. The park road winds south through high desert and crosses over I-40 (no access to the interstate at this point), the Santa Fe Railway tracks, and the Puerco River to arrive at the Puerco Indian Ruins. This pueblo was expanded in the fourteenth century and was home to about 70 inhabitants. Its exact cultural affiliation is still uncertain; it was possibly a mixture of Anasazi and Mogollon people. Hopi tradition says that these occupants eventually migrated north to the Hopi country. A few rooms have been excavated and partially restored.

About 1 mile south, an overlook permits views of Newspaper Rock, a huge sandstone block covered with ancient petroglyphs.

At The Tepees pullout are colorful badlands. A 3-mile spur road climbs Blue Mesa, where numerous petrified logs are perched on pedestals of soft clay. A short interpretive trail explains this spot's geology. The Jasper Forest Overlook dramatically reveals the area's topography with logs strewn below. Petrified logs with attached root systems suggest that the trees grew nearby; otherwise the fragile roots would have been broken off.

Fossil destruction in the Crystal Forest area in the early 1900s by souvenir hunters and gem collectors prompted Arizona Territory citizens to petition Congress to preserve the petrified wood sites. Cracks and hollows in the logs here once held beautiful clear quartz and amethyst crystals.

The Flattops are massive remnants of a once-continuous layer of sandstone capping parts of this area. The remaining capstone protects softer deposits, which have long been eroded from other parts of the park. Flattops wilderness campers should park here and hike at least 0.5 mile from the road before camping.

The Long Logs and Agate House trails, both quite short and easy, explore the Rainbow Forest, where iron, manganese, carbon, and other minerals lend bright colors to the petrified wood. Agate House is a partially restored pueblo that was constructed a century or so earlier than the Puerco Indian Ruins.

The trail through Giant Logs behind the Rainbow Forest Museum climbs up and down the slopes. The fence serves as a constant reminder that the petrified wood and all other natural and historic objects in the park are protected by law. No collecting please, not even a tiny sliver of stone. Petrified wood, fossils, and other rocks collected on private lands can be purchased at local gift shops.

From the Rainbow Forest Museum, the park road continues 2 miles south to the park boundary and highway US 180.

About 220 million years ago during the Late Triassic Period, Arizona was only about 500 miles north of the equator (today it is over 2,000 miles north). The climate was hot and tropical and many streams crossed a vast floodplain. To the south, tall, stately pine-like trees grew along the headwaters. Crocodile-like reptiles, giant fish-eating amphibians, and small dinosaurs lived among a variety of ferns, cycads, and other plants and animals that are known only as fossils today. All of the plants species, over 200 kinds known from the Chinle Formation that once lived here are now extinct. In some cases, their descendants are still living, usually in humid tropical regions of the world. For example, horsetails, or scouring rushes, are represented in the Petrified Forest National Park by two well-known Triassic Period genera—*Neocalamites* and *Equisetites*. Modern horsetails of the genus Equisetum rarely grow taller than 6 to 10 feet (in arid Arizona, most are 1 or 2 feet tall) and are less than 0.5 inch in diameter. The Late Triassic Period horsetails had trunks up to 16 inches in diameter and attained heights of up to 30 feet.

The 100-foot tall Triassic Period conifers—*Araucarioxylon arizonicum*, *Woodworthia*, and *Schilderia adamanica*—fell and were washed by muddy rivers into the floodplain. There they were quickly buried by silt, mud, and volcanic ash, and this blanket of deposits cut off oxygen and slowed the logs' decay. Slowly, mineral-bearing ground waters seeped through the logs and gradually encased the original wood tissues with silica, usually as a form of quartz variously known as jasper, chalcedony, opal, amethyst, or agate, and other minerals. The logs became petrified.

Plants were not the only things petrified. Hard parts from animals, such as teeth, bones, shells, scales, and sometimes even ligaments were replaced with minerals. Various kinds of freshwater fish lived in the ponds and rivers of the Late Triassic Period. One was *Chinlea*, a small coelacanth related to the famous living coelacanth, *Latimeria*, which was discovered about 50 years ago in oceanic waters off the east coast of Africa. Until then, it was thought that the coelacanths became extinct some 60 million years ago.

The dominant inhabitants of the waterways were giant amphibians known as metoposaurs and giant reptiles known as phytosaurs. Remains of these animals are the most abundant fossils of backboned creatures found in the park. The amphibian giant was 6 to 8 feet long and had an inordinately large, flat skull with a jaw bristling with small, sharply pointed teeth. It was obviously a fish eater. One of the typical phytosaurs was Rutiodon, which grew commonly to 10 or more feet in length and looked very much like a modern crocodile.

On land dwelt a great variety of reptiles, large and small. Some were herbivores, such as the large, heavily armored aetosaurs, which looked a little like a 15-foot-long cross between a modern crocodile and a horned lizard. Their armor plates helped protect them from the most fearsome of the Chinle Formation predators—*Postosuchus. Postosuchus* attained lengths of 20 feet or more. Its hind legs were much longer than its fore legs, thus this predator very likely rose to a more or less upright position to search for its prey. Possibly it could run short distances bipedally. Its skull was not unlike that of the gigantic carnivorous dinosaurs that were dominant in the Jurassic and Cretaceous Periods, millions of years later.

After millions of years, the area sank, was flooded, and was covered with more freshwater sediments. Later the area was lifted far above sea level. The buried logs cracked from the stress of this uplifting. Still later, in recent geologic time, wind and water eroded away the accumulated layers of sediment and exposed the massive petrified logs and other fossilized plant and animal remains. Although there are other petrified forests (Yellowstone National Park has an exceptionally good one), nowhere else in the world are petrified logs found in such quantity and in such a rainbow of colors.

Besides the remarkable geologic story here, archaeological sites record a rich human history extending back at least 8,000 years. There is evidence of early wandering hunting and gathering families up to settled agricultural villages or pueblos, which had trading ties with neighboring villages. Then the archaeological record fades about 1450.

In the mid-1800s U.S. Army mappers and surveyors traversed the area and reported fantastic stories of a painted desert and its trees turned to stone. Next, farmers, ranchers, and sightseers came to the area. Where there had been abundant deposits of petrified wood in the 1850s, wood gathering for souvenirs and numerous commercial ventures had denuded many locations by 1900. Arizona territorial residents recognized that the supply of petrified wood was not endless. In 1906 selected "forests" were set aside as Petrified Forest National Monument. In 1932, another 2,500 acres of Painted Desert were added to the monument. In 1962, the area became Petrified Forest National Park and eight years later, 50,000 acres were further designated as wilderness.

Directions: North entrance is about 26 miles northeast of Holbrook on I-40. South entrance is about 20 miles southeast of Holbrook on US 180.

Activities: Sightseeing by vehicle and foot; backcountry hiking and camping.

Facilities: Painted Desert Visitor Center: exhibits, restrooms, restaurant, service station, gift shop. Rainbow Forest Visitor Center: exhibits, restrooms, soda fountain, gift shop. No campgrounds in park; picnic areas at Chinde Point and Rainbow Forest.

Dates: Open year-round, except Christmas and New Year's Day. Hours vary seasonally.

Fees: There is an entrance fee.

Closest town: Holbrook, about 20 to 26 miles, see above.

For more information: Superintendent's Office, PO Box 2217, Petrified Forest National Park, AZ 86028. Phone (520) 524-6228. Web site www.nps.gov/pefo.

Lyman Lake State Park

[Fig. 24(1)] Eleven miles south of St. Johns is Lyman Lake State Park. This 1,500-acre reservoir is located on the Little Colorado River. Anglers try for channel catfish (*Ictalurus punctatus*), largemouth bass (*Micropterus salmoides*), walleye (*Stizostedion vitreum*), crappie (*Pomoxis* sp.), and northern pike (*Esox lucius*) including the legendary lunker Ike the Pike. There is handicapped accessible camping and fishing. On summer weekdays, tours are given to a petroglyph site. Reservations for the tour are required.

Birders have spotted such species as the great blue heron (*Ardea herodias*), Canada goose (*Branta canadensis*), mallard (*Anas platyrhynchos*), northern pintail (*Anas acuta*), American kestrel (*Falco sparverius*), rufous hummingbird (*Selasphorus rufus*), violet-green swallow (*Tachycineta thalassina*), northern mockingbird (*Mimus polyglottos*), Wilson's warbler (*Wilsonia pusilla*), black-headed cowbird (*Molothrus ater*), bald eagle (*Haliaeetus leucocephalus*), and osprey (*Pandion haliaetus*). Besides native mammals, such as the desert cottontail (*Sylvilagus audubonii*), prairie dog (*Cynomys gunnisoni*), beaver (*Castor canadensis*), and white-tailed deer (*Odocoileus virginianus*), there is a small herd of bison (*Bison bison*) maintained by the Lyman Lake Buffalo Club.

Directions: Located 11 miles south of St. Johns or about 17 miles north of Springerville on US 180/191.

Activities: Camping, boating, fishing, water skiing, swimming, mountain biking, hiking, and wildlife viewing.

Facilities: 67 camping sites, marina with camping and fishing supplies, boat rentals, restrooms, showers, hookups, grocery store, and snack bar.

Dates: Lake open year-round but facilities available only during summer.

Fees: There is a day use fee, camping fee, and tour fee.

Closest town: St. Johns, 11 miles.

For more information: Arizona State Parks, 1300 West Washington Street, Phoenix, AZ 85007. Phone (602) 542-4174 or (520) 337-4441.

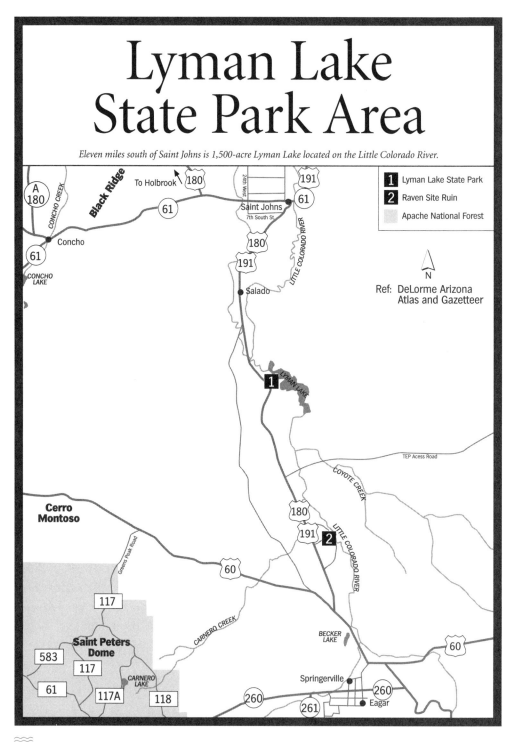

Lyman Lake State Park Area

Eleven miles south of Saint Johns is 1,500-acre Lyman Lake located on the Little Colorado River.

A 180

CONCHO CREEK

Black Ridge

To Holbrook 180

24th West

191

61

Saint Johns

7th South St.

61

Concho

180

191

61

CONCHO LAKE

LITTLE COLORADO RIVER

Salado

1 Lyman Lake State Park

2 Raven Site Ruin

Apache National Forest

N

Ref: DeLorme Arizona Atlas and Gazetteer

1 LYMAN LAKE

TEP Acess Road

COYOTE CREEK

Cerro Montoso

180

191 **2**

LITTLE COLORADO RIVER

Greens Peak Road

60

117

CARNERO CREEK

BECKER LAKE

60

Saint Peters Dome

583

117

CARNERO LAKE

61

117A

118

260

Springerville

260

Eagar

261

✹ RAVEN SITE RUIN

[Fig. 24(2)] About 5 miles south of Lyman Lake is Raven Site Ruin, a 500- to 800-room multistory pueblo overlooking the Little Colorado River that was home to the Anasazi and Mogollon cultures. The site was occupied continuously from as early as A.D. 1000 to at least A.D. 1475. It may have still been in use when Coronado marched by in the sixteenth century. About 80 different pottery types have been found and most were manufactured locally, indicating that this was a major population and trading center. There is also a replica of a pueblo room complete with the accouterments the occupants would have had. Tours are available as well as the opportunity to participate in ongoing research.

Directions: Look for the signed Raven Site Ruin turnoff from US 180/191 about 12 miles north of Springerville.

Activities: Site tours, petroglyph hikes, hands-on archaeology.

Facilities: Small museum, gift shop, picnic area, and campground.

Dates: Open daily from May through Sept.

Fees: There is a small charge for a tour; participatory programs also have a fee.

Closest town: Springerville, 12 miles.

For more information: White Mountain Archaeological Center, 1737 E. Winter Drive, Phoenix, AZ 85020. Phone (520) 333-5857 or (602) 943-8882. Web site www.ravensite.com.

Winslow Area

✹ HOMOLOVI RUINS STATE PARK

[Fig. 25(1)] Homolovi Ruins (*Homolovi* is Hopi for "place of the little hills") is a very important archaeological location because it spans the time when some of the prehistoric Anasazi were migrating in stages northward to the Hopi mesas. This site was a major trade center and staging area for the migrations.

Four main pueblo ruins reveal the story of Homolovi. Homolovi I Pueblo consists of about 350 rooms. It is located near the Little Colorado River and is reached via a paved road and a short dirt trail. Homolovi II is about 2.5 miles north of the visitor center and is accessed by a 0.25-mile round-trip trail. This pueblo was occupied from A.D. 1250 to 1450 with a population of perhaps 3,000. The village contained 700 to 1,200 rooms arranged around three plazas and may have stood two or three stories high.

Archaeologist Jesse W. Fewkes, while working for the Smithsonian, excavated at Homolovi in 1896 and sent over 700 artifacts to the museum in Washington, DC.

Ask at the visitor center for directions to other pueblo ruins and rock art sites.

Directions: Take I-40 Exit 257 for AZ 87 (just east of Winslow), and go north 1.3 miles to entrance.

Homolovi Ruins State Park Area

Homolovi Ruins is an important archaeological location because it spans the time when prehistoric Anasazi were migrating northward to the Hopi mesas.

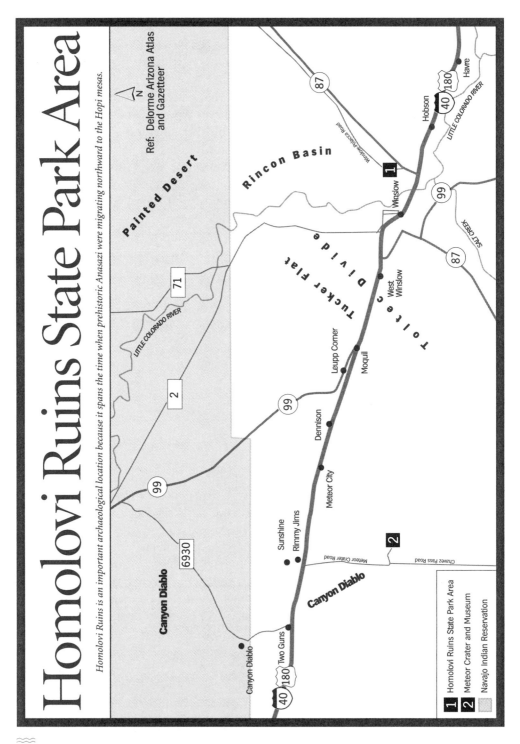

Ref: Delorme Arizona Atlas and Gazetteer

N

Painted Desert

Rincon Basin

Tucker Flat

Toltec Divide

Little Colorado River

Salt Creek

Winslow-Pueblo Road

Hobson

Havre

Winslow

West Winslow

Leupp Corner

Moqui

Dennison

Meteor City

Rimmy Jims

Sunshine

Meteor Crater Road

Chavez Pass Road

Canyon Diablo

Two Guns

Canyon Diablo

Canyon Diablo

Little Colorado River

87

40 180

99

87

99

99

99

71

2

6930

40 180

2

1 Homolovi Ruins State Park Area
2 Meteor Crater and Museum
  Navajo Indian Reservation

Activities: Easy walks around the ruins and to rock art sites. During the summer, there are ongoing excavations and tours. Wildlife viewing along the Little Colorado River; obtain a checklist of the over 100 bird species recorded from the visitor center.

Facilities: Visitor center, restrooms, 53 campsites, water hookups and showers available in summer. Park facilities are handicapped accessible.

Dates: Open daily except Christmas.

Fees: There is an entrance fee and camping fee.

Closest town: Winslow, 5 miles.

For more information: Arizona State Parks, 1300 West Washington Street, Phoenix, AZ 85007. Phone (602) 542-4174 or (520) 289-4106.

▓ METEOR CRATER AND MUSEUM

[Fig. 25(2)] In the late 1880s, Dr. D.M. Barringer was the first person to believe that this deep crater was created by the impact of a meteorite. Ironically, geologist G. K. Gilbert, who correctly advocated a meteorite impact origin for the craters on the moon, did not recognize this crater as having the same origin. In 1892, Gilbert proposed that the crater was the result of a steam explosion brought on by volcanic activity. For 20 years, Dr. Barringer scoured the area for evidence to support his impact theory. Unfortunately, he couldn't find any large, recognizable meteorites. He finally drilled a hole in the crater and at 1,346 feet hit extraterrestrial material.

Contemporary geologists believe that 50,000 years ago, a meteorite weighing millions of tons smashed into the northern Arizona desert at a speed of nearly 45,000 miles per hour. Over 300 million tons of rock were blasted into the sky leaving behind a crater that today is about 600 feet deep and nearly 1 mile across.

The Museum of Astrogeology offers a self-guided tour of exhibits and video presentations portraying the formation of the crater and the role the feature plays in the study of the earth and space sciences. In the 1960s, Meteor Crater was one of the training places for potential lunar astronauts. The Astronaut Hall of Fame depicts man's exploration of space.

Meteor vs. Meteorite

Technically, Meteor Crater is misnamed. A meteor is the stony object that, upon entering the earth's atmosphere, is heated by friction to the point where the outer surface of the meteor melts and incandesces. If the meteor is not completely vaporized and strikes the ground, it is then called a meteorite. Most meteors originate as asteroids, which are members of our solar system and are thought to have been produced at the time of creation of the solar system some 4.6 billion years ago. Meteor "showers" are produced by swarms of cometary debris that follow their parents around the sun. Every comet produces such a swarm, but the earth's atmosphere only encounters a few of them each year.

And new as of 1999 is a big screen digital theater showing the meteor impact film *Collisions and Impacts*. Outside the visitor center is an Apollo space capsule.

Directions: Located 35 miles east of Flagstaff or 20 miles west of Winslow, just off I-40.

Activities: Learn about meteorite impact craters and the exploration of space.

Facilities: Visitor center, crater viewing platform, picnic area, coffee shop, store, gas station, RV park (phone 520-289-4002).

Dates: Open year-round. Hours vary seasonally.

Fees: There is an entrance fee.

Closest town: Winslow, 20 miles.

For more information: Meteor Crater Enterprises, PO Box 70, Flagstaff, AZ 86002. Phone (520) 289-5898 or 2362 or (800) 289-5898. Web site www.meteorcrater.com.

Flagstaff Area

GRAND FALLS NAVAJO TRIBAL PARK

The 185-foot-high, chocolate brown Grand Falls was created when a lava flow spilled into the canyon carved by the Little Colorado River and dammed the river. The seasonal river must now meander around the terminal end of the lava flow and fall back into the canyon. Usually the only times to actually see water in the riverbed are early spring when snows are melting in the White Mountains (the headwaters of the Little Colorado River) or in late summer when the rainy season is in full swing, but it can be quite a spectacle. It may be difficult to appreciate that the drop is about 25 feet higher than Niagara Falls since there are no trees or buildings for scale.

The lava flow probably originated from Merriam Crater, a cinder cone squatting about 8 miles southwest of the falls. Geologists disagree on the exact age of this eruption, but it may have been between several thousand or tens of thousands of years ago. The lava filled the entire 200-foot-deep canyon and spread a short distance over the east bank. A finger of lava flowed downstream for about 15 miles. A lake was created behind the lava dam, but eventually it filled with sediment, forcing the river to follow the lower ground around the east edge of the lava flow before dropping back into the canyon.

Although a dirt road approaches the river above the falls, **do not attempt to cross if there is any water in the riverbed**. Your vehicle may be swept over the falls or become mired in mud, only to be washed away later. Instead, follow the dirt track leading to the left to a few ramadas and picnic tables.

About 0.25 mile below the falls, there is an unmarked, rough but short trail down to the river's edge. Protect camera gear since the spray from the falls is more mud than water.

Directions: From Flagstaff, take US 89 north 1.8 miles and turn right onto the Camp Townsend-Winona Road. After 8 miles, turn left onto the Leupp Road. Go about 13 miles and turn left at the sign "Grand Falls 10 Miles." There may also be a sign that reads "Navajo Road 70." This road is dirt but usually passable to ordinary passenger vehicles except when wet.

Activities: Scenic view, limited hiking along rim and to canyon floor, picnicking.

Facilities: Rustic ramadas with picnic tables.

Dates: Open year-round.

Fees: None.

Closest town: Flagstaff, about 35 miles.

For more information: Navajo Nation Parks and Recreation Department, PO Box 9000, Window Rock, AZ 86515. Phone (520) 871-6647.

The drop of Grand Falls is about 25 feet higher than that of Niagara Falls.

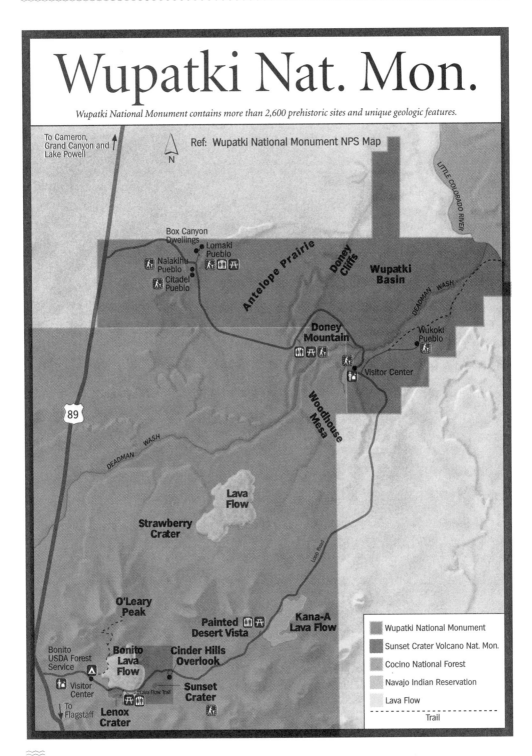

Wupatki Nat. Mon.

Wupatki National Monument contains more than 2,600 prehistoric sites and unique geologic features.

To Cameron,
Grand Canyon and
Lake Powell

N

Ref: Wupatki National Monument NPS Map

LITTLE COLORADO RIVER

Box Canyon
Dwellings

Lomaki
Pueblo

Nalakihu
Pueblo

Citadel
Pueblo

Antelope Prairie

Doney
Cliffs

Wupatki
Basin

DEADMAN WASH

Doney
Mountain

Wukoki
Pueblo

Visitor Center

89

WASH

DEADMAN

Woodhouse
Mesa

Lava
Flow

Strawberry
Crater

Loop Road

O'Leary
Peak

Painted
Desert Vista

Kana-A
Lava Flow

Bonito
USDA Forest
Service

Bonito
Lava
Flow

Cinder Hills
Overlook

Lava Flow Trail

Visitor
Center

To
Flagstaff

Lenox
Crater

Sunset
Crater

■	Wupatki National Monument
■	Sunset Crater Volcano Nat. Mon.
■	Cocino National Forest
■	Navajo Indian Reservation
■	Lava Flow
- - - -	Trail

▨ WUPATKI NATIONAL MONUMENT

[Fig. 26] Wupatki National Monument, northeast of Flagstaff, contains more than 2,600 prehistoric sites and many unique geologic features. The archaeological sites are the remnants of three separate and distinct cultures—the Kayenta Anasazi, the Sinagua, and the Cohonina—that lived in the area about 800 years ago. Archaeologists believe that these three groups shared and exchanged goods and ideas.

The Kayenta Anasazi are responsible for many of the pueblos found throughout the monument, especially those found in the northern section such as Lomaki and Crack-in-the-Rock. Most of the petroglyphs are also thought to be Anasazi.

Early in the twelfth century, Sinagua (Spanish for "without water") people from the Flagstaff area moved northward into the Wupatki Basin and occupied the Wupatki Pueblo area. At Wupatki Pueblo, there is evidence of both Sinagua and Anasazi cultures; the community room or amphitheater is probably Kayenta Anasazi while the ball court is most likely of Sinaguan origin.

Although the Cohonina (a corruption of the Hopi name for the Havasupai people) generally lived north and west of the San Francisco Peaks, their ceramics are found within the monument. However, there is no evidence that they inhabited any of the larger pueblos.

One remarkable geologic feature is a natural blowhole located a few yards from the Wupatki ball court. Other blowholes are known to exist throughout the monument and seem to be connected to a large underground system of fissures. When the barometric pressure is low, air may blow out of the opening at up to 35 miles per hour. Conversely, when the pressure is high, air flows into the ground. Blowholes may have held special significance to the early residents since many of the larger pueblos are situated near them. Even today, one is used by Navajo medicine men for curing ceremonies.

The prehistoric dwellings were long abandoned when Captain Lorenzo Sitgreaves arrived in 1851. Sitgreaves was looking for an overland route through the recently acquired New Mexico territory, and his account was the first written documentation of these ruins. Around 1900, Smithsonian archaeologist Jesse W. Fewkes mapped and photographed the Wupatki area and used Hopi terms to label geographic and cultural features. President Calvin Coolidge established Wupatki National Monument in 1924.

Directions: Entrance is on the right (east) 27 miles north of Flagstaff on US 89. The visitor center is another 14 miles.

Activities: Self-guided walks through ruins. Occasionally there are guided-tours and other interpretive programs; check at the visitor center for a schedule.

Facilities: Visitor center, picnic tables, and restrooms.

Dates: Visitor center open every day except Christmas and New Year's Day.

Fees: There is an entrance fee that is also good for nearby Sunset Crater Volcano National Monument.

Closest town: Flagstaff, 27 miles.

For more information: Wupatki National Monument, HC 33, Box 444A, Flagstaff, AZ 86004. Phone (520) 679-2365. Web site www.nps.gov/wupa.

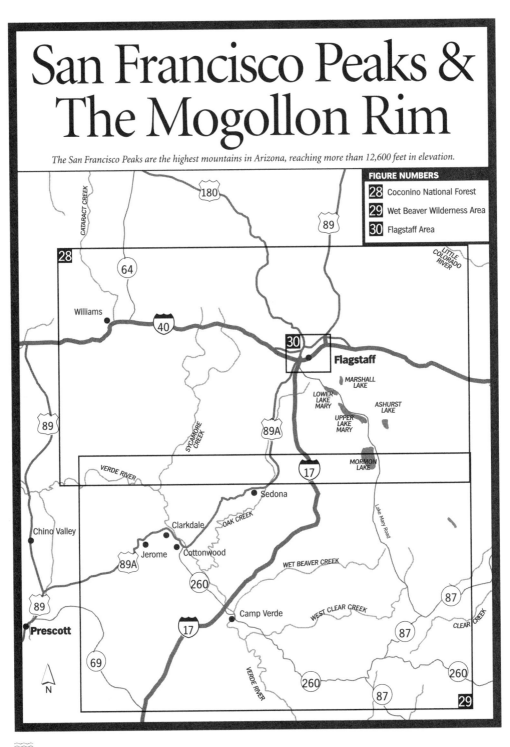

San Francisco Peaks & The Mogollon Rim

The San Francisco Peaks are the highest mountains in Arizona, reaching more than 12,600 feet in elevation.

FIGURE NUMBERS

28	Coconino National Forest
29	Wet Beaver Wilderness Area
30	Flagstaff Area

San Francisco Peaks
And The Mogollon Rim

T he San Francisco Peaks, the highest mountains in Arizona, tower over a volcanic field of more than 600 cinder cones, lava domes, and other igneous features. This is one of the largest volcanic fields in North America, covering a 1,800-square-mile area roughly centered on Flagstaff.

About 20 miles to the south is the rather abrupt southern edge of the Colorado Plateau known as the Mogollon Rim. (Locals pronounce it "muggy-own," but it's the name of an early Spanish governor, so it probably should be pronounced "mo-go-yon") The Rim extends more than 200 miles across Arizona and continues east into New Mexico. In places, the cliff below the Rim exceeds 2,000 feet.

The Mogollon Rim area extending back to the Peaks is cloaked in the world's largest stand of ponderosa pine forest. But the vegetation changes quickly to pinyon-juniper woodland or desert scrub at the base of the cliff. Where deep, narrow canyons

[*Above:* The snow-covered San Francisco Peaks in the Coconino National Forest]

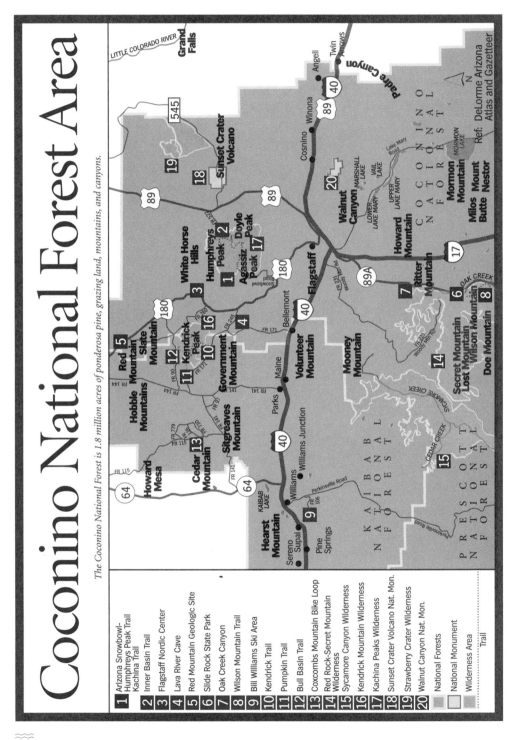

Coconino National Forest Area

The Coconino National Forest is 1.8 million acres of ponderosa pine, grazing land, mountains, and canyons.

Ref: DeLorme Arizona Atlas and Gazetteer

1 Arizona Snowbowl–Humphreys Peak Trail Kachina Trail
2 Inner Basin Trail
3 Flagstaff Nordic Center
4 Lava River Cave
5 Red Mountain Geologic Site
6 Slide Rock State Park
7 Oak Creek Canyon
8 Wilson Mountain Trail
9 Bill Williams Ski Area
10 Kendrick Trail
11 Pumpkin Trail
12 Bull Basin Trail
13 Coxcombs Mountain Bike Loop
14 Red Rock–Secret Mountain Wilderness
15 Sycamore Canyon Wilderness
16 Kendrick Mountain Wilderness
17 Kachina Peaks Wilderness
18 Sunset Crater Volcano Nat. Mon.
19 Strawberry Crater Wilderness
20 Walnut Canyon Nat. Mon.

National Forests
National Monument
Wilderness Area
Trail

have been incised into the rim, shadowed slopes often harbor moisture-loving species like Douglas fir (*Psuedotsuga menziesii*), spruce (*Picea* sp.), bigtooth maple (*Acer grandidentatum*), and, sometimes, aspen (*Populus tremuloides*). Most of the forest above the Rim is managed by the U.S. Forest Service as the Coconino, Kaibab, and Apache-Sitgreaves national forests.

Coconino National Forest

[Fig. 28] The Coconino National Forest, one of the most productive in the Southwest, covers 1.8 million acres of magnificent ponderosa pine timber and grazing land, soaring mountains, and deep canyons.

Two of the most popular sections of the Coconino National Forest are the San Francisco Peaks area and Oak Creek Canyon, made famous by Western writer Zane Grey and by more than 20 major films. The Peaks area includes the Kachina Peaks, Kendrick Mountain, and Strawberry Crater wilderness areas and the Lamar Haines Wildlife Area. Oak Creek Canyon and the surrounding red sandstone country include more than 60 hiking trails.

Within the Coconino National Forest, there are a number of natural and man-made lakes stocked with fish. To the southeast of Flagstaff are Lower and Upper Lake Mary, Marshall, Ashurst, Mormon, Kinnikinick, Long, Soldiers, Stoneman, Blue Ridge, and a few smaller lakes. A variety of fish can be caught in these lakes, including rainbow (*Oncorhynchus mykiss*) and brown trout (*Salmo trutta*), channel catfish (*Ictalurus punctatus*), walleye (*Stizostedion vitreum*), largemouth bass (*Micropterus salmoides*), green sunfish (*Lepomis cyanellus*), yellow perch (*Perca flavescens*), black crappie (*Pomoxis nigromaculatus*), northern pike (*Esox lucius*), and bluegill (*Lepomis macrochirus*). For a recorded message of fishing conditions, call the fishing hotline at (602) 789-3701. There is also a regional office of the Arizona Game and Fish Department in Flagstaff at 3500 S. Lake Mary Road. Phone (520) 774-5045.

Shallow Mormon Lake is the largest natural lake in Arizona and is a very important resting stop for migrating waterfowl and other birds. Along the lake's south shore is the Mormon Lake Ski Center, which has more than 20 miles of groomed Nordic trails. A trail fee is collected and ski rentals are available. PO Box CC, Flagstaff, AZ 86002. Phone (520) 354-2250.

Mountain biking is very popular in the Coconino National Forest. The many Forest Service roads and trails outside the wilderness areas offer rides of varying length and difficulty. Cosmic Ray's regularly updated mountain biking guide, *Fat Tire Tales and Trails*, has plenty of trip ideas.

One easy ride from Flagstaff is to Fisher Point, which overlooks Walnut Canyon.

Directions: Start at the intersection of Lone Tree Road and Zuni Drive. Take the dirt road that heads southeast. At mile 2.9, take the right fork another 2 miles to

Fisher Point. Bikes are not permitted in Walnut Canyon, but bikers can hike in.

Trail: About 9.8 miles round-trip.

Degree of difficulty: Easy to moderate.

Elevation: 6,800 to 7,500 feet.

Surface and blaze: Dirt and gravel roads.

For more forest information: Supervisor's Office, Coconino National Forest, 2323 E. Greenlaw Lane, Flagstaff, AZ 86004. Phone (520) 527-3600. Web site www.fs.fed.us/r3/coconino.

THE GRAND CANYON-FLAGSTAFF STAGECOACH LINE

From 1892 until 1901, stagecoaches carried tourists the 70 miles from Flagstaff to the Grand Canyon. A number of different routes developed based on the terrain and the season. Once the railroad tracks from Williams reached the South Rim of the Grand Canyon in 1901, the early tourists opted for the three-hour train ride instead of one or two dusty days in a stagecoach. Today, many hikers, mountain bikers, horseback riders, and four-wheel drivers try to follow the old routes, which vary from regularly maintained Forest Service roads to faint, rocky tracks. There are no visitor facilities, but plenty of magnificent scenery. The best way to locate these trails is with a copy of Richard and Sherry Mangum's excellent book, *Grand Canyon-Flagstaff Stagecoach Line: A History and Exploration Guide*, plus the appropriate topographic and Forest Service maps, a compass, and maybe a GPS (Global Positioning System).

Directions: The Flagstaff trailhead is the easiest part to locate. Early stagecoach passengers boarded at the railroad station in downtown Flagstaff. Maps in the Mangums' book are very helpful, but topographic and Forest Service maps are needed, too. One of the main routes discussed in the Mangums' book is marked with signs and a good place to start.

Trail: Up to 70 miles or more one-way.

Surface: Dirt and gravel roads.

For more information: Peaks Ranger District, 5075 N. Hwy. 89, Flagstaff, AZ 86004. Phone (520) 526-0866.

KACHINA PEAKS WILDERNESS

[Fig. 28(17)] Located 10 miles north of Flagstaff, the 18,960 acres of the Kachina Peaks Wilderness encompasses the upper slopes and summits of the San Francisco Mountains, including Humphreys Peak (12,633 feet), the highest point in Arizona. Locally, the mountain is known as the San Francisco Peaks. The ring of summits—Humphreys, Agassiz, Fremont, and Doyle—almost encloses the interior valley called the Inner Basin.

At one time, this composite or stratovolcano was several thousand feet higher and probably had a fairly symmetrical shape, like Mt. Shasta or Mt. Fuji. This type of volcano is the accumulation of many eruptions over many tens of thousands of years to as many as a half-million years. Some geologists believe that between 200,000 and 400,000 years ago, the San Francisco Peaks blew its top, forming the Inner Basin, an event strikingly similar to what Mount St. Helens, in Washington State, did in 1980. Then followed a series of glacial periods that further carved the mountain's slopes.

Arizona's only arctic-alpine habitat, about two square miles worth, is found within this wilderness area. It is home to the endemic and threatened San Francisco Peaks groundsel (*Senecio franciscanus*), a dwarf member of the sunflower family. The San Francisco Peaks' steep U-shaped valleys and moraines are the best examples of Ice Age glaciation in Arizona.

The mountain is sacred to numerous Indian tribes including the Zuni, Havasupai, Hopi, and Navajo. Please treat the area respectfully by treading lightly and taking nothing but photos and memories.

Directions: Travel north about 7 miles from Flagstaff on US 180. Turn right on Snowbowl Road and continue about 7 miles to the ski area and signs for the Humphreys Peak and Kachina trailheads.

Activities: Hiking, camping except in the Inner Basin and above timberline, cross-country skiing, hunting, and nature study.

Facilities: None.

Dates: Open year-round.

Fees: None.

Closest town: Flagstaff, about 14 miles.

For more information: Peaks Ranger District, 5075 N. Hwy. 89, Flagstaff, AZ 86004. Phone (520) 526-0866.

HUMPHREYS PEAK TRAIL

[Fig. 28(1)] Bagging the highest peak in Arizona is a popular activity. Remember, though, that the weather above tree line can be severe, especially during the summer rainy season when thunderstorms can build very rapidly. Start early and don't become a lightning rod. Many of the trees near timberline are bristlecone pines (*Pinus aristata*), one of the longest-living plants on earth. Some of the pines growing on the San Francisco Peaks are well over 1,000 years old.

Directions: At the Arizona Snowbowl, there are two trailheads; the upper one is located at the far end of the deck of the Upper Ski Lodge and is signed.

Trail: 4.5 miles one-way.

Degree of difficulty: Moderate.

Elevation: 9,500 to 12,633 feet.

Surface: Forest floor to rocky.

KACHINA TRAIL

[Fig. 28(1)] Unlike the Humphreys Trail, the Kachina is a relatively level traverse around the south side of the San Francisco Peaks. It's a lovely walk through old-growth coniferous forest and aspen groves. The trail ends at the old Weatherford Trail, originally built in the 1920s as a toll road to the top of the Peaks.

Directions: The trailhead is at the far end of the first parking area when arriving at the Arizona Snowbowl. Look for signs along the road for the trailhead.

Trail: About 6 miles one-way.

Degree of difficulty: Moderate.

Elevation: 9,300 to 8,800 feet.

Surface: Forest floor.

INNER BASIN TRAIL

[Fig. 28(2)] The Inner Basin Trail follows an old road to several springs that provide some of Flagstaff's municipal water. There are extensive stands of quaking aspen (*Populus tremuloides*) in the Inner Basin, partly as a result of large wildfires in the late 1800s, which make this a particularly popular hike in the autumn when the leaves have turned gold. Because it is part of Flagstaff's watershed, no camping, horses, or dogs are allowed in the Inner Basin.

Directions: Take US 89 north from Flagstaff about 17 miles and turn left on the graded dirt Lockett Meadow Road (FR 522). Watch for signs at any forks until it ends at Lockett Meadow Campground, about 4 miles from the highway.

Trail: 2 miles one-way.

Degree of difficulty: Moderate.

Elevation: 8,600 to 11,200 feet.

Surface: Dirt road.

ARIZONA SNOWBOWL

[Fig. 28(1)] In a west-facing valley between Agassiz and Humphreys peaks is the Arizona Snowbowl. This downhill ski area boasts a total vertical drop of 2,300 feet, 31 trails, four chairlifts, and an annual average of 250 inches of snow for skiing from mid-December to mid-April. From mid-June to mid-October, the main chairlift takes visitors to 11,500 feet on the west ridge of Agassiz Peak, where they have a breathtaking view of the Grand Canyon to Arizona's central mountains.

Directions: Go north from Flagstaff on US 180 about 7 miles. Turn right on Snowbowl Road and continue another 7 miles to the ski area.

Activities: Downhill skiing and snowboarding.

Facilities: Full service rental shop, repair shop, ski school, and restaurant.

Dates: Mid-December to mid-April.

Fees: There is a fee for chairlift tickets.

Closest town: Flagstaff, 14 miles.

For more information: Arizona Snowbowl, PO Box 40, Flagstaff, AZ 86002. Phone (520) 779-1951. Snow report (520) 779-4577. Web site www.arizonasnowbowl.com.

FLAGSTAFF NORDIC CENTER

[Fig. 28(3)] The lower slopes of the San Francisco Peaks offer great cross-country skiing. For those who tire of breaking their own trail through the deep snow, the Flagstaff Nordic Center offers more than 20 miles of groomed cross-country trails winding through the Coconino National Forest. The center operates usually from December until April.

Directions: Go north about16 miles from Flagstaff on US 180. The center is on the right.

Activities: Groomed track skiing.

Facilities: Rentals, lessons, snowshoeing, and group packages.

Dates: December to April.

Fees: There is a trail fee.

Closest town: Flagstaff, 16 miles.

For more information: Arizona Snowbowl, PO Box 40, Flagstaff, AZ 86002. Phone (520) 779-1951. Snow report (520) 779-4577. Web site www.arizonasnowbowl.com.

LAVA RIVER CAVE

[Fig. 28(4)] At 3,820 feet, Lava River Cave is the longest lava tube in Arizona. The tube formed between 650,000 and 700,000 years ago when molten lava erupted from a volcano near the present-day site of Michelbach Ranch on Hart Prairie. As the outer surface of the flow cooled and hardened, the interior continued to flow, leaving a hollow tube. Some of the lava flow features to look for include flow ripples, splashdowns (where rocks from the ceiling fell onto the still-molten floor), cooling cracks (formed as the lava cooled and shrank), and lavasicles (very small icicle-like "drips" of remelted lava). Please be careful not to damage any of these unique features as you explore the cave.

No special spelunking equipment is needed other than a strong dependable light (three sources of light per person is a good idea). Sturdy shoes and a hard hat are recommended. The cave entrance angles downward and requires a little bit of scrambling. Watch out for the low ceiling in places. Once inside the lava tube, the walking is fairly easy and for most of its length, spelunkers can stand upright.

About 1915, lumbermen working for the Saginaw and Manestee Lumber Company discovered this lava tube. In those early days, ice inside the cave left over from winter was "mined" during the spring and summer to provide Flagstaff residents with cool drinks and occasionally to make ice cream. The temperature just inside the cave entrance hovers around 45 degrees Fahrenheit; but at the tube's far end, the temperature is rarely above 35 degrees Fahrenheit, so dress accordingly.

Sometimes squirrels and porcupines visit the cave. Look for their droppings. Bats, too, inhabit the cave and play an important role as the only major night-flying predator of insects.

Directions: Drive about 14 miles north of Flagstaff on US 180 to milepost 230. Turn left onto the unpaved Forest Road 245 and go 3 miles to FR 171 then left.

Go 1 mile and turn left onto FR 171A. The cave is less than 0.5-mile down this track.

Activities: Spelunking.

Facilities: None.

Dates: Open year-round, although forest roads may be impassable when wet. Also snow and ice may block the entrance to the cave.

Fees: None.

Closest town: Flagstaff, 18 miles.

For more information: Peaks Ranger District, 5075 N. Hwy. 89, Flagstaff, AZ 86004. Phone (520) 526-0866.

RED MOUNTAIN GEOLOGIC SITE

[Fig. 28(5)] About halfway to the Grand Canyon from Flagstaff on US 180 is the intriguing volcanic cone known as Red Mountain. The eruptions that created Red Mountain occurred about 740,000 years ago. Erosion has cut away the side of the volcano, dramatically revealing its interior geology. Even people with no interest in geology are drawn to the amphitheater-like bowl containing strange, colorful pinnacles and fantastic pillars.

Directions: Drive about 32 miles northwest of Flagstaff on US 180. Turn left at the Red Mountain sign. The dirt road continues another 0.3 mile to the trailhead.

Activities: Hiking and nature study.

Facilities: None.

Dates: Open year-round.

Fees: None.

Closest town: Flagstaff, 32 miles.

For more information: Peaks Ranger District, 5075 N. Hwy. 89, Flagstaff, AZ 86004. Phone (520) 526-0866.

Trail: About 0.5 miles one-way.

Degree of difficulty: Easy.

Elevation: 6,900 to 7,050 feet.

Surface and blaze: An old cinder road with a few rock cairns.

STRAWBERRY CRATER WILDERNESS

[Fig. 28(19)] Strawberry Crater is just one of more than 600 volcanic craters and cones on the San Francisco Peaks Volcanic Field. This 50,000- to 100,000-year-old cinder cone is set in rolling pinyon-juniper woodland with sagebrush (*Artemesia* sp.), rabbitbrush (*Chrysothamnus* sp.), four-wing saltbush (*Atriplex canescens*), and Apache plume (*Fallugia paradoxa*). A few taller ponderosa pines are scattered about.

Running from the northeast base of the crater is a jagged lava flow that makes for challenging hiking. There are no maintained trails. The small archaeological sites, found within the 10,141-acre wilderness, should not be disturbed.

Directions: The easiest access is from FR 545, which is the Sunset Crater-Wupatki

Loop Road. About 3 miles east of the Sunset Crater Volcano National Monument boundary, turn left into the Painted Desert Vista parking lot. The wilderness boundary begins there. Strawberry Crater is 4.5 miles directly north.

Activities: Hiking, camping, and nature study.

Facilities: None.

Dates: Open year-round, although forest roads may be impassable when wet.

Fees: None.

Closest town: Flagstaff, 20 miles.

For more information: Peaks Ranger District, 5075 N. Hwy. 89, Flagstaff, AZ 86004. Phone (520) 526-0866.

SYCAMORE CANYON WILDERNESS

[Fig. 28(15)] The Sycamore Canyon Wilderness was established in 1935. Intermittent Sycamore Creek and its tributaries have carved a 20-mile long canyon into the Mogollon Rim about 15 miles west of busy Oak Creek Canyon. In places the canyon is as much as 7 miles wide and more than 2,000 feet deep. Wildlife, including mountain lion (*Felis concolor*), black bear (*Ursus americanus*), bobcat (*Felis rufus*), mule deer (*Odocoileus hemionus*), javelina (*Tayassu tajacu*), gray fox (*Urocyon cinereoargenteus*), and ringtail (*Bassariscus astutus*), is abundant especially along the lower creek and in the dense forest and chaparral of the northern section of the canyon.

Besides Arizona sycamores, other trees along the canyon bottom include cottonwood, willow, and netleaf hackberry.

The 55,937-acre wilderness is managed by three national forests—the Coconino, Prescott, and Kaibab. There are 11 trailheads to the wilderness with most of them on the east or Coconino side. One main trailhead is at the mouth of the canyon.

In the northwest head of Sycamore Canyon, on the Kaibab National Forest, is a popular rock climbing area called The Pit. Here basalt cliffs are broken by vertical cracks that challenge climbers' skills.

BOBCAT
(Felis rufus)

Directions: Most of the trailheads in the upper canyon can be reached from Flagstaff. Drive 2 miles west on Old Route 66 (Bus. 40) and turn left onto the Woody Mountain Road (FR 231). Stay on FR 231 about 14 miles and then refer to the Coconino National Forest map to locate the various trailheads. The mouth of Sycamore Canyon is reached by turning off the Tuzigoot National Monument road onto FR 131. Follow FR 131 for 10.6 miles to its end.

Activities: Hiking, camping, nature study, and hunting.

Facilities: None.

Dates: Open year-round, although winter snows usually close roads to the northern end of the canyon.

Fees: None.

Closest town: Flagstaff, about 20 miles from the upper canyon; Clarkdale, about 12 miles from the canyon's mouth.

For more information: Sedona Ranger District, PO Box 300, Sedona, AZ 86339. Phone (520) 282-4119. Chino Valley Ranger District, PO Box 485, Chino Valley, AZ 86323-0485. Phone (520) 636-2302. Williams/Forest Service Visitor Center, 200 Railroad Ave., Williams, AZ 86046. Phone (520) 635-4061.

PARSONS TRAIL

[Fig. 29(1)] This trail is probably the most popular in the wilderness because it follows the only perennial stretch of Sycamore Creek. No camping is allowed along this 3-mile riparian zone, but a trek there is a great day trip to watch birds or wade in the creek.

Directions: From Tuzigoot National Monument near Clarkdale, drive 10.6 miles north on FR 131 to its end.

Trail: 3.7 miles one-way to Parsons Spring.

Degree of difficulty: Easy.

Elevation: 3,600 to 4,000 feet.

Surface: Gravel, sand, and some wading.

Oak Creek Canyon, Sedona, and the Red Rock Country

The 12-mile drive through Oak Creek Canyon is one of northern Arizona's most delightful and scenic drives. In that short distance, the traveler descends from pine and fir forest to bubbling Oak Creek and passes through oak and juniper woodland to scattered stands of Arizona cypress (*Cupressus glabra*) and juniper set against the base of red sandstone cliffs and buttes. An equally glorious drive runs from I-17 down Schnebly Hill Road (FR 153) to its junction with AZ 179 in Sedona. This dirt road can be impassable when wet but is usually fine for sedans if drivers go slowly.

At the mouth of Oak Creek Canyon, set against a majestic backdrop of red and white cliffs, is Sedona. This community began in the late 1800s as a few farms and ranches along Oak Creek. While examining prehistoric ruins in the area, turn-of-the-century archaeologist Jesse Fewkes predicted that someday many people would come to see the beautiful red rocks and buttes. Little did he realize that less than 100 years after his visit, millions of tourists would be arriving annually for Jeep tours and shopping, hot-air balloon flights, fine dining, tennis and golf at area resorts.

Fishing Oak Creek is a major draw. Rainbow and brown trout lurk in the cold and clear waters of the upper creek. Downstream of Sedona, the creek warms from the desert sun, and bass and catfish are common.

The riparian habitat of Oak Creek hosts many species of wildlife. Some of the more unusual or special ones include the Arizona gray squirrel (*Sciurus arizonensis*), Arizona myotis bat (*Myotis occultus*), yellow-billed cuckoo (*Coccyzus americanus*), narrow-headed garter snake (*Thamnophis rufipunctatus*), Arizona toad (*Bufo microscaphus microscaphus*), common black hawk (*Buteogallus anthracinus*), and Mexican spotted owl (*Strix occidentalis*). Historically, the creek was home to river otter (*Lutra canadensis*). At least half of the 250 vertebrate species use the riparian habitats during some part of their life cycle, and of these, about 75 species require these streamside habitats for survival.

The Forest Service maintains five campgrounds (*see* table on page 348) and three day-use areas where hikers and anglers can access the creek. There are parcels of private land along the creek, and many landowners do not allow trespassing. Also, fishing is not allowed from bridges.

There are more than 60 trails in the Red Rock Country. All are used by hikers; some are appropriate for mountain biking and horseback riding.

Rock climbers test their skills on the sandstone mesas and buttes around Sedona and the basalt cliffs at the head of Oak Creek Canyon.

Directions: Oak Creek Canyon is located along AZ 89A.

Activities: Hiking, camping, swimming, fishing, and nature study.

Facilities: Forest Service campgrounds and picnic areas, private resorts.

Dates: Open year-round.

Fees: There are parking and camping fees.

Closest town: Sedona.

For more information: Sedona Ranger District, PO Box 300, Sedona, AZ 86339. Phone (520) 282-4119. Sedona-Oak Creek Canyon Chamber of Commerce, PO Box 478, Sedona, AZ 86339. Phone (520) 282-7722 or (800) 288-7336. Web site www.sedonachamber.com or www.sedona.net.

🏵 SLIDE ROCK STATE PARK

[Fig. 28(6)] This state park is located in the heart of Oak Creek Canyon. A natural 30-foot water slide worn in the creek's bottom attracts visitors. Much of the park is an old homestead where apple orchards and original buildings are being preserved.

Directions: Drive 7 miles north of Sedona on AZ 89A.

Activities: Wading, nature study, hiking, and fishing.

Facilities: Visitor center, restrooms, picnic area, and concession stand.

Dates: Open year-round.

Fees: There is an entrance fee.

Closest town: Sedona, 7 miles south.

For more information: Slide Rock State Park, PO Box 10358, Sedona, AZ 86339. Phone (520) 282-3034. Arizona State Parks, 1300 W. Washington St., Phoenix, AZ 85007. Phone (602) 542-4174.

RED ROCK-SECRET MOUNTAIN WILDERNESS

[Fig. 28(14)] The Red Rock-Secret Mountain Wilderness takes in much of the Mogollon Rim between Oak Creek Canyon on the east and Sycamore Canyon on the west. The wilderness plunges as much as 1,500 feet into canyons that drain into Oak Creek and the Verde River. Secret Mountain and Wilson Mountain are high, forested mesas jutting into the lower desert country.

The wide variety of vegetation, including more than 600 species of flowering plants, provides habitat for an equally diverse wildlife population. More than 250 species of mammals, birds, reptiles, and amphibians are found in the area, including elk (*Cervus elaphus*), mule and white-tailed deer, javelina, coyote (*Canis latrans*), desert and mountain cottontail (*Sylvilagus* sp.), mountain lion, black bear, band-tailed pigeon (*Columba fasciata*), rufous hummingbird (*Selasphorus rufus*), hairy woodpecker (*Picoides villosus*), hermit thrush (*Catharus guttatus*), Arizona alligator lizard (*Elgaria kingi*), and Woodhouse's toad (*Bufo woodhousei*).

Sixteen trailheads are scattered along the perimeter of this 43,950-acre wilderness, allowing for hikes or horseback rides of various lengths, from one day to several, to routes only to be attempted by experienced canyoneers.

Directions: Some trailheads are accessible from along AZ 89A in Oak Creek Canyon; others can be reached by various Forest Service roads northwest of Sedona.

Activities: Hiking, camping, nature study, and hunting.

Facilities: None.

Dates: Open year-round, although roads may be impassable when wet.

Fees: Parking fee at some trailheads.

Closest town: Flagstaff, about 15 miles; Sedona, about 2 miles.

For more information: Peaks Ranger District, 5075 N. Hwy. 89, Flagstaff, AZ 86004. Phone (520) 526-0866. Sedona Ranger District, PO Box 300, Sedona, AZ 86339. Phone (520) 282-4119.

WEST FORK TRAIL

[Fig. 29(5)] West Fork is the setting for one of Western writer Zane Grey's most famous novels—*Call of the Canyon*. The canyon walls soar over the tiny stream. A day hike up the West Fork Trail is one not to be soon forgotten.

Directions: Drive 11 miles north of Sedona on AZ 89A to the Call of the Canyon Day Use Area. Turn left and pay parking fee.

Trail: 3 miles one-way.

Degree of difficulty: Easy, but may require wading.

Elevation: 5,300 to 5,600 feet.

Surface and blaze: Forest floor, rocky to sandy.

WILSON MOUNTAIN TRAIL

[Fig. 29(6)] This trail climbs to the top of Wilson Mountain to reveal the entire Verde Valley spread out to the south, Oak Creek Canyon to the east, more of the Red Rock Country to the west, and the San Francisco Peaks on the northern horizon.

Directions: Drive north from Sedona on AZ 89A about 1.5 miles, cross Midgley Bridge, and turn left and park. A small sign marks the beginning of the trail.

Trail: 5.6 miles one-way.

Degree of difficulty: Moderate.

Elevation: 4,600 to 6,960 feet.

Surface and blaze: Rocky, marked by cairns.

RED ROCK STATE PARK

[Fig. 29(7)] This state park on lower Oak Creek is a nature center for environmental education with many interesting exhibits, programs, and ranger-led hikes. Surrounded by the red sandstone buttes and mesas that make Sedona famous, this is a lovely spot to watch birds or enjoy a picnic. Call ahead for a schedule of programs.

Directions: 5 miles southwest of Sedona on Red Rock Loop Road.

Activities: Hiking, horseback riding, and nature study.

Facilities: Visitor center, restrooms, picnic area, and concession stand.

Dates: Open year-round.

Fees: There is an entrance fee.

Closest town: Sedona.

For more information: Red Rock State Park, 4050 Lower Red Rock Loop Road, Sedona, AZ 86336. Phone (520) 282-6907. Arizona State Parks, 1300 W. Washington St., Phoenix, AZ 85007. Phone (602) 542-4174.

MUNDS MOUNTAIN WILDERNESS

[Fig. 29(12)] Taking AZ 179 south from Sedona to I-17 is another spectacular drive. Motorists pass Courthouse Butte and Cathedral Rock as well as skirt the edge of the Munds Mountain Wilderness. Another notable feature is Bell Rock, shaped very much like the Liberty Bell. According to New Age guru Page Bryant, and her spiritual guide, Albion, Bell Rock is the location of one the seven vortexes or psychic-energy points around Sedona and a "refueling" place for alien visitors. For "true believers" (or just the curious), stop by one of the many New Age bookstores or gift shops for more information. Nature lovers should take the 3.7-mile Bell Rock Pathway,

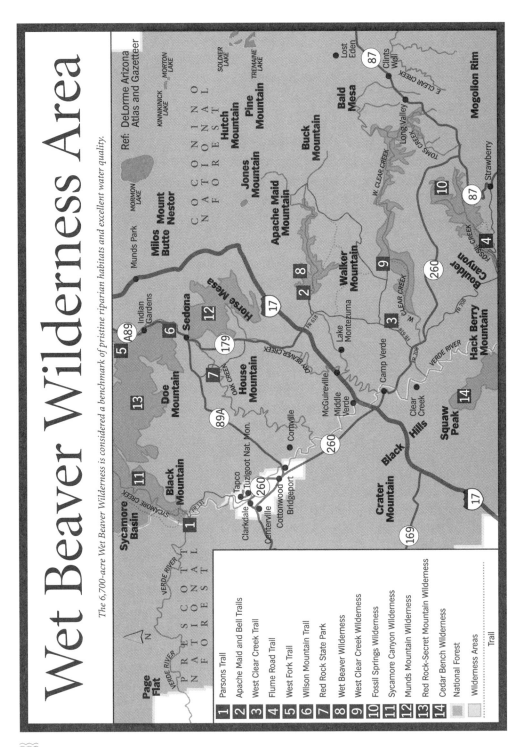

Wet Beaver Wilderness Area

The 6,700-acre Wet Beaver Wilderness is considered a benchmark of pristine riparian habitats and excellent water quality.

Ref: DeLorme Arizona
Atlas and Gazetteer

1 Parsons Trail
2 Apache Maid and Bell Trails
3 West Clear Creek Trail
4 Flume Road Trail
5 West Fork Trail
6 Wilson Mountain Trail
7 Red Rock State Park
8 Wet Beaver Wilderness
9 West Clear Creek Wilderness
10 Fossil Springs Wilderness
11 Sycamore Canyon Wilderness
12 Munds Mountain Wilderness
13 Red Rock-Secret Mountain Wilderness
14 Cedar Bench Wilderness

National Forest

Wilderness Areas

Trail

which goes from near milepost 310 to the Village of Oak Creek and meanders through a pinyon-juniper-Arizona cypress woodland.

Munds Mountain Wilderness preserves 18,150 acres of the unique red sandstone formations just east of Sedona, as well as part of the spectacular Mogollon Rim. Elevations range from 3,600 to 6,800 feet.

The steep sides of Munds and Lee mountains expose cliffs of Coconino Sandstone and the Schnebly Hill Formation. Several "ramps" of basalt flows allow access, albeit difficult walking, to their summits.

There is a great assortment of vegetation and wildlife species. Besides mule deer, white-tailed deer (*Odocoileus virginianus*) live here. Upper Woods Canyon contains outstanding riparian habitat consisting of Arizona black walnut (*Juglans major*), willow (*Salix* sp.), cottonwood (*Populus* sp.), velvet ash (*Fraxinus pennsylvanica velutina*), and Arizona sycamore (*Plantanus wrightii*) that is vital to many animals.

Directions: Eighteen miles of trails penetrate this wilderness with several trail-heads conveniently located along AZ 179, near the end of Jacks Canyon Road, and off the Schnebly Hill Road. The Forest Service can supply trail information.

Activities: Hiking, camping, horseback riding, swimming, nature study, rock climbing, and hunting.

Facilities: None.

Dates: Open year-round, although snow may block access to the higher areas in winter.

Fees: None.

Closest town: Sedona.

For more information: Sedona Ranger District, PO Box 300, Sedona, AZ 86339. Phone (520) 282-4119.

🌐 WET BEAVER WILDERNESS

[Fig. 29] Wet Beaver is a steep-walled canyon cutting into the Mogollon Rim. Red Schnebly Hill, Supai, and Hermit sandstones and shales form striking cliffs along the lower canyon. This 6,700-acre wilderness is considered by the Forest Service to be a benchmark of pristine riparian habitats and excellent water quality. Wet Beaver is also one of Arizona's rarest natural resources—it features a perennially flowing desert stream. Rainbow and brown trout and smallmouth bass (*Micropterus dolomieui*) are popular sport fish here. The native roundtail chub (*Gila robusta*) also lives in this stream with about 18 other species. And as the area's name suggests, beaver are residents, too. In the upper reaches of the canyon, beaver (*Castor canadensis*) successfully build dams; but along the lower stream, flash floods usually prevent the beaver from constructing dams or typical beaver lodges. Instead, the "desert" beaver live in burrows they dig into the stream banks.

Two major trails, Apache Maid and Bell, offer easy access to this wilderness. Following the length of Wet Beaver Creek is a challenge best left to experienced canyoneers.

Arizona Treefrogs

When the summer rains come to the mountains, Arizona treefrogs (*Hyla wrightorum*) emerge from underground in the evening, breed in ephemeral rain pools in the ponderosa pine forest, and then climb into the pines to feed on bark beetles and other invertebrates. After a few weeks, the original adult treefrogs and the newly metamorphosed adults retire to their underground burrows. In the glow of a flashlight, the moist green skin of these half-dollar-size frogs reflects like an emerald jewel.

Directions: The best access is from I-17 Exit 298. Travel east on FR618 for 2.1 miles, then turn left at the sign for the Apache Maid and Bell trails. The trailhead is 0.25 mile.

Activities: Hiking, camping, nature study, swimming, and fishing.

Facilities: None.

Dates: Open year-round.

Fees: None.

Closest town: Camp Verde, 15 miles.

For more information: Beaver Creek Ranger District, PO Box 670, Camp Verde, AZ 86322. Phone (520) 567-4121.

APACHE MAID AND BELL TRAILS

[Fig. 29(2)] These trails start out as one. After about 2 miles, the Apache Maid Trail forks to the left and eventually climbs to the west rim of Wet Beaver Canyon. The Bell Trail continues down to the creek.

Trail: About 4.5 miles one-way to the rim; about 3 miles one-way to the creek.

Degree of difficulty: Moderate to rim; easy to creek.

Elevation: 3,000 to 5,200 feet at rim.

Surface and blaze: Rocky to sandy; cairns.

WEST CLEAR CREEK WILDERNESS

[Fig. 29(9)] Located 25 miles northeast of Camp Verde, West Clear Creek has carved one of the most rugged and remote canyons in northern Arizona. It is the longest of the canyons cutting through the Mogollon Rim.

Plant growth within the canyon is lush, with hanging gardens of maidenhair fern (*Adiantum capillus-veneris*), crimson monkey flower (*Mimulus cardinalis*), and scarlet penstemon (*Penstemon eatoni*). Trees and shrubs along the creek and slopes include cottonwood, Arizona black walnut, box elder (*Acer negundo*), willow, alder (*Alnus* sp.), Gambel oak (*Quercus gambelii*), bigtooth maple, Douglas fir, ponderosa pine, white fir (*Abies concolor*), New Mexico locust (*Robinia neomexicana*), and Arizona sycamore. The rare Arizona bugbane (*Cimicifuga arizonica*) lives in the moist canyon depths.

Wildlife is abundant. Species include mule and white-tailed deer, elk, black bear, mountain lion, river otter (which have been introduced), bald eagle (*Haliaeetus leucocephalus*), osprey (*Pandion haliaetus*), peregrine falcon (*Falco peregrinus*), common black hawk, Mexican spotted owl, and many song birds such as red-faced warblers (*Myioborus picta*) and Bewick's wren (*Thryomanes bewickii*).

A trail starts at Bull Pen Ranch near the canyon's mouth and follows the creek eastward for a few miles before climbing up the northern slope to the rim. This access is fairly easy and attracts anglers and inexperienced hikers. Rainbow and brown trout and smallmouth bass are the popular sport fish here. The roundtail chub, spikedace, and other native fish also live in this stream.

The upper end of the canyon is accessed by steep and rocky rim-to-creek trails, such as the Calloway, Maxwell, and Tramway. To find the trailheads requires at the very least a high-clearance vehicle and careful use of the Coconino National Forest map.

**ARIZONA
TREEFROG**
(Hyla wrightorum)

In the main, narrow part of the West Clear Creek, there are no trails. Wading or swimming dozens of pools is necessary in many places. Flash floods and hypothermia are very real dangers, especially during the summer rainy season. Hikers must plan trips carefully.

Directions: Drive east from Camp Verde about 5 miles on AZ 260, turn left onto FR 618, go 2 miles, then right 4 miles on FR 215 to the east end of the Bull Pen dispersed camping area and the signed West Clear Creek trailhead.

Activities: Hiking, camping, swimming, nature study, and fishing.

Facilities: None.

Dates: Open year-round, although the higher rims may be inaccessible in winter.

Fees: None.

Closest town: Camp Verde, about 10 miles.

For more information: Long Valley Ranger District, HC 31, Box 68, Happy Jack, AZ 86024. Phone (520) 354-2216. Beaver Creek Ranger District, PO Box 670, Camp Verde, AZ 86322. Phone (520) 567-4121.

WEST CLEAR CREEK TRAIL

[Fig. 29(3)] The first 6 miles of this trail follow West Clear Creek past swimming holes and good fishing spots. Then the trail turns northwest and climbs steeply 2 miles to the canyon rim and FR 214A.

Trail: About 8 miles one-way to FR 214A.

Degree of difficulty: Moderate to strenuous.

Elevation: 3,700 to 5,780 feet.

Surface: Rocky, some wading necessary.

FOSSIL SPRINGS WILDERNESS

[Fig. 29(10)] Fossil Springs is located at the bottom of a steep-sided, wide canyon cut some 1,600 feet into the Mogollon Rim. Each minute, 20,000 gallons of 72-degree water gushes from the springs. The abundant water supports one of the most botanically diverse riparian habitats in the state. More than 30 species of trees and shrubs

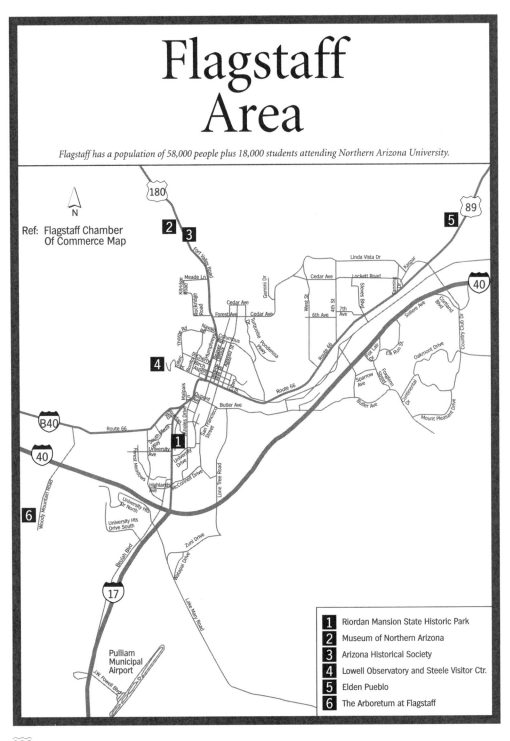

Flagstaff Area

Flagstaff has a population of 58,000 people plus 18,000 students attending Northern Arizona University.

Ref: Flagstaff Chamber
Of Commerce Map

1 Riordan Mansion State Historic Park
2 Museum of Northern Arizona
3 Arizona Historical Society
4 Lowell Observatory and Steele Visitor Ctr.
5 Elden Pueblo
6 The Arboretum at Flagstaff

grow along the creek—in sharp contrast to the surrounding desert shrubs. More than 100 species of birds have been recorded near the springs. The roundtail chub and Gila topminnow (*Poeciliopsis occidentalis*), both endangered species, live in Fossil Creek.

In 1909, a small dam was built below the springs to divert water into a flume that runs down to the Childs-Irving Power Plant on the Verde River. The electricity produced went to the mines around Jerome and Prescott. The flume is no longer in use but is on the National Register of Historic Places.

The Mail, Flume Road, and Fossil Spring trails allow access to the 11,550-acre wilderness area.

Directions: The most direct approach is to take FR 708 either from Camp Verde or Strawberry to the Irving trailhead.

Activities: Hiking, camping, swimming, nature study, and hunting.

Facilities: None.

Dates: Open year-round, although wet weather may make forest roads impassable.

Fees: None.

Closest town: Strawberry, 10 miles.

For more information: Beaver Creek Ranger District, PO Box 670, Camp Verde, AZ 86322. Phone (520) 567-4121.

FLUME ROAD TRAIL

[Fig. 29(4)] **Directions:** Follow FR 708 about 10 miles from Strawberry until the signed trailhead on the right just before the Irving Power Plant.

Trail: 3.5 miles to the springs.

Degree of difficulty: Easy to moderate.

Elevation: 3,800 to 4,240 feet.

Surface: An old gravel road, except for a short climb at the beginning to get on the road.

COCONINO NATIONAL FOREST CAMPGROUNDS

Dispersed camping is allowed throughout most of the Coconino National Forest except for heavily used or ecologically sensitive places such as Oak Creek Canyon or the Inner Basin. There are 21 developed campgrounds in this national forest. See Appendix G for a table of information on individual campgrounds.

Flagstaff Area

[Fig. 30] Local legend relates that in July 1876, a passing wagon train stopped near the southern base of the San Francisco Peaks to celebrate the country's centennial. The pioneers stripped the branches from a tall ponderosa pine and fastened an American flag to the trunk. For years that flagpole stood alongside the trail. In the spring of 1881, citizens of a budding community decided to name their town after that staff.

The following year, the transcontinental railroad arrived in Flagstaff, bringing new opportunities, stores, saloons, banks, and more settlers. Today, Flagstaff is a city of about 58,000 plus another 18,000 students attending Northern Arizona University.

One of the best ways to get acquainted with Flagstaff's rich frontier history is to take a free guided history walk with local historians Richard and Sherry Mangum. These tours are offered some weekends from spring until fall. Check with the Flagstaff Visitor Center for their schedule. If a tour is not possible, their book, *Flagstaff Historic Walk: A Stroll Through Old Downtown,* will provide plenty of information or visit their Web site (www.flagguide.com/mainstreet/historicwalk/walk.htm) for a virtual tour.

If your interests lean more toward geology, take Marie Jackson's *Stone Landmarks: Flagstaff's Geology and Historic Building Stones* on a walk around downtown for a delightfully different perspective on this mountain town.

A system of urban and nearby Forest Service trails allows visitors to easily explore the town and surrounding forest on foot or mountain bike.

For more information: Flagstaff Visitors Center in the historic Santa Fe (now Amtrak) Railroad Station, 1 E. Route 66, Flagstaff, AZ 86001. Phone (520) 774-9541 or (800) 842-7293. Web sites www.flagstaff.az.us or www.flagguide.com or www.flagstaffarizona.com. Peaks Ranger Station, 5075 N. Hwy 89, Flagstaff, AZ 86004. Phone (520) 526-0866. Mormon Lake Ranger District, 4373 S. Lake Mary Road, Flagstaff, AZ 86001. Phone (520) 774-1182.

▓ RIORDAN MANSION STATE HISTORIC PARK

[Fig. 30(1)] Timothy and Michael Riordan were prominent pioneer Flagstaff businessmen who developed a successful logging industry around the turn of the century. After marrying Caroline and Elizabeth Metz, their two families lived together on a 50-acre estate in a unique twentieth century mansion constructed in duplex fashion. The elegant 1904 home contains 40 rooms, over 13,000 square feet of living area plus servants' quarters. Charles Whittlesey, the creator of Grand Canyon's El Tovar Lodge, designed the residence.

Directions: In Flagstaff at 1300 Riordan Ranch St.

Activities: Guided tours.

Facilities: Visitor center, museum, and picnic area.

Dates: Open daily; 8 to 5 (summer), 11 to 5 (winter).

Fees: There is an entrance fee.

Closest town: Flagstaff.

For more information: Riordan Mansion State Historic Park, 1300 Riordan Ranch Road, Flagstaff, AZ 86001. Phone (520) 779-4395. Arizona State Parks, 1300 W. Washington St., Phoenix, AZ 85007. Phone (602) 542-4174. Web site www.pr.state.az.us.

Ice Age Relics

During the Pleistocene Epoch, from about 2 million to 10,000 years ago, North America was subjected to a series of ice ages. The great continental glaciers never reached the American Southwest, but the climate was much wetter and cooler than today and relatively small mountain glaciers existed on Arizona's higher mountains.

During these times, plant communities were often quite different than those seen today. Broadleaf, deciduous trees were more widely distributed, not confined riparian communities. One of these trees was the Arizona black walnut (*Juglans major*), whose meaty nuts are relished by the Arizona gray squirrel (*Sciurus arizonensis*).

Over the last 10,000 years, as Arizona has warmed and become more arid, the walnut trees died off—except those near water. The range of the gray squirrel also shrank. Today, the gray squirrel is only found in the riparian communities along the Mogollon Rim and a few other similar settings in southern Arizona.

Other animals in Arizona that are thought to be Ice Age relics include the Gila chub (*Gila intermedia*), longfin dace (*Agosia chrysogaster*), Gila topminnow (*Poeciliopsis occidentalis*), narrow-headed garter snake (*Thamnophis rufipunctatus*), Arizona toad (*Bufo microscaphus microscaphus*), and water shrew (*Sorex palustris*).

MUSEUM OF NORTHERN ARIZONA

[Fig. 30(2)] The museum is the ideal introduction to the natural and human history of the Colorado Plateau. The museum's bookstore is a wealth of information about the region. A visit to the gift shop is recommended for anyone interested in learning more about native arts and crafts. Annual shows display the best artwork from the Navajo, Hopi, Zuni, and Pai people.

Directions: About 3 miles north of Flagstaff on US 180.

Activities: Tours, educational programs, and lectures.

Facilities: Museum with permanent and changing exhibits on geology, anthropology, biology, and fine art; nature trail, gift shop, bookstore, and restrooms.

Dates: Open year-round.

Fees: There is an entrance fee.

Closest town: Flagstaff.

For more information: Museum of Northern Arizona, 3101 N. Fort Valley Road, Flagstaff, AZ 86001. Phone (520) 774-5213. Web site www.musnaz.org.

ARIZONA HISTORICAL SOCIETY PIONEER MUSEUM

[Fig. 30(3)] The old county hospital houses the Pioneer Museum, which contains many items and photographs from northern Arizona's past including an early physicians' exhibit and a popular seasonal exhibit called "Playthings of the Past." A barn contains Flagstaff's second motorized fire truck, a 1923 American La France.

In 1967, one of Flagstaff's earliest surviving cabins was moved from the east side of town to this location and now serves as a center for craft demonstrations.

Directions: About 2 miles north of downtown Flagstaff on US 180 (Fort Valley Road). Look for the old 1929 Baldwin articulated locomotive and Santa Fe Caboose parked out front.

Activities: Self-guided tours, special events, and demonstrations.

Facilities: Museum, gift shop, restrooms, and changing exhibits.

Dates: Open Monday-Saturday; closed Christmas Day, New Year's Day, Easter, and Thanksgiving.

Fees: A donation is suggested.

Closest town: Flagstaff.

For more information: AHS Pioneer Museum, 2340 N. Fort Valley Road, Flagstaff, AZ 86001. Phone (520) 774-6272.

▒ LOWELL OBSERVATORY AND STEELE VISITOR CENTER

[Fig. 30(4)] In 1894, Percival Lowell set up his 24-inch refracting telescope on a mesa above Flagstaff so he could observe Mars. The private observatory has been studying the heavens ever since. And it's no coincidence that Pluto's abbreviation, PL, is also Percival's initials: One of the observatory's proudest discoveries was the planet Pluto in 1930.

The Steele Visitor Center contains many interactive exhibits explaining the astounding world of astronomy. Daytime tours feature discussions about the history Lowell Observatory and the research done there, followed by tours of the Pluto Discovery Telescope, the 24-inch Clark Telescope, the historic Rotunda Library, and the 16-inch reflecting telescope housed in the McAllister Public Observatory. Safe viewing of the sun through a specially filtered telescope is also available. Evening tours include indoor discussions of the constellations and other features of the night sky, followed by telescope viewing (weather permitting).

Directions: The observatory is located about 1 mile west of downtown Flagstaff at 1400 W. Mars Hill Road.

Activities: Tours and programs including night-sky viewing.

Facilities: Visitor center with hands-on exhibits, gift shop, and restrooms.

Dates: Open year-round except Easter, Thanksgiving, Christmas, and New Year's Day; occasional evening programs.

Fees: There is an entrance fee.

Closest town: Flagstaff.

For more information: Lowell Observatory, 1400 W. Mars Hill Road, Flagstaff, AZ 86001. Phone (520) 774-2096 or 3358. Web site www.lowell.edu.

▒ ELDEN PUEBLO

[Fig. 30(5)] Located on the east side of Flagstaff, just minutes from downtown, is the prehistoric ruin known as Elden Pueblo. From about A.D. 600 to 1400, the

Sinagua people lived in the Flagstaff area while growing plots of corn, beans, and squash. Initially they lived in pit houses and later built above-ground pueblos. They made fine brownware and redware pottery and traded for painted pottery with other prehistoric groups throughout the Southwest. Through trade, the Sinagua also acquired seashells, jewelry, macaw parrots (*Ara* sp.), minerals, and copper bells.

Directions: Located just off US 89, south of the traffic light at the Camp Townsend-Winona Road.

Activities: Archaeology camps for children and adults, amateurs and professionals.

Facilities: None.

Dates: Open year-round, but most activities are held in spring, summer, and fall.

Fees: None to visit site, but most camps have fees.

Closest town: Flagstaff.

For more information: Elden Pueblo Archaeological Project, PO Box 3496, Flagstaff, AZ 86003-3496. Phone (520) 523-8797. Or contact Coconino National Forest, Archaeology Section, 2323 East Greenlaw Lane, Flagstaff, AZ 86004. Phone (520) 527-3600.

THE ARBORETUM AT FLAGSTAFF

[Fig. 30(6)] The Arboretum at Flagstaff, also known as the Transition Zone Horticultural Institute, was founded in 1981 to help visitors and residents better understand the plants and plant communities of the Colorado Plateau. The arboretum is also involved in conserving rare and endangered species of plants and native animals. An artificial pond and brook harbor Little Colorado spinedace (*Lepidomeda vittata*), a threatened fish. The arboretum takes in 200 acres of ponderosa pine forest and is a delightful place for a quiet walk or picnic. Annual native plant sales are a highly anticipated event by local gardeners.

Directions: Located about 4 miles southwest of Flagstaff on the Woody Mountain Road.

Activities: Nature walks, workshops, lectures, native plant sales, and guided tours.

Facilities: Visitor center, gift shop, passive solar greenhouse, constructed wetlands, nature trail, riparian area, gardens, picnic tables, and restrooms.

Dates: Open Apr. 1-Dec. 15.

Fees: There is an admission fee.

Closest town: Flagstaff, 4 miles.

For more information: The Arboretum at Flagstaff, PO Box 670, Flagstaff, AZ 86002. Phone (520) 774-1441. Web site www.flagguide.com/arboretum.

SUNSET CRATER VOLCANO NATIONAL MONUMENT

[Fig. 28(18)] During the winter of A.D. 1064-65, this volcano began to form as ash and cinders exploded from a fissure. Lava flowed from its base, leaving black rivers of jagged basalt. For about 200 years, periodic eruptions added more igneous debris around the vent until a 1,000-foot-high cone was formed. The wind carried the lightest, smallest volcanic particles over 800 square miles of northern Arizona. This volcanic activity initially caused the Sinaguan inhabitants of the area to flee, but they and others soon returned to farm in the new volcanic soils (and quite coincidently experienced slightly warmer and wetter conditions for the next century or so, which helped their crops grow).

A final burst of activity around 1250 deposited iron- and sulfur-rich lava on the rim of the cone giving the volcano a permanent "sunset" glow. Nineteenth century explorer and geologist John Wesley Powell is credited with giving the cone its present name.

A mile-long self-guiding loop trail at the base of the volcano allows visitors to examine volcanic features. Climbing Sunset Crater is not allowed due to the fragile nature of its slopes; however, hikers can explore other cinder cones nearby, such as Lenox Crater and Doney Mountain. Inquire at the visitor center for hiking information.

The road to Sunset Crater continues north to Wupatki National Monument (*see* page 135) and then west back to US 89, allowing a loop drive to be done.

Directions: Drive about 12 miles northeast of Flagstaff on US 89, and then turn right (east) on the Sunset Crater Road. It's about 3 miles to the visitor center and another 2 miles to Sunset Crater.

Activities: Nature trails, summer programs, and viewpoints.

Facilities: Visitor center, restrooms, picnic areas, and a Forest Service campground across from the visitor center.

Dates: Open daily except Christmas Day.

Fees: There is an entrance fee.

Closest town: Flagstaff, 15 miles southwest.

For more information: Sunset Crater Volcano National Monument, Route 3, Box 149, Flagstaff, AZ 86004. Phone (520) 526-0502. For camping information, contact the Coconino National Forest, Peaks Ranger Station, 5010 N. Hwy 89, Flagstaff, AZ 86004. Phone (520) 526-0866 or 527-1474.

▒ WALNUT CANYON NATIONAL MONUMENT

[Fig. 28(20)] A short distance southeast of Flagstaff, intermittent Walnut Creek has carved a 400-foot deep gorge that visitors can hike down to see cliff dwellings built about 800 years ago by the Sinagua. These early people were able to live in an area that lacks water, a region the Spanish called the *Sierra Sin Agua*—"mountains without water."

The Sinagua first appeared in the Flagstaff area about A.D. 600. Possibly they were attracted by the abundant game and wild plants. But they were also farmers. The Sinagua built one-room pit houses near their agricultural fields, relying on the scant rain to grow corn and other crops. Archaeologists once thought that the eruption of nearby Sunset Crater in A.D. 1064-65 made the land more fertile, creating a prehistoric land rush. Recent findings, however, suggest that it was increased rainfall and slightly warmer temperatures in the mid-eleventh century that made farming more productive. During this time, large above-ground villages were built, such as those at Wupatki National Monument (*see* page 135) and Elden Pueblo, and many pit houses were abandoned. The cliff dwellings in Walnut Canyon were built mostly between 1125 and 1250.

By the mid-thirteenth century, Walnut Canyon was abandoned and some of the Sinagua occupied new villages a few miles to the southeast along Anderson Mesa. The reasons for this move are not clear. Archaeologists believe that some of the Sinagua were eventually assimilated into the Hopi culture.

Walnut Canyon has a remarkable array of plant communities. The rim area is ponderosa pine forest; but in the canyon, the south-facing slopes have pinyon pine, juniper, banana yucca (*Yucca baccata*), claret cup hedgehog cactus (*Echinocereus triglochidiatus*), and prickly pear (*Opuntia* sp.). The shady, north-facing slopes are covered with a variety of shrubs and even Douglas fir. At the canyon bottom, the intermittent Walnut Creek supports a diverse riparian community including box elder and Arizona black walnut.

Two paved foot trails begin at the visitor center. The Island Trail, a 0.9-mile loop, passes 25 of the cliff dwelling rooms and takes visitors through the different plant communities. There is a 185-foot climb (240 stairs) back to the canyon rim. Remember the rim is nearly 7,000 feet above sea level. The 0.7-mile Rim Trail overlooks the canyon and takes visitors by the ruins of Sinagua rim-top structures.

Directions: Go about 7 miles east of downtown Flagstaff on I-40 to Exit 204 and follow the entrance road 3 miles to the visitor center.

Activities: Hiking to the cliff dwellings and nature study.

Facilities: Visitor center, restrooms, and picnic area.

Dates: Open daily except Christmas Day.

Fees: There is an entrance fee.

Closest town: Flagstaff, about 10 miles west.

For more information: Walnut Canyon National Monument, Walnut Canyon Road, Flagstaff, AZ 86004-9705. Phone (520) 526-3367. Web site www.nps.gov/waca.

Kaibab National Forest

[Fig. 28] The Kaibab National Forest has the distinction of being divided by one of nature's greatest spectacles—the Grand Canyon. The North Kaibab District, north of the Canyon, is discussed in the Arizona Strip chapter. The Kaibab National Forest that lies south of Grand Canyon National Park is broken into two districts—Tusayan and Williams—separated by the high desert country of the Coconino Plateau. The

Tusayan Ranger District is adjacent to the south boundary of Grand Canyon National Park and has a developed campground (*see* below).

The Williams Ranger District encircles the city of Williams. The district is cut east and west by I-40. Elevations range from 5,500 feet in the southwestern part of the district to 10,418 feet at the summit of Kendrick Mountain near the northeastern boundary, with an average of 7,000 feet. Much of the terrain is relatively level, except for numerous small knolls, which are mainly volcanic cinder cones. The few larger mountains are lava domes, formed by thick, viscous lavas such as andesite, dacite, and rhyolite.

In 1851, Captain Lorenzo Sitgreaves led a government expedition past the mountain that would eventually bear his name. An escort for this party, Brevet Major H.L. Kendrick, also had a mountain named for him. The Sitgreaves party labeled Bill Williams Mountain after famed trapper and mountain man William Sherley Williams.

A few years later, ranchers settled the well-watered open meadows of Spring Valley, Garland Prairie, Pitman Valley, and Red Lake. After the turn of the century, homesteaders tried farming root crops, such as potatoes, but were largely unsuccessful because of the high elevation, short growing season, and lack of moisture. Remains of these homesteads and ranches dot the landscape today.

The timber industry got started in this area to supply ties for the transcontinental Atlantic and Pacific Railroad (now the Burlington Northern-Santa Fe) line built in 1882. Later, the railroad transported lumber to a growing nation. In 1893, the Saginaw Lumber Company was established in Williams. The company built railroad spur lines into the forest to reach new timber stands. With the completion of railroad logging in the Williams area in the mid-1920s, operations moved to the Tusayan Ranger District between 1928 and 1935. After that time, trucks transported logs from the forest to the mills.

The natural resources of the area were first protected in 1893 with the establishment of the Grand Canyon Forest Reserve; another forest reserve was established around Williams in 1898. These reserves became the Tusayan National Forest in 1910. In 1934, the Tusayan National Forest was combined with the Forest Service land north of the Grand Canyon to become today's Kaibab National Forest.

Forest Service rangers began a program to regulate forest uses such as ranching, lumbering, and homesteading. They built lookouts in trees, and later constructed towers, to help spot wildfires. Many of the forest's trails were originally built to reach fire lookout points.

There are more than 230 developed campsites with running water, fire rings, and tables at four fee-area campgrounds. Boating, fishing, and picnicking are also permitted. Sunflower Flat Wildlife Area, southeast of Williams on FR 747, is a good spot to see deer, elk, wild turkey (*Meleagris gallopavo*), and other animals. Coleman Lake and Bixler Mountain are also excellent areas to find wildlife including a variety of birds such as western meadowlark (*Sturnella neglecta*), horned lark (Eremophila alpestris), western and mountain bluebirds (*Sialia mexicana* and *S. currucoides*), chipping sparrow (*Spizella passerina*), red-winged blackbird (*Agelaius phoeniceus*), Steller's jay (*Cyanocitta stelleri*), common raven (*Corvus corax*), American crow (*Corvus brachyrhynchos*), and many others.

Surprisingly, within the 550,411 acres of national forest land, there are no perennial streams and only a few reliable springs. However, within a few miles of Williams are six small lakes and reservoirs—Cataract, Kaibab, and White Horse lakes and Dogtown, Santa Fe, and Williams City reservoirs. Fishing in the small lakes scattered within the Kaibab National Forest is a popular activity and is at its best from early spring through May and then later in the summer. Catch rates decline in early

Merriam's Elk

Northern Arizona is home to elk, but these are not native animals. Once there was a race of unusually large elk [called Merriam's elk (*Cervus elaphus merriami*)] existing in the high country. Legend has it that the antlers were often palmated like those of moose. However, by the turn of the century, Merriam's elk were extinct, victims of overhunting. Today's herds are Roosevelt's or Rocky Mountain elk (*C. e. nelsoni*), a variety from the Yellowstone country. They were introduced to Arizona beginning in 1913.

These elk have done so well in northern Arizona that they may be eating themselves, and other browsers, out of a home. Where fires have occurred in the forest, quaking aspen is often the first tree species to return. However, aspen regeneration has been effectively prevented by hungry elk. Elk and cattle have also overgrazed some meadows. In a few of these areas, elk-proof fences have been erected around young aspen groves and meadows, but a more effective, long-term solution may be increased hunting to lower elk populations. The elk herd south of Flagstaff peaked at about 19,600 animals in 1993-94 and has since been reduced to about 14,600. The state has about 28,000 animals. However, the Arizona Game and Fish Department's long-term goal is to cut this number in half. Biologists believe that this will help other species such as deer, turkeys, and even native fish, which become threatened when riparian habitat is overgrazed.

summer until the July and August monsoons stimulate feeding. Game fish include brown and rainbow trout, channel catfish, largemouth bass, black crappie, bluegill, yellow perch, and green sunfish. Brook trout (*Salvelinus fontinalis*) can be taken in several small ponds south of Williams. For a recorded message about fishing conditions, call the fishing hotline at (602) 789-3701. Or write the Arizona Game and Fish Department, 2221 W. Greenway Road, Phoenix, AZ 850023. Phone (602) 942-3000.

There is a small downhill ski area on Bill Williams Mountain and a cross-country ski area, Spring Valley, 6 miles north of Parks on FR 141. Other popular places for cross-country skiing include Sevier and Barney flats southeast of Williams about

6 miles. About 8 miles east of Williams on historic Route 66 is the Oak Hill Snow Play Area, which is popular with tubers.

Be sure to stop at the Williams/Forest Service Visitor Center located in the restored historic train station depot on the corner of Grand Canyon Boulevard and Railroad Avenue. The visitor center contains exhibits on the history and natural resources of the region.

For more information: Williams/Forest Service Visitor Center, 200 W. Railroad Ave., Williams, AZ 86046. Phone (520) 635-4061 or (800) 863-0546. Web site www.fs.fed.us/r3/kai.

OVERLAND ROAD

In the summer of 1863, the U.S. Army blazed a road from the Beale Road (precursor to Route 66, *see* page 333) near Flagstaff to Whipple Creek near Prescott, which experienced a short-lived gold rush. The road continued west through Garland Prairie to Lockett Spring, then turned southwest to cross Hell Canyon and from there to Prescott. About 30 miles of this historic route is within the Kaibab National Forest and has been marked for hikers and horseback riders. There are several trailheads. A map and more information can be obtained from the Williams Ranger District office.

Directions: There are trailheads at Dow Springs and Pomeroy Tanks and 3 more along or near County Road 73. Get detailed instructions from Williams Ranger District office.

Trail: About 30 miles.

Degree of difficulty: Easy to moderate.

Elevation: About 6,800 feet.

Surface and blaze: Rocky to forest floor; marked with rock cairns, distinctive brass caps, and tree blazes.

For more information: Williams/Forest Service Visitor Center, 200 W. Railroad Ave., Williams, AZ 86046. Phone (520) 635-4061 or (800) 863-0546. Web site www.fs.fed.us/r3/kai.

COXCOMBS MOUNTAIN BIKE LOOP

[Fig. 28(13)] The numerous Forest Service roads and some trails offer endless possibilities for the mountain biker. One ride that has it all—history, scenery, and wildlife—is the Coxcombs Loop. Its length is perfect for a half-day ride and picnic. The route winds through a transitional area of ponderosa pine forest and pinyon-juniper woodland and an occasional meadow. There are distant views of Kendrick and Sitgreaves mountains to the east as well as Picacho Peak and Mt. Floyd to the west.

In some areas, the route crosses cleared pastures created to grow more forage for livestock. Keep a sharp lookout for pronghorn (*Antilocapra americana*) in these openings. You may encounter a sheepherder's camp or two. Usually these are occupied by herders whose ancestry traces to Mexico, South America, or the Basque region of Spain.

At one point, a short spur (FR 2030) leads to historic Laws Spring. This perennial seep was visited by Lieutenant Edward Beale, a retired Navy officer, who constructed the first federal road across the Southwest in 1857 (*see* page 333). There are prehistoric petroglyphs and historic inscriptions at the spring.

Directions: Drive east from Williams on I-40 to the Parks Exit. Turn north then west to the Pines General Store. Turn north on FR 141 and drive about 9 miles to FR 97. Take FR 97 to where it meets FR 141 again, turn left, drive about 2.7 miles, and turn right onto FR 730. Go 2.2 miles to FR 115. In another 0.5 mile, park at the intersection of FR 115 and FR 136. A high-clearance vehicle is recommended. On a bike, follow FR 730 to FR779 to FR 115. Return on FR 115 with a short side trip on FR 2030 to Laws Spring.

Trail: 7.7-mile loop.

Elevation: Rolling terrain at about 7,100 feet.

Degree of difficulty: Moderate.

Surface: Dirt and gravel road.

For more information: Williams/Forest Service Visitor Center, 200 W. Railroad Ave., Williams, AZ 86046. Phone (520) 635-4061 or (800) 863-0546. Web site www.fs.fed.us/r3/kai.

KENDRICK MOUNTAIN WILDERNESS

[Fig. 28(16)] The Kendrick Mountain Wilderness straddles the Coconino and Kaibab national forests. The mountain, which rises to 10,418 feet, is one of the larger volcanoes of the San Francisco Peaks Volcanic Field. The slopes are cloaked in ponderosa pine, fir, spruce, oak, and aspen. The upper steep slopes are covered with old-growth forest that shelters Mexican spotted owls, northern goshawks (*Accipiter gentilis*), blue grouse (*Dendragapus obscurus*), and black bear. Meadows on the north and west slopes attract mule deer and elk.

There are three established trails that climb to the summit of Kendrick allowing for a variety of loop hikes.

Directions: Drive about 14 miles north of Flagstaff on US 180 to milepost 230. Turn left onto the unpaved FR 245 and go 3 miles to FR 171. Turn right. The wilderness is about 3 miles down the road.

PRONGHORN
(*Antilocapra americana*)

BLACK
BEAR
(Ursus
americanus)

Activities: Hiking, camping, nature study, and hunting.

Facilities: None.

Dates: Open year-round, but Forest Service roads may be impassable when wet.

Fees: None.

Closest town: Flagstaff, 21 miles.

For more information: Williams Ranger District, 501 W. Bill Williams Ave., Williams, AZ 86046. Phone (520) 635-2676. Peaks Ranger District, 5075 N. Hwy. 89, Flagstaff, AZ 86004. Phone (520) 526-0866.

KENDRICK TRAIL

[Fig. 28(10)] The first half of this trail is an old logging road with a fairly gentle grade. Each switchback takes hikers higher and higher and into less disturbed forest. Eventually the road ends and the trail becomes just a footpath.

Nearing the summit, the trail crosses a relatively open, flat area and passes the Old Lookout Cabin built in 1911-12. Another 0.3-mile climb delivers hikers at the modern fire lookout on the top of Kendrick.

Directions: Drive about 14 miles north of Flagstaff on US 180 to milepost 230. Turn left onto the unpaved Forest Road 245 and go 3 miles to FR 171. Turn right and travel 3 miles to reach the turnoff for the trailhead.

Trail: 4.6 miles one-way.

Degree of difficulty: Moderate.

Elevation: 7,980 to 10,418 feet.

Surface and blaze: Packed dirt and rock.

PUMPKIN TRAIL

[Fig. 28(11)] The Pumpkin Trail climbs the west ridge of Kendrick. At mile 1.6, it intersects with the Connector Trail, which goes 2 miles to meet the Bull Basin Trail.

Directions: Instead of turning off at the Kendrick Trail, stay on FR 171 another 4 miles to the turnoff for the Pumpkin trailhead.

Trail: 5.5 miles one-way.

Degree of difficulty: Moderate.

Elevation: 7,300 to 10,418 feet.

Surface and blaze: Packed dirt and rock.

BULL BASIN TRAIL

[Fig. 28(12)] Going up the Pumpkin Trail, down the Bull Basin, and across on the Connector makes a pleasant 11-mile loop hike. The lucky hiker may see elk, black bear, mule deer or blue grouse (*Dendragapus obscurus*) along this heavily wooded trail.

Directions: Stay on FR 171 instead of turning off to the Pumpkin trailhead. In another 3 miles, turn right onto FR 144. Go 1.5 miles and turn right onto FR 90. Go 4.7 miles and then turn right onto FR 90A. In about 0.5 mile turn right again to reach the trailhead.

Trail: 4.5 miles one-way.

Degree of difficulty: Moderate.

Elevation: 8,100 to 10,418 feet.

Surface and blaze: Packed dirt and rock.

BILL WILLIAMS SKI AREA

[Fig. 28(9)] This small downhill ski area, on the slopes of Bill Williams Mountain, can accommodate about 250 skiers. The ski area consists of 35 acres geared to beginner and intermediate skiers. There is a Poma lift with 600 feet of rise and a towrope. However, adequate snow is sometimes a problem. Be sure to call ahead to see if the area is open.

Directions: Drive 3 miles south of Williams on County Road 73. Turn right at FR 106 and go another 2 miles.

Activities: Downhill skiing and snow boarding.

Facilities: Lodge, ski and board rentals, and instruction.

Dates: Open Thursday through Sunday during winter season.

Fees: There is a fee for the ski lifts.

Closest town: Williams.

For more information: Williams Ski Area, PO Box 953, Williams, AZ 86046. Phone (520) 635-9330. Web site www.thegrandcanyon.com.

KAIBAB NATIONAL FOREST CAMPGROUNDS

Dispersed camping is allowed through most of the Kaibab except for heavily used areas. There are four developed campgrounds. See Appendix G for a table of information on individual campgrounds.

White Mountains

The White Mountains are the highest overall region in Arizona, averaging 8,000 feet in elevation.

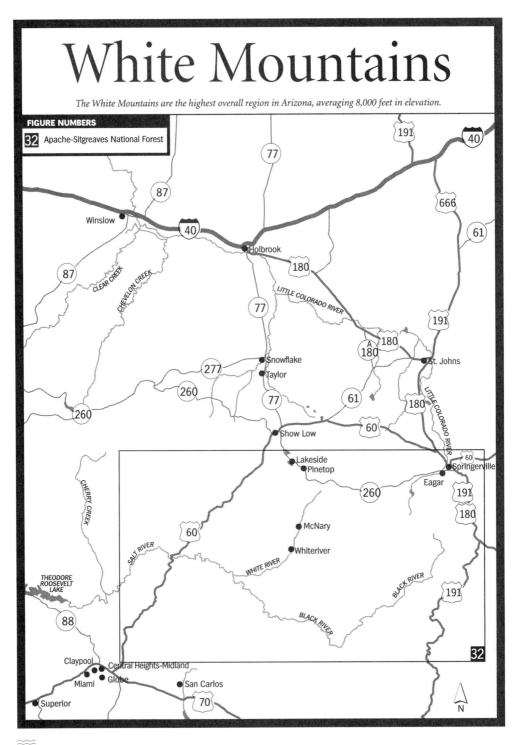

FIGURE NUMBERS

32 Apache-Sitgreaves National Forest

White Mountains

I n east-central Arizona are the White Mountains, which are another extensive volcanic field perched on top of the Mogollon Rim. The general elevation is quite high, about 8,000 feet on average. The numerous volcanic mountains and mesas rise another couple thousand feet to produce the highest overall region in Arizona.

The Apache-Sitgreaves National Forests cover 2 million acres in the White Mountains and along the Mogollon Rim. The forests are administered as one unit and include more than 800 miles of trail and 400 species of wildlife. With more than 450 miles of rivers and streams and 50 cold-water lakes, Apache-Sitgreaves is one of the top national forests in the nation for fishing. In the winter, visitors come to the forest to ice fish and cross-country ski.

In the White Mountains, there are many lovely forest drives. Two of the best are AZ 260, between Springerville and Pinetop-Lakeside, and the Coronado Trail (*see* page 180).

[*Above:* The Black River winds through the lush landscape of the Apache-Sitgreaves National Forest]

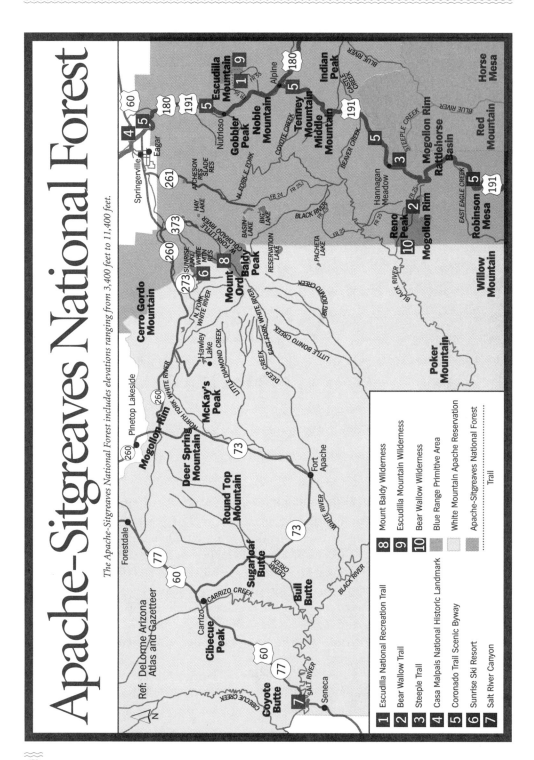

The Apache-Sitgreaves National Forest includes elevations ranging from 3,400 feet to 11,400 feet.

Ref: DeLorme Arizona Atlas and Gazetteer

1 Escudilla National Recreation Trail
2 Bear Wallow Trail
3 Steeple Trail
4 Casa Malpais National Historic Landmark
5 Coronado Trail Scenic Byway
6 Sunrise Ski Resort
7 Salt River Canyon
8 Mount Baldy Wilderness
9 Escudilla Mountain Wilderness
10 Bear Wallow Wilderness
Blue Range Primitive Area
White Mountain Apache Reservation
Apache-Sitgreaves National Forest
Trail

Apache-Sitgreaves National Forests

[Fig. 32] The Apache-Sitgreaves National Forests are administered from the supervisor's office in Springerville as one national forest. The forests encompass 2 million acres of magnificent mountain country along the Mogollon Rim and the White Mountains of east-central Arizona. Elevations range from below 3,400 feet near Clifton to more than 11,400 feet on Mt. Baldy, resulting in a diverse climate and a variety of vegetation types—everything from desert scrub to spruce-fir forest.

While tranquil today, the Apache-Sitgreaves country has had a stormy past. Evidence of prehistoric people is found in ruins and petroglyphs. Potsherds and stone arrowheads are common (and protected) throughout the area. The Sitgreaves Forest is named after Capt. Lorenzo Sitgreaves, a government topographical engineer who conducted the first scientific expedition across northern Arizona in the early 1850s. The Apache Forest commemorates the Indian tribes still residing on the neighboring reservations.

In the late nineteenth century, the U.S. Army established a series of forts in New Mexico and Arizona. To supply these forts and settlements, a military road was built linking Fort Apache, Fort Verde, and Fort Whipple near Prescott. Each mile of the 200-mile road was marked by counting the revolutions of a wagon wheel and then carving the mileage into a tree trunk or rock. A few of these mileage posts are still visible today. A telegraph line was strung along the route, too. Part of this old road, the General Crook Trail, runs almost the length of the Sitgreaves National Forest and the adjoining Coconino National Forest. In many places, the trail follows the brink of the Mogollon Rim. The scenic Rim Road, FR 300, follows much of the old trail, and other portions are suitable for hiking or horseback riding. Today the trail is marked with cairns and white and yellow chevrons placed on trees.

The Apache-Sitgreaves forests provide important habitat for more than 400 species of wildlife. There are more than 450 miles of rivers and streams, and more than 50 cold-water lakes cover nearly 2,000 surface acres. The forest is considered to be one of the top national forests in the nation for fishing. The types of fish include native Apache trout (*Oncorhynchus apache*); rainbow, brown, and brook trout; cutthroat trout (*Oncorhynchus clarki*); bass; catfish; walleye, northern pike; and Arctic grayling (*Thymallus arcticus*). Ice fishing is also popular, but anglers need to be well equipped for the potentially harsh winter conditions. Many of the forest's lakes offer campgrounds operated by the Forest Service or private concessionaires. For a recorded message of current fishing conditions, call the fishing hotline at (602) 789-3701. There is also a regional office of the Arizona Game and Fish Department in Pinetop. Phone (520) 367-4281.

More than 800 miles of trail allow exploration of the forest by foot or horseback. Some trails outside of designed wilderness areas and many of the Forest Service roads are suitable for mountain biking. The district offices can offer suggestions. There are

MEXICAN WOLF
(*Canis lupus baileyi*)

cross-country ski trails located near Greer, Alpine, and Forest Lakes, but this activity is by no means confined to these three areas. For skiing ideas, read Dugald Bremner's *Ski Touring Arizona*.

Besides the various ranger stations, the Mogollon Rim Visitor Center, located on AZ 260 at the edge of the rim, also offers maps, information, restrooms, and 100-mile vistas. There is also a Forest Service Visitor Center at Big Lake.

The Mogollon Rim country offers outstanding opportunities for wildlife viewing. Visit the Allen Severson Wildlife Area or the Jacques Marsh Wildlife Area, both near Show Low.

For more information: Supervisor's Office, Apache-Sitgreaves National Forest, PO Box 640, Springerville, AZ 85938. Phone (520) 333-4301. Web site www.fs.fed.us/r3/asnf.

MOUNT BALDY WILDERNESS

[Fig. 32(8)] In the early 1870s, Capt. George Wheeler climbed Mount Baldy and commented that the view was "the most magnificent and effective of any among the large number that have come under my observation. Outstretched before us lay the tributaries of seven principal streams…four main mountain peaks…valley lands far surpassing any I have before seen."

Mount Baldy is a stratovolcano and was carved extensively during the Pleistocene Epoch. Today it is mantled with dense spruce-fir forest. Elk are very common and black bear, mule deer, golden-mantled ground squirrel (*Spermophilus lateralis*), blue grouse, and wild turkey may be seen. Sign of mountain lion, bobcat, and coyotes may be in evidence. Beaver dams span the streams. Look for wild orchids (*Calypso bulbosa* and *Spiranthes romanzoffiana*) along the trail as well as Rocky Mountain iris (*Iris missouriensis*), lupine (*Lupinus* sp.), penstemon (*Penstemon* sp.), cinquefoil (*Potentilla* sp.), fleabane (*Erigeron* sp.), yellow columbine (*Aquilegia chrysantha*), and Indian paintbrush (*Castilleja* sp.).

Two trails, the West Fork and the East Fork, each about 6.5 miles long, lead into the wilderness and join near the top. The streams paralleling the trails join northeast of the wilderness area to become the Little Colorado River. A 0.5-mile spur trail leads to Baldy Peak on the White Mountain Apache Indian Reservation; however, the peak is considered sacred and is closed to non-Apaches. Violators are subject to arrest by tribal law enforcement officers, so it is advised to end your hike at the reservation boundary, which is usually marked with a sign.

Ironically, the highest point along the summit ridge is not the named 11,403-foot Baldy Peak. Careful examination of the topographic map will show that a short distance to the north, on Forest Service land, is a point enclosed by the 11,400-foot contour, but the U.S. Geologic Survey neglected to mark the highest elevation within that oval. The elevation is estimated to be 11,420 feet. So hikers can legally climb to the true summit of Mount Baldy.

Directions: From Springerville, take AZ 260 about 18 miles west to AZ 273. Drive about 11 miles to FR 113J. The signed West Fork trailhead is located at the end of FR 113J, about 0.5 mile from AZ 273 (FR 113). To reach the East Fork Trail, stay on AZ 273 (FR 113) another 4 miles. The signed trail begins at the Phelps Cabin site, 0.2 mile in from AZ 273 (FR 113).

Activities: Hiking, camping, horseback riding, nature study, trout fishing, and hunting.

Mexican Wolves

The Mexican wolf (*Canis lupus baileyi*) is the rarest, southernmost, and most genetically distinct subspecies of the North American gray wolf. The adults are about the size of a German shepherd and have a distinctive, richly colored coat of buff, gray, rust and black. Confirmed sightings of Mexican wolves in the United States had ceased by 1970. Yet another six years passed before the Mexican wolf was listed as an endangered species. Between 1977 and 1980, Mexican wolves were obtained from Mexico to establish a captive breeding programs. There are now over 40 facilities raising wolves.

In March 1998, 11 Mexican wolves from several different breeding facilities were released into the Apache-Sitgreaves National Forest. Two more were released later in the year and an additional 21 were released in 1999. They are all radio collared to help researchers keep track of them. The plan is to release about 15 pairs or family groups during a five-year period into the Blue Range Primitive Area and/or adjacent Gila Wilderness in New Mexico. Scientists hope that by 2008, the population will number at least 100 and be self-sustaining.

Despite many folktales and campfire horror stories, wolves are naturally fearful of humans and present no significant threat to human safety. However, like other predators, wolves do sometimes kill livestock. The reintroduction program calls for wolves to be removed or relocated when such conflicts occur. The private conservation group Defenders of Wildlife has established a fund to compensate ranchers at market value for documented losses of livestock to wolves.

For updates on this program, contact the Mexican Wolf Recovery Leader at the Web site http://ifw2es.fws.gov/MexicanWolf.

Facilities: None.

Dates: Usually can be hiked from June to Oct. Heavy winter snows close the area except to well-prepared cross-country skiers and snowshoers.

Fees: None.

Closest town: Springerville, about 30 miles northeast.

For more information: Springerville Ranger District, PO Box 760, Springerville, AZ 85938. Phone (520) 333-4372.

ESCUDILLA WILDERNESS

[Fig. 32(9)] Escudilla Wilderness, designated in 1984 and containing 5,200 acres, encompasses a large, hulking mountain with a challenging hike to the top. Its 10,912-foot elevation provides marvelous vistas across the White Mountains to the Painted Desert to the north and the Basin and Range country to the south. Several pristine, high elevation meadows comprise relatively rare plant associations.

Aldo Leopold, one of the founders of the Wilderness Society, wrote in *A Sand County Almanac*, "Escudilla still hangs on the horizon, but when you see it you no longer think of bear. It's only a mountain now." Leopold was referring to the fact that one of the last grizzlies (*Ursus arctos*) in Arizona was killed here in the early 1900s. This notorious bear was known locally as Big Foot. After many unsuccessful attempts to hunt the bear, a government hunter set up a trap gun. According to notes in the National Museum, "a .303 Savage was set the first night but Big Foot went around it, sprung it, and chewed up the stock; the second night both the Winchester and Savage were set and the Winchester got him. There was no way in which to weigh him but the carcass was very fat and his weight was estimated at 1000 lbs."

Black bear still roam the area, plus deer, wild turkey, and many other species.

Directions: From Alpine, drive about 6 miles north on US 191. Between mileposts 420 and 421, turn right (east) onto FR 56 and go 4.6 miles to Terry Flat Loop. Take the left fork 0.4 mile to the signed trailhead.

Activities: Hiking, horseback riding, nature study, and hunting.

Facilities: None.

Dates: Heavy winter snows close the area except to well-prepared cross-country skiers and snowshoers.

Fees: None.

Closest town: Alpine, about 11 miles south.

For more information: Alpine Ranger District, PO Box 469, Alpine, AZ 85920. Phone (520) 339-4384.

ESCUDILLA NATIONAL RECREATION TRAIL

[Fig. 32(1)] The 3.3-mile, well-graded Escudilla National Recreation Trail takes the visitor from Terry Flat to the highest fire lookout in Arizona on top of Escudilla Mountain, where on very clear days, you can see the San Francisco Peaks near Flagstaff and the Pinaleno Mountains near Safford.

Trail: 3.3 miles one-way.
Degree of difficulty: Moderate.
Elevation: 9,600 to 10,876 feet at lookout.
Surface: Forest floor, sometimes rocky.

BEAR WALLOW WILDERNESS

[Fig. 32(10)] The 11,080-acre Bear Wallow Wilderness, established in 1984, boasts some of the largest acreage of virgin ponderosa pine forest in the Southwest. About 21 miles of trail penetrate the wilderness, allowing hikers, horseback riders, hunters, and anglers to access the area. The western boundary abuts the San Carlos Apache Reservation. A permit from the Apaches is required to enter their land.

Beautiful Bear Wallow Creek is perennial and contains threatened Apache trout (*Oncorhynchus apache*) (*see* Native Trout sidebar). Stream barriers have been constructed at the national forest and reservation boundary to help prevent upstream migration of non-native fish such as rainbow trout. Wildlife is abundant—not only black bear but also elk, mule deer, bobcat, coyote, various species of squirrel, gray fox, turkey, Mexican spotted owl, and blue grouse. A majestic view from atop the Mogollon Rim awaits the hiker who follows the Rose Spring Trail along the southern boundary of the wilderness.

Directions: The easiest access is from US 191 about 6 miles south of Hannagan Meadow. Turn right (west) onto FR 25 and drive 3.3 miles to the signed trailhead for the Bear Wallow Trail.

Activities: Hiking, camping, nature study, fishing, and hunting.
Facilities: None.
Dates: Heavy winter snows close the area except to well-prepared cross-country skiers and snowshoers.
Fees: None.
Closest town: Alpine, about 30 miles north.
For more information: Alpine Ranger District, PO Box 469, Alpine, AZ 85920. Phone (520) 339-4384.

BEAR WALLOW TRAIL

[Fig. 32(2)] This easy trail gives quick access to the creek.
Trail: About 1.5 miles to Bear Wallow Creek and another 6.1 miles to the reservation boundary.
Degree of difficulty: Moderate.
Elevation: 8,700 to 6,700 at reservation boundary.
Surface: Forest floor, rocky in places.

BLUE RANGE PRIMITIVE AREA

[Fig. 32] These 200,000-acres were designated a primitive area in 1933. Another 22,500 acres in adjacent New Mexico became the Blue Range Wilderness in 1980. A

Native Trout

Historically, Arizona streams contained two native species of trout. The Apache trout (*Oncorhynchus apache*), handsome fish of deep, golden-yellow color with bold, dark spots, are endemic to the White Mountains and once occupied all suitable habitats in the headwaters of the Black, White, and Little Colorado rivers. Gila trout (*Oncorhynchus gilae*) were native to the headwaters of the Agua Fria, Verde, and San Francisco rivers in Arizona and the Gila River in New Mexico. Gila trout have a golden-yellow belly with silvery-yellow and blue reflections along their upper sides and back. Fine dark spots profusely cover their backs and tail. (Some ichthyologists believe the Gila trout in Arizona may not have been the same species as that found in New Mexico.) By the mid-twentieth century, the introduction of non-native fish, dam and diversion projects, and water pollution reduced the Apache trout to only a few limited areas, and the Gila trout was completely extirpated in Arizona.

The Arizona Game and Fish Department began a recovery and reintroduction program in the late 1960s. Today 26 Apache trout populations occupy approximately 150 miles of streams in historic habitat on the White Mountain Apache Reservation and the Apache-Sitgreaves National Forest. About 15 lakes in northeastern Arizona are also stocked and managed for sport fishing. Additionally, there is an introduced population in North Canyon on the Kaibab National Forest, which is outside of the trout's historic range (*see* page 36).

In 1999, 120 Gila trout were reintroduced into Dude Creek, a tributary of the East Verde River northeast of Payson, Arizona. Once the population is considered established, the process to remove the trout from endangered species status will begin; and possibly, anglers will be able to reel one of these beauties in.

Many of the streams containing Apache trout are open to fishing but are managed under a variety of regulations. Check with local authorities for the latest rules. Gila trout cannot be legally fished in Arizona or New Mexico because they are still considered endangered.

primitive area is simply a local Forest Service administrative decision to manage a particular part of the national forest as wilderness—a decision that can be easily changed later. On the other hand, a wilderness area is established by Congress and has more permanence. Ironically, although the Blue Range Primitive Area was one of the first areas in the nation to be managed as wilderness, it has not yet achieved full legal status as a wilderness area.

The Blue Range is rugged and beautiful with high, timbered ridges and deep, shadowy canyons. The Mogollon Rim, made famous as the "Tonto Rim" in Zane Grey's Westerns, crosses the area from west to east. The rim, unique from both geological and ecological standpoints, is further enhanced by the spectacular Blue River Canyon and river. There are spruce and fir in the high country and ponderosa, pinyon, and juniper in the lower canyons, as well as a diverse mix of conifers and deciduous trees along the Blue River, which is the abode of the threatened loach minnow (*Tiaroga cobitis*) and a few trout.

Mule and white-tailed deer, elk, bighorn sheep (*Ovis canadensis*), black bear, wild turkey, javelina, and other game find food and shelter in the primitive area. Mexican wolves (*Canis lupus baileyi*) have recently been reintroduced after being eliminated back in the early 1900s (*see* Mexican Wolves sidebar). Their haunting howl epitomizes wilderness.

One tiny but special mammal in this region is the New Mexico jumping mouse (*Zapus hudsonius*). Its distinctive coloration—yellow sides, a dark, broad band down the middle of the back, and white belly—makes it impossible to confuse with any other small mammal in the Southwest. Its large hind feet and legs are built for jumping, which is a curious method of locomotion for an animal that lives in meadows of dense grass and herbs.

Birders also enjoy the primitive area. Besides many typical forest and riparian birds, there are a number of rare species such as the southern bald eagle, Mexican spotted owl, peregrine falcon, aplomado falcon (*Falco femoralis*), Arizona (Strickland's) woodpecker (*Picoides stricklandii*), black-eared bushtit (*Psaltriparus* sp.), and olive warbler (*Peucedramus taeniatus*).

Descendants of many of the original pioneer settlers still reside along the Blue and have retained a remarkably traditional ranching lifestyle. A one-room schoolhouse is still used to educate the children of Blue River. The school is located near the confluence of Johnson Canyon and the Blue River about 1 mile north of the Blue Crossing Campground (*see* campground table below). The teacher welcomes visitors, but the school is closed on Fridays. Phone (520) 339-4346. The rich cultural history of the area has been recorded in *Down the Blue*, compiled by the Blue River Cowbelles.

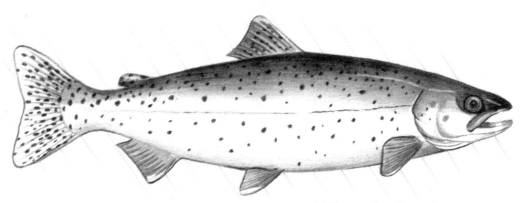

APACHE TROUT
(Oncorhynchus apache)

Orchids

Orchids are a family of mainly tropical plants not usually associated with the dry, hot Southwest. However, nearly two-dozen different orchid species live in Arizona's cool, moist forests. One of the most beautiful is the delicate calypso or fairy slipper (*Calypso bulbosa*) with its rose-pink flowers bearded with yellow hairs. Arizona also has three species of coral root (*Corallorhiza* sp.), orchids that lack chlorophyll. Since they cannot photosynthesize food for themselves, they draw nourishment from a fungus that decomposes dead plant material.

Long before the pioneers, people of the Mogollon culture lived throughout the area. They built pit house villages, small multiple room blocks, small to moderately sized masonry pueblos, cliff dwellings, and a few large multi-storied pueblos with kivas. Petroglyphs and pictographs are visible at several locations.

Access to more than 300 miles of trail is fairly good, but prospective visitors should remember that this is big, rough, generally dry, remote country. Go properly prepared. Study the Forest Service's *Blue Range Wilderness and Primitive Area Map*, and get the latest trail information from either the Alpine or Clifton Ranger Offices.

Directions: There are many trailheads along US 191 south of Alpine. Another approach is the dirt road FR 281 that goes south from US 180 about 4 miles east of Alpine. After 30 rough miles following the Blue River, FR 281 dead-ends at the Smith Place, which consists of a cabin, barn, and corral. The last several miles of road include river crossings that may be impassable during high water. Again, there are many trailheads along this road.

Activities: Hiking, camping, horseback riding, nature study, fishing, and hunting.

Facilities: None.

Dates: Higher areas closed by heavy winter snows, but can make for excellent snowshoeing and cross-country skiing.

Fees: None.

Closest town: Alpine, about 14 miles north of the northwest boundary.

For more information: Alpine Ranger District, PO Box 469, Alpine, AZ 85920. Phone (520) 339-4384. Clifton Ranger District, PO Box 698, Clifton, AZ 85533. Phone (520) 687-1303.

STEEPLE TRAIL

[Fig. 32(3)] This long trail takes visitors from the high country down to the Blue River for a great introduction to what the Blue Range has to offer.

Directions: The trailhead is located at Hannagan Meadow. Take FR 29A east a short distance to the signed trailhead.

Trail: 13.2 miles one-way.

Degree of difficulty: Strenuous.

Elevation: 9,200 to 5,280 feet.

Surface: Forest floor, occasionally rocky and marshy.

🗆 APACHE-SITGREAVES NATIONAL FORESTS CAMPGROUNDS

Camping is permitted in nearly all areas of the forest. However, at several heavily used locations (e.g., Lee Valley Reservoir, Greer Lakes, Woods Canyon Lake, Willow Springs Lake, and Big Lake), camping is restricted to developed campgrounds. The operation and maintenance of some campgrounds is under contract to concessionaires. Fees are charged in most developed areas to assist in the maintenance of facilities. Campers may stay a maximum of 14 days at any one location. A reservation is advised to ensure a campsite during the busy summer months. Sites can be reserved by calling (800) 280-2267 and paying by credit card, money order, or personal check. See Appendix G for a table of information on individual campgrounds.

CALYPSO OR
FAIRY SLIPPER
(Calypso bulbosa)

🗆 CASA MALPAIS NATIONAL HISTORIC LANDMARK

[Fig. 32(4)] Situated on terraces above the Little Colorado River, the thirteenth century Casa Malpais was home to the Mogollon people for almost 200 years. It is one of the largest and most complex Mogollon communities. The main pueblo contains more than 120 ground-level rooms. In places there was a second story. Besides the large masonry pueblo, there is a great kiva, an enclosing wall, three masonry stairways, a prehistoric trail, numerous isolated rooms, sacred chambers, rock art, and formal trash middens. Many unique artifacts have been uncovered here and are on display in the Casa Malpais Museum.

But what really sets Casa Malpais apart from other ancient Southwestern ruins is the intricate series of passages and rooms deep inside natural fissures in the underlying terraces of basalt lava. These underground chambers were used as burial sites and are the only known catacombs north of Mexico.

The only way to see the ruins is with a guide. The tours begin at the Casa Malpais Museum in Springerville.

Directions: Meet at the Casa Malpais Museum in Springerville.

Activities: Guided 1.5-hour tour of the ruins.

Facilities: Museum and bookstore in Springerville.

Dates: Open year-round.

Fees: There is a tour fee.

Closest town: Springerville.

For more information: Casa Malpais Museum, PO Box 807, 318 E. Main St., Springerville, AZ 85938. Phone (520) 333-5375.

Coronado Trail Scenic Byway

[Fig. 32(5)] The 130-mile section of US 191 between Springerville and Clifton is locally known as the Coronado Trail because it goes through part of Arizona that was traversed by the Spanish conquistador Francisco Vásquez de Coronado (1510-1554) and his expedition party in 1540. Coronado was seeking the fabled Seven Cities of Cibola but instead discovered the stone and mud pueblos of Zuni in New Mexico.

Near Springerville, the Wenima Riparian Corridor, the Becker Lake Wildlife, and Sipe White Mountain Wildlife Area all attract a variety of birds and wildlife. From Springerville south to Alpine, the terrain changes from rolling grasslands into spruce-fir forest at elevations of more than 8,000 feet. Surrounding mountains extend up to 11,000 feet.

The tiny community of Alpine was founded by Mormon pioneers in 1879. Learn more about the fascinating history of this area by visiting the web site www.geocities.com/Heartland/Orchard/6586.

South of Alpine, the road becomes narrow with sharp curves. About 26 miles beyond Alpine, you come to Hannagan Meadow. At the edge of the meadow is a lodge built in 1926 to accommodate travelers who needed a break in what was then a two-day drive to Clifton. Authentic log cabins, each with it own character and furnished with antiques, are available for rent. This is a good year-round base for outdoor activities such as hiking, fishing, hunting, and cross-country skiing. Hannagan Meadow Lodge, HC 61 PO Box 335, Alpine, AZ 85920. Phone (520) 339-4370 or (800) 547-1416.

At the brink of the Mogollon Rim, about 33 miles south of Alpine, is Blue Vista. Stop here for an amazing view of wave after wave of mountains to the south. Just beyond the overlook, the road drops steeply, then continues winding round and round, following ridges and hillsides. Locals say that when you're absolutely sure that you have seen your last switchback, you're only half way to Clifton. The spruce-fir forest gives way to pinyon-juniper woodland and finally desert scrub is encountered at an elevation of about 3,500 feet.

Just before reaching Clifton, the road passes by the huge open pit copper mine at "new" Morenci; the original town of Morenci was quarried away in the 1960s as the mine expanded. This mine is one of North America's leading copper producers. In Clifton is the historic Chase Creek District, where territorial-style architecture speaks of past glories. Locals claim that the Apache patriot and warrior Geronimo was born here.

The drive takes about four to five hours and sections may be closed during or following winter snowstorms. An interpretive audiotape is available from either the Alpine or Clifton District Offices.

For more information: Alpine Ranger District, PO Box 469, Alpine, AZ 85920. Phone (520) 339-4384. Clifton Ranger District, PO Box 698, Clifton, AZ 85533.

Phone (520) 687-1303. Additional general area information may be obtained from the Greenlee County Chamber of Commerce, housed in the old train station in Clifton, PO Box 1237, Clifton, AZ 85533. Phone (520) 865-3313.

White Mountain Apache Reservation

[Fig. 32] The 1.6 million-acre White Mountain Apache Reservation (usually called the Fort Apache Indian Reservation by the federal government) takes in a portion of the Mogollon Rim and most of the headwaters feeding into the Salt River. The reservation offers some of Arizona's best outdoor recreation opportunities. There are many developed campsites, lakes, streams, hiking trails, and a modern ski area. Hunting for elk, deer, pronghorn, black bear, mountain lion, javelina, rabbit, turkey, quail, duck and goose is popular.

Anglers try their luck catching rainbow and native Apache trout in a number of mountain streams or even rent a lake for an exclusive fishing experience. The state record for brown trout was a 22.9-pounder caught at Reservation Lake in 1999. No state license is required, but a tribal permit is needed.

Anyone interested in fish, not just anglers, may wish to visit the Alchesay National Fish Hatchery on the picturesque North Fork of the White River. It is accessible from AZ 73 between the towns of Indian Pine and Whiteriver. Another hatchery is on Williams Creek and found by driving 4 miles south of Hon-Dah on AZ 73 then turning left (east) between mileposts 353 and 354 and following signs for 9 miles. Each year, approximately 350,000 rainbow trout fingerlings are brought to Alchesay from the Williams Creek National Fish Hatchery. When the fish are 8 inches long, they are taken to stock waters on Apache lands and other federally managed waters in Arizona.

For more information about visiting either hatchery: Alchesay National Fish Hatchery, PO Box 398, Whiteriver, AZ 85941.

For a different kind of "wild life" experience, the White Mountain Apaches operate the Hon-Dah Resort and Casino located about 3 miles south of Pinetop at the intersection of AZ 260 and AZ 73.

For more information: Hon-Dah Resort and Casino, 777 Hwy 260, Hon-Dah, AZ 85935. Phone (520) 369-0299 or (800) WAY-UP-HI. Web site www.hon-dah.com. There are other Indian-owned and -operated casinos around the state, too. The Arizona Office of Tourism [2702 N. Third St., Suite 4015, Phoenix, AZ 85004; phone (888) 520-3434. Web site www.arizonaguide.com.] can supply further details.

In 1870, a U.S. Army post was established near what is today the town of Whiteriver, and soon after, the post and surrounding area were designated as a reservation. The old fort complex is undergoing renovation and conversion to a historic park that will serve as the home for the White Mountain Apache Tribe's rapidly growing Heritage

Program. In addition to the historic buildings of the old fort, the complex includes the Apache Culture Center and Museum. The site features changing exhibits and video presentations on White Mountain Apache culture, arts, and crafts. There is also a bookstore and gift shop. Weekend demonstrations of local arts and crafts are offered in the fall and spring. The Fort Apache complex also includes a replica of a 1800s Apache village located on the riverbank below the cliffs, about a ten-minute walk. Information can be obtained by calling the center at (520) 338-4625.

For more information: White Mountain Apache Tribe, Office of Tourism, PO Box 710, Fort Apache, AZ 85926. Phone (520) 338-1230. For hunting, fishing, and other outdoor recreation permits, contact the White Mountain Apache Game and Fish Department, PO Box 220, Whiteriver, AZ 85941. Phone (520) 338-4385 or 4386. Web site www.wmat.nsn.us. or www.wmatoutdoors.com.

SUNRISE SKI RESORT

[Fig. 32(6)] The Sunrise Ski Resort is owned and operated by the White Mountain Apache Tribe. Sixty-five runs descend from three adjacent mountain peaks; the highest is 11,300-foot Apache Peak, providing winter fun for skiers of all abilities. The eight chairlifts are capable of transporting 16,000 skiers per hour. The total vertical drop is 1,800 feet. The resort has snowmaking equipment to augment the usually generous snowfall, so the ski season typically spans November to mid-April. The nearby 100-room Sunrise Hotel on Sunrise Lake is available for winter and summer lodging.

Directions: Take AZ 260 about 18 miles west of Springerville then turn left (south) onto AZ 273. The ski area and hotel are about 3.5 miles.

Activities: Downhill and cross-country skiing, snowboarding, tubing, sleigh rides, snowmobile tours, and ice fishing.

Facilities: Hotel, restaurant, general store, equipment rentals, and lessons.

Dates: Late November to mid-April.

Fees: There are fees for the chairlifts and other activities.

Closest town: Springerville, about 22 miles east.

For more information: Sunrise Park Resort, PO Box 217, McNary, AZ 85930. Phone (520) 735-7669 or 7600 or (800) 55-HOTEL. Web site www.sunriseskipark.com.

SALT RIVER CANYON

[Fig. 32(7)] One of the most exciting and scenic river trips in Arizona is running the 52 miles of the Salt River between highway US 60 and AZ 288. Where US 60 bridges the river, the Salt River Canyon is 2,000 feet deep. Some enthusiasts claim the ride is Arizona's most technically challenging whitewater run, exceeding even the Colorado River through the Grand Canyon. The 27 rapids range in difficulty from Class II to the sometimes unrunnable Quartzite Falls. At most flows, the river is a solid Class III-IV run and not recommended for novices. Commercial outfitters offer river trips. The big-water season lasts from January to May, but some people run the river in small inflatable boats at low water and enjoy nearly year-round boating.

While most of the river's course is within the Salt River Canyon Wilderness managed by the Tonto National Forest (*see* page 204), the launch point is on the White Mountain Apache side of the river, and the first 20 river miles cross reservation land. Entering this area requires a recreation permit from the tribe.

Additionally, the Forest Service also requires a river permit between March 1 and May 15. The application period for these limited permits is December 1 through January 31 each year. This Forest Service permit covers the portion of river from Gleason Flat to approximately 32 miles downstream at the take-out point immediately downstream of the AZ 288 bridge.

The Forest Service offers a *Salt River Recreation Opportunity Guide* that gives detailed information concerning "leaving no trace" practices, general information about the rapids, and a detailed river map. Also considered essential is a copy of Glenn Rink's *A Guide to Salt River Canyon Natural History and River Running*.

The river receives steady use by anglers, picnickers, campers, hikers, hunters in season, and sightseers.

Directions: Drive north from Globe on US 60 about 57 miles to where the highway crosses the Salt River. On the north side of the bridge, turn left and stop at the trading post for permits, information, and directions to the put-in.

Activities: White-water boating, fishing, camping, hiking, hunting, and nature study.

Facilities: Near the US 60 bridge is a store that sells permits.

Dates: Open year-round, although the most exciting boating is in the spring.

Fees: There is a fee for recreation and boating permits.

Closest town: Globe, about 57 miles south.

For more information: For the reservation permits, contact White Mountain Game and Fish Department, PO Box 220, Whiteriver, AZ 85941. Phone (520) 338-4385. For the Forest Service permit, contact the River Permit Coordinator, Globe Ranger District, Rte. 1, Box 33, Globe, AZ 85501. Phone (520) 402-6200. For commercial rafting trips, contact Far Flung Adventures, PO Box 2804, Globe, AZ 85502. Phone (800) 231-7238.

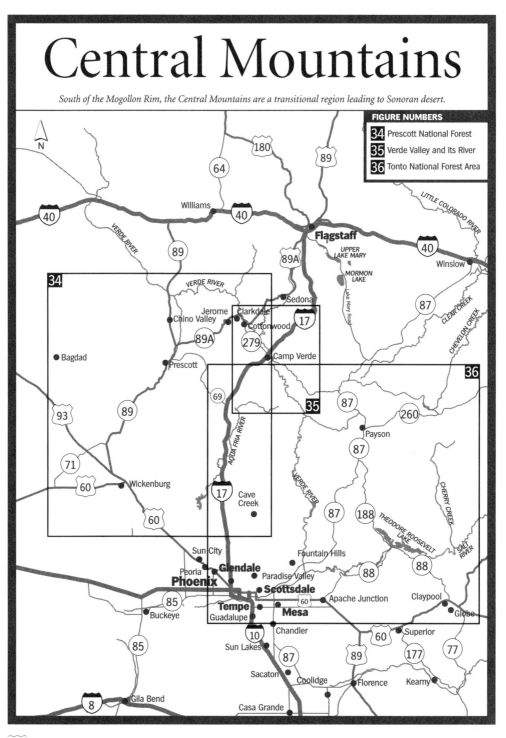

Central Mountains

South of the Mogollon Rim, the Central Mountains are a transitional region leading to Sonoran desert.

FIGURE NUMBERS
34 Prescott National Forest
35 Verde Valley and its River
36 Tonto National Forest Area

Central Mountains

ৎ

S outh of the Mogollon Rim is a broad transitional region of mountains and canyons leading to the low, hot Sonoran desert. Within this transitional area are mountains high enough to support ponderosa pine forest and some firs and spruce. Lower hills are generally covered with woodlands of pinyon pine, a variety of junipers, evergreen oaks, and Arizona cypress. These forests and woodlands are mostly contained in the Prescott and Tonto national forests and the southern part of the Apache-Sitgreaves National Forest.

Farther south, and at lower elevations still, chaparral and Sonoran desert begin to make an appearance. Perhaps incongruously, some of this treeless terrain is also under Forest Service management. However, much of the desert falls under the Bureau of Land Management's jurisdiction.

[*Above:* Montezuma Castle National Monument protects a very well-preserved cliff dwelling]

Prescott National Forest

This national forest contains lower hills covered with pinyon pines, junipers, evergreen oaks, and Arizona cypress.

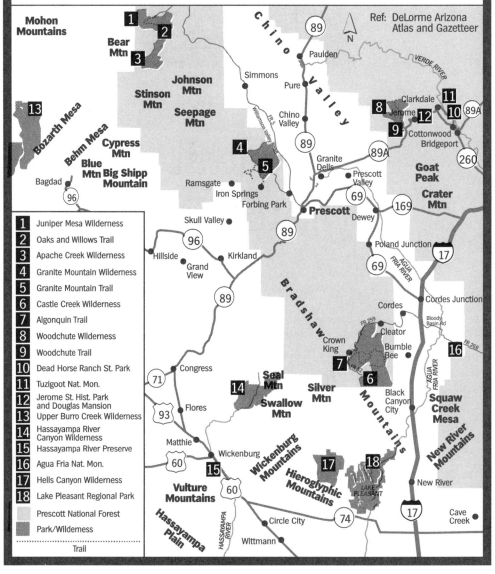

Ref: DeLorme Arizona Atlas and Gazetteer

1. Juniper Mesa Wilderness
2. Oaks and Willows Trail
3. Apache Creek Wilderness
4. Granite Mountain Wilderness
5. Granite Mountain Trail
6. Castle Creek Wilderness
7. Algonquin Trail
8. Woodchute Wilderness
9. Woodchute Trail
10. Dead Horse Ranch St. Park
11. Tuzigoot Nat. Mon.
12. Jerome St. Hist. Park and Douglas Mansion
13. Upper Burro Creek Wilderness
14. Hassayampa River Canyon Wilderness
15. Hassayampa River Preserve
16. Agua Fria Nat. Mon.
17. Hells Canyon Wilderness
18. Lake Pleasant Regional Park

Prescott National Forest
Park/Wilderness
Trail

Prescott National Forest

[Fig. 34] Pronghorn (*Antilocapra americana*) are common in the Prescott area, but increasing development is quickly destroying their preferred habitat. The Arizona Game and Fish Department has caught and moved some of the herds to other parts of Arizona. Conservationists oppose the controversial practice.

Fishing in the small lakes and ponds scattered across the Prescott National Forest is popular. Near the town of Prescott are Lynx, Watson, Willow, and Granite lakes. All have nearby developed campgrounds. For a recorded message about fishing conditions, call the fishing hotline at (602) 789-3701.

Mountain biking is a wonderful way to explore Prescott National Forest. Old mining and lumber roads penetrate almost every part of the forest and make superb bike routes.

For more information: Prescott National Forest, 344 South Cortez St., Prescott, AZ 86303-4398. Phone (520) 771-4700. Web site www.fs.fed.us/r3/prescott.

JUNIPER MESA WILDERNESS

[Fig. 34(1)] This seldom-visited wilderness area, located in the remote northwest corner of the Prescott National Forest, was established in 1984. A large mesa lies in the center of 7,554 acres of solitude. Elevations range from 5,600 feet on the southeast side near Juniper Spring to 7,000 feet on the west side near George Wood Canyon and Gobbler Knob. The primary vegetation on the steep south-facing slopes is pinyon and Utah juniper (*Juniperus osteosperma*) and on the north-facing slopes, ponderosa and alligator juniper (*Juniperus deppeana*). Various oaks, cliffrose (*Cowania mexicana*), mountain mahogany (*Cercocarpus* sp.), beargrass (*Nolina* sp.), prickly pear, and agave grow here, too.

A great variety of wildlife can be found, including Gambel's quail (*Callipepla gambelii*), mourning dove (*Zenaida macroura*), Cooper's hawk (*Accipiter cooperii*), curve-billed thrasher (*Toxostoma curvirostre*), greater roadrunner (*Geococcyx californianus*), western kingbird (*Tyrannus verticalis*), and great horned owl (*Bubo virginianus*). Black bear, elk, mule deer, bobcat, and Abert's squirrel (*Sciurus aberti*) are relatively common. There are no perennial streams, and the reliability of springs is questionable during long periods of dry weather.

PARRY'S AGAVE
(*Agave parryi*)

Riparian Birds

In the late 1960s and early '70s, biologists discovered just how important riparian habitats are to nesting birds. One study done along the Verde River revealed upwards of 847 pairs of nesting birds per 100 acres of habitat. By comparison, an Eastern deciduous forest may have 200 pairs. The biologists wondered how could the riparian densities be so high. In a typical forest situation, most of the breeding birds defend a fairly large feeding territory around their individual nest site. Thus, only a limited number of each species can occupy the forest.

It turned out that the riparian-dependent species were not setting up this kind of a territory. Instead, they were defending the nest itself but were flying into the adjacent desert to feed. The biologists learned that there were very few nesting birds in that adjacent desert, probably because there are only a few species, such as Gambel's quail and common poorwills, who nest on the ground or in the short desert shrubs.

Because the riparian-dependent birds did not have a feeding territory encircling their nest site, the nests could be built much closer together.

Carry plenty of water. There are about 17 miles of trail within the wilderness area, but the use of topographic maps is recommended.

Directions: From Prescott take County Road 5 north about 36 miles then turn left onto FR 125. The wilderness area is north of the road.

Activities: Hiking, camping, horseback riding, nature study, and hunting.

Facilities: None.

Dates: Open year-round, although wet weather may make forest roads impassable.

Fees: None.

Closest town: Prescott, about 40 miles.

For more information: Chino Valley Ranger District, PO Box 485, Chino Valley, AZ 86323-0485. Phone (520) 636-2302.

OAKS AND WILLOWS TRAIL

[Fig. 34(2)] This trail crosses the western end of the wilderness and ascends Juniper Mesa.

Directions: From CR 5 drive 8 miles west on FR 125 to the signed trailhead.

Trail: 6.6 miles one-way.

Degree of difficulty: Moderate.

Elevation: 6,000 to 7,000 feet.

Surface and blaze: Rocky; cairns.

APACHE CREEK WILDERNESS

[Fig. 34(3)] This wilderness lies immediately south of the Juniper Mesa Wilderness. Rolling hills of pinyon-juniper woodland interspersed with granite outcrops grace this small, remote, and relatively rugged terrain. Established in 1984, the 5,628-acre wilderness contains three springs and several important riparian areas including Apache Creek. Along the washes grow Arizona black walnut, cottonwoods, and box elder. Elevations range from 5,200 to 6,900 feet. This is excellent habitat for mountain lion and numerous species of birds. The plentiful oak trees encourage acorn woodpeckers (*Melanerpes formicivorus*) to be residents. There are two maintained trails within the wilderness area, but the use of topographic maps is highly recommended.

Directions: From Prescott take County Road 5 north about 36 miles then turn left onto FR 125. The wilderness area is south of the road.

Activities: Hiking, camping, horseback riding, nature study, and hunting.

Facilities: None.

Dates: Open year-round, although wet weather may make forest roads impassable.

Fees: None.

Closest town: Prescott, about 40 miles.

For more information: Chino Valley Ranger District, PO Box 485, Chino Valley, AZ 86323-0485. Phone (520) 636-2302.

GRANITE MOUNTAIN WILDERNESS

[Fig. 34(4)] An easily identifiable landmark located on the northwest outskirts of Prescott, this 9,799-acre wilderness is characterized by gigantic granite boulders, some the size of houses, stacked to elevations that exceed 7,600 feet. The wilderness area contains several trails, but only one, the Granite Mountain Trail, climbs to the summit. Because of the area's proximity to Prescott and resulting popularity, hiking groups are limited to 15 people; equestrian groups to 10 animals. Dogs must be on a leash at all times. Campfires are prohibited; however, stoves fueled by propane or white gas are permitted. There is no camping within 200 feet of the Granite Mountain Trail.

Rock climbing is perhaps more popular than hiking. Maintenance of existing fixed anchors is permitted, but no new anchors are allowed. Some of the best climbing routes are closed between February and July to protect nesting peregrine falcons.

Other trails skirt the south and eastern wilderness boundaries and therefore are open to mountain bike use.

Directions: Drive about 5 miles west from Prescott on the Iron Springs Road to the Granite Basin Lake Road (FR 374). Turn right and continue about 4 more miles to Granite Basin Lake, the end of the road, and the signed main trailhead.

Activities: Hiking, camping, horseback riding, nature study, and climbing.

Facilities: Campground.

Dates: Open year-round, although winter snows occasionally occur.

Fees: There is a fee for overnight camping.

Closest town: Prescott, 8 miles.

For more information: Prescott National Forest Supervisor's Office, 344 S. Cortez St., Prescott, AZ 86303-4398. Phone (520) 771-4700.

GRANITE MOUNTAIN TRAIL

[Fig. 34(5)] This trail will take you to the summit of Granite Mountain for panoramic views of the Prescott National Forest.

Trail: 3.8 miles one-way.
Degree of difficulty: Moderate.
Elevation: 5,300 to 7,626 feet.
Surface: Rocky to sandy.

CASTLE CREEK WILDERNESS

[Fig. 34(6)] This extremely rugged wilderness of 25,517 acres sits on the eastern slopes of the Bradshaw Mountains not far from Crown King, once a mining camp but now a hodgepodge collection of summer cabins. Prominent granite peaks overlook the Agua Fria River. Elevations range from 2,800 feet to more than 7,000 feet. At the lower elevations, saguaro (*Cereus giganteus*), palo verde (*Cercidium* sp.), and mesquite (*Prosopis* sp.) are common. Gaining elevation, one passes through grassland, then chaparral, and finally, forests of ponderosa, Arizona white oak (*Quercus arizonica*), and alligator juniper.

There are nine maintained trails, totaling 27 miles, within this wilderness, but the use of a topographic map is helpful. After a long, exhilarating hike, return to Crown King and have a cool one in the Crown King Saloon. This bar was originally built in the mining town of Oro Belle, 8 miles away, in 1895. When the mines closed in 1916, the saloon was dismantled and transported by mule and wagon to its present location.

Directions: Reaching this wilderness area is half of the adventure. Take I-17 north from Phoenix about 50 miles to Exit 259, the Bloody Basin/Horsethief Basin exit. Take FR 259 and follow the signs for Crown King, another 28 miles. You will pass through the old and nearly abandoned mining towns of Cordes and Cleator. Pass Crown King, go another 0.5 mile, then make a left on FR 52. Go another 2.5 miles to the signed trailhead on the left.

Activities: Hiking, camping, horseback riding, nature study, and hunting.

Facilities: None.

Dates: Open year-round, although wet weather may make Forest Service roads impassable.

Fees: None.

Closest town: Prescott, 35 miles.

For more information: Prescott National Forest Supervisor's Office, 344 S. Cortez St., Prescott, AZ 86303-4398. Phone (520) 771-4700. For Forest Service road conditions, call (520) 632-7740. For the saloon, call (520) 632-7053.

ALGONQUIN TRAIL

[Fig. 34(7)] This trail descends through catclaw acacia, manzanita, mountain mahogany, and other dense shrubs to finally reach the remains of the Algonquin mine by a beautiful little creek.

Trail: 4 miles one-way.
Degree of difficulty: Moderate.
Elevation: 6,850 to 4,600 feet.
Surface: Rocky.

CEDAR BENCH WILDERNESS

[Fig. 34(7), Fig. 36(1)] Located along the Verde Rim, the dividing line between the Verde and Agua Fria drainages, the Cedar Bench Wilderness is 16,005 acres. Elevations range from 4,500 feet to 6,700 feet with the primary vegetative cover of chaparral with pockets of pinyon and Utah juniper.

The Verde National Wild and Scenic River forms a portion of the eastern boundary of this little-used wilderness. While there are nine maintained trails within the area, the use of topographic maps is highly recommended.

Directions: Rim trailheads can be reached from the Dugas Road from I-17 Exit 268.

Activities: Hiking, camping, horseback riding, nature study, and hunting.

Facilities: None.

Dates: Open year-round, although wet weather may make Forest Service roads impassable.

Fees: None.

Closest town: Camp Verde, about 40 miles.

For more information: Verde Ranger District, PO Box 670, Camp Verde, AZ 86322-0670. Phone (520) 567-4121.

PINE MOUNTAIN WILDERNESS

[Fig. 34(8), Fig. 36(2)] This 20,100-acre wilderness straddles the boundary between the Prescott and Tonto national forests. Lying along the high Verde Rim, Pine Mountain at 6,800 feet stands as an island of tall, green timber, primarily ponderosa pine, surrounded by brush-covered desert mountains. A great variety of wildlife haunts the steep slopes and deep canyons.

Six maintained trails penetrate the wilderness, but topographic maps are a must.

Directions: To reach the Pine Mountain trailhead, take the Dugas Road from I-17 Exit 268. Drive the 25 miles to its end and various trailheads.

Activities: Hiking, camping, horseback riding, nature study, and hunting.

Facilities: None.

Dates: Open year-round, although wet weather may make Forest Service roads impassable.

Fees: None.

Closest town: Camp Verde, about 45 miles.

For more information: Verde Ranger District, PO Box 670, Camp Verde, AZ 86322-0670. Phone (520) 567-4121.

WOODCHUTE WILDERNESS

[Fig. 34(8)] Perched above and to the west of the old copper-mining town of Jerome, this small wilderness offers relatively easy access and spectacular views of the San Francisco Peaks and panoramic vistas of central Arizona. Created in 1984, the 5,923-acre wilderness ranges in elevation from 5,500 to 7,800 feet. Ponderosa pine dominates at the higher elevations giving way to pinyon-juniper woodland at lower sites. In late summer, this can be a good place to observe migrating warblers and other birds. Some sightings include hermit warbler (*Dendroica occidentalis*), Townsend's warbler (*Dendroica townsendi*), black-throated gray warbler (*Dendroica nigrescens*), Nashville warbler (*Vermivora ruficapilla*), Virginia's warbler (*Vermivora virginiae*), and painted redstart (*Myioborus picta*).

The wilderness is named after a wooden chute constructed to carry ponderosa timbers down the mountain to the copper mines of Jerome.

There is only one maintained trail, the 6-mile Woodchute Trail, into the wilderness.

Directions: Drive 8 miles southwest of Jerome on AZ 89A, and turn north at the Potato Patch Campground at Mingus Pass. Take FR 106 about 0.3 mile to the Woodchute trailhead.

Activities: Hiking, camping, horseback riding, nature study, and hunting.

Facilities: None.

Dates: Open year-round, but may be snowy during the winter.

Fees: None.

Closest town: Jerome, 10 miles.

For more information: Verde Ranger District, PO Box 670, Camp Verde, AZ 86322-0670. Phone (520) 567-4121. Chino Valley Ranger District, PO Box 485, Chino Valley, AZ 86323-0485. Phone (520) 636-2302.

WOODCHUTE TRAIL

This trail ends at the north rim of Woodchute Mountain, where you can see into the Verde Valley and beyond.

Trail: 5 miles one-way.

Degree of difficulty: Moderate.

Elevation: 7,000 to 7,700 feet.

Surface: Forest floor.

PRESCOTT NATIONAL FOREST CAMPGROUNDS

At-large camping is permitted in much of the Prescott National Forest except in heavily used areas, mostly near the town of Prescott. This national forest has 13 developed campgrounds. See Appendix G for a table of information on individual campgrounds.

Prescott Area

[Fig. 34] The mile-high city of Prescott was founded soon after gold was discovered in the nearby hills in 1863, the same year that Abraham Lincoln signed the act that created the Arizona Territory. Prescott became Arizona's first territorial capital and the region's economic center. Many of the buildings constructed in those early days still stand: infamous Whiskey Row, where in the 1890s more than 20 saloons served liquor and vice day and night; the downtown Courthouse and plaza; and the first territorial governor's residence, now part of the Sharlot Hall Museum (phone (520) 445-3122). There are approximately 525 buildings in Prescott on the National Register of Historic Places. Prescott also claims to have the world's oldest rodeo, which is held each July 4th week.

Granite hills near town lure hikers, rock climbers, and nature lovers. On the northeast side of town is Watson Woods, the last remaining intact floodplain along Granite Creek. More than 350 different kinds of plants grow there. Sonoran mud turtles (*Kinosternon sonoriense*) swim in a large pond in the woods. Great blue herons (*Ardea herodias*), mallards (*Anas platyrhynchos*), mule deer, javelina, skunks, and squirrels regularly come for a drink. Nature trails are being developed.

For more information: Prescott Chamber of Commerce, PO Box 1147, Prescott, AZ 86302. Phone (520) 445-2000 or (800) 266-7534.

MULE DEER
(*Odocoileus hemionus*)
In Arizona, mule deer tend to live in pine forests or low desert areas

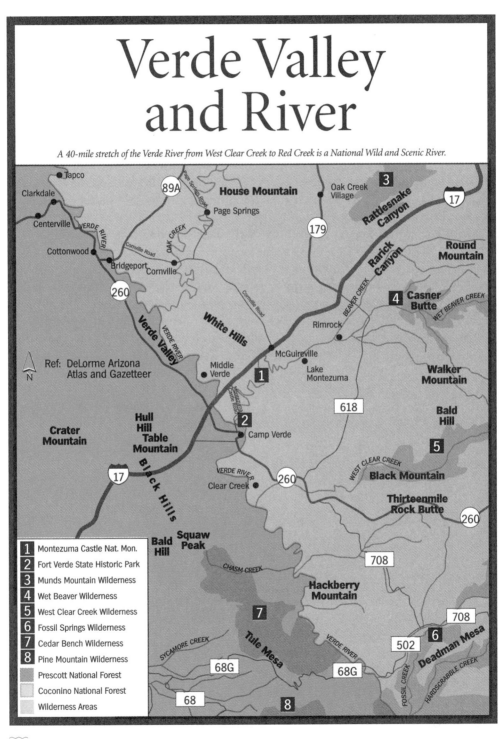

Verde Valley and River

A 40-mile stretch of the Verde River from West Clear Creek to Red Creek is a National Wild and Scenic River.

Ref: DeLorme Arizona Atlas and Gazetteer

1 Montezuma Castle Nat. Mon.
2 Fort Verde State Historic Park
3 Munds Mountain Wilderness
4 Wet Beaver Wilderness
5 West Clear Creek Wilderness
6 Fossil Springs Wilderness
7 Cedar Bench Wilderness
8 Pine Mountain Wilderness
Prescott National Forest
Coconino National Forest
Wilderness Areas

Verde Valley and River

[Fig. 35] About midway between Prescott and Flagstaff is the broad Verde Valley, bounded on its northeast side by the Mogollon Rim and its southwest side by the Black Hills. The Verde River and its numerous tributaries drain the valley. The river meanders through the small communities of Clarkdale, Cottonwood, and Camp Verde and past state parks and national monuments before plunging over a basalt lava ledge and beginning a whitewater race south through Sonoran desert wilderness toward the Salt River near Phoenix. Just before reaching the Salt River, the Verde's flow is interrupted by two dams—Horseshoe and Bartlett.

The upper Verde River has cut a scenic canyon between Perkinsville and Clarkdale that is unusual among Arizona streams in that it still maintains a fairly strong, native fish community. In addition to the federally protected, endangered spikedace (*Meda fulgida*), native species include longfin dace (*Agosia chrysogaster*), desert sucker (*Catostomus clarki*), roundtail chub (*Gila robusta*), and speckled dace (*Rhinichthys osculus*). Amazingly, these natives are able to dominate despite introduced species such as the red shiner (*Richardsonius hydrophlox*), mosquitofish (*Gambusia affinis*), yellow bullhead (*Ameiurus natalis*), carp (*Cyprinus carpio*), channel catfish, and smallmouth bass.

Waterfowl can be common, especially during spring and fall migration. Expect to see green-wing and blue-winged teal (*Anas crecca* and *A. discors*), cinnamon teal (*Anas cyanoptera*), mallard, common merganser (*Mergus merganser*), and other types of ducks and wading birds. The river's riparian habitat also hosts a plethora of nesting and migrating birds. Serious birders will want a copy of *Birding Sedona and the Verde Valley* by Virginia Gilmore.

One of the best ways to experience the upper Verde is to take the Verde Canyon Train. The tracks were laid to connect Clarkdale and Jerome with the Ash Fork-Prescott Railroad. The early train was called the "Verde Mix" because of the variety of products and people carried on the line. Today's four-hour round trip train ride goes about 15 miles from Clarkdale to the tiny ranching settlement of Perkinsville, which had a starring role in the 1962 classic movie *How the West Was Won*. Board the train at 300 N. Broadway in Clarkdale.

For the train's schedule, information, and ticket purchase: Verde Canyon Railroad, 300 N. Broadway, Clarkdale, AZ 86324. Phone (520) 639-0010 or (800) 320-0718. Web site www.verdecanyonrr.com.

The section of river from a few miles upstream of Clarkdale to Beasley Flat, a few miles downstream of Camp Verde, is usually a relatively calm float that can be done in a canoe or kayak. Venturing beyond Beasley Flat, though, requires whitewater experience, especially when the river is high (usually after storms or during the spring runoff).

The whitewater run is about 59 miles and drops more than 1,000 feet. Most boaters exit at Sheep Bridge at the top of Horseshoe Reservoir. Peaceful pools alternate with long stretches of rock-dodging Class II-III rapids. Virtually all are runnable, although a few Class IV ledge drops may require lining or portage. The Forest Service offers a free *Verde River Recreation Opportunity Guide* with more detailed information about the rapids of the Verde. Also very useful is Jim Slingluff's *Verde River Recreation Guide* or Bob Williams' *A Floater's Guide to the Verde River*. Not only do these books contain boating and rapid information, but both are storehouses of natural history information about the river.

Besides the exciting rapids, the Verde offers access to some great hiking in side canyons, where the ruins of ancient Indian cultures await discovery. There is also a hot spring near the confluence with Fossil Creek, good catfishing, and wildlife watching. Look for javelina, river otter, ringtail, beaver, bobcat, black bear, mountain lion, mule and white-tailed deer, and coyotes. Birds include bald and golden eagles, common black hawk, turkey vulture (*Cathartes aura*), kingbirds (*Tyrannus* sp.), black phoebes (*Sayornis nigricans*), vermilion flycatchers (*Pyrocephalus rubinus*), belted kingfishers (*Ceryle alcyon*), Gambel's quail, and many others. The Verde is one of the few places in Arizona to catch a glimpse of the rare Sonoran mud turtle (*Kinosternon sonoriense*) or the Mexican garter snake (*Thamnophis eques*). Endangered Colorado squawfish (*Ptychocheilus lucius*) and razorback suckers (*Xyrauchen texanus*) have been reintroduced.

In 1984, largely due to the persistence and vision of the late Arizona Congressman Morris Udall, 40 miles of the Verde River—from its confluence with West Clear Creek to Red Creek, about 10 miles upstream from Bartlett Lake—was selected to be a National Wild and Scenic River.

Two major dams have been built on the lower Verde River to create the artificial reservoirs of Horseshoe Lake and Bartlett Lake. Besides bass, bluegill, and crappie fishing, anglers occasionally hook flathead catfish (*Pylodictis olivaris*) that weigh 30 pounds or more.

For more information: Verde Ranger District, PO Box 670, Camp Verde, AZ 86322-0670. Phone (520) 567-4121. Or contact the Cave Creek Ranger District, 40202 N. Cave Creek Road, Scottsdale, AZ 85262. Phone (520) 595-3300.

DEAD HORSE RANCH STATE PARK

[Fig. 34(10)] Despite the name, Dead Horse Ranch is a delightful respite from the desert sun and makes a good base to explore the Verde Valley area. The park is nestled along the tree-lined Verde River. Bird-watching in the spring and summer can be very rewarding. Sightings of verdin (*Auriparus flaviceps*), northern cardinal (*Cardinalis cardinalis*), spotted sandpiper (*Actitis macularia*), wood duck (*Aix sponsa*), great blue heron, lesser nighthawk (*Chordeiles acutipennis*), blue-winged teal, peregrine falcon, bald eagle, osprey, northern harrier (*Circus cyaneus*), orioles (*Icterus* sp.), kingbirds and many other songbirds are common.

Directions: From Cottonwood, take AZ 89A (Cottonwood Street) to Main Street, turn right onto 10th Street, cross the Verde River, and go about 1 mile to the park.

Activities: Hiking, horseback riding, camping, picnicking, bird-watching, canoeing, and fishing.

Facilities: 67-unit campground, visitor center, picnic area, restrooms, showers, RV hook-ups.

Dates: Open year-round.

Fees: There is an entrance and camping fee.

Closest town: Cottonwood.

For more information: Dead Horse Ranch State Park, 675 Dead Horse Ranch Road, Cottonwood, AZ 86326. Phone (520) 634-5283. Arizona State Parks, 1300 W. Washington St., Phoenix, AZ 85007. Phone (602) 542-4174.

TUZIGOOT NATIONAL MONUMENT

[Fig. 34(11)] Tuzigoot (Apache for "crooked water") is a large hilltop dwelling constructed by the Sinagua people between 1125 and 1400. It sits atop a long ridge that rises 120 feet above a big meander of the Verde River. Originally, the pueblo was two stories in places and had 77 ground-floor rooms. There were few exterior doors; entry was by way of ladders through openings in the roofs. This design suggests that protection from other people was a guiding element in its construction. Who they may have been afraid of is not clear. A short, paved path with interpretive signs winds through the pueblo.

Just west of the monument is Peck's Lake, an oxbow lake that is an abandoned meander of the Verde River. At the north end of the lake is Tavasci Marsh, an outstanding area to look for birds and other wildlife. The Phelps Dodge Mining Corp. owns the lake and marsh, but certain areas are open to the public. Ask the monument rangers about access.

Directions: Take AZ 279 (Broadway) east out of Clarkdale to the Tuzigoot Road. Turn left and drive 1.5 miles to the site.

Activities: Short walk through the ruin.

Facilities: Visitor center and restrooms.

Dates: Open year-round.

Fees: There is an entrance fee.

Closest town: Clarkdale.

For more information: Tuzigoot National Monument, PO Box 219, Camp Verde, AZ 86324. Phone (520) 634-5564. Web site www.nps.gov/tuzi.

JEROME STATE HISTORIC PARK AND DOUGLAS MANSION

[Fig. 34(12)] Perched on the side on Cleopatra Hill, overlooking the Verde Valley, is the lively ghost town of Jerome. Prehistoric Indians were the first to discover and mine the copper ore found here. Spanish explorers came in the late sixteenth century looking for gold but were disappointed. Anglo-Americans staked the first mining claims in 1876, but profitable mining didn't occur until about a half-dozen years later.

After 1883, Jerome grew rapidly from a tent city into a prosperous company town.

Underground mining was phased out in 1918 after uncontrollable fires erupted in the 88 miles of tunnels under the town. Open pit mining was begun, but the dynamiting combined with the maze of subterranean tunnels, and natural faulting along the mountainside caused homes and buildings to crack and shift on their foundations. Jerome's jail has slid more than 225 feet through the years.

The copper market crashed in the early 1950s, so the mines closed and residents left in droves. From a peak of about 15,000 people, the population dropped to about 50 hardy souls. During the 1960s and '70s, hippies, artists, writers, and entrepreneurs discovered Jerome. The Douglas Mansion, built in 1916 by James "Rawhide Jimmy" Douglas as a hotel for visiting mining officials, was made a state park in 1965, and Jerome became a National Historic Landmark in 1976. Today the ghost town boasts about 500 residents and is a popular destination for tourists looking for shops, galleries, lodging, eateries, and old-time saloons set in a picturesque mining town.

Directions: The state park is located just off AZ 89A adjacent to the historic mining town of Jerome.

Activities: Touring the old Douglas Mansion and learning about the area's copper mining and history.

Facilities: Visitor center, museum, picnic area, and restrooms.

Dates: The state park is open year-round except Christmas.

Fees: There is a state park entrance fee.

For more information: Jerome Chamber of Commerce, PO Drawer K, Jerome, AZ 86331. Web site www.sedona.net/jerome. Jerome State Historic Park, PO Box D, Jerome, AZ 86331. Phone (520) 634-5381. Arizona State Parks, 1300 W. Washington St., Phoenix, AZ 85007. Phone (602) 542-4174.

MONTEZUMA CASTLE NATIONAL MONUMENT

[Fig. 35(1)] This national monument protects a very well-preserved five-story, 20-room cliff dwelling built by Sinagua farmers during the twelfth and thirteenth centuries. A short paved path takes visitors to the base of the cliff where the ruin is located. Early Anglo settlers thought mistakenly that the structure was Aztecan in origin, thus giving it the name it still carries. Nearby, against the same limestone cliff, was once an imposing six-story, 45-room dwelling. Unfortunately, this structure burned while occupied, or shortly after abandonment in the early 1400s. Its remains are exposed to the deteriorating effects of the weather.

Both dwellings face Wet Beaver Creek, a permanent stream that has its source in springs hidden deep in a canyon cut into the Mogollon Rim to the north. Along the streams banks are lovely old, white-barked Arizona sycamores, netleaf hackberry trees (*Celtis reticulata*), velvet ash, and Fremont cottonwoods (*Populus fremontii*). Above this riparian area are arid slopes covered with creosote (*Larrea tridentata*), four-wing saltbush (*Atriplex canescens*), and canotia (*Canotia holacantha*).

A separate section of the monument, about a 15-minute drive away, includes

Montezuma Well, a remarkable natural limestone sinkhole, and more Sinagua dwellings, including an excavated pit house, small cliff houses, and a couple of pueblos. A short, paved loop walk takes you to an overlook of the well where springs continually feed the pond. The sinkhole never fills, however, because water leaks out through cracks in the southeast wall. A short side path leads to the place where the water emerges outside the hill surrounding the well. Here the water is channeled into an irrigation ditch originally built by the ancient Indians.

Directions: To reach Montezuma Castle, exit I-17 at Exit 289, go past the Cliff Castle Casino, turn left onto the signed Montezuma Castle Road.

Activities: Short walks, nature study, and archaeology.

Facilities: Visitor center, restrooms, picnic area.

Dates: Open year-round.

Fees: There is an entry fee.

Closest town: Camp Verde, about 4 miles south.

For more information: Montezuma Castle National Monument, PO Box 219, Camp Verde, AZ 86322. Phone (520) 567-3322. Web site www.nps.gov/moca.

FORT VERDE STATE HISTORIC PARK

[Fig. 35(2)] For the Western history buff, Fort Verde is a required stop. The fort was a base for General George Crook's scouts and soldiers during the Indian campaigns of the 1870s. Along "Officers' Row," several of the original buildings have been restored. You will see the officers' quarters, doctor's quarters, bachelor officers' quarters, and the commanding officer's house.

Directions: In the town of Camp Verde on Hollamon Street, 2 miles east of I-17 Exit 287.

Activities: Learning about the life of frontier soldiers.

Facilities: Visitor center, museum, picnic area, and restrooms.

Dates: Open daily year-round.

Fees: There is an entrance fee.

Closest town: Camp Verde.

For more information: Fort Verde State Historic Park, 125 E. Hollaman St., Camp Verde, AZ 86322. Phone (520) 567-3275. Arizona State Parks, 1300 W. Washington St., Phoenix, AZ 85007. Phone (602) 542-4174.

Bureau of Land Management Areas

Where the central mountains of Arizona meet the Sonoran Desert, the Bureau of Land Management administers much of the public land.

▓ UPPER BURRO CREEK WILDERNESS

[Fig. 34(13)] Although difficult to access, this 27,440-acre wilderness encompasses part of Burro Creek, one of the last streams in Arizona to flow relatively undisturbed by human activity into the lowland desert. Adventuresome hikers equipped with binoculars can expect to see a wide variety of wildlife. The BLM counts 267 vertebrate species, over a quarter of Arizona's wildlife species, as residents. Golden and bald eagles, a large breeding colony of common black hawks, and prairie falcons (*Falco mexicanus*) are found here. The BLM notes that the area has the greatest diversity of birds of prey anywhere in the United States.

Burro Creek drains the Mohon Mountains to the north, the Santa Maria Mountains to the south, and the Aquarius Mountains to the northwest. The slopes enclosing the creek are steep and rocky. The creek, which has been proposed as a National Wild and Scenic River, flows through gorges, boulder-strewn narrows, gentle open stretches, and small waterfalls, and past a side stream containing hidden hot springs.

The roundtail chub (*Gila robusta*), a candidate for endangered status, and the lowland leopard frog (*Rana* sp.), a threatened species, live here. Along the stream grow Fremont cottonwood, Goodding willow (*Salix gooddingii*), mesquite, and other trees. The Wilderness Society has called this type of riparian community the "rarest forest in North America." Near Goodwin Mesa is desert grassland and at higher elevation, pinyon-juniper woodland. Farther downstream (and lower in elevation) are healthy stands of palo verde and saguaro.

Burro Creek, with its permanent flow, served as a travel corridor for prehistoric people. The Prescott Culture (Patayan) built multi-storied pueblos here during the thirteenth century. They apparently also mined obsidian, a black volcanic glass.

Downstream from the wilderness area, about 1.5 miles off US 93, is the BLM Burro Creek Recreation Area and campground, a great base for exploring the surrounding area. Visitors enjoy picnicking, bird-watching, swimming, or rock-hounding for agates and Apache tears. Interpretive signs introduce the desert plant life. The campground has drinking water. Day use is free, but there is a fee for camping.

Directions: The wilderness area is about 65 miles northwest of Wickenburg and about 15 miles north of US 93. Only very rough four-wheel-drive tracks approach the wilderness boundary. There are no established trails in the wilderness area.

Activities: Rough cross-country hiking, camping, swimming, deer and small game hunting, and nature study.

Facilities: None.

Dates: Open year-round.

Fees: None to enter wilderness area; there is a campground fee.

Closest town: Wikieup, about 18 miles northwest.

For more information: BLM, Kingman Field Office, 2475 Beverly Ave., Kingman, AZ 86401. Phone (520) 692-4400 or 757-3161. Web site www.az.blm.gov.

HASSAYAMPA RIVER CANYON WILDERNESS

[Fig. 34(14)] The Hassayampa River begins in the mountains south of Prescott. The river flows south eventually reaching the Gila River. Though the origin and true meaning of the word "Hassayampa" is debated, a local poet wrote:

You've heard about the wondrous stream, they call the Hassayamp.

They say it turns the truthful guy into a lying scamp.

And if you quaff its water once, it's sure to prove your bane.

You'll ne'er forsake the blasted stream or tell the truth again.

During the late 1800s, prospectors swarmed to the region. One of them, Henry Wickenburg, discovered a fabulously rich gold deposit in the nearby Vulture Mountains, but most others went home empty-handed.

Within this 11, 840-acre wilderness is a 15-mile stretch of the Hassayampa River. Although the river flows only intermittently, it supports a rich and diverse riparian community of Arizona black walnut, ash, Fremont cottonwood, willow, box elder, and Arizona cypress. The sensitive species flannelbush (*Fremontia californica*) is also found in the area. Farther from the stream bed, the plant life is more typical of the Sonoran desert: saguaro, mesquite, barrel cactus (*Ferocactus* sp.), prickly pear, palo verde, catclaw acacia (*Acacia greggii*), and ocotillo (*Fouquieria splendens*).

Expect wildlife such as mule deer, javelina, rattlesnakes (*Crotalus* sp.), gopher snake (*Pituophis melanoleucus*), desert tortoise (*Gopherus agassizi*), Gila monster (*Heloderma suspectum*), black-tailed jackrabbit (*Lepus californicus*), mountain lion, coyote, and Harris' antelope squirrel (*Ammospermophilus harrisi*). Some rare or threatened wildlife include spotted bat (*Euderma maculatum*), great egret (*Casmerodius albus*), black-crowned night-heron (*Nycticorax nycticorax*), common black hawk, zone-tailed hawk (*Buteo albonotatus*), and prairie falcon.

Bird-watching is very good in the spring, when the riparian habitat attracts many birds such as Harris's hawk (*Parabuteo unicinctus*), yellow-billed cuckoo, willow flycatcher (*Empidonax traillii*), Bell's vireo (*Vireo bellii*), summer tanager (*Piranga olivacea*), yellow warbler (*Dendroica petechia*), belted kingfisher, vermilion flycatcher, yellow-breasted chat (*Icteria virens*), and common yellowthroat (*Geothlypis trichas*).

The cottonwood, willow, and mesquite bottomlands also shelter the very rare Arizona skink (*Eumeces gilberti arizonensis*), a foot-long, tan-colored lizard with shiny, smooth scales and a brick-red tail.

There are no trails into this wilderness, and the four-wheel-drive Constellation Road, which approaches the southern boundary, crosses private land so access is difficult. Check with the BLM for the latest access information.

BELTED
KINGFISHER
(Ceryle alcyon)

Directions: The wilderness area is located about 20 miles north-northeast from Wickenburg. Only very poor four-wheel-drive tracks come near the boundaries. Once there, it is possible to hike cross-country to Sam Powell Peak or The Needle, an igneous monolith.

Activities: Cross-country hiking, camping, and nature study.

Facilities: None.

Dates: Open year-round, but summers are very hot.

Fees: None.

Closest town: Wickenburg, 20 miles.

For more information: Bureau of Land Management, Phoenix Field Office, 2015 W. Deer Valley Road, Phoenix, AZ 85027-2099. Phone (602) 580-5500.

HASSAYAMPA RIVER PRESERVE

[Fig. 34(15)] Birders can enjoy another section of the Hassayampa River downstream of the wilderness area. About 3 miles along US 60 southeast of Wickenburg, the "dude ranch capital of Arizona" (*see* Appendix F) is the Hassayampa River Preserve, managed by The Nature Conservancy since 1986. A 5-mile stretch of perennially flowing water has created a lush stand of Fremont cottonwood and Goodding willow.

More than 230 species of birds have been observed at this location. Nesting species include pied-billed grebe (*Podilymbus podiceps*), green heron (*Butorides virescens*), black-crowned night-heron (*Nycticorax nycticorax*), ruddy duck (*Oxyura jamaicensis*), Cooper's hawk (*Accipiter cooperii*), sora (*Porzana carolina*), black-chinned hummingbird (*Archilochus alexandri*), Costa's hummingbird (*Calypte costae*), gilded flicker (*Colaptes chrysoides*), yellow warbler (*Dendroica petechia*), blue grosbeak (*Guiraca caerulea*), and bronzed cowbird (*Molothrus aeneus*).

Three 0.5-mile loop trails wander through woodland, along the riverbank, or around a small lake. Trail and natural history information can be picked up at the visitor center.

Directions: Take US 60 about 3 miles southeast of Wickenburg. Turn right at the preserve sign.

Activities: Bird-watching, self-guided nature walks, and guided walks on the last Saturday of every month.

Dates: Open Wednesday through Sunday.

Facilities: Visitor center, trail guides, restrooms, and gift shop.

Fees: A small donation is suggested.

Closest town: Wickenburg, 3 miles northwest.

For more information: Hassayampa River Preserve, 49614 Hwy 60, Wickenburg, AZ 85390. Phone (520) 684-2772. Web site www.tnc.org.

HELLS CANYON WILDERNESS

[Fig. 34(17)] This 9,900-acre wilderness, next to the old Castle Hot Springs Resort, has no maintained trails, but game and livestock trails crisscross the area providing access to some lovely Sonoran desert country with saguaro, cholla (*Opuntia* sp.), ocotillo, and palo verde. In the northwest corner of the wilderness is chaparral habitat at an elevation of 2,600 feet, nearly 2,000 feet below its normal occurrence in Arizona. Besides the native desert animals such as deer, javelina, desert tortoises, and black-tailed jackrabbits, a few feral burros, descended from those left by prospectors, roam the area.

The wilderness includes part of the Hieroglyphic Mountains, which received their name from the many petroglyphs and pictographs in the area.

Directions: Drive north from Phoenix on I-17 to Exit 223 for AZ 74 (Carefree Highway) and travel west. Continue to the Lake Pleasant Regional Park turnoff and head north. After about 5.5 miles, turn left onto the Castle Hot Springs Road. Another 5 miles brings you to a narrow wash on the left side of the road. Here 2 unmarked trails begin: one that trends westerly, the other that goes south.

Activities: Hiking, camping, and nature study.

Facilities: None.

Dates: Open year-round, but summers are hellishly hot.

Fees: None.

Closest town: Phoenix, 25 miles.

For more information: Bureau of Land Management, Phoenix Field Office, 2015 W. Deer Valley Road, Phoenix, AZ 85027-2099. Phone (602) 580-5500.

AGUA FRIA NATIONAL MONUMENT

[Fig. 34(16)] During the summer of 1999, Secretary of the Interior Bruce Babbitt proposed that Perry Mesa and Black Mesa, which sits between Black Canyon City and Cordes Junction, receive some sort of additional federal protection. Because of area's rich archaeological resources and its proximity to Phoenix, the Bureau of Land Management feared that heavy use of these public lands would prompt vandalism of its Native American sites. On January 11, 2000, President Bill Clinton signed a proclamation creating the 71,100-acre Agua Fria National Monument.

Pueblos and ruins in the area date from the 1200s and 1300s, a period of great cultural upheaval when residents were changing the way that they built structures, made pottery, and buried their dead. By the early 1400s, the area was abandoned. Some archaeologists speculate that the Hohokam, who lived in the Salt River Valley where Phoenix is now, drove out these people.

The Agua Fria River separates Perry Mesa and Black Mesa and has been proposed as a National Wild and Scenic River. The riparian habitat is first-rate and includes mature galleries of cottonwood, willow, and Arizona sycamore. This north-south corridor attracts wintering bald eagles, zone-tailed hawks, and migrating waterfowl. It's believed that relict populations (*see* Ice Age Relicts sidebar) of the native Gila chub (*Gila intermedia*), longfin dace, and Gila topminnow still exist here. The massive New Waddell Dam on the lower Agua Fria River, outside the boundaries of the new monument, creates Lake Pleasant, a reservoir popular with motorboaters and anglers. The riverbed below the dam is usually dry. Water from the reservoir is diverted into irrigation canals. Anglers go after largemouth and white bass (*Morone chrysops*), and there are unverified reports of striped bass (*Morone saxatilis*).

The mesa tops are also important pronghorn habitat. Hunting for them, as well as deer and quail, is popular. The area includes part of the Black Canyon Trail, an old route that once connected Phoenix and Flagstaff.

Directions: One approach is to take the Bloody Basin Exit (Exit 259) on I-17, about 25 miles north of Black Canyon City. Follow the rough dirt road east and south about 15 miles to reach the Perry Mesa area. Although this area is not on Forest Service land, the Prescott National Forest map is handy for navigation as well as the appropriate topographic maps. There are no established trails.

Activities: Cross-country hiking, archaeological and nature study, and hunting.

Facilities: None.

Dates: Open year-round, although the dirt roads are quite rough and may be impassable in wet weather.

Fees: None.

Closest town: Black Canyon City.

For more information: Bureau of Land Management, Phoenix Field Office, 2015 W. Deer Valley Road, Phoenix, AZ 85027-2099. Phone (602) 580-5500. Web site www.az.blm.gov/aguafria/afriafactsht.htm.

Tonto National Forest

[Fig. 36] The Tonto National Forest abuts the escarpment of the Mogollon Rim and runs south to where the central mountains of Arizona begin to meet the Sonoran desert. Two Apache reservations run along the east boundary, and the greater Phoenix metropolitan area and the I-17 corridor essentially follow the west boundary. Within this 2.9 million acres is a mind-boggling array of plant and animal communities—everything from spruce trees to giant saguaro cacti and dark-eyed juncos to Gila monsters.

From 1886 to 1892, the notorious Pleasant Valley War occurred in the area. The "war" was actually a feud between two rival families, the Tewksburys and the Grahams. Although sometimes described as a fight between sheepmen and cattlemen, it apparently began over some stolen horses but quickly escalated and may have resulted in as many as 50 deaths from the towns of Holbrook to Globe. The feud finally ended when the last Tewksbury killed the last Graham on the streets of Tempe. Don Dedera's *A Little War of Our Own* relates this tragic tale.

Any mention of Tonto National Forest must include Zane Grey. From 1908 to

1939, Grey wrote 65 Western novels, many set in the canyons, draws, and forests of the Tonto. In 1920, locals built the writer a cabin under the Mogollon Rim (which in this area is also called the Tonto Rim) about 23 miles northeast of Payson. The cabin was a favorite tourist spot until it burned in 1990. There are plans to build a replica. In the meantime, there is a Zane Grey exhibit in the Rim Country Museum in Payson. Phone (520) 474-3483.

A small section of the Tonto National Forest lies south of Globe and includes the Pinal Mountains. Geologically it is more part of the southeastern Basin and Range Country, so dealt with in that chapter as the Pinal Mountain Recreation Area (*see* page 314).

For more information: Supervisor's Office, Tonto National Forest, 2324 E. McDowell Road, Phoenix, AZ 85006. Phone (602) 225-5200. Web site www.fs.fed.us/r3/tonto.

THE BOULDERS MOUNTAIN BIKE ADVENTURE

One of the best ways to explore the woods is by mountain bike. The district offices can offer suggestions, but just outside of Payson is a moderate ride to "The Boulders" that can be combined with a little rock climbing.

Directions: Drive east out of Payson on Granite Dells Road until it becomes a dirt road and park to the side. Bike down Sutton Road. At 0.5 mile, the road makes a sharp right; you make a left onto a dirt trail. It ends in another 1.5 miles. Take a break, do a little bouldering, or if the creek is running, have a swim. Then look up the hillside across the creek to find a little game trail. This is your route to a sandy arroyo. Cross it to a dirt road (FR 435) that will take you back to your vehicle.

Trail: About a 5.4-mile loop.

Degree of difficulty: Moderate.

Elevation: From 4,970 to 4,600 feet.

Surface: Rocky to sandy.

TONTO NATURAL BRIDGE STATE PARK

[Fig. 36(3)] Not far from Payson and surrounded by the Tonto National Forest, this state park protects what may be the world's largest natural travertine (a hard, dense, finely crystalline spring-deposited form of limestone) bridge and an historic lodge. The bridge is 183 feet high and spans a 400-foot tunnel that measures 150 feet at its widest point. Pine Creek dissolved and eroded through the travertine to form the tunnel. Beneath the bridge, Pine Creek flows into a deep, clear pool. The nearby cliffs are of hard Precambrian igneous and sedimentary rocks.

Visitors can chose from three trails. Pine Creek Trail follows the creek above the bridge for 0.5 mile to a view of the upstream side of the bridge. Waterfall Trail is about 300 feet long and leads to a view of a small waterfall on the creek. The Gowan Loop Trail is a steep, rough 0.5 mile that goes to the downstream side of the bridge.

Tonto National Forest Area

Tonto National Forest covers 2.9 million acres from the Mogollon Rim to Sonoran desert.

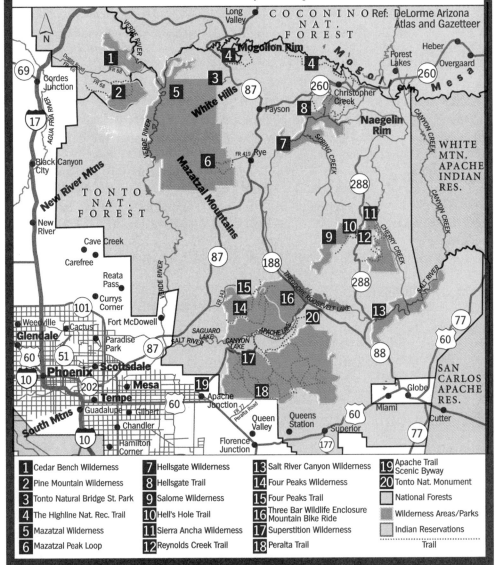

1 Cedar Bench Wilderness	**7** Hellsgate Wilderness
2 Pine Mountain Wilderness	**8** Hellsgate Trail
3 Tonto Natural Bridge St. Park	**9** Salome Wilderness
4 The Highline Nat. Rec. Trail	**10** Hell's Hole Trail
5 Mazatzal Wilderness	**11** Sierra Ancha Wilderness
6 Mazatzal Peak Loop	**12** Reynolds Creek Trail

13 Salt River Canyon Wilderness	**19** Apache Trail Scenic Byway
14 Four Peaks Wilderness	**20** Tonto Nat. Monument
15 Four Peaks Trail	National Forests
16 Three Bar Wildlife Enclosure Mountain Bike Ride	Wilderness Areas/Parks
17 Superstition Wilderness	Indian Reservations
18 Peralta Trail	Trail

Directions: Drive about 10 miles north of Payson on AZ 87 and then turn left at the park sign.

Activities: Hiking, picnicking, and touring an historic lodge.

Facilities: Picnic tables.

Dates: Open year-round.

Fees: There is an entrance fee.

Closest town: Payson, 10 miles.

For more information: Tonto Natural Bridge State Park, PO Box 1245, Payson, AZ 85547. Park office phone (520) 476-4202. Lodge tours phone (520) 476- 2261.

THE HIGHLINE NATIONAL RECREATION TRAIL

[Fig. 36(4)] Another trail popular with hikers, mountain bikers, and equestrians is the Highline Trail that hugs the base of the Mogollon Rim from Pine to AZ 260 east of Christopher Creek. Rim country pioneers built this trail for horseback commerce.

The 51-mile long trail crosses several roads and 15 trails at convenient intervals, allowing you to do it as a series of day trips and/or loops. (Runners may be interested in the annual Zane Grey Ultramarathon that follows the trail. The winner in 1999 finished the 51 miles in 8 hours and 31 minutes.) Located at an average 5,500 feet elevation, the Highline is generally open year-round. Vegetation ranges from manzanita and juniper to pine and fir. The trail crosses a number of perennial streams.

Directions: The trail's western end is in the small community of Pine. Its eastern end is located where AZ 260 begins its ascent of the Mogollon Rim, near milepost 279, about 27 miles northeast of Payson.

Trail: 51 miles one-way.

Degree of difficulty: Moderate.

Elevation: From 5,400 to 6,800 feet.

Surface and blaze: Varies from rocky to sandy to forest floor; tree blazes, cairns, and signs.

For more information: Payson Ranger District, PO Box 100, Payson, AZ 85541. Phone (520) 474-7900.

MAZATZAL WILDERNESS

[Fig. 36(5)] The Mazatzal Wilderness contains more than 252,000 acres, making it one of the state's largest wilderness areas and a favorite with backpackers and equestrians. Established in 1940, it was expanded to its present size in 1984. Its name is supposedly derived from an Aztec word meaning "land of the deer." But Aztecs never lived in Arizona, so how the mountain range was named remains a mystery. Locals often pronounce it "mat-ta-zal," but a more correct way is "mah´-zat-zahl."

Native Americans have occupied the Mazatzal area for at least 5,000 years. By 1400, overpopulation and overuse of key natural resources apparently led to abandonment. But within a century, Southeastern Yavapai people had entered the area and were eventually joined by a few Tonto Apache, who lived primarily to the east of the range.

One of the first Anglo-Americans known to have entered the Mazatzals was Kit Carson. In 1829, Carson was trapping along the Salt River and then went upstream along the Verde. Indian hostility curtailed more permanent use of the area until General George Crook's campaign in the 1870s subjugated both the Apache and Yavapai and confined them to reservations.

The southern half of the Mazatzal Mountains consists almost entirely of Precambrian granitic rocks and some gneiss. The lower rolling hills on the west side of the range are covered by volcanic flows and igneous tuffs. The steep, rugged topography of the eastern portion has been greatly influence by the hardness of the rocks. Outcrops of rhyolite and porphyry jasper resist erosion and form cliffs, while softer slate areas in the south form more rounded slopes. The hard quartzites make up the higher peaks.

The eastern side of this wilderness consists predominately of chaparral or pine-covered mountains broken by narrow, vertical-walled canyons. On its west side below brush-covered foothills, the Verde River flows through Sonoran desert terrain.

Elevations range from 2,100 feet along the Verde to 7,903 feet at the summit of Mazatzal Peak. There is an extensive 240-mile trail system, but their condition ranges from very good to hardly worth hiking. Several are unsuitable for horses. Just locating some of the 14 or so trailheads can be challenging. Group sizes are limited to no more than 15 and no more than 15 head of pack or saddle animals. Directions to the various trailheads and trail descriptions are available from the Forest Service in its *Recreation Opportunity Guide* for the area.

Directions: Probably the easiest access to the wilderness is from the east side, which parallels AZ 87, the highway between Phoenix and Payson.

Activities: Hiking, camping, horseback riding, nature study, fishing, and hunting.

Facilities: None.

Dates: Open year-round, although wet weather may make some Forest Service roads impassable.

Fees: None.

Closest town: Carefree, 25 miles.

For more information: For the west side of the wilderness, contact the Cave Creek Ranger District, 40202 N. Cave Creek Road, Scottsdale, AZ 85262. Phone (520) 595-3300. For the east side, contact the Payson Ranger District, PO Box 100, Payson, AZ 85541. Phone (520) 474-7900.

MAZATZAL PEAK LOOP

[Fig. 36(6)] This two-or three-day loop hike is a super introduction to the Mazatzal Wilderness. The trail climbs to the crest of the range and circumnavigates Mazatzal Peak.

Directions: From Payson drive 14.5 miles south on AZ 87 to the signed turnoff for the Barnhardt Trail. Turn right onto FR 419 and drive 5 miles to its end. Three trails begin here. Start on the Barnhardt. In about 6.2 miles, take the Mazatzal Divide Trail south for about 3.3 miles before turning left onto the Y Bar Basin Trail, which leads back to the parking area some 7.5 miles and 2,500 vertical feet away.

Trail: 17 miles round-trip.

Degree of difficulty: Strenuous.

Elevation: 4,200 to 6,500 feet.

Surface: Rocky, look for cairns.

HELLSGATE WILDERNESS

[Fig. 36(7)] This 37,440-acre wilderness was established in 1984 and holds two perennial streams running through major canyons. Deep pools of water separated by falls make travel along Tonto and Haigler creeks extremely difficult. Those wanting to explore along the creek will need to be wary of flash floods, be properly prepared for swimming in cold water, and have the necessary equipment to climb around the falls. Less strenuous hikes can be found on the trails.

Elevations range from 3,000 feet along the lower end of Tonto Creek to more than 6,400 feet on Horse Mountain. Spring and fall are the ideal times to visit. The tiny area known as Hell's Gate, where Tonto and Haigler creeks join, is too fragile to be used by livestock, plus the last 0.5 mile is unsafe for horses; however, pack or saddle animals may be used elsewhere in the wilderness. Directions to the six trailheads and trail descriptions are available from the Forest Service in its *Recreation Opportunity Guide* for the area.

Wildlife includes black bear, white-tailed and mule deer, coyote, bobcat, gray fox, javelina, beaver, and many other small mammals. The creeks hold brown and rainbow trout, catfish, and smallmouth bass.

Directions: From Payson, drive about 11 miles east on AZ 260. Turn right onto FR 405A, go 0.3 mile and turn right at a cement water trough onto FR 893 to reach the signed trailhead.

Activities: Hiking, camping, swimming, nature study, and fishing.

Facilities: None.

Dates: Open year-round.

Fees: None.

Closest town: Payson, 18 miles.

For more information: Payson Ranger District, PO Box 100, Payson, AZ 85541. Phone (520) 474-7900. Pleasant Valley Ranger District, PO Box 450, Young, AZ 85554. Phone (520) 462-4300.

HELLSGATE TRAIL

[Fig. 36(8)] This is one way to reach the spectacular confluence of Tonto and Haigler creeks known as Hell's Gate where the canyon walls rise straight up 1,500 feet.

Trail: About 7 miles one-way to Tonto Creek.

Degree of difficulty: Strenuous.

Elevation: 5,300 to 4,000 feet.

Surface: Rocky.

SALOME WILDERNESS

[Fig. 36(9)] This 18,530-acre wilderness, established in 1984, contains a major canyon system carved by two streams. The upper reaches of Salome and Workman creeks are small but perennial streams that snake their way through the bottom of this scenic canyon wilderness. There are rumors of brown and rainbow trout, too. Bigtooth maple, alder, ash, Arizona sycamore, and box elder flourish along the banks while the canyon slopes are covered with chaparral or pinyon-juniper woodland. The higher elevations support scattered stands of ponderosa pine; the lower areas are deserts of jojoba (*Simmondsia chinensis*), palo verde, prickly pear cactus, and saguaro inhabited by canyon wrens (*Catherpes mexicanus*) and phainopeplas (*Phainopepla nitens*). Black phoebes hunt insects above the water, and belted kingfishers dive for tiny minnows. In the lower reaches of the canyon, pools of water can be found year-round, but cross-country travel is very difficult and often requires climbing gear.

Elevations range from 2,600 feet at the lower end of Salome Creek to 6,500 feet on Hopkins Mountain. Spring and fall are the best times to explore its 12 miles of difficult trails. There are four main trailheads. Directions can be obtained from the Pleasant Valley Ranger Station.

Spanish-speaking settlers named the creek for the biblical Salome, daughter of Herodias.

Directions: From Young, drive south on AZ 288 about 16 miles to the entrance of the Reynolds Creek Campground. Hell's Hole Trail starts right here.

Activities: Hiking, camping, swimming, and nature study.

Facilities: None.

Dates: Open year-round, but summers are unbearably hot.

Fees: None.

Closest town: Young, about 16 miles north.

For more information: Pleasant Valley Ranger District, PO Box 450, Young, AZ 85554. Phone (520) 462-4300.

HELL'S HOLE TRAIL

[Fig. 36(10)] **Trail:** About 5.3 miles to Hell's Hole.

Degree of difficulty: Strenuous.

Elevation: 5,500 to 3,920 feet.

Surface: Forest floor to brushy and rocky.

SIERRA ANCHA WILDERNESS

[Fig. 36(11)] First established in 1933 as a primitive area, this 20,850-acre wilderness is full of surprises and is delightful to explore. Sierra Ancha, which means "wide mountains," includes precipitous box canyons, high cliffs, and pine-covered mountains. The extremely rough topography often prohibits cross-country travel; however, there is an extensive 57-mile system of trails varying in condition. Directions to the 15 trailheads and trail descriptions are available from the Forest Service in its *Recre-*

ation Opportunity Guide for the area.

The mountains here are primarily made of Precambrian-age rocks that have been extensively faulted. The oldest are the Pinal Schist. Resting on its eroded surface is the Scanlan Conglomerate, followed by the Pioneer Shale, the Barnes Conglomerate, the thick Dripping Springs Quartzite, and remnants of the gray Mescal Limestone. Igneous basalt dikes of younger age (exact age unknown) have intruded on the Precambrian deposits.

Growing at the higher elevations are ponderosa pines, Douglas firs, and maples. The threatened Chiricahua dock (*Rumex* sp.), a wild relative of rhubarb, is found here, too. In the deep canyons like the one carved by Workman Creek are stands of Arizona sycamore, box elder, various kinds of evergreen oaks, scarlet sumac (*Rhus glabra*), and wild grape (*Vitis arizonica*).

The Salado people built small cliff houses here between the thirteenth and fourteenth centuries but soon abandoned them. Some archaeologists believe these homes were timber camps where prehistoric loggers lived while harvesting timber for other villages.

Just outside the eastern wilderness boundary flows beautiful Cherry Creek, another wonderful place to explore.

Directions: Several trailheads can be reached by driving south about 20 miles from Young on AZ 288.

Activities: Hiking, camping, nature study, and hunting.

Facilities: None.

Dates: Open year-round, although higher areas may become snowbound.

Fees: None.

Closest town: Globe, 45 miles; Young, about 20 miles north.

For more information: Pleasant Valley Ranger District, PO Box 450, Young, AZ 85554. Phone (520) 462-4300.

REYNOLDS CREEK TRAIL

[Fig. 36(12)] This trail climbs nearly 1,500 feet and traverses scenic Knoles Hole. It can be used to connect with other trails to cross the wilderness to its east boundary.

Directions: Drive south from Young on AZ288 about 20 miles then turn east onto FR 410 and drive about 4 miles to the trailhead.

Trail: 3.7 miles one-way.

Degree of difficulty: Moderate.

Elevation: 6,200 to 7,600 feet.

Surface: Rocky and brushy.

Chaparral And Bears

In the relatively open ponderosa pine forest, black bears are not very common—maybe one bear in every 6 to 10 square miles. However, in dense chaparral, bear populations can be as dense as one per square mile. Black bears relish their privacy and require a certain amount of plant growth for cover. Also, many of the chaparral plants produce fruits, berries, nuts, or other edibles that bears like to eat.

SALT RIVER CANYON WILDERNESS

[Fig. 36(13)] This wilderness, established in 1984, contains 32,100 very rugged and trailless acres. Thirty-two miles of the Salt River and its spectacular 2,000-foot-deep canyon bisect the wilderness. Elevations range from 2,200 feet to 4,200 feet on White Ledge Mountain. There are no maintained trails. Most visitors come to this wilderness by raft or kayak on the Salt River and its 27 rapids during the short and dangerous river-running season (*see* page 182).

Directions: Although access is possible via primitive four-wheel-drive roads at Gleason Flat and Horseshoe Bend, there are no developed hiking trails.

Activities: Cross-country hiking, camping, nature study, and whitewater boating.

Facilities: None.

Dates: Open year-round.

Fees: There is a fee for the mandatory river permits.

Closest town: Globe, 30 miles.

For more information: Globe Ranger District, Rt. 1, Box 33, Globe, AZ 85501. Phone (520) 402-6200 or 425-7189.

FOUR PEAKS WILDERNESS

[Fig. 36(14)] The Four Peaks Wilderness was established in 1984 and contains about 60,740 acres at the southern end of the Mazatzal Mountains. The Four Peaks are visible for many miles rising from the desert foothills. They are one of the most widely recognized landmarks of central Arizona and thus attract many hikers.

The mountains are a fascinating geologic complex. The bulk of the peaks consists of Precambrian granites and schists, clearly exposed along Buckhorn Ridge and in Boulder and Cottonwood canyons. A cap of deformed shale and quartzite, also of Precambrian age, forms the sheer face of the peaks. Farther to the south, the Painted Cliffs are composed of volcanic tuffs and ash flows of Cenozoic age. They were deposited during the same time period as similar formations in the nearby Superstition Wilderness. The unconformity, or difference in age, between the younger rock and the older rock is estimated to be a mind-boggling 2 billion years.

Elevations range from 1,600 feet near Mormon Flat Dam to 7,657 feet, the summit of Brown's Peak. This wide altitudinal span allows a great variety, and in some cases unique, plant and animal communities. It's possible to hike from Sonoran desert to ponderosa pine forest. Even a few Douglas firs and quaking aspens manage to survive on the north slope of Brown's Peak. Desert bighorn sheep scramble over the rugged terrain, and black bears are common. A small herd of feral burros descended from those left by prospectors roams the backcountry.

Unfortunately, a large part of the wilderness was burned in 1996 in the largest wildfire ever in Arizona's history. Two campers left a fire smoldering near Lone Pine Saddle. During the next 11 days, the flames consumed more than 61,000 acres of wilderness and adjacent land. It will take many decades for the area to fully recover.

In some ways worse than the fire is the erosion that followed. Several trails have been badly damaged with deep ditches cutting across the route. In other areas, the brush is growing so rapidly that passage is difficult.

There are seven major trailheads leading to 11 trails. Directions to the various trailheads and trail descriptions are available from the Forest Service in its *Recreation Opportunity Guide* for the Four Peaks area.

Directions: Various trailheads are accessible from either AZ 87 or AZ 188.

Activities: Hiking, camping, nature study, and hunting.

Facilities: None.

Dates: Open year-round, but lower elevations are dangerously hot during summer.

Fees: None.

Closest town: Mesa, 25 miles.

For more information: Mesa Ranger District, PO Box 5800, Mesa, AZ 85211-5800. Phone (602) 379-6446.

FOUR PEAKS TRAIL

[Fig. 36(15)] This route is popular and easy to follow. The trail skirts the east end of Browns Peak, the highest of the four.

Directions: Drive north from Mesa about 21 miles on AZ 87 to FR 143, which is about 11.5 miles north of the Verde River bridge and just past the Desert Vista Rest Stop. Turn east and follow FR 143 almost 19 miles to El Oso Divide. Then turn right (south) onto FR 648 and continue 1.3 miles to the trailhead at Lone Pine Saddle. A high-clearance vehicle is recommended.

Trail: 4 miles one-way.

Degree of difficulty: Moderate.

Elevation: 5,700 to 6,100 feet.

Surface: Rocky.

THREE BAR WILDLIFE ENCLOSURE MOUNTAIN BIKE RIDE

[Fig. 36(16)] Adjacent to the east boundary of the wilderness area is the Three Bar Wildlife Enclosure, a fenced area being studied by the Arizona Game and Fish Department biologists. Mountain bikers enjoy pedaling FR 647 from AZ 188 into the wildlife enclosure and back to the highway. The route is a 6.6-mile loop (with another mile along the highway to complete the loop) that takes you past riparian habitat and chaparral. At either end of your ride, you can take a cooling dip in Roosevelt Lake. While bikes are welcome on established Forest Service roads and some trails, they are not allowed inside the wilderness area.

For more information: Mesa Ranger District, PO Box 5800, Mesa, AZ 85211-5800. Phone (602) 379-6446.

SUPERSTITION WILDERNESS

[Fig. 36(17)] The Superstition Mountains, alleged site of the legendary Lost Dutchman Mine, were first designated as wilderness in 1940 and expanded in 1984 to include a total of 160,200 acres. The area is starkly beautiful and rugged and attracts many hikers, horseback riders, and budding prospectors. Habitats range from Sonoran desert to oak woodland to pinyon-juniper woodland to riparian communities of netleaf hackberry, Arizona black walnut, Fremont cottonwood, and Arizona sycamore. At the highest elevations are a few pockets of ponderosa pine.

Summer visitors must contend with searing heat and lack of water. Bitter cold, rains and even snowstorms may occur in the winter, but spring and fall are usually delightful. After a wet winter, spring visitors are rewarded with carpets of Mexican gold poppy (*Eschscholtzia mexicana*) and bajada lupine (*Lupinus concinnus*). This is also a good time for birding, with cactus wrens (*Campylorhynchus brunneicapillus*), curve-billed thrashers (*Toxostoma curvirostre*), Gambel's quail (*Callipepla gambelii*), Gila woodpeckers (*Melanerpes uropygialis*), ash-throated flycatchers (*Myiarchus cinerascens*), black-throated sparrows (*Amphispiza bilineata*), and greater roadrunners (*Geococcyx californianus*) commonly observed.

People probably have used the Superstition Mountains for millennia. The earliest known use was by hunting and gathering groups making forays from nearby river valleys in 700 and 800. The agrarian Hohokam later settled the area. After about 1200, new forms of architecture and culture appeared. Either the Hohokam adopted new ideas from the Salado or were replaced by them.

Between 1200 and 1400, the Salado occupied a number of places within the wilderness area. The broken terrain, poor soils, and general lack of water kept most of their villages and cliff dwellings quite small. One of their hilltop structures may have functioned as a calendric observatory; however, little is known about this culture.

By 1400, various economical and political stresses caused the downfall of prehistoric civilizations throughout most of Arizona. For the next century or two, the Superstitions became what the early Spanish explorers called a *despoblado* or depopulated area. The Pima Indians of the Salt-Gila River Basin continued to hunt and visit the area. After about 1500, the Southeastern Yavapai occupied the vicinity. From that time until the arrival of the Anglo-Americans in the mid-1800s, these mountains were almost exclusively Southeastern Yavapai territory.

Although frequent references to the Apaches are heard in the Superstitions, they actually made little use of the area. Much of the confusion probably resulted from the tendency of Anglo-Americans in the Southwest to label all Indians as Apaches.

The Coronado Expedition passed to the east of the area in 1540 (*see* page 180), but few Europeans, if any, explored the Superstitions until the 1800s. After Arizona became part of the U.S. territory at the end of the Mexican-American War in 1848, Anglo-Americans began to filter into the area. The 1870s and 1880s were boom times in central Arizona, with substantial mining activity around the edge of the Superstition volcanic field.

Rumors still abound concerning the Lost Dutchman Mine and other gold deposits supposedly located in the Superstitions. Jacob Waltz, who was actually German, not Dutch, claimed to have rediscovered gold mines originally developed by the Peralta family of Sonora, Mexico. After Waltz's death in 1891, his story became embellished to legendary proportions. Despite the fact that the area's geology is not conducive to these types of deposits, many hopeful prospectors have combed the Superstitions for decades. Robert Sikorsky's *Quest for the Dutchman's Gold* details the facts, myths, and legends of this "lost mine."

Around the turn of the century, several ranches were established in and around the Superstitions. They supplied beef to the military and to the mining towns of Silver King and Pinal. The Miles Ranch in the southeast corner of the wilderness and the Reavis Ranch were purchased by the U.S. government in 1966.

The geologic history of the Superstition Wilderness is quite complex. During the Tertiary Period, there was much volcanic activity, including lava flows and explosive eruptions. These lavas, tuffs, and agglomerates were deposited on deeply eroded Precambrian granites and schists.

Some 12 trailheads allow access to about 180 miles of trail in varying condition. Some are unsuitable for horses. The western end of the wilderness receives heavy use during the cooler months, but the eastern side is less visited. Directions to the various trailheads and trail descriptions are available from the Forest Service in its *Recreation Opportunity Guide* for the area and in *Hiker's Guide to the Superstitions* by Jack Carlson and Elizabeth Stewart. Rock climbers test their skill in ascending Weaver's Needle, a 4,553-foot volcanic plug in the southeast corner of the wilderness. Remember that climbers' bolts and pitons are forbidden in the wilderness.

Directions: Most of the trailheads are accessible from either the Apache Trail (AZ 88) or US 60.

Activities: Hiking, camping, horseback riding, nature study, rock climbing, and hunting.

Facilities: None.

Dates: Open year-round, although summers are dangerously hot.

Fees: Although there is no permit or entrance fee required, some of the popular trailheads do have a parking fee.

Closest town: Apache Junction, 7 miles.

For more information: Mesa Ranger District, PO Box 5800, Mesa, AZ 85211-5800. Phone (602) 379-6446.

PERALTA TRAIL

[Fig. 36(18)] The Peralta Trail climbs 1,300 feet in about 2 miles to Fremont Saddle where you have a great view of Weaver's Needle. The pinnacle was named for Pauline Weaver, a locally famous mountain man.

Directions: Drive 8.5 miles southeast from Apache Junction on US 60 to the Peralta Road (FR 77). Turn left and drive 8 miles to the trailhead. Parking fee required.

Trail: 6.3 miles.
Degree of difficulty: Moderate.
Elevation: 1,680 to 3,000 feet.
Surface: Rocky.

▨ TONTO NATIONAL FOREST CAMPGROUNDS

Camping at large is generally allowed throughout the Tonto National Forest except in high-use areas and recreation areas. The Tonto does have 29 developed campsites. See Appendix G for a table of information on individual campgrounds.

Apache Trail Scenic Byway

[Fig. 36(19)] Running between Globe and Apache Junction and roughly following the course of the Salt River is the highly scenic Apache Trail (AZ 88). This route traverses beautiful Sonoran desert, forbidding canyons, and skirts sparkling man-made lakes. The road also allows access to the Superstition Wilderness. The 38-mile stretch from Apache Junction was built in 1904 to carry supplies and equipment to the 4,000 laborers constructing Roosevelt Dam. Within a year, 1.5 million pounds of freight were arriving every month by mule train. More than 30 men died during the dangerous construction of the dam and road including Al Sieber, a legendary scout during the Apache Wars, who was crushed by a boulder.

In 1988, this section was designated a National Forest Scenic Byway. Only the first 17 miles from Apache Junction are paved. The remaining 21 miles are winding and occasionally narrow but safe to careful, slow drivers. One highlight is Fish Creek Hill, where the one-lane road (with turnouts) drops more than 1,000 feet at a 15 to 17 percent grade. Check your brakes.

From Roosevelt Dam to Globe, about 40 miles, the road is paved. The old copper mining town of Globe has preserved many of its historic buildings. Pick up a free tour pamphlet at the Globe Chamber of Commerce. Also, just 1.25 miles southwest of downtown are the Besh-Ba-Gowah ruins and museum. The name is an Apache phrase meaning "place of metal." Here visitors are encouraged to enter the rooms of this 700-year-old Salado pueblo, climb ladders into the upper stories, and see the utensils, pottery, and other items that were a part of life in pre-Columbian times.

Some of the pueblo is original, while other sections have been stabilized and some completely reconstructed. There are also earlier habitation sites here—pit houses built by the Hohokam around 900 and abandoned two centuries later. A museum houses a wide range of Salado pottery, clothing, tools, and other artifacts. An ethno-botanical garden illustrates how native plants were used by the Salado to provide food, fibers, construction materials, and dyes. Adjacent is the newly opened Globe Botanical Garden.

For more information: Mesa Ranger District, 26 MacDonald, Suite 120, Mesa, AZ 85201. Phone (602) 379-6446. Besh-Ba-Gowah Archaeological Park, 150 N. Pine St., Globe, AZ 85501. Phone (480) 425-0320. Globe Chamber of Commerce, phone (800) 804-5623.

🏜 SALT RIVER LAKES

Beginning in 1905, a series of dams were built on the Salt River to create reservoirs to provide irrigation water and hydroelectric power for the Phoenix metropolitan area.

Roosevelt Lake Recreation Area is formed by the 284-foot high Theodore Roosevelt Dam, which was built between 1905 and 1911. It was renovated between 1991 and 1995. The lake is 23 miles long and has more than 88 miles of shoreline. The 23,200-acre lake sprawls across a wide desert valley. There are six boat ramps scattered along the south and west shores. There are also several developed campgrounds as well as a marina resort, trailer park, grocery store, gas station, ranger station, and a visitor center with maps, exhibits and bookstore. Anglers go after largemouth bass and crappie.

Adjacent to the north shore of the lake is the Roosevelt Lake Wildlife Area. Tonto Creek, which flows into the north arm of the lake, is popular with waterfowl, quail, and small game hunters.

Those interested in history should stop at the Tonto Basin Ranger Station, located about 1.5 miles southeast of the dam on AZ 88 and ask for directions to the old Roosevelt Cemetery. A free Forest Service pamphlet, *Roosevelt Cemetery: Reminiscing a Lost Era*, tells the story of the community of Roosevelt that emerged from the desert in 1905. The 2,000 residents had come to build the world's highest masonry dam.

Horse Mesa Dam, constructed between 1924 and 1927, created Apache Lake Recreation Area. The 2,656-acre lake is 17 miles long and has more than 40 miles of shoreline squeezed between the high rugged slopes of the Four Peaks Wilderness and the Superstition Wilderness. There are two boat ramps accessible from the Apache Trail and a small marina with gas, motel, coffee shop, and supplies.

Smallmouth bass and crappie fishing is usually good. Largemouth bass and walleye also lurk in the shallows.

Canyon Lake Recreation Area resulted from the construction of Mormon Flat Dam, which was built between 1923 and 1925. This 950-acre reservoir is 10 miles long and has more than 28 miles of shoreline. There are two boat ramps at the southwest end of the lake and a small marina with a restaurant, gas, a convenience store, boat rentals, and camping. Smallmouth bass and catfish fishing can be excellent.

Saguaro Lake Recreation Area was formed by the construction of Stewart Mountain Dam, built between 1928 and 1930. The 1,280-acre lake is about 10 miles long and has about 22 miles of shoreline. There are two boat ramps at the lake's west end, which are accessed from the Bush Highway (FR 204) about 5 miles south of AZ 87.

This is a favorite lake for catfish. Below Stewart Mountain Dam, trout fishing can be very good. For a recorded message of fishing conditions, call the fishing hotline at (602) 789-3701.

For more information: Roosevelt Lake Visitor Center, HC 02, Box 4800, Roosevelt, AZ 85545. Phone (520) 467-3200.

TONTO NATIONAL MONUMENT

[Fig. 36(20)] Tonto National Monument protects two cliff dwellings built by the Salado culture about 700 years ago. A 0.5 mile self-guiding trail climbs 350 feet to the 19-room lower ruin. Allow about an hour for the round trip. The 40-room upper ruin may be visited only on a conducted tour; contact the park staff before your visit.

Today, these ruins overlook Roosevelt Lake in the Tonto Basin, but in the fourteenth century, only the Salt River and Tonto Creek meandered through the valley. These two streams nourished thick stands of mesquite, Arizona black walnut, and Arizona sycamore. The hillsides and mesas, then as now, supported saguaro, cholla, prickly pear, agave, and jojoba. A few pinyon and junipers survive on the higher hilltops. Deer, rabbit, quail, and other game flourished.

By 850, people from the lower Gila and Salt River valleys (near present-day Phoenix), the Hohokam, were living in pit house villages in the Tonto Basin. After several centuries, for reasons not yet understood, the Hohokam seem to have been replaced by a new culture, the Salado.

Like their predecessors, the Salado also farmed the basin, irrigating fields of corn, beans, pumpkins, amaranth (*Amaranthus* sp.), and cotton. They hunted and gathered wild plant foods from the surrounding hills. They exchanged surplus food and goods with neighboring tribes, joining a trade network that reached from Colorado to Mexico. As the Salado prospered, their numbers increased. By the early 1300s, some people had migrated up into the foothills.

The Salado constructed apartment-style dwellings for sleeping, storage, cooking, and protection. The lower dwelling consisted of 16 ground level rooms, three of which had a second story. Next to this was a 12-room annex. The upper site had 32 ground floor rooms, eight with a second story. Apparently, some hill-dwellers began to specialize in weaving and pottery making, trading their wares for food and cotton grown in the valley. Sometime between 1400 and 1450, the Salado abandoned the area. Exactly why they left and where they went is still not known.

When construction of the nearby Roosevelt Dam began in 1906, the ruins became a target for pothunters and vandals. To help protect the site, then-President Theodore Roosevelt proclaimed the area a national monument.

Directions: The monument is located on AZ 88 about 29 miles northwest of Globe.

Activities: Self-guided hike to the lower cliff dwelling or ranger-led hike to the upper site.

Facilities: Visitor center, picnic area, and restrooms.

Dates: Open daily except Christmas.

Fees: There is an entry fee.

Closest town: Globe, about 29 miles southeast.

For more information: Tonto National Monument, PO Box 707, Roosevelt, AZ 855545. Phone (602) 467-2241. Web site www.nps.gov/tont.

SAN CARLOS APACHE RESERVATION

The 1.8 million-acre San Carlos Apache Reservation lies immediately south of the White Mountain Apache Reservation (*see* page 181). The Salt River and the Black River (which a National Park Service national river inventory concluded was "the one of the wildest rivers in Arizona") comprise the natural boundary between the two reservations. The natural setting ranges from cool, coniferous forest to blazing Sonoran desert. The 10,000 or so San Carlos Apaches live primarily in San Carlos, the tribal headquarters, and Bylas. Smaller settlements include Peridot, Eight Mile Wash, Calva, and Cutter.

Visitors can witness some of the traditional dances and ceremonies. The most popular of these is the Sunrise Ceremony, which celebrates the coming of age of Apache girls. This and other ceremonial dances often take place on summer weekends in or near San Carlos. The Tribal Rodeo and Fair held over Veterans Day weekend is another important event. For more information, contact the tribal office at (480) 475-2361.

Trout, bass, catfish, and crappie fishing are plentiful in the more than 100 lakes and ponds to be found on the reservation. Anglers, boaters, and hikers can find developed campsites at Point of Pines and San Carlos, Talkalai, and Seneca lakes. When full, the man-made San Carlos Lake is the largest body of water on the reservation (*see* page 181). There are endless opportunities for backcountry exploration, too.

Hunting on the reservation is also a thriving business. Pronghorn, bighorn sheep, deer, small game, and birds attract hunters. Record-size elk are not uncommon.

Remember that permits are required to camp, picnic, hunt, fish, boat, hike, or venture onto the back roads. And go properly equipped. Seneca and San Carlos Lakes can be reached via paved roads, but roads to other recreation sites may be rough. Particularly during the July and August rainy season and following winter snowfalls in the high country, the unpaved reservation roads are best traveled by high-clearance, four-wheel-drive vehicles.

Like their Apache neighbors to the north, the San Carlos Apaches have their own casino called Apache Gold. It is located 6 miles east of Globe on US 70.

For more information: San Carlos Recreation and Wildlife Department, PO Box 97, San Carlos, AZ 85550. Phone (520) 475-2343 or (888) 275-2653.

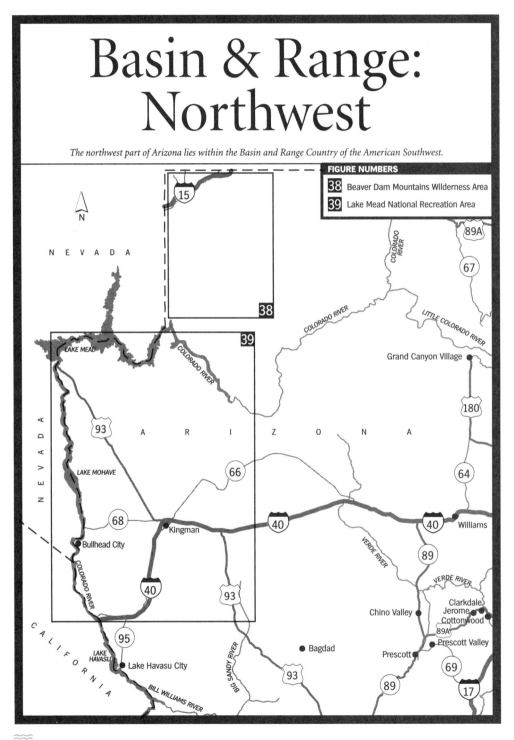

Basin & Range: Northwest

The northwest part of Arizona lies within the Basin and Range Country of the American Southwest.

FIGURE NUMBERS

38 Beaver Dam Mountains Wilderness Area

39 Lake Mead National Recreation Area

NEVADA

NEVADA

ARIZONA

CALIFORNIA

COLORADO RIVER

COLORADO RIVER

COLORADO RIVER

LITTLE COLORADO RIVER

VERDE RIVER

VERDE RIVER

BIG SANDY RIVER

BILL WILLIAMS RIVER

LAKE MEAD

LAKE MOHAVE

LAKE HAVASU

Grand Canyon Village

Kingman

Bullhead City

Lake Havasu City

Bagdad

Chino Valley

Clarkdale
Jerome
Cottonwood

Prescott Valley

Prescott

Williams

Basin and Range: Northwest

The northwest part of Arizona lies within the Basin and Range Country of the American Southwest. Here elements of the Great Basin, Mohave, and Sonoran deserts come together, giving the plant and animal communities eclectic mixtures. For example, juniper, Joshua tree (*Yucca brevifolia*), and saguaro cactus (*Cereus giganteus*) can be found living together, as well as reptiles such as the racer (*Coluber constrictor*), Mohave sidewinder (*Crotalus cerastes cerastes*), and Gila monster (*Heloderma suspectum*).

In spite of the fact that three very busy highways—I-15, I-40, and US 93—cross the region, this is lonesome country. Once the visitor leaves the pavement, he needs to be well prepared. From a distance, the scattered mountain ranges shimmer in the summer heat and are not inviting (*see* warnings about mountain and desert travel, page IX), but return in the spring or fall to explore their secret places and a world of delicate beauty set amidst naked rock will be revealed.

[*Above:* 1,500-foot-deep Black Canyon is popular with canoeists and kayakers]

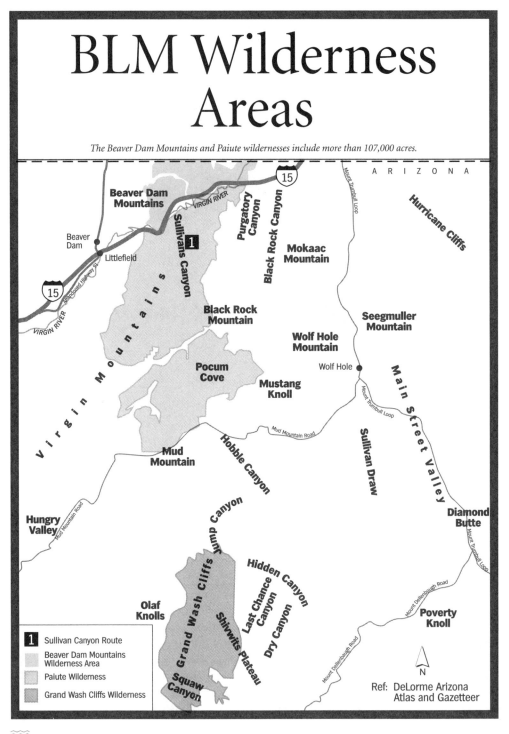

BLM Wilderness Areas

The Beaver Dam Mountains and Paiute wildernesses include more than 107,000 acres.

ARIZONA

15

Beaver Dam Mountains

VIRGIN RIVER

Purgatory Canyon

Black Rock Canyon

Mount Trumbull Loop

Hurricane Cliffs

Beaver Dam

Littlefield

Sullivans Canyon

1

Mokaac Mountain

15

Abandoned Highway 91

VIRGIN RIVER

Virgin Mountains

Black Rock Mountain

Seegmuller Mountain

Wolf Hole Mountain

Wolf Hole

Main Street Valley

Pocum Cove

Mustang Knoll

Mud Mountain Road

Mount Trumbull Loop

Sullivan Draw

Hobble Canyon

Mud Mountain

Mud Mountain Road

Hungry Valley

Diamond Butte

Jump Canyon

Mount Trumbull Loop

Grand Wash Cliffs

Hidden Canyon

Last Chance Canyon

Dry Canyon

Mount Dellenbaugh Road

Poverty Knoll

Olaf Knolls

Shivwits Plateau

Mount Dellenbaugh Road

Squaw Canyon

1	Sullivan Canyon Route
	Beaver Dam Mountains Wilderness Area
	Paiute Wilderness
	Grand Wash Cliffs Wilderness

N

Ref: DeLorme Arizona Atlas and Gazetteer

Bureau of Land Management Wilderness Areas

⬛ BEAVER DAM MOUNTAINS WILDERNESS

[Fig. 38] This 19,600-acre wilderness is located in the extreme northwest corner of Arizona and spills over into Utah. There are no designated trails, but the wilderness is accessible from I-15 and from a dirt road that bisects the area.

This is a land of Joshua trees and desert tortoises (*Gopherus agassizi*). Peregrine falcon (*Falcon peregrinus*), common black-hawk (*Buteogallus anthracinus*), California leaf-nosed bat (*Macrotus californicus*), and spotted bat (*Euderma maculatum*) also reside here.

A 5-mile section of the Virgin River, one of the few remaining wild tributaries to the Colorado River, runs through this wilderness. The riparian corridor through this desert region is especially valuable to wildlife, including desert bighorn sheep (*Ovis canadensis*). The river has cut a spectacular gorge several hundred feet deep, exposing dramatic faulting and folding of the region's rock layers. Sometimes in the spring there is enough water to float a kayak or small raft. River runners put in at Bloomington, Utah and take out at the BLM Virgin River Campground, for a float of about 21 river miles, or they continue another 16 miles to Littlefield. Because of the shallow, rocky nature of the river and fast, strong currents, only experienced whitewater boaters should attempt this trip.

The river is also home to the endangered woundfin minnow (*Plagopterus argentissimus*) and Virgin River roundtail chub (*Gila robusta seminuda*), as well as the Virgin River spikedace (*Lepidomeda mollispinus*).

Directions: Take I-15 about 16 miles southwest of St. George, UT and exit at the Cedar Pocket Road and BLM Virgin River Campground. The dirt Cedar Pockets Road goes north and for the next 7 miles passes through the wilderness area.

Activities: Hiking, camping, river running, and nature study.

Facilities: None in wilderness, but there is a BLM campground at the interstate exit.

Dates: Open year-round.

Fees: None for the wilderness. There is a fee for the BLM campground.

Closest town: Littlefield, 10 miles southwest.

For more information: BLM, Arizona Strip Field Office, 345 East Riverside Dr., St. George, UT 84790. Phone (435) 688-3200. Web site www.az.blm.gov.

⬛ PAIUTE WILDERNESS

[Fig. 38] Lying immediately south of I-15 in the northwest corner of Arizona is the 87,900-acre Paiute Wilderness. The Virgin Mountains form the backbone of this

Rattlesnakes

Arizona has 11 species of rattlesnakes (*Crotalus* sp.), the most of any state. Rattlesnakes are members of the pit viper family, named for a depression in the loreal scale, which is slightly behind and below the nostril. The snake uses the pit to sense heat. This organ is so sensitive that it can detect heat from a candle flame 30 feet away. The snakes use this pit to hunt in the dark and to avoid larger, non-prey animals that give off larger heat images.

Rattlesnakes have long, curved fangs that lie parallel to the jaw line when not in use. During a strike, the fangs rotate to a perpendicular position. They are hollow and pump venom into the victim like a hypodermic needle. Their venom, which is actually toxic saliva, is a complex mixture of enzymes unique to pit vipers. The venom probably evolved not so much to be a defensive weapon (though it can be quite effective) but rather to help in capturing prey and partially digesting the meal.

Rattlesnakes do not have to be coiled to strike, nor do they always rattle. Fortunately, with a little care, rattlesnake encounters can be avoided. Most bites to adult humans are the result of human provocation or reaching under rocks or bushes, where snakes like to rest. Those who are bitten rarely die, less than 1 percent.

area, rising more than 5,600 feet above the desert floor. Mount Bangs, the highest peak in the area at 8,012 feet, provides a commanding view of the Basin and Range country to the north and west and the Arizona Strip to the east and south. A section of the Virgin River runs through the wilderness and attracts river runners experienced with floating capricious desert streams.

The area's vegetation varies, ranging from ponderosa pine (*Pinus ponderosa*) on top of Mount Bangs, through singleleaf pinyon (*Pinus monophylla*) woodlands on the higher slopes, to scrub oak (*Quercus* sp.) and sagebrush (*Artemesia* sp.) on the lower slopes. Around the area's perimeter are Joshua trees, yucca (*Yucca* sp.), and barrel cactus (*Ferocactus* sp.). These plant communities host over 250 animal species, including mule deer (*Odocoileus hemionus*), mountain lion (*Felis concolor*), desert bighorn sheep, and desert tortoise.

Part of this wilderness area is now included in the new Grand Canyon-Parashant National Monument (*see* page 23), but it will remain under BLM management.

Directions: Take I-15 about 16 miles southwest of St. George, UT and exit at the Cedar Pocket Road and BLM Virgin River Campground. The wilderness lies south of I-15 and the Virgin River.

Activities: Hiking, camping, river running, and nature study.

Facilities: None in the wilderness, but there is a BLM campground at the interstate exit.

Dates: Open year-round.

Fees: None for the wilderness. There is a fee for the BLM campground.

Closest town: Littlefield, 10 miles southwest.

For more information: BLM, Arizona Strip Field Office, 345 East Riverside Dr., St. George, UT 84790. Phone (435) 688-3200. Web site www.az.blm.gov.

SULLIVAN CANYON ROUTE

[Fig. 38(1)] There are no established trails leading into the wilderness from the BLM campground, but a popular route follows Sullivan Canyon. This canyon is a good introduction to the natural features of the Paiute Wilderness.

Directions: From the BLM campground's upper loop, follow a trail down to the Virgin River. If possible, ford the river and follow the south bank 1.5 miles downstream to the mouth of Sullivan Canyon. If the river is running high, do not attempt to cross it.

Trail: This is not an established trail, but you can follow the canyon bottom 8 miles or more. Additional routes (not trails) lead out of the canyon to Mount Bangs.

Degree of difficulty: Strenuous.

Elevation: 2,000 feet up to 8,012 feet at the summit of Mount Bangs.

Surface: Rocky.

MOUNT WILSON WILDERNESS

[Fig. 39(4)] This 23,900-acre wilderness encompasses 5,445-foot-high Mount Wilson, the highest and most prominent topographic point in the Hoover Dam region. Wilson Ridge extends from the summit north and south about 18 miles. Roughly half of its length is within Lake Mead National Recreation Area. From the summit, you can see the entire Lake Mead-Lake Mohave area; Eldorado, McCullough, and Spring mountains in Nevada; and the Cerbat and Hualapai ranges near Kingman. Wilson Ridge breaks off dramatically on the west towards Lake Mohave and on the east towards the flat, broad Detrital Valley.

Vegetation is sparse except in the washes; only creosote (*Larrea tridentata*) and bursage (*Ambrosia* sp.) survive on the stark granitic rock. Nonetheless the landscape is impressive with richly colored rocks, intricately carved canyons, and more than 3,000 feet of vertical relief. Much of the area is critical range for the more than 100 desert bighorn sheep that live here.

Directions: From Kingman, travel 50 miles north on US 93 to the Temple Bar Road turnoff. Continue on the paved Temple Bar Road for 10.7 miles to an unpaved jeep trail that heads northwest 3 miles to the wilderness boundary. From here, it is possible to hike cross-country to Mount Wilson. The Lake Mead

RATTLESNAKE
(*Crotalus* sp.)

Desert Tortoise

Desert tortoises (*Gopherus agassizi*) are one of four species of North American land turtles. Desert tortoises live in the Mohave and Sonoran deserts. They court and mate in the spring, then the females lay from three to seven eggs in sandy soil, where they incubate for approximately 90 days. When the eggs hatch in August or September, the hatchlings are less than 2 inches long and do not have a hard shell. In the four to five years it takes for the shell to ossify, they are vulnerable to predation by ravens, coyotes, and other animals. If they survive, biologists believe the tortoises can live 50 to 60 years in the wild. Older adults may be more than 1 foot in length and weigh nearly 10 pounds.

Tortoises store their metabolic waste not as urine, which is water soluble, but as uric acid, which is not. Because of this, tortoises can use their bladders as internal canteens, storing water when it is available for reuse during times of drought. They can also extract moisture from succulent vegetation.

Tortoise populations have been drastically reduced in recent years because of illegal collection as pets, competition with livestock for food, urban development of their habitat, and a mysterious, fatal bacterial upper respiratory disease possibly introduced by the release of pet tortoises.

National Recreation Area administers most of the lands surrounding the wilderness. Obey all National Park Service public use and off-road-vehicle restrictions when accessing the Mount Wilson wilderness. Some lands around the wilderness are privately owned; please respect the property rights of the owners and do not cross or use these lands without their permission. Check with the BLM for current accessibility.

Activities: Hiking, camping, and nature study.

Facilities: None.

Dates: Open year-round, but summers are too hot for hiking.

Fees: None.

Closest town: Kingman, about 64 miles south.

For more information: BLM, Kingman Field Office, 2475 Beverly Avenue, Kingman, AZ 86401. Phone (520) 692-4400. Web site www.az.blm.gov.

MOUNT TIPTON WILDERNESS

[Fig. 39(5)] The 30,706-acre Mount Tipton Wilderness takes in the entire northern half of the imposing Cerbat Mountains. Elevations range from 3,400 feet near Cane Spring up to the 7,148-foot summit of Mount Tipton. The mountains rise abruptly from flat valleys—Detrital Valley on the west and Hualapai Valley on the east. Located north of and below Mount Tipton are the Pinnacles, immense tusk-like rows of maroon-colored spires, standing majestically above open, tawny-colored valleys.

Large and topographically complex, the Mount Tipton Wilderness provides a wide range of hiking, backpacking, photography, and horseback riding opportunities.

Vegetation ranges from Mohave Desert scrub consisting of creosote, blackbrush

DESERT TORTOISE
(Gopherus agassizi)

(*Colegyne ramosissima*), and Joshua trees to stands of ponderosa pine at the upper elevations. In between are areas covered with chaparral and grasslands of primarily black grama (*Bouteloua eriopoda*). Canyon bottoms contain pockets of riparian vegetation, which is extremely important to the wildlife, including mule deer, bobcat (*Felis rufus*), mountain lion, various raptors, and many of the other 200-plus species of vertebrates.

The Mount Tipton Wilderness is also home to herds of mustangs or feral horses. They are descended from animals released by or escaped from early prospectors and other people traveling through the area. In spite of BLM efforts to eliminate the wild horses, the herds continue to thrive and compete with the native animals for forage.

Directions: From Kingman, travel approximately 35 miles north along the Stockton Hill Road to the Cane Springs Ranch Road turnoff. Continue along Cane Springs Ranch Road for 2 miles and stop at the ranch house for permission to continue on the final mile to the wilderness boundary, much of which is across private property. The southern boundary of the wilderness can also be easily accessed via the BLM-maintained Chloride/Big Wash Road. The Chloride/Big Wash Road turnoff is located 1.5 miles north of the Chloride turnoff on US 93. The wilderness lies immediately to the north of the Chloride/Big Wash Road as it begins its steep, switchbacking ascent to the crest of the Cerbat Range. Please respect the property rights of private landowners and do not cross or use these lands without their permission. Check with the BLM for current accessibility.

Activities: Hiking, camping, and nature study.

Facilities: None.

Dates: Open year-round, but summers are too hot for hiking.

Fees: None.

Closest town: Kingman, about 38 miles south.

For more information: BLM, Kingman Field Office, 2475 Beverly Avenue, Kingman, AZ 86401. Phone (520) 692-4400. Web site www.az.blm.gov.

🏵 MOUNT NUTT WILDERNESS

[Fig. 39(6)] There are no established trails in the Mount Nutt Wilderness, but many of the wash and canyon bottoms provide access to hikers. Hiking, camping, hunting, photography, and rock scrambling opportunities are varied and challenging. Map study is essential.

Animals That Don't Drink

Wouldn't it be handy for desert animals if they didn't have to drink water or even acquire it from succulent food? In Arizona, the kangaroo rat (*Dipodomys* sp.) and pocket mouse (*Perognathus* sp.) can do just that. These mammals have no sweat glands, a complex nasal passageway that recovers water vapor as the animal exhales, extremely efficient kidneys that produce urine twice as concentrated as sea water, and feces five times drier than a lab rat's droppings. More moisture is conserved by only coming out of their burrows at night, when the ambient temperature is lower and relative humidity higher. They eat primarily dry, high carbohydrate seeds, which, when metabolized produce enough water for survival.

Mount Nutt, at 5,216 feet, caps the southern portion of the Black Mountains. Within the 27,660-acre wilderness, craggy peaks and pinnacles, varying in color from pink to buff to brown, tower over deep canyons. Along the main ridgeline, prominent mesas have been cut into a series of steep mazelike canyons. Outward from the main ridgeline, numerous huge volcanic plugs ring the entire wilderness. Prehistoric red, black, and white pictographs have been discovered here, and a cave shows human occupation extending from 3,500 years ago to about A.D. 1400.

The lower slopes support Mohave Desert scrub, whereas the higher elevations have juniper and grassland. Several springs feed riparian areas of netleaf hackberry (*Celtis reticulata*), cottonwood, willow, and oak. At Fig Tree Spring, introduced figs (*Ficus* sp.) flourish.

The wilderness is critical bighorn sheep habitat. Other wildlife residents include desert tortoise, Gila monster, and ferruginous and Swainson's hawk (*Buteo regalis* and *B. swainsoni*). There is also the endemic Mount Nutt snail, a species of gastropod found nowhere else.

Directions: From Kingman, travel 3 miles south on I-40 to the Oatman Road Exit. Travel approximately 10 miles west on Oatman Road to the Navajo Road junction. Travel west on Navajo Road 2 miles to the wilderness boundary. The west side of the wilderness can also be accessed from several weathered jeep trails (four-wheel-drive required) that intersect the Silver Creek Road. The Silver Creek Road is an unpaved, county-maintained road that connects Oatman and Bullhead City. Some lands around and within the wilderness are not federally administered. Please respect the property rights of the owners and do not cross or use these lands without their permission.

Activities: Hiking, camping, and nature study.

Facilities: None.

Dates: Open year-round, but too hot in the summer for hiking.

Fees: None.

Closest town: Kingman, about 15 miles east.

For more information: BLM, Kingman Field Office, 2475 Beverly Avenue, Kingman, AZ 86401. Phone (520) 692-4400. Web site www.az.blm.gov.

WARM SPRINGS WILDERNESS

[Fig. 39(7)] Several miles southeast of the old mining town of Oatman is the 112,400-acre Warm Springs Wilderness. The wilderness area encircles an immense and pristine desert landscape. One thousand feet above the surrounding desert, the 10-mile-long Black Mesa dominates the wilderness. Its edges are dissected into a maze of winding canyons. Remnant mesas and isolated hills dot a vast, encircling alluvial apron.

The steep mountain slopes are covered with brittlebush (*Encelia* sp.) and Bigelow nolina (*Nolina bigelovii*). The summit of Black Mesa has prominent stands of Mohave yucca (*Yucca schidigera*), a plant that is harvested (outside the wilderness area) for fertilizer and landscaping. Smoke trees (*Dalea spinosa*) are also found here. In the spring following a wet winter, this area unveils a notably colorful wildflower display, including ocotillos (*Fouquieria splendens*), blooming annuals, shrubs, and cacti.

Besides the usual Mohave Desert animals, there is quite a population of feral burros, descended from animals released by early miners. The burros eat almost any kind of vegetation and are major competitors with the native bighorn sheep and other mammals. The BLM claims to have trapped and removed more burros from this area than any other location in Arizona.

Water at Warm Springs and other springs allows for extended camping trips. Also near these water sources are often found petroglyphs, providing clues to early Indian use of the area. There are no maintained trails, but equestrians and hikers often utilize the numerous burro trails. Carry plenty of water and a good map.

Directions: From Kingman, travel 3 miles south on I-40 to the Oatman Road Exit. Beginning about 12 miles down the Oatman Road, several four-wheel-drive roads lead south to the wilderness boundary. Some lands around the wilderness are not federally administered. Please respect the property rights of the owners and do not cross or use these lands without their permission.

Activities: Hiking, horseback riding, camping, and nature study.

Facilities: None.

Dates: Open year-round, but summers are too hot for hiking.

Closest town: Kingman, about 20 miles northeast.

For more information: BLM, Kingman Field Office, 2475 Beverly Avenue, Kingman, AZ 86401. Phone (520) 692-4400. Web site www.az.blm.gov.

KANGAROO RAT
(*Dipodomys* sp.)

WABAYUMA PEAK WILDERNESS

[Fig. 39(3)] At the southern end of the Hualapai Mountains is Wabayuma Peak, towering and tortuous at 7,610 feet. A series of massive ridges that extend from the peak in a semicircle to the north, south, and west plunge nearly 5,000 feet to the desert floor below.

At the base of the range, the vegetation is a curious mix of Mohave and Sonoran desert species, with Joshua trees growing next to saguaro cactus. The mountain summits rise high enough above the desert to support stands of ponderosa pine. Hikers and horseback riders enjoy this wilderness year-round, but especially during the winter, when other parts of northern Arizona are snowbound.

Along the 40,000-acre wilderness's southeast boundary is Boriana Canyon, where rock hounds can look for ores of copper, lead, zinc, gold, and silver. However, do not enter any signed closed areas or mine shafts.

Directions: From Kingman, drive 14 miles southeast on the Hualapai Mountain Road to the Hualapai Mountain County Park. Continue 5 miles to Pine Lake, then turn right at the Pine Lake firehouse onto unpaved BLM Road 2123. Go another 13.5 miles to the wilderness area and trailhead. The Wabayuma Peak area can also be accessed via the rough four-wheel-drive McKensie Wash/Boriana Canyon Road out of Yucca, which is 20 miles south of Kingman along I-40. Just past the Boriana Mine, the Boriana Canyon Road becomes BLM Road 2123. Some lands around and within the wilderness are not federally administered. Please respect the property rights of the owners and do not cross or use these lands without their permission.

Activities: Hiking, horseback riding, camping, rock hounding, and nature study.

Facilities: None in wilderness, but there is a BLM campground at Pine Lake.

Dates: Open year-round.

Fees: None for wilderness, but there is a campground fee.

Closest town: Kingman, about 20 miles north.

For more information: BLM, Kingman Field Office, 2475 Beverly Avenue, Kingman, AZ 86401. Phone (520) 692-4400. Web site www.az.blm.gov.

WABAYUMA PEAK TRAIL

[Fig. 39(1)] The Wabayuma Peak Trail begins as an old jeep road. After about 2 miles, you reach the end of the jeep road in a saddle. The trail continues uphill to the northwest. Near the summit the trail becomes faint, but blaze marks on the large ponderosa pines will guide you to the top. From the peak are spectacular views of the Black Mountains to the west, the Aquarius Mountains to the east, and the Hualapai Mountain range to the north and south.

Directions: From Kingman, drive 14 miles on the paved Hualapai Mountain Road through the Hualapai Mountain County Park into the small community of Pine Lake. Turn right at the Pine Lake Fire Station onto an unpaved one-lane road. Follow signs to Wild Cow Springs Campground, but continue past the campground 13.5 miles to the trailhead. Park opposite the old jeep trail that takes off steeply up the hill.

Trail: 3 miles one-way.
Degree of difficulty: Moderate.
Elevation: 6,047 to 7,601 feet.
Surface and blaze: Rocky; marked with rock cairns and blazes.

Lake Mead National Recreation Area

[Fig. 39] In 1935, the 726-foot-high Hoover Dam was completed, the first of a series of dams built on the lower Colorado River in an effort to tame the muddy river that was "too thick to drink but too thin to plow." The 144-mile-long Lake Mead, the reservoir behind Hoover Dam, is the largest man-made lake in the U.S. Downstream, Davis Dam, completed in 1953, creates Lake Mohave. Together, Lake Mead and Lake Mohave, plus the surrounding desert in Arizona and Nevada, make up Lake Mead National Recreation Area.

Lake Mead National Recreation Area offers a wealth of things to do and places to go year-round. Twice the size of Rhode Island, its huge lakes cater to motor boaters, sailors, canoeists, and swimmers. A handy reference is Geoffrey Schneider and Rose Houk's *Lake Mead National Recreation Area Guide to Boating: Places to go and things to see.* Anglers try to hook striped bass (*Morane saxatilis*), largemouth bass (*Micropterus salmoides*), channel catfish (*Ictalurus punctatus*), black crappie (*Pomoxis nigromaculatus*), and bluegill (*Lepomis macrochirus*). Lake Mohave also contains

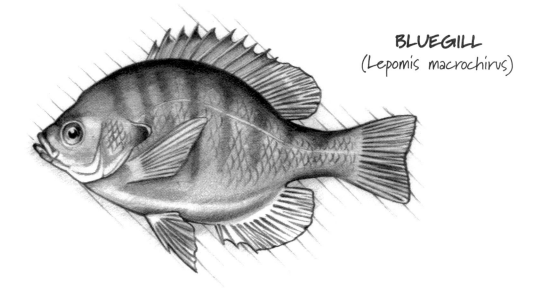

BLUEGILL
(Lepomis macrochirus)

Lake Mead N.R.A.

At 144-miles-long, Lake Mead is the largest man-made lake in the United States.

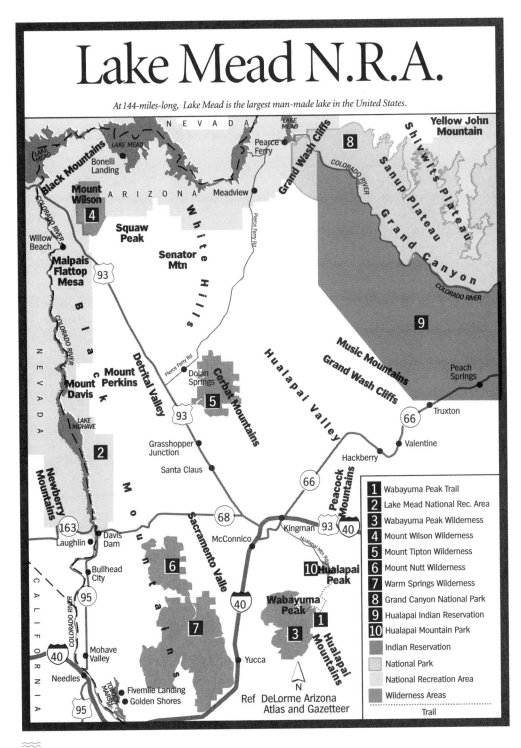

1 Wabayuma Peak Trail
2 Lake Mead National Rec. Area
3 Wabayuma Peak Wilderness
4 Mount Wilson Wilderness
5 Mount Tipton Wilderness
6 Mount Nutt Wilderness
7 Warm Springs Wilderness
8 Grand Canyon National Park
9 Hualapai Indian Reservation
10 Hualapai Mountain Park
   Indian Reservation
   National Park
   National Recreation Area
   Wilderness Areas
   Trail

Ref DeLorme Arizona
Atlas and Gazetteer

rainbow and cutthroat trout (*Oncorhynchus mykiss* and *O. clarki*). For a recorded message of fishing conditions, call the fishing hotline at (602) 789-3701.

The surrounding desert rewards hikers, wildlife photographers, and roadside sightseers. A good place to begin a visit is at the Alan Bible Visitor Center, 4 miles northeast of Boulder City, Nevada. The park staff can provide up-to-date information on park activities and services. An introductory movie, exhibits, books, brochures, and maps are available.

Willow Beach National Fish Hatchery, located along the upper reaches of Lake Mohave, raises large numbers of rainbow trout and conducts research on threatened and endangered fish species of the Colorado River. Visitors are welcome. Contact them at Willow Beach National Fish Hatchery, PO Box 757, Boulder City, NV 89005. Phone (520) 767-3456.

One part of the NRA of special interest to non-motorized boaters is 1,500-foot-deep **Black Canyon**. From the base of Hoover Dam to Willow Beach is a popular 12-mile float trip. For more information and permits, contact the Bureau of Reclamation, Attn: Canoe Launch Permits, PO Box 60400, Boulder City, NV 89006-0400. Phone (702) 293-8204.

Lake Mead National Recreation Area is one of the best places in Arizona to see the elusive desert bighorn sheep. Bighorn populations have been doing so well in the Black Mountains, along the eastern side of Lake Mohave, that the Arizona Game and Fish Department occasionally captures some of these animals for transplanting in other areas. For example, in 1999, the biologists captured 65 sheep. Forty-four were relocated to the Grand Wash Cliffs and Kanab Canyon, both on the Arizona Strip. The rest were traded to Utah for future introductions of pronghorn antelope and buffalo.

Directions: To reach Lake Mead from Kingman, drive 71 miles northwest on US 93 to Hoover Dam; the Alan Bible Visitor Center is another 4 miles into Nevada. To reach Lake Mohave from Bullhead City, drive about 6 miles north on AZ 95 to Davis Dam. From the dam, follow the signed road leading several miles to the lakeshore.

Activities: Guided tours of the dams, RV and tent camping, hiking, scenic driving, fishing, boating, swimming, and water skiing.

Facilities: Alan Bible and Hoover Dam visitor centers, marinas, lodges, swimming beaches, boat rentals, and campgrounds.

Dates: Open year-round.

Fees: There are recreational fees.

Closest town: Boulder City, NV.

For more information: Superintendent, Lake Mead National Recreation Area, 601 Nevada Highway, Boulder City, NV 89005-2426. Phone (702) 293-8907. Web site for Lake Mead NRA www.nps.gov/lame. Web site for Hoover Dam www.hooverdam.com.

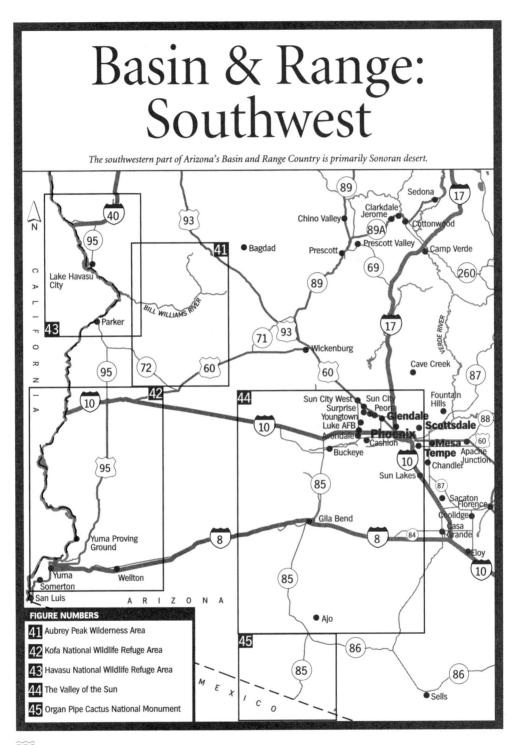

Basin & Range: Southwest

The southwestern part of Arizona's Basin and Range Country is primarily Sonoran desert.

FIGURE NUMBERS

- **41** Aubrey Peak Wilderness Area
- **42** Kofa National Wildlife Refuge Area
- **43** Havasu National Wildlife Refuge Area
- **44** The Valley of the Sun
- **45** Organ Pipe Cactus National Monument

Basin and Range: Southwest

The southwest section of Arizona's Basin and Range Country is primarily Sonoran desert. The relatively flat desert floor is punctuated by isolated mountain ranges. However, few of these ranges rise high enough for there to be significant changes in the kinds of plant and animal communities that live there. Flowing through this desert is the Colorado River and two of its major tributaries—the Bill Williams and Gila rivers.

The Sonoran desert can be an unforgiving place to visit, especially during the summer (*see* warning about mountain and desert travel, page IX). But travelers prepared with plenty of water and choosing the milder late fall through early spring months will discover one of the most unique biological areas in the United States.

The Bureau of Land Management administers much of the land within this area. There are also sizeable national wildlife refuges operated by the U.S. Fish and Wildlife

[*Above:* A stretch of El Camino del Diablo within the Cabeza Prieta National Wildlife Refuge]

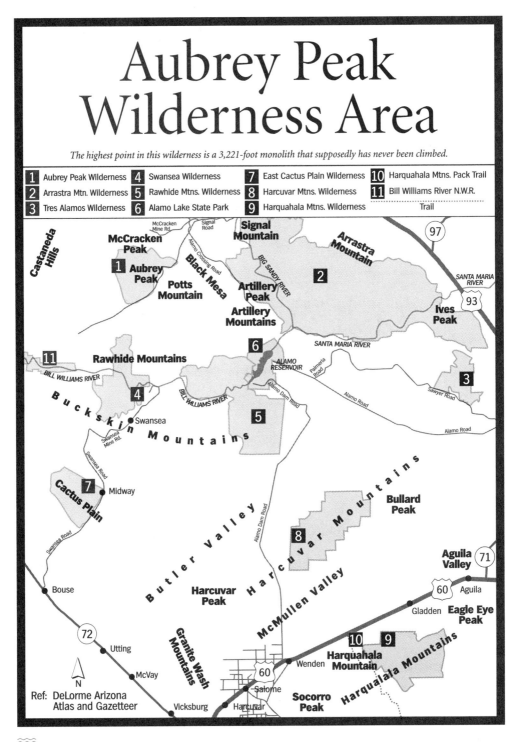

Aubrey Peak Wilderness Area

The highest point in this wilderness is a 3,221-foot monolith that supposedly has never been climbed.

1 Aubrey Peak Wilderness	**4** Swansea Wilderness	**7** East Cactus Plain Wilderness	**10** Harquahala Mtns. Pack Trail
2 Arrastra Mtn. Wilderness	**5** Rawhide Mtns. Wilderness	**8** Harcuvar Mtns. Wilderness	**11** Bill Williams River N.W.R.
3 Tres Alamos Wilderness	**6** Alamo Lake State Park	**9** Harquahala Mtns. Wilderness	Trail

McCracken Mine Rd   Signal Road

Signal Mountain

Castaneda Hills

McCracken Peak

1 Aubrey Peak

Black Mesa

Alamo Crossing Road

Arrastra Mountain

2

97

SANTA MARIA RIVER

Potts Mountain

Artillery Peak

BIG SANDY RIVER

93

Ives Peak

Artillery Mountains

6

SANTA MARIA RIVER

11

BILL WILLIAMS RIVER

Rawhide Mountains

ALAMO RESERVOIR

Palmeria Road

Alamo Dam Road

3

Sawyer Road

4

BILL WILLIAMS RIVER

Buckskin Mountains

5

Alamo Road

Alamo Road

• Swansea

Swansea Mine Rd.

Swansea Road

Cactus Plain

7 • Midway

Butler Valley

Alamo Dam Road

Harcuvar Mountains

Bullard Peak

Swansea Road

8

Aguila Valley

71

• Bouse

Harcuvar Peak

Harcuvar Mountains

McMullen Valley

60 Aguila

Gladden **Eagle Eye Peak**

72

• Utting

Granite Wash Mountains

10 **9**

Harquahala Mountains

↑ N

• McVay

60

Wenden **Harquahala Mountain**

Ref: DeLorme Arizona Atlas and Gazetteer

Salome

Socorro Peak

Vicksburg • Harcuvar

Service, a number of state parks, one national monument, and several Indian reservations, including the expansive Tohono O'odham Nation.

The Desert Ranges West of Phoenix

▓ AUBREY PEAK WILDERNESS

[Fig. 41(1)] The 15,400-acre Aubrey Peak Wilderness is a volcanic wonderland of buttes, dikes, plugs, tafoni caves, spires, overhangs, and slickrock. The highest point in the wilderness is a spectacular sheer-sided, unnamed 3,221-foot monolith that supposedly has never been climbed. The 2,953-foot Aubrey Peak, a large cliff-encircled mesa that dominates the eastern portion of the wilderness along with numerous other large mesas, buttes, and volcanic plugs, is more accessible, but still a challenge to experienced hikers.

The Aubrey Peak Wilderness boasts stands of large saguaro (*Carnegiea gigantea*), palo verde (*Cercidium microphyllum*), ironwood (*Onleya tesota*), and smoke trees (*Dalea spinosa*), typical of the Sonoran desert. This vegetation often merges with Joshua trees and other species more characteristic of the Mohave Desert, creating a visually intriguing, quilt-like mosaic of plants throughout the area. A unique and protected spurge (*Stillingia linearifolia*) grows along Centennial Wash. Desert rosy boas (*Lichanura trivirgata*), a rare and beautiful snake, are also known to reside here.

The wilderness offers excellent opportunities for primitive types of recreation. Hiking, backpacking, and photography have become increasingly popular in recent years. There are no established trails in the wilderness area, so map and compass are necessary.

Directions: From Kingman, travel 22 miles south on I-40 to the Yucca/Alamo Road turnoff. From Yucca, continue another 50 miles southeast on Alamo Road to where a wooden pole power line crosses the road. The wilderness boundary lies a short distance west of Alamo Road on the power line maintenance road. Once at the wilderness boundary, jeep trails running southwest and northwest basically define the boundaries of the wilderness. From US 93, Alamo Road can also be accessed from Wikieup via the county-maintained Chicken Springs Road. The Aubrey Peak Wilderness boundary is 15 miles south of the Chicken Springs Road/Alamo Road junction. Some lands around and within the wilderness are not federally administered. Please respect the property rights of the owners and do not cross or use these lands without their permission.

Activities: Hiking, camping, and nature study.
Facilities: None.
Dates: Open year-round, but summer is too hot for hiking.
Fees: None.

Closest town: Wikieup, about 35 miles northeast.

For more information: BLM, Kingman Field Office, 2475 Beverly Avenue, Kingman, AZ 86401. Phone (520) 692-4400. Web site www.az.blm.gov.

ARRASTRA MOUNTAIN WILDERNESS

[Fig. 41(2)] This 129,800-acre, trailless wilderness is a rugged, scenic, and diverse area that offers plenty of solitude for experienced hikers. The Poachie Mountains trend southeast to northwest through the wilderness, culminating in the Arrastra Mountain at 4,807 feet. The southern and western slopes of the range are drained by long canyons and washes that empty into one of two ephemeral desert rivers, the south-flowing Big Sandy or the west-flowing Santa Maria. Both of these rivers have been recommended as National Wild and Scenic Rivers.

Cutting into the northern slope of the Poachies, and just outside the wilderness boundary, is Black Canyon, a winding volcanic gorge with flowing springs and outstanding petroglyph panels. People's Canyon, a tributary to the Santa Maria River, is a true desert oasis of lush riparian habitat within a colorful rhyolitic gorge. Surprisingly, a fern (*Thelypteris puberula*), considered to be of tropical origin, has been recorded growing in People's Canyon. The only other locale known for this plant in the state is in extreme southeastern Arizona. Much of the wilderness is critical habitat for desert tortoises. An estimated 600 adults live in the area.

Directions: Due to its remoteness from major highways or secondary roads, this wilderness is difficult to access. US 93 roughly parallels portions of the wilderness from 3 to 6 miles to the north and east. A rugged and usually passable jeep trail that approaches the Peoples Canyon area from the north can be accessed along US 93 at the AZ 97 (Bagdad) turnoff. The wilderness boundary is about 4 miles from here. The unmaintained Wendon/Yucca Road, accessible from Alamo Road, comprises several miles of the western boundary, giving access to Artillery Peak and the Big Sandy River. Roads in this area are not marked and are often impassable due to erosion. Study the maps thoroughly, and refer to them frequently along the way. Some lands around the wilderness are not federally administered. Please respect the property rights of the owners and do not cross or use these lands without their permission.

Activities: Hiking, camping, and nature study.

Facilities: None.

Dates: Open year-round, but too hot in summer for hiking.

Fees: None.

Closest town: Wikieup, about 30 miles northwest.

For more information: BLM, Kingman Field Office, 2475 Beverly Avenue, Kingman, AZ 86401. Phone (520) 692-4400. Web site www.az.blm.gov.

TRES ALAMOS WILDERNESS

[Fig. 41(3)] Immediately southeast of the Arrastra Mountain Wilderness is the 8,300-acre *Tres Alamos*, which means "three cottonwood trees," a small but quite diverse wilderness area. The eastern part of the wilderness takes in the scenic ridgelines, canyons, and washes of the southern Black Mountains, whereas the western side consists mainly of lower desert bajada and plains. Sawyer Peak, at 4,293 feet, is the highest point in the wilderness and in the Black Mountains. The monolith of Tres Alamos is the area's most striking landscape feature. Saguaro and palo verde cover the hills and bajadas. Joshua trees and creosote dot the plains, and mesquite and acacia line the washes. Wildlife includes the Gila monster (*Heloderma suspectum*), prairie falcon (*Falcon mexicanus*), golden eagle (*Aquila chrysaetos*), and possibly, Cooper's hawks (*Accipiter cooperii*) and kit fox (*Vulpes macrotis*). Endangered desert pupfish (*Cyprinodon* sp.) and Gila topminnow (*Poecilopsis occidentalis*) inhabit two ponds fed by the ephemeral stream originating from Tres Alamos Spring, which is just outside the wilderness boundary. The willow-lined stream plunges 60 feet into one of the ponds.

All of the area offers terrain suitable for hiking, backpacking, nature study, photography, and camping. Equestrian use can be enjoyed on the bajadas and plains. The area can be equally enjoyed by both experienced and novice backcountry users.

Directions: Take US 93 to the Lake Alamo Road. Drive about 6.5 miles westward on the Lake Alamo Road to a road fork and take the right fork. Drive about 7 more miles to reach the southern boundary of the wilderness. Roads along the western and northern wilderness boundaries require four-wheel-drive; high-clearance vehicles are needed for access elsewhere. Some lands around and within the wilderness are not federally administered. Please respect the property rights of the owners and do not cross or use these lands without their permission.

Activities: Hiking, horseback riding, rock climbing, camping, and nature study.

Facilities: None.

Dates: Open year-round, but too hot in the summer for hiking.

Fees: None.

Closest town: Wickenburg, about 35 miles southeast.

For more information: BLM, Kingman Field Office, 2475 Beverly Avenue, Kingman, AZ 86401. Phone (520) 692-4400. Web site www.az.blm.gov.

SWANSEA WILDERNESS

[Fig. 41(4)] A section of the Bill Williams River divides this 16,400-acre wilderness into two parts, north and south. The northern area's main feature is Black Mesa; the south is largely hilly, with several peaks rising more than 1,000 feet. But the river is the "crown jewel" of this wilderness and has been recommended as a National Wild and Scenic River. Along the river grow Fremont cottonwood (*Populus fremontii*), willow (*Salix* sp.), mesquite (*Prosopis* sp.), tamarisk (*Tamarix* sp.), seepwillow

Gila Monsters

The Gila monster (*Heloderma suspectum*) is the only poisonous lizard in Arizona and only one of two venomous lizards in the world. Biologists estimate that these large, chunky lizards with beadlike, black and pink scales spend up to 98 percent of their time in their subterranean shelters. When they do emerge, they hunt for newborn rodents, rabbits, hares, ground nesting birds, lizards, and bird and reptile eggs.

The Gila monster's venom is produced in glands in the lower jaw and is expressed along grooved teeth as the animal bites. Should desert visitors be concerned? According to a nineteenth century Phoenix doctor, "I have never been called to attend a case of Gila monster bite, and I don't want to be. I think a man who is foolish enough to get bitten…ought to die. The creature is so sluggish and slow of movement that the victim of its bite is compelled to help largely in order to get bitten."

(*Baccharis* sp.), and arrowweed (*Pluchea* sp.). This rich riparian habitat supports many birds, including Bell's vireo (*Vireo bellii*), yellow-billed cuckoo (*Coccyzus americanus*), summer tanager (*Piranga rubra*), and white-faced ibis (*Plegadis chihi*). In the river's waters swim green sunfish (*Lepomis cyanellus*), red shiner (*Richardsonius hydrophlox*), channel catfish, and bullhead catfish (*Ameiurus natalis*). Native fish may include longfin dace (*Agosia chrysogaster*), desert sucker (*Catostomus clarki*), Gila sucker (*Catostomus insignis*), and roundtail chub (*Gila robusta*).

The river flows through a canyon whose walls consist of a remarkable layering of schist and gneiss. So unique is this feature that geologists have recommended the area be recognized as the Banded Canyon National Natural Landmark.

Backpackers, day hikers, horseback riders, canoeists, kayakers, inner-tubers, hunters, photographers, birders, and nature lovers enjoy this special place.

Directions: At Bouse on AZ 72, take the Swansea Road north, through Midway to the Swansea ghost town. Roads near the wilderness include pipeline and power line maintenance roads on the northeast, east, and south. High-clearance or four-wheel-drive vehicles are recommended for access to the wilderness boundary. Some lands around and within the wilderness are not federally administered. Please respect the property rights of the owners and do not cross or use these lands without their permission.

Activities: Hiking, camping, river running, horseback riding, and nature study.

Facilities: None.

Dates: Open year-round.

Fees: None.

Closest town: Bouse, about 25 miles south.

For more information: BLM, Lake Havasu Field Office, 2610 Sweetwater Avenue, Lake Havasu City, AZ 86406. Phone (520) 505-1200. Web site www.az.blm.gov.

▨ RAWHIDE MOUNTAINS WILDERNESS AND ALAMO LAKE STATE PARK

[Fig. 41(5)] Like the Swansea Wilderness, the Bill Williams River also bisects the 38,470-acre Rawhide Mountains Wilderness. The river has carved a 600-foot-deep gorge through the Rawhide Mountains, which are mostly low hills composed of highly eroded schist, gneiss, and granite. The mountains are cut by several washes and canyons, most notably the Mississippi Wash, which winds down a narrow canyon with several small, seasonal waterfalls. Evidence of prehistoric hunters and gatherers can be found in rock art and ancient trails.

Most of the wilderness is Sonoran desert composed of palo verde-saguaro and creosote-bursage communities. Of course, along the riverbanks are riparian species such as cottonwood, willow, seep willow, tamarisk, arrowweed, and mesquite.

Bald eagles (*Haliaeetus leucocephalus*) utilize the area, as do endangered black rails (*Laterallus jamaicensis*). Threatened species include yellow-billed cuckoo, snowy egret (*Egretta thula*), ferruginous hawk, osprey (*Pandion haliaetus*), and lowland leopard frog (*Rana yavapaiensis*). Other birds of concern include American bittern (*Botaurus lentiginosus*), least bittern (*Ixobrychus exilis*), common black-hawk (*Buteogallus anthracinus*), and belted kingfisher (*Ceryle alcyon*). Long-billed curlew (*Numenius americanus*), Swainson's hawk, white-faced ibis, Bell's vireo, yellow-breasted chat (*Icteria virens*), ruby-crowned kinglet (*Regulus calendula*), yellow warbler (*Dendroica petechia*), Lucy's warbler (*Vermivora luciae*), vermilion flycatcher (*Pyrocephalus rubinus*), black phoebe (*Sayornis nigricans*), and numerous migrating ducks and geese can be observed here, too.

The large size of this wilderness, the varied and colorful terrain, and the presence of year-round water enhance wilderness opportunities for hikers, backpackers, birdwatchers, photographers, and river-runners (flows permitting).

Directions: The Bill Williams River gorge, located downstream from Alamo Dam, is accessible from Alamo Lake State Park, along the south shore of Alamo Lake. To reach the state park, take Alamo Road 30 miles north from Wenden. Parking is available at the dam overlook. It is 1.5 miles from the overlook to the bottom of the dam, where the gorge begins. The gorge may be closed to hikers from late winter through spring to lessen disturbance of nesting bald eagles. Some lands around the wilderness are not federally administered. Please respect the property rights of the owners and do not cross or use these lands without their permission.

Activities: Hiking, camping, river running, and nature study.

Facilities: None.

Dates: Open year-round, except specific eagle nesting sites. Summers are too hot for hiking.

GILA MONSTER
(Heloderma suspectum)

BALD
EAGLE
(Haliaeetus
leucocephalus)

Fees: None.

Closest town: Wenden, about 30 miles south.

For more information: BLM, Lake Havasu Field Office, 2610 Sweetwater Avenue, Lake Havasu City, AZ 86406. Phone (520) 505-1200. Web site www.az.blm.gov.

GIBRALTAR MOUNTAIN WILDERNESS

[Fig. 43] The 18,790-acre Gibraltar Mountain Wilderness, which includes the western end of the Buckskin Mountains, is one of the most impregnable in the Yuma BLM District. The steep, convoluted mountain mass is deeply incised by narrow washes. Elevations range from 640 feet to nearly 1,900 feet above sea level. Most of the area is critical bighorn sheep habitat and includes two lambing grounds.

There are no established trails, but washes and canyon bottoms allow access for hikers and challenging horseback riding. The area is well suited for primitive recreation pursuits such as rock climbing, nature study, photography, orienteering, and contemplation.

Directions: Drive 2 miles south of Parker, and then turn east onto Shea Road and follow this road for 10 miles to an unmarked dirt road to the north. Follow this track about 1 mile to the wilderness boundary. Other roads near the wilderness include a power line road on the northeast, Cienega Springs road on the west, and a mining road on the south. High-clearance or four-wheel-drive vehicles are recommended for access to the wilderness boundary. All lands within and around the wilderness are federally administered.

Activities: Hiking, camping, horseback riding, rock climbing, and nature study.

Facilities: None.

Dates: Open year-round, but summers are too hot for hiking.

Fees: None.

Closest town: Parker, about 15 miles west.

For more information: BLM, Lake Havasu Field Office, 2610 Sweetwater Avenue, Lake Havasu City, AZ 86406. Phone (520) 505-1200. Web site www.az.blm.gov.

EAST CACTUS PLAIN WILDERNESS

[Fig. 41(7)] The name is a little misleading; don't expect a perfectly flat plain. The 14,630-acre East Cactus Plain Wilderness takes in rolling terrain of stabilized sand dunes, sand sculptures, smaller flats of sand dotted with pebbles, and rounded hills of silky red sand. Both Mohave and Sonoran desert plant communities exist here along with some unique plant groupings. In the dunes live the unusual Mohave fringed-toed lizard (*Uma scoparia*) and flat-tailed horned lizard (*Phrynosoma m'calli*).

Recreational opportunities include horseback riding and backpacking trips, sight-seeing, photography, and botanical and wildlife study.

Directions: At Bouse on AZ 72, take the Swansea Road north. Roads near the wilderness include Swansea Road on the southeast and a power line maintenance road on the northeast, which will take you within walking distance of the wilderness boundary.

Activities: Hiking, camping, horseback riding, and nature study.

Facilities: None.

Dates: Open year-round, but summers are too hot for hiking.

Fees: None.

Closest town: Bouse, about 12 miles south.

For more information: BLM, Lake Havasu Field Office, 2610 Sweetwater Avenue, Lake Havasu City, AZ 86406. Phone (520) 505-1200. Web site www.az.blm.gov.

▨ HARCUVAR MOUNTAINS WILDERNESS

[Fig. 41(8)] The rock-strewn Harcuvar Mountains rise abruptly more than 2,500 feet from the desert floor. Large bajadas stretch out for miles toward the McMullen Valley to the south and the Butler Valley to the north. Within the 25,050-acre wilderness, many boulder-choked canyons dissect the main range. The ridges between the canyons are covered with massive boulders. The high northern ridgeline features an "island" of chaparral and grassland habitat, perhaps a relictual community left from the last Ice Age. Within this island can be found Gilbert's skink (*Eumeces gilberti*), rosy boa (*Lichanura trivirgata*), and desert night lizards (*Xantusia vigilis*); all three species are isolated from other similar populations. Desert bighorn sheep, mountain lion, fox, prairie falcon, various hawks, golden eagles, and desert tortoises can also be seen here.

Pictographs and prehistoric agricultural sites provide a few clues to earlier residents. *Harcuvar* may be an old Mohave Indian word meaning "there is little sweet water." In addition to historical exploring, day hiking and backpacking are popular. Hunting, horseback riding, and rock climbing may also be done.

Directions: Access to the area is via the Alamo Dam Access Road north from Wenden on US 60. Between 8 and 20 miles from Wenden, jeep roads lead east to the wilderness boundary. High-clearance and four-wheel-drive vehicles are recommended. Some lands around and within the wilderness are not federally administered. Please respect the property rights of the owners and do not cross or use these lands without their permission.

Activities: Hiking, horseback riding, rock climbing, camping, and nature study.

Facilities: None.

Beep Beep

Yes, roadrunners do exist; and no, they do not cry, "Beep Beep." The greater roadrunner (*Geococcyx californianus*) is a member of the cuckoo family. One tall tale relates how roadrunners find a sleeping rattlesnake and build a fence of cactus joints around it. However, the facts are no less impressive. Roadrunners can reach running speeds of 15 miles per hour. They can fly, but rarely do. They are very effective predators, capturing snakes, lizards, large insects, rodents, and small birds. On cool mornings, the bird erects its feathers to expose its darkly pigmented skin to the sun, thus heating its body without unnecessary expenditure of metabolic energy.

Dates: Open year-round, but summers are too hot for hiking.

Fees: None.

Closest town: Wenden, about 12 miles south.

For more information: BLM, Lake Havasu Field Office, 2610 Sweetwater Avenue, Lake Havasu City, AZ 86406. Phone (520) 505-1200. Web site www.az.blm.gov.

HARQUAHALA MOUNTAINS WILDERNESS

[Fig. 41(9)] About 30 miles west of Wickenburg, the Harquahala Mountains rise like a tall ship on a desert sea. Harquahala Peak at 5,681 feet is almost a mile above the desert floor and dominates this 22,880-acre wilderness. These are the highest mountains in southwestern Arizona. On a clear day, the view from Harquahala Peak is breathtaking. Four Peaks in the Mazatzals, 118 miles to the east, and the Chemehuevi Mountains in California, about 90 miles away, are visible.

The name *Harquahala* is a European corruption of a Mohave Indian word meaning "there is running water up high." Many of the canyons have springs and seeps where water is available year-round. During rainy periods, streams flow through the canyons, creating many picturesque waterfalls. Of course, this relative abundance of water in the desert attracts many species of wildlife.

An old road leads to the summit of Harquahala Peak where the remains of a 1920 observatory stand. The Smithsonian Astrophysical Observatory measured and studied solar activity for five years in hopes of aiding weather forecasting. Now it shares the summit with a microwave communications facility that is used to control water flow in the Central Arizona Project canals cutting across the desert below.

Directions: High-clearance and four-wheel-drive vehicles are needed to travel to the boundary of the wilderness. Paved US 60 provides access to jeep trails extending to the wilderness area's northern boundary. The paved Eagle Eye Road provides access to numerous jeep trails along the area's southern side. Harquahala Peak can be reached by a 10.5-mile four-wheel-drive road off of the Eagle Eye Road, but erosion and steep grades will be encountered. Only experienced backcountry drivers should attempt this road. Some lands around and within the wilderness are not federally administered. Please respect the property rights of the owners and do not cross or use these lands without their permission.

Activities: Hiking, camping, and nature study.

Facilities: None.

Dates: Open year-round, but summers are too hot for hiking.

Fees: None.

Closest town: Aguila, 15 miles northeast.

For more information: BLM, Phoenix Field Office, 2015 West Deer Valley Road, Phoenix, AZ 85027-2099. Phone (623) 580-5500. Web site www.az.blm.gov.

HARQUAHALA MOUNTAINS PACK TRAIL

[Fig. 41(10)] Although a four-wheel-drive road climbs to the summit from the south, this trail offers a more challenging way to the top. The last 0.75 mile climbs over 1,400 vertical feet. Views from the top are incredible.

Directions: Drive 13.6 miles southwest of Aguila on US 60 and turn left onto a four-wheel-drive road. Continue 2.2 miles to the trailhead.

Trail: 5.4 miles one-way.

Degree of difficulty: Strenuous.

Elevation: 2,400 to 5,681 feet.

Surface: Rocky.

HUMMINGBIRD SPRINGS WILDERNESS

[Fig. 44(1)] This 31,200-acre wilderness is dominated by the 3,418-foot eminence of Sugarloaf Mountain, a colorful and spectacular landmark surrounded by lower peaks, ridges, bajadas, and the Tonopah Desert plains. Sheer cliff faces, fins and pinnacles, winding canyons, and a large natural arch high on the east slope of the mountain add to the topographic interest of the area.

Saguaro, cholla (*Opuntia* sp.), hedgehog (*Echinocereus* sp.), prickly pear (*Opuntia* sp.), ocotillo, mesquite, palo verde, and jojoba (*Simmondsia chinensis*) grow profusely here. Unusual plants include nakedwood (*Colubrina californica*), night-blooming cereus (*Peniocereus greggii*), Wiggins' cholla (*Opuntia wigginsii*), and selaginella (*Selaginella eremophilia*). Most of the wilderness is excellent habitat for desert bighorn sheep, mule deer, and desert tortoise. Cooper's hawks, prairie falcons, golden eagles, kit foxes, and Gila monsters may also be encountered.

Directions: It can be accessed from the south by exiting I-10 at the Tonopah or Salome Road exits. The Eagle Eye Road south of Aguila provides access from the north. Dirt roads extend to the wilderness boundary from these roads and other unnamed roads nearby. Road conditions vary, and high-clearance and

GREATER
ROADRUNNER
(*Geococcyx californianus*)

four-wheel-drive vehicles are recommended. Some lands around and within the wilderness are not federally administered. Please respect the property rights of the owners and do not cross or use these lands without their permission.

Activities: Hiking, camping, and nature study.

Facilities: None.

Dates: Open year-round.

Fees: None.

Closest town: Tonopah, about 15 miles southeast.

For more information: BLM, Phoenix Field Office, 2015 West Deer Valley Road, Phoenix, AZ 85027-2099. Phone (623) 580-5500. Web site www.az.blm.gov.

SUGARLOAF MOUNTAIN ROUTE

One of the easier ways to get into this desert wilderness is by walking an old road to the top of Sugarloaf Mountain. The road, now closed to vehicles, leads hikers through stark but spectacular scenery to the 3,418-foot summit and a panoramic view the area.

Directions: From Aguila, take the Eagle Eye Road to the Aguila microwave facility road. About 3 miles before reaching the microwave tower, turn left onto a four-wheel-drive road, which reaches the wilderness boundary in about 1 mile.

Trail: About 2.5 miles one-way.

Degree of difficulty: Moderate.

Elevation: About 2,600 to 3,418 feet.

Surface: Rocky.

BIG HORN MOUNTAINS WILDERNESS

[Fig. 44(2)] This 21,000-acre wilderness area is separated from the Hummingbird Springs Wilderness only by an old jeep road. The two areas are really all the same mountain range. Golden eagles, prairie falcons, barn owls (*Tyto alba*), and great horned owls (*Bubo virginianus*) nest in the cliffs.

Smaller hills, fissures, chimneys, narrow canyons, and desert plains surround the central mountainous core. Hikers find easy going around the base of the range, while rock climbers tackle steep cliffs on Big Horn Peak.

After a dusty, long hike in the Big Horns, you may want to go for a long soak at **El Dorado Hot Spring** (no phone; Web site www.el-dorado.com) in Tonopah, about 10 miles southwest of the wilderness area.

Directions: Access to the wilderness can be gained by exiting I-10 at the Tonopah or Salome Road exits. Unmaintained dirt roads extend to the wilderness

SAGUARO
(*Carnegiea gigantea*)

area's eastern, northern, and western boundaries. Because road conditions vary and some routes are primitive, high-clearance and four-wheel-drive vehicles are recommended. Some lands around and within the wilderness are not federally administered. Please respect the property rights of the owners and do not cross or use these lands without their permission.

Activities: Hiking, camping, and nature study.

Facilities: None.

Dates: Open year-round.

Fees: None.

Closest town: Tonopah, about 15 miles southeast.

For more information: BLM, Phoenix Field Office, 2015 West Deer Valley Road, Phoenix, AZ 85027-2099. Phone (623) 580-5500. Web site www.az.blm.gov.

MUGGINS MOUNTAINS WILDERNESS

[Fig. 42(9)] This relatively small but rugged 7,674-acre wilderness is dominated by Klothos Temple, Muggins Peak, and Long Mountain. Washes snake their way up into and around these peaks, making excellent hiking routes. Some signs of old placer mine workings from the late 1800s in the western half of the wilderness lends some historic interest to the area.

Typical Sonoran desert vegetation covers the area. Along washes may be found blue palo verde (*Cercidium floridum*), ironwood , mesquite, smoke tree, and bitter condalia (*Condalia* sp.). Other species of notable interest are holly-leaved bursage (*Franseria* sp.), hoffmanseggia (*Hoffmanseggia microphylla*), Wiggins' cholla (*Opuntia wigginsii*), and a red-spined barrel cactus (*Ferocactus* sp.).

Wildlife includes chuckwalla (*Sauromalus obesus*), Gila monster, cactus wren (*Campylorhynchus brunneicapillus*), desert bighorn sheep, and possibly desert tortoise and elf owl (*Micrathene whitneyi*).

Directions: To reach the southwest boundary, take the Dome Valley Exit off I-8. Travel 1.25 miles on the frontage road then turn northwest and go to County Avenue 20E. Continue to County 7th Street. Turn right (east) and drive to the foot of the mountains, where the Muggins Wash Road continues northeast and drops into a Muggins Wash and the wilderness boundary.

Activities: Hiking, camping, horseback riding, and hunting.

Facilities: None.

Dates: Open year-round, but summers are too hot for outdoor recreation.

Fees: None.

Closest town: Yuma, about 25 miles west.

For more information: BLM, Yuma Field Office, 2555 Gila Ridge Road, Yuma, AZ 85365. Phone (520) 317-3200. Web site www.az.blm.gov.

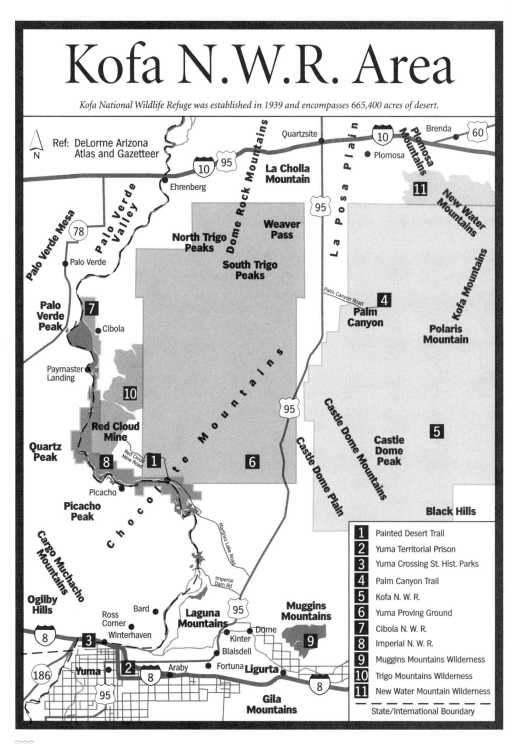

Kofa N.W.R. Area

Kofa National Wildlife Refuge was established in 1939 and encompasses 665,400 acres of desert.

N

Ref: DeLorme Arizona
Atlas and Gazetteer

Quartzsite

10 **60** Brenda

95

Plomosa

Plomosa Mountains

La Cholla Mountain

10

Ehrenberg

11

Dome Rock Mountains

New Water Mountains

La Posa Plain

95

78

Palo Verde Valley

Weaver Pass

Palo Verde Mesa

Palo Verde

North Trigo Peaks

South Trigo Peaks

Kofa Mountains

Palm Canyon Road

4

Palo Verde Peak

7

Cibola

Palm Canyon

Polaris Mountain

Paymaster
Landing

10

Chocolate Mountains

95

Castle Dome Mountains

Red Cloud Mine

Quartz Peak

8

Red Cloud Mine Road

1

6

Castle Dome Plain

Castle Dome Peak

5

Picacho

Picacho Peak

Black Hills

Cargo Muchacho Mountains

Martinez Lake Road

1	Painted Desert Trail
2	Yuma Territorial Prison
3	Yuma Crossing St. Hist. Parks
4	Palm Canyon Trail
5	Kofa N. W. R.
6	Yuma Proving Ground
7	Cibola N. W. R.
8	Imperial N. W. R.
9	Muggins Mountains Wilderness
10	Trigo Mountains Wilderness
11	New Water Mountain Wilderness
	State/International Boundary

Imperial
Dam Rd

Ogilby Hills

Ross
Corner

Bard

Winterhaven

Laguna Mountains

95

Muggins Mountains

8

3

Kinter

Dome

9

Blaisdell

186

Yuma

2

8

Araby

Fortuna **Ligurta**

8

95

Gila Mountains

🟤 KOFA NATIONAL WILDLIFE REFUGE

[Fig. 42(5)] Kofa National Wildlife Refuge was established in 1939 and encompasses 665,400 acres of pristine desert, including two mountain ranges—the Kofa and Castle Dome. The Kofa Mountains were named after the King of Arizona Mine, a gold mine active in the late 1800s. The refuge is home to Arizona's only native palms, Kofa Mountain barberry (*Berberis harrisoniana*), an endemic species, and bighorn sheep. Approximately 800 to 1,000 desert bighorn sheep live in the refuge and provide animals for transplanting throughout Arizona and neighboring states.

Most of the refuge is designated wilderness, but several four-wheel-drive roads cross the area and are open to public use.

Directions: From Yuma, drive north on US 95 about 30 miles. US 95 parallels the west boundary for the next 40 miles. Several dirt roads, some signed, lead from 1 to several miles east to the refuge boundary.

Activities: Hiking, rock climbing, camping, limited hunting, mineral collecting in the Crystal Hill Area only, and nature study.

Facilities: None.

Dates: Open year-round, but summers are very hot.

Fees: None.

Closest town: Quartzsite, about 18 miles north.

For more information: Refuge Manager, Kofa National Wildlife Refuge, PO Box 6290, Yuma, AZ 85366. Phone (520) 783-7861.

PALM CANYON TRAIL

[Fig. 42(4)] This short trail leads into a magnificent, narrow canyon where about 42 California fan palms (*Washingtonia filifera*) grow. These are the only native palms in the state. Some botanists believe this grove is descended from palm groves that were more wide spread during the last Ice Age. As the region warmed to desert conditions, a few palms survived in this protected spot. Other botanists have suggested that birds or coyotes carrying seeds in their digestive tracts may have brought the trees here.

Directions: From Quartzsite, drive south on US 95 for 18 miles to the Palm Canyon Road. Turn left and drive another 9 miles to the mouth of Palm Canyon. Park at road's end.

Trail: About 0.5 mile one-way.

Degree of difficulty: Easy to moderate.

Elevation: 2,120 to 2,520 feet.

Surface: Sandy and rocky.

🟤 NEW WATER MOUNTAIN WILDERNESS

[Fig. 42(11)] The stony 24,600-acre New Water Mountain Wilderness is 10 miles east of Quartzsite, home base for nine major gem, mineral, and rock shows each year, and about 4 miles south of I-10. Located adjacent to and north of the Kofa National Wildlife Refuge, this area is characterized by strings of craggy spires, sheer rock outcrops, natural arches, slickrock canyons, and deep sandy washes. Black Mesa, a large volcanic butte rising 1,200 feet above the desert plain, dominates the western part of the wilderness. A large, natural arch at the northwest end of the range is a locally well-known landmark.

Vegetation is sparse with saguaro, creosote, ocotillo, and cholla dotting the hills, and palo verde and ironwood lining the washes. The rare night-blooming cereus (*Peniocereus greggii*) and Wiggins' cholla (*Opuntia wigginsii*) also grow here. The wilderness is important habitat to the desert bighorn sheep, including the New Water and Dripping Springs lambing areas. The wilderness offers many types of primitive recreation, such as extended backpacking and hiking trips, day hikes, and wildlife watching. Opportunities to photograph and hunt deer and desert bighorn sheep and collect interesting minerals and rocks are plentiful.

Directions: The western boundary of the wilderness can be accessed via the Gold Nugget Road south of I-10 (Exit 26). The north-central part of the wilderness can be reached by the Ramsey Mine Road south of US 60. The Kofa Wilderness forms the southern boundary of the New Water Mountain Wilderness. Some lands around and within the wilderness are not federally administered. Please respect the property rights of the owners and do not cross or use these lands without their permission.

Activities: Hiking, camping, and nature study.

Facilities: None.

Dates: Open year-round, but very hot in the summer.

Fees: None.

Closest town: Quartzsite, about 15 miles northwest.

For more information: BLM, Yuma Field Office, 2555 Gila Ridge Road, Yuma, AZ 85365. Phone (520) 317-3200. Web site www.az.blm.gov.

EAGLETAIL MOUNTAINS WILDERNESS

[Fig. 44(3)] A few miles southwest of the Big Horn Mountains and south of I-10 is the 100,600-acre Eagletail Mountains Wilderness. The Eagletail Mountains stretch across the desert for about 15 miles in a northwest to southeast direction. The upper weathered basaltic cliffs and jagged peaks form the backbone of this spectacular mountain range. The lower eroded slopes are embedded with horizontal flows of Tertiary age lava.

There are relict stands of juniper and oak (*Quercus turbinella*) on the north-facing slopes near Eagletail Peak. Also found in the wilderness area are four rare plants—nakedwood (*Colubrina californica*), selaginella (*Selaginella eremophila*), night-blooming cereus (*Peniocereus greggii*), and wild onion (*Allium parishii*).

Equestrians and hikers enjoy the Ben Avery Trail, which crosses the desert wilderness. Courthouse Rock and Eagletail Peak attract rock climbers.

Directions: Drive about 13 miles west of Tonopah on I-10 and take Exit 81. Turn south toward the Harquahala Valley and drive 5 miles to the Courthouse Rock Road. Follow this road west about 5 miles to a major fork. The right fork, a gas pipeline maintenance road, and the left fork, the East Clanton Well Road, both offer access to the wilderness. High-clearance or four-wheel-drive vehicles are recommended for access to the wilderness boundary. Some lands around and within the wilderness are not federally administered. Please respect the property rights of the owners and do not cross or use these lands without their permission.

Activities: Hiking, horseback riding, rock climbing, camping, and nature study.
Facilities: None.
Dates: Open year-round.
Fees: None.
Closest town: Tonopah, about 25 miles east.
For more information: BLM, Yuma Field Office, 2555 Gila Ridge Road, Yuma, AZ 85365. Phone (520) 317-3200. Web site www.az.blm.gov.

BEN AVERY TRAIL

[Fig. 44(4)] This trail is named after a well-known Phoenix outdoor writer and covers about 12 miles in all. A nice day hike is a walk as far as Indian Spring. This is a good area to see desert wildlife, such as mule deer, bobcat, gray fox, kit fox, coyote, black-tailed jackrabbit, cactus wren, and red-tailed hawk, and perhaps evidence of prehistoric cultures.

Directions: From the major fork described above, take the right branch about 6 miles to a marked road going south. Follow this track about 1.5 miles to the Ben Avery trailhead at the wilderness boundary.
Trail: About 3.5 miles one-way.
Degree of difficulty: Easy.
Elevation: About 1,600 to 1,800 feet.
Surface: Old jeep road.

SIGNAL MOUNTAIN WILDERNESS

[Fig. 44(5)] Only a four-wheel-drive road separates the Signal Mountain and Woolsey Mountain wilderness areas; they are both part of the Gila Bend Mountains. This 13,350-acre wilderness offers a variety of scenery, including sharp volcanic peaks, steep-walled canyons, arroyos, craggy ridges, and outwash plains. Signal Mountain, at the area's center, rises 1,200 feet above the desert floor, to an elevation of 2,182 feet. The mountain received its name from an aircraft beacon which once stood on the summit. Palo verde-saguaro and creosote-bursage plant communities are found throughout bajada and upland areas, while washes are lined with mesquite, ironwood, acacia, and palo verde.

In the past, desert bighorns roamed these mountains but disappeared probably due to overhunting. As part of their continuing program to increase the desert bighorn population in Arizona, the Arizona Game and Fish Department re-introduced a herd of bighorn sheep here in the 1980s.

Of interest to archaeologists are rock alignments, possible habitation sites, and prehistoric lithic sites, where stone tools were manufactured. It is hard to imagine people being able to survive in this harsh desert environment.

Directions: Exit I-10 west of Phoenix at AZ 85. Drive south 5.5 miles to Old US 80, turn right, and go 6 miles to Hassayampa. Continue for another 8 miles to the Aqua Caliente Road. Follow this road about 5 miles to an unnamed road bearing left. Follow this road a few miles until you see the signed wilderness boundary to the north. High-clearance vehicles are required and four-wheel-drive vehicles are recommended. Some lands around and within the wilderness are not federally administered. Please respect the property rights of the owners and do not cross or use these lands without their permission.

Activities: Hiking, camping, and nature study.

Facilities: None.

Dates: Open year-round, but too hot summer recreation.

Fees: None.

Closest town: Buckeye, about 30 miles northeast.

For more information: BLM, Phoenix Field Office, 2015 West Deer Valley Road, Phoenix, AZ 85027-2099. Phone (623) 580-5500. Web site www.az.blm.gov.

WOOLSEY PEAK WILDERNESS

[Fig. 44(6)] One of the appealing aspects of the 64,000-acre Woolsey Peak Wilderness is its highly varied topography. The 3,270-foot Woolsey Peak, rising 2,500 feet above the Gila River, is a geographic landmark visible throughout southwestern Arizona. The area contains flat desert plains, low rolling hills, basalt-capped mesas, jagged desert mountains, wide valleys, and numerous washes. The complex geology ranges from Precambrian-age to recent era deposits of pegmatites, red and brown sandstones, blue-green marine sediments, and black volcanics.

The wilderness contains a surprising variety of vegetation, including saguaro, cholla, palo verde, creosote and bursage. The washes are lined with desert mesquite, ironwood, and palo verde. The diversity, ruggedness, and size of the wilderness offer excellent opportunities for solitude and primitive recreation. The desert enthusiast will enjoy hiking and camping here.

Directions: Exit I-10 west of Phoenix at AZ 85. Drive south 5.5 miles to Old US 80, turn right, and go 6 miles to Hassayampa. Continue for another 8 miles to the Aqua Caliente Road. Follow this road about 5 miles to an unnamed road bearing left. Follow this road a few miles until you see the signed wilderness boundary to the south. High-clearance vehicles are needed and four-wheel-drive vehicles are recommended. Some lands around and within the wilderness are not federally administered. Please respect the property rights of the owners and do not cross or use these lands without their permission.

Activities: Hiking, camping, and nature study.

Facilities: None.

Dates: Open year-round, but too hot in the summer for hiking.

Fees: None.

Closest town: Buckeye, about 30 miles northeast.

For more information: BLM, Phoenix Field Office, 2015 West Deer Valley Road, Phoenix, AZ 85027-2099. Phone (623) 580-5500. Web site www.az.blm.gov.

SIERRA ESTRELLA WILDERNESS

[Fig. 44(7)] Tucked between the Gila River Reservation, occupied by both Maricopa and Pima Indians, and the Estrella Mountain County Regional Park, the 14,400-acre Sierra Estrella Wilderness is considered to be one of the most impregnable and least explored mountain ranges in the state. The mountains have knife-edge ridgelines, inaccessible peaks, and steep, rubble-strewn talus slopes. There are few trails, and the canyon bottoms are usually a disarray of boulders.

Along with desert bighorns, mule deer, javelina, and coyotes, mountain lions reside here. Besides the usual Sonoran desert plants, there are a few elephant trees (*Bursera microphylla*). This is the northernmost occurrence of this species. Surprisingly, there are also a few junipers growing in the extreme upper part of the sierra in protected locations.

Nearby is the Gila River, formerly perennial, which allowed Indians to live in the area. Prehistoric petroglyphs and artifacts, such as stone tools, are scattered about. But remember, that all archaeological remains are protected by law. Observe, photograph, study them, but do not disturb.

Directions: Although distinguished as one of the closest wilderness areas to metropolitan Phoenix, four-wheel-drive vehicles are required to approach the wilderness boundary. Primitive dirt roads near the wilderness boundary are extremely sandy or silty, and wash crossings are rough and deep. Only the western boundary of the wilderness is accessible to the public; elsewhere the area is bounded by the Gila River Indian Reservation.

To reach the western boundary of the wilderness, take I-10 to Exit 126 and travel 8.3 miles south to Elliot Road. Turn right and go 2.6 miles to Rainbow Valley Road. Turn left and drive 9.3 miles south, until the pavement ends. Turn left on Riggs Road and continue 4 miles to an intersection, but continue through the intersection another 5.3 miles to a power line road. Turn right and drive 1.9 miles to an unnamed road to the left. Take it 1.9 miles east to the Quartz Peak Trailhead. Some lands around and within the wilderness are not federally administered. Please respect the property rights of the owners and do not cross or use these lands without their permission.

Activities: Hiking, camping, and nature study.

Facilities: None.

Dates: Open year-round, but too hot during summer for hiking.

Fees: None.

Closest town: Phoenix, about 25 miles north.

For more information: BLM, Phoenix Field Office, 2015 West Deer Valley Road, Phoenix, AZ 85027-2099. Phone (623) 580-5500. Web site www.az.blm.gov.

QUARTZ PEAK TRAIL

[Fig. 44(7)] Quartz Peak Trail, in the 14,400-acre Sierra Estrella Wilderness, leads visitors from the floor of Rainbow Valley (elevation 1,550 feet) to the summit ridge of the Sierra Estrella at Quartz Peak (elevation 4,052 feet) in just 3 miles. Along the way, visitors are treated to a variety of Sonoran desert plants and wildlife, scenic vistas, and evidence of the area's volcanic history. The views from the summit are spectacular—to the west is a dramatic panorama of rugged mountain ranges and desert plains, and to the east metropolitan Phoenix unfolds over the valley of the lower Salt River. Quartz Peak Trail is extremely steep and sometimes difficult to follow. **This is a hike for experienced and well-conditioned hikers only!**

The trail begins at Quartz Peak trailhead by following a closed four-wheel-drive track approximately 0.25 mile. Look to the left as you walk up the old road and see the narrow Quartz Peak trail ascending the ridge to the north. The trail is poorly marked in places and does not extend to the summit. The final 0.25 mile to Quartz Peak is a scramble over boulder and talus slopes that require careful footing. Quartz Peak is a point on the spine of the Sierra Estrella capped with an outcrop of white quartz.

Directions: See directions to the Sierra Estrella Wilderness, page 253.

Trail: 3 miles one-way.

Degree of difficulty: Strenuous. Horses and pack stock are not allowed on Quartz Peak Trail.

Elevation: 1,550 to 4,052 feet.

Surface: Rocky.

NORTH MARICOPA WILDERNESS

[Fig. 44(8)] This 63,200-acre wilderness area lies about 12 miles northeast of Gila Bend. Unlike most of the desert mountain ranges that have a single ridgeline, the North Maricopa Mountains is a jumble of long ridges and isolated peaks, which are separated and bisected by numerous washes. Vegetation includes saguaro, cholla, ocotillo, and other Sonoran desert plant species. Desert bighorn sheep, desert tortoise, coyotes, bobcat, fox, deer, Gambel's quail (*Callipepla gambelii*), and raptors inhabit the wilderness.

A segment of the 1850s Butterfield Overland Stageline Route runs along the southern boundary of the wilderness. This stageline was the first reliable, relatively fast method of transportation between the eastern United States and California. The stage carried people, mail, and freight over 2,700 miles in less than 25 days. In its three-year history, the stage was late only three times.

The wilderness provides outstanding opportunities for solitude and primitive recreation, including hiking, backpacking, horseback riding, camping, wildlife observation, and photography. The Margie's Cove and Brittlebush trails take visitors through the heart of the North Maricopa Mountains Wilderness.

Directions: Access to the wilderness from the south can be attained using dirt roads extending northward from AZ 238 (Maricopa Road). Four-wheel-drive is needed to negotiate parts of the route along the southern boundary. Access from the north can be gained via dirt roads extending south from Rainbow Valley Road and the gas pipeline maintenance road. A primitive dirt road parallels the eastern boundary. The western boundary is inaccessible. Some lands around and within the wilderness are not federally administered. Please respect the property rights of the owners and do not cross over or use these lands without their permission.

Activities: Hiking, camping, horseback riding, and nature study.

Facilities: None.

Dates: Open year-round, but too hot during the summer for hiking.

Fees: None.

Closest town: Maricopa, about 30 miles east.

For more information: BLM, Phoenix Field Office, 2015 West Deer Valley Road, Phoenix, AZ 85027-2099. Phone (623) 580-5500. Web site www.az.blm.gov.

MARGIE'S COVE AND BRITTLEBUSH TRAILS

[Fig. 44(9)] Margie's Cove Trail is a nearly level, 9-mile route through the heart of the 63,200-acre North Maricopa Mountains Wilderness. The North Maricopa Mountains are a jumble of long ridges and isolated peaks separated by extensive, saguaro-studded bajadas and wide desert washes. Cholla, ocotillo, prickly pear, palo verde, ironwood, and Mexican jumping bean (*Sapium biloculare*) complement the thick stands of saguaro to form classic Sonoran desert vistas. Commonly seen wildlife include desert mule deer, javelina, desert bighorn sheep, coyote, desert tortoise, and numerous varieties of lizards and birds. During wet spring months, the hillsides adjacent to the trail are awash with brilliant yellow blooms of the brittlebush (*Encelia* sp.).

Margie's Cove Trail follows a combination of former vehicle tracks and wide, unmarked desert washes. No trail signs or directional markers are available along the route; therefore, this trail is recommended only for experienced hikers skilled in reading topographic maps. Margie's Cove Trail intersects the northern terminus of the Brittlebush Trail in the interior of the North Maricopa Mountains Wilderness. The Brittlebush Trail leads about 6 miles south to its trailhead.

Directions: To access Margie's Cove West trailhead, exit AZ 85 about 14 miles north of Gila Bend onto a primitive dirt access road. Use extreme caution when turning from AZ 85 onto the dirt road. Drive 3.8 miles and then turn south for 1.2 miles to the trailhead. A high-clearance, two-wheel-drive vehicle is suitable for this road. Margie's Cove East trailhead is accessed from Maricopa Road (AZ 238). Drive about 17 miles east of Gila Bend, turn left onto a dirt road, go about 7 miles, and then turn left. The trailhead is 1.6 miles more. A four-wheel-drive vehicle is recommended for safe access to this trailhead. To reach the Brittlebush trailhead, drive from Gila Bend about 10.4 miles east on Maricopa Road (AZ 238) to a primitive dirt road entering from the north. Follow that road about 6 miles to the trailhead. A high-clearance, two-wheel-drive vehicle is recommended.

Facilities: Margie's Cove West trailhead includes day-use parking for ten vehicles, three campsites with picnic tables and steel fire rings, a vault toilet, and informational signs. Margie's Cove East trailhead has day-use parking for five vehicles and informational signs. None at Brittlebush trailhead.

Trail: About 9 miles one-way between the two Margie's Cove trailheads; Brittlebush is about 6 miles one-way.

Degree of difficulty: Moderate.

Elevation: Trailheads are about 1,200 feet and the trail is fairly level.

Surface: Rocky.

SOUTH MARICOPA WILDERNESS

[Fig. 44(10)] The 60,100-acre South Maricopa Mountains Wilderness is located 16 miles east of Gila Bend and a few miles south of the North Maricopa Wilderness. This wilderness includes 13 miles of the Maricopa Mountain range and extensive desert plains. The eastern part of the wilderness has an isolated and screened mountainous interior formed by long ridges and isolated peaks and separated by plains and washes. The western part is dominated by desert flats fronting the east-west trending Maricopa Mountains ridgeline.

Desert bighorn sheep, desert tortoise, coyotes, bobcat, fox, deer, Gambel's quail, and various raptors also inhabit the wilderness. Saguaro, cholla, ocotillo, palo verde, and mesquite are among the many plant species found here. Hiking, backpacking, horseback riding, camping, wildlife observation, and photography are activities both experienced and family-oriented outdoor enthusiasts can enjoy.

Directions: Access is difficult. Because road conditions vary, high-clearance and four-wheel-drive vehicles are recommended. I-8 parallels the southern boundary of the wilderness, but offers no access to the wilderness. The northern boundary can be accessed from primitive dirt roads south of Maricopa Road, but active railroad tracks and rights-of-way restrict public crossings. No roads lead to the western and eastern boundaries of the wilderness. Some lands around and within the wilderness are not federally administered. Please respect the property rights of the owners and do not cross or use these lands without their permission.

Activities: Hiking, camping, and nature study.

Facilities: None.

Dates: Open year-round, but too hot in summer for hiking.

Fees: None.

Closest town: Maricopa, about 30 miles east.

For more information: BLM, Phoenix Field Office, 2015 West Deer Valley Road, Phoenix, AZ 85027-2099. Phone (623) 580-5500. Web site www.az.blm.gov.

▨ TABLE TOP WILDERNESS

[Fig. 44(11)] The Table Top Range consists of several craggy basalt-covered peaks over 3,500 feet high. Table Top Mountain is the dominant feature; its steep basalt sides rise 4,356 feet to a flat-topped summit. Within this 43,400-acre wilderness, there are several deep canyons with wide, sandy washes that cut into the mountain range.

The vegetation is typical Sonoran desert. The washes are lined with mesquite, ironwood, and palo verde. In some locations the saguaro cacti are as numerous as in Saguaro National Park and Organ Pipe Cactus National Monument.

Visitors may see Cooper's hawk, red-tailed hawk (*Buteo jamaicensis*), prairie falcon, kestrel (*Falco sparverius*), or turkey vulture (*Cathartes aura*) circling on thermals. Mule deer, javelina, and antelope jackrabbit (*Lepus alleni*) are also present. Desert bighorn sheep, coyote, Gambel's quail, Gila spotted whiptail lizard (*Cnemidophorus flagellicaudus*), and the Ajo mountain whipsnake (*Masticophis* sp.) abound.

Directions: Exit I-8 at the Vekol Road (Exit 144). Cross to the south of the interstate, and go over the cattle guard. The pavement ends. In about 2.5 miles, continue to the right as you pass the junction at the Vekol Ranch entrance. Approximately 6.5 miles south of the ranch is a corral to the east and another cattle guard. Cross through and continue easterly on the main track about 6 miles to the road's end. High-clearance and four-wheel-drive vehicles recommended.

Activities: Hiking, camping, horseback riding, and nature study.

Facilities: Small, three-site campground at Table Top trailhead.

Dates: Open year-round, but summers are too hot for hiking.

Fees: None.

Closest town: Casa Grande, about 25 miles east.

For more information: BLM, Phoenix Field Office, 2015 West Deer Valley Road, Phoenix, AZ 85027-2099. Phone (623) 580-5500. Web site www.az.blm.gov.

TABLE TOP TRAIL

[Fig. 44(12)] Table Top Trail takes visitors from the floor of Vekol Valley (elevation 2,299 feet) to the summit of Table Top Mountain (elevation 4,356 feet) in just 3.5 miles. Along the way, visitors are treated to a variety of Sonoran desert plants and wildlife, scenic vistas, and evidence of the area's volcanic history. The view from atop the summit is a dramatic panorama of rugged mountain ranges and desert plains. The trail begins by crossing several small washes and bajadas (desert outwash plains), and winds northeasterly toward Table Top Mountain through forests of saguaro, cholla, prickly pear, palo verde, and ironwood. At the base of the mountain, the trail begins a series of switchbacks on its steep ascent to the summit. Near the summit, the east edge of the trail is bordered by a 4-foot-tall wall of loosely piled stones, the origin and purpose of which are unknown. The trail ends 0.2 mile below the summit, but it is an easy cross-country walk. Vegetation on the summit includes an unusual 40-acre island of desert grassland and chaparral.

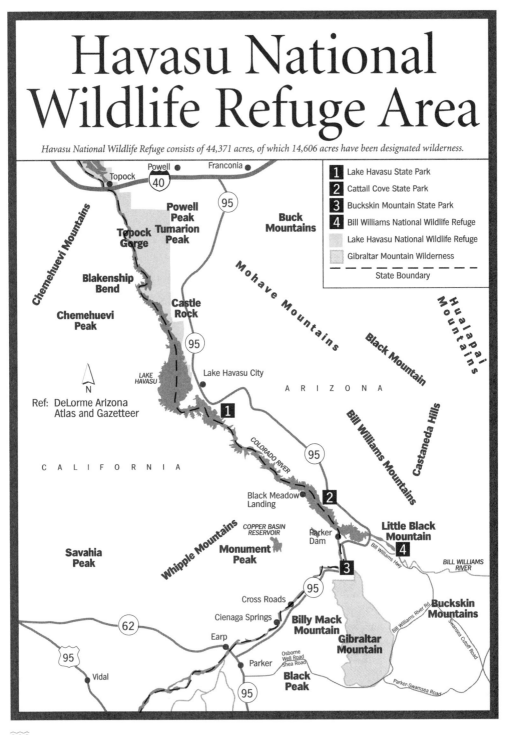

Havasu National Wildlife Refuge Area

Havasu National Wildlife Refuge consists of 44,371 acres, of which 14,606 acres have been designated wilderness.

1 Lake Havasu State Park
2 Cattail Cove State Park
3 Buckskin Mountain State Park
4 Bill Williams National Wildlife Refuge
  Lake Havasu National Wildlife Refuge
  Gibraltar Mountain Wilderness
  State Boundary

Topock
Powell
Franconia
40
95
Powell Peak
Tumarion Peak
Buck Mountains
Topock Gorge
Chemehuevi Mountains
Blakenship Bend
Castle Rock
Chemehuevi Peak
Mohave Mountains
Black Mountain
Hualapai Mountains
95
LAKE HAVASU
Lake Havasu City
N
ARIZONA
Ref: DeLorme Arizona Atlas and Gazetteer
1
Bill Williams Mountains
Castaneda Hills
CALIFORNIA
COLORADO RIVER
95
Black Meadow Landing
2
Little Black Mountain
4
COPPER BASIN RESERVOIR
Parker Dam
Bill Williams Hwy
BILL WILLIAMS RIVER
Savahia Peak
Whipple Mountains
Monument Peak
3
95
Cross Roads
Cienaga Springs
Billy Mack Mountain
Buckskin Mountains
Bill Williams River Rd
Swansea Cutoff Road
62
Earp
Gibraltar Mountain
Osborne Well Road
Shea Road
95
Parker
Vidal
Black Peak
Parker-Swansea Road
95

Directions: The trail begins at the road's end in the directions to the Table Top Wilderness, page 257. About 0.2 mile down the trail is a trailhead marker and visitor registration box.

Facilities: Table Top Trailhead includes a small, three-site campground with picnic tables, fire-rings, a vault toilet, and day-use parking for approximately 10 vehicles. No water or trash collection is provided.

Trail: 3.5 miles one-way.

Degree of difficulty: Moderate.

Elevation: 2,299 to 4,374 feet.

Surface: Rocky.

LAVA FLOW TRAIL

[Fig. 44(13)] Lava Flow Trail, in the 34,400-acre Table Top Wilderness, offers moderately difficult hiking in a varied and dramatic Sonoran desert landscape. Three trailheads are linked by a relatively level 7.25-mile trail. From south to north, the trail meanders through dense forests of saguaro, palo verde, ironwood, and cholla; skirts the jumbled basaltic slopes of Black Mountain; traverses an extensive creosote-bush flat; and crosses several large washes. Lava Flow Trail provides sweeping views of Vekol Valley and the Sand Tank Mountains to the west, while flat-topped Table Top Mountain looms to the east.

Directions: Lava Flow Trail is accessed at three points. Exit I-8 at the Vekol Valley Interchange (Exit 144), approximately 26 miles east of Gila Bend and 34 miles west of Casa Grande. To access Lava Flow West and South trailheads, travel south on Vekol Valley Road 2.1 miles to the Vekol Ranch turnoff and continue south on the dirt road to the right. From I-8, it is 9.8 miles to Lava Flow West trailhead and 14.5 miles to Lava Flow South trailhead. To access Lava Flow North trailhead, travel south on Vekol Valley Road 0.7 mile from I-8 and turn east onto the primitive four-wheel-drive road. It is 9.1 miles from I-8 to Lava Flow North trailhead. A high-clearance vehicle is required for access to Lava Flow South trailhead, and four-wheel-drive is required for access to Lava Flow North and West trailheads.

Trail: About 7 miles from the north trailhead to the south trailhead.

Degree of difficulty: Moderate.

Elevation: Trailhead is about 2,200 feet and the trail is fairly level.

Surface: Rocky.

The Lower Colorado River Valley

HAVASU NATIONAL WILDLIFE REFUGE

[Fig. 43] Havasu National Wildlife Refuge is located along the Colorado River, extending 24 miles between Needles, California and Lake Havasu City. When the gates closed at Parker Dam in 1941, President Franklin D. Roosevelt created the refuge to provide habitat and protect wildlife resources. The refuge consists of 44,371 acres, of which 14,606 acres have been designated wilderness. The Colorado River and its backwaters provide over 300 miles of shoreline within the refuge.

There are three distinct sections of the refuge—Topock Marsh, Topock Gorge, and Needles Wilderness. The marsh area is a very popular place for boaters to enjoy fishing, bird-watching, or just relaxing. The scenic, narrow, 16-mile-long Topock Gorge has become a favorite destination with canoeists. Boats may enter either end of the gorge, but no water skiing or overnight camping is permitted. The eastern bank forms the boundary for the Needles Wilderness, a range of sharp desert peaks that are popular with rock climbers.

The refuge headquarters is located in Needles, California. River access is available from a variety of public and private boat launching ramps at each end of the refuge.

In the lower Colorado River valley, the natural habitat provides critical winter food supply for thousands of geese, ducks, sandhill cranes (*Grus canadensis*), and many other species. The endangered Yuma clapper rail (*Rallus longirostris*), peregrine falcon, and southern bald eagle can be found at the refuge. Herons and egrets nest in rookeries within Topock Marsh. The Clark's grebe (*Aechmophorus clarkii*) nests in Topock Gorge and visitors often see bighorn sheep.

Directions: The refuge is accessible from I-40, where it crosses the Colorado River, and from several side roads heading west off of AZ 95, south of I-40.

Activities: Boating, water skiing, swimming, fishing, hunting, camping, and nature study.

Facilities: Boat ramp.

Dates: Open year-round.

Fees: None.

Closest town: Lake Havasu City.

For more information: Refuge Manager, Havasu National Wildlife Refuge, PO Box 3009, Needles, CA 92363. Phone (760) 326-3853.

BILL WILLIAMS RIVER NATIONAL WILDLIFE REFUGE

[Fig. 43(4)] The Bill Williams River National Wildlife Refuge includes the marshy delta area at the confluence of the Colorado and Bill Williams rivers, a 9-mile riparian corridor along the Bill Williams River, and 6,000 acres of upland desert habitat. Prior to the construction of the Alamo Dam in 1968, the flow of the Bill Williams River could vary between 10 cubic feet per second (cfs)—barely a trickle—and a raging 86,000 cfs. Vegetation along the river was well adapted to these fluctuating flows. Cottonwood and willow trees grew fast and dropped their seeds in the silt beds exposed by receding floodwaters. In drier areas, arrowweed and screwbean mesquite (*Prosopis pubescens*) mixed with other cottonwoods and willows. Farther from the river, honey mesquite, saltbush, and quailbush were found. However, since the 1930s,

99 percent of the cottonwood and willow forests of the lower Colorado River valley have disappeared for a variety of reasons, including invasion of exotic species such as salt cedar or tamarisk, deliberate cutting of the native trees, flooding by reservoirs, and the diversion of water. Most of the remaining 1 percent of forest is found along the Bill Williams River.

Like the other wildlife refuges along the lower Colorado River, this refuge is a magnet for birds. More than 275 species have been recorded here. Some of the summer residents include summer tanagers, southwestern willow flycatchers, vermilion flycatchers, and yellow-billed cuckoos. Frequent migrants include Townsend's and black-throated gray warblers (*Dendroica townsendi* and *D. nigrescens*), western tanagers (*Piranga ludoviciana*), and Lazuli buntings (*Passerina amoena*). These species are entirely dependent upon the cottonwood and willow forests. The marsh at the delta attracts mallards (*Anas platyrhynchos*), northern pintails (*Anas acuta*), and common mergansers (*Mergus merganser*). The endangered Yuma clapper rail also nests here in the spring.

Muskrat (*Ondatra zibethicus*), beaver (*Castor canadensis*), raccoon (*Procyon lotor*), bobcat (*Felis rufus*), gray fox (*Urocyon cinereoargenteus*), skunk (*Mephitis mephitis*), and coyote (*Canis latrans*) also rely on the riparian habitat. Desert cottontails (*Sylvilagus audubonii*), black-tailed jackrabbits (*Lepus californicus*), mountain lions (*Felis concolor*), desert bighorn sheep, mule deer, and javelina (*Tayassu tajacu*) can be found in the refuge as well.

Many reptiles and amphibians can be seen in the uplands including western diamondback and sidewinder rattlesnakes (*Crotalus atrox* and *C. cerastes*), common kingsnakes (*Lampropeltis getulus*), desert tortoises, desert iguanas (*Dipsosaurus dorsalis*), and Gila monsters. Checkered gartersnakes (*Thamnophis marcianus*), collared lizards (*Crotaphytus* sp.), and mud turtles (*Kinosternon* sp.) are found closer to the river.

Most of the original native species of fish are long gone, but razorback suckers (*Xyrauchen texanus*) and bonytail chubs (*Gila elegans*) have recently been reintroduced into the delta area. Other fish include channel catfish, carp (*Cyprinus carpio*), and red shiner.

Directions: The refuge is located halfway between Parker and Lake Havasu City, along AZ 95. The delta can be viewed from several turnouts off AZ 95. The riparian area along the Bill Williams River is best seen by driving the road, which begins 0.3 mile south of the Bill Williams River bridge and ends about 3 miles east of AZ 95.

Activities: Hiking, hunting in season, fishing, boating, and nature study.

Facilities: Visitor center, 1 mile south of river on AZ 95.

Dates: Open year-round.

SKUNK
(Mephitis
mephitis)

Fees: None.

Closest town: Lake Havasu City, about 15 miles northwest.

For more information: Refuge Manager, Bill Williams River National Wildlife Refuge, 60911 Highway 95, Parker, AZ 85344. Phone (520) 667-4144.

LAKE HAVASU AND CATTAIL COVE STATE PARKS

[Fig. 43(1), Fig. 43(2)] These two state parks lie adjacent to each other between Lake Havasu City and the Bill Williams River. They both offer access to the southern part of Lake Havasu. Lake Havasu State Park has a swimming beach and a campground. Cattail Cove State Park has a modern lakeside campground, as well as offering more than 140 boat-access-only campsites. An alternative name to this park could be smoke tree (*Dalea* sp.), since they are very abundant along the shore.

The low elevation of the lake, about 450 feet above sea level, and thus warm to hot year-round temperatures, make these parks popular with boaters, swimmers, water skiers, and anglers.

Directions: Lake Havasu State Park is accessible at Windsor Beach just west of London Bridge in Lake Havasu City. The main entrance to Cattail Cove State Park Drive is about 15 miles south of Lake Havasu City on AZ 95.

Activities: Hiking, swimming, water skiing, boating, fishing, camping, and nature study.

Facilities: Boat ramps, boat-access-only campsites, swimming beaches, nature trails, and drive-in campgrounds.

Dates: Open year-round.

Fees: There are entrance and camping fees.

Closest town: Lake Havasu City.

For more information: Lake Havasu State Park, 1350 West McCulloch Boulevard, Lake Havasu City, AZ 86403. Phone (520) 855-7851. Cattail Cove State Park, 1350 West McCulloch Boulevard, Lake Havasu City, AZ 86403. Phone (520) 855-1223. Web site www.pr.state.az.us.

BUCKSKIN MOUNTAIN STATE PARK

[Fig. 43(3)] This scenic park is located on a secluded bend of the Colorado River backed by low cliffs. The park attracts nature lovers and water enthusiasts, who also enjoy the neatly manicured campground. Human anglers compete with great blue and black-crowned night-herons (*Ardea herodias* and *Nycticorax nycticorax*) and great and snowy egrets (*Ardea alba* and *Egretta thula*) for largemouth bass, crappie, channel catfish, and bluegill. Hikers will find three short developed trails that ascend the steep bluff to panoramic overlooks.

Directions: Located 11 miles north of Parker off AZ 95.

Activities: Hiking, swimming, boating, fishing, nature study, and camping.

Facilities: Swimming beach, boat ramp, playground, volleyball and basketball courts, horseshoe pit, showers, and nature trails.

Dates: Open year-round.

Fees: There are entrance and camping fees.

Closest town: Parker, about 11 miles southwest.

For more information: Buckskin Mountain State Park, PO Box BA, Parker, AZ 85344. Phone (520) 667-3231. Web site www.pr.state.az.us.

🦎 CIBOLA NATIONAL WILDLIFE REFUGE

[Fig. 42(7)] The 17,000-acre Cibola National Wildlife Refuge was established in 1964 as mitigation for dam construction on the Colorado River in the 1930s and 1940s and channelization work to prevent flooding. The refuge is located in the floodplain of the lower Colorado River and provides important habitat for migrating birds, wintering waterfowl, and resident species. About 240 species of birds use the refuge during the year. The refuge contains several miles of historic river channels and several backwaters that provide key habitats in a changed environment. About 1,600 acres are farmed to provide food for migrating and wintering waterfowl, including sandhill cranes, the Great Basin subspecies of Canada geese (*Branta canadensis moffitti*), brown pelicans (*Pelecanus occidentalis*), herons, and other species.

The headquarters and visitor center are located at the north end of the refuge. An auto tour route offers wildlife viewing, which is especially good in the winter. Hunting for deer, waterfowl, dove, rabbit, and quail is possible in season. Fishing is another popular activity.

Directions: From Blythe, CA, drive south on Cibola Road about 17 miles and follow signs to the refuge headquarters.

Activities: Wildlife watching, hunting, boating, and fishing.

Facilities: Visitor center and auto tour route.

Dates: Refuge open year-round, although some sections may be closed seasonally; visitor center open weekdays.

Fees: None.

Closest town: Blythe, CA, about 17 miles north.

For more information: Refuge Manager, Cibola National Wildlife Refuge, Route 2, Box 138, Cibola, AZ 85328-9801. Phone (520) 857-3253.

🦎 IMPERIAL NATIONAL WILDLIFE REFUGE

[Fig. 42(8)] The Imperial National Wildlife Refuge takes in more than 25,000 acres along the lower Colorado River. Spring and fall offer the greatest variety of birds—more than 270 species—but the sheer numbers of wintering waterfowl can be amazing.

One of the best ways to experience the Imperial and Cibola national wildlife refuges is from water level in a canoe or kayak. *A Boating Trail Guide to the Colorado River: Canoeing from Blythe to Imperial Dam* is available from either refuge office.

Directions: The refuge headquarters is located 3 miles north of the resort community of Martinez Lake. Take US 95 north from Yuma to Martinez Road. Follow the signs to the headquarters.

Activities: Hiking, boating, fishing, hunting, and nature study.

Facilities: Refuge headquarters has literature and natural history exhibits; viewing tower; lookout points along the Red Cloud Mine Road; and interpretive trail.

Dates: Refuge open year-round; headquarters open Monday through Friday.

Fees: None.

Closest town: Yuma, about 30 miles south.

For more information: Imperial National Wildlife Refuge, PO Box 72217, Yuma, AZ 85365. Phone (520) 783-3371 or 783-3372.

PAINTED DESERT TRAIL

[Fig. 42(1)] This self-guided interpretive trail provides a closer look at desert plants, unique geological features, and a splendid view across the river valley. November through April is the best period for this hour-long hike. A leaflet obtained at the trailhead is your guide.

Directions: Drive 2.8 miles north of the refuge headquarters on the Red Cloud Mine Road.

Trail: 1-mile loop.

Degree of difficulty: Easy.

Elevation: Trailhead is about 200 feet; the trail is fairly level.

Surface: Maintained trail.

TRIGO MOUNTAINS WILDERNESS

[Fig. 42(10)] The Trigo Mountains lie east of the Colorado River and adjacent to the Imperial National Wildlife Refuge. The 30,300-acre trailless wilderness area is bisected by an old dirt road into two sections, north and south. The wilderness includes 14 miles of the Trigo Mountain ridgeline with Red Cloud Wash to the south, Clip Wash in the center, and Hart Mine Wash to the north. The area is characterized by sawtooth ridges and steep-sided canyons, and is heavily dissected by washes. Elevations range from a mere 220 feet above sea level to about 1,250 on the highest peaks.

Understandably the hot, dry deserts of southwestern Arizona are not the best habitats for a large predator such as a mountain lion; yet, the elusive and rare Yuma puma (*Felis concolor browni*) is believed to still prowl in this wilderness area. Though rarely glimpsed by visitors, you should keep an eye out for lion tracks and scat. Perhaps they prey on the feral burros that are common in the area.

Recreation such as extended horseback riding and backpacking trips, sight-seeing, hiking, and rock climbing are enhanced by the topographic diversity and scenic character, as well as botanical, wildlife, and cultural values.

Directions: From Yuma, travel north along AZ 95 to the Martinez Lake Road. Then go west on Martinez Lake Road to the Imperial National Wildlife Refuge. Travel northwest on Red Cloud Mine Road to Red Cloud Wash. Roads near the wilderness include Cibola Road, Hart Mine Wash Road, and Lopez Wash Road. High-clearance or four-wheel-drive vehicles are recommended for access to the wilderness boundary. Some lands around the wilderness are not federally administered. Please respect the property rights of the owners and do not cross or use these lands without their permission. North of Clip Wash, the easternmost wilderness boundary is adjacent to the U.S. Army Yuma Proving Ground. Observe all warning signs.

Activities: Hiking, camping, and nature study.

Facilities: None.

Dates: Open year-round, but very hot in the summer.

Fees: None.

Closest town: Yuma, about 30 miles south.

For more information: BLM, Yuma Field Office, 2555 Gila Ridge Road, Yuma, AZ 85365. Phone (520) 317-3200. Web site www.az.blm.gov.

🔲 YUMA TERRITORIAL PRISON STATE HISTORIC PARK AND YUMA CROSSING STATE HISTORIC PARK

[Fig. 42(2), Fig. 42(3)] Before the advent of bridges, places to easily wade across the Colorado River were difficult to find. However, on the lower Colorado, just below the mouth of Gila River, is a good crossing place. For millennia, Indians have used this crossing; later came the Spanish, and after them, American trappers and soldiers. Here the town of Yuma grew up on the east bank. Two state parks present some of the area's rich history.

Although considered a model facility in the late 1800s, the Yuma Territorial Prison was known as the "hellhole of Arizona." Prisoners endured summer temperatures close to 120 degrees Fahrenheit. Photo exhibits show past "residents," and visitors can wander through cellblocks, climb the watchtower, and see the prison graveyard.

The Yuma Crossing State Historic Park's visitor center shows a video that explains the changes and conflicts brought by Indians, the Spanish, mountain men, the '49ers, and pioneers. Restored nineteenth century military buildings invite exploration.

Directions: Yuma Territorial Prison State Historic Park is located on Prison Hill Road off Giss Parkway. Yuma Crossing State Historic Park is located at 201 N. Fourth Avenue just before the Colorado River bridge.

Activities: Self-guided tours.

Facilities: Both have visitor centers and exhibits.

Dates: Yuma Territorial Prison State Historic Park, open year-round; Yuma

The Valley of the Sun

Two thousand years ago the Hohokam people built canals to divert water from the Salt River to grow crops in this desert region.

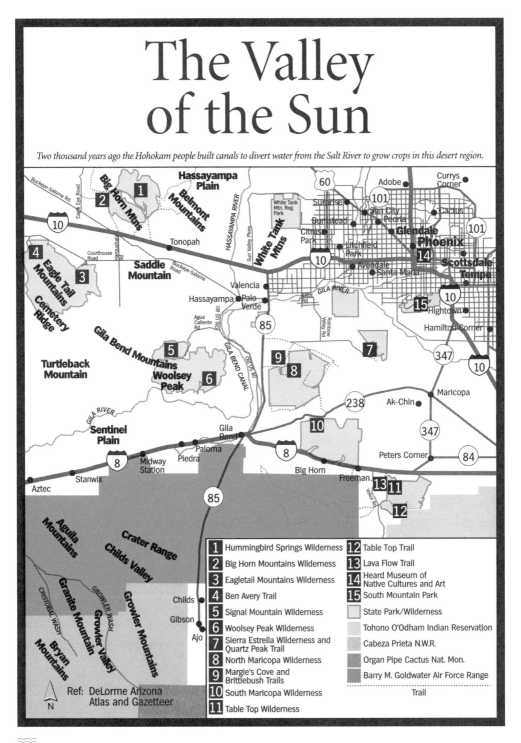

1 Hummingbird Springs Wilderness	**12** Table Top Trail
2 Big Horn Mountains Wilderness	**13** Lava Flow Trail
3 Eagletail Mountains Wilderness	**14** Heard Museum of Native Cultures and Art
4 Ben Avery Trail	**15** South Mountain Park
5 Signal Mountain Wilderness	☐ State Park/Wilderness
6 Woolsey Peak Wilderness	Tohono O'Odham Indian Reservation
7 Sierra Estrella Wilderness and Quartz Peak Trail	Cabeza Prieta N.W.R.
8 North Maricopa Wilderness	Organ Pipe Cactus Nat. Mon.
9 Margie's Cove and Brittlebush Trails	Barry M. Goldwater Air Force Range
10 South Maricopa Wilderness	········· Trail
11 Table Top Wilderness	

Ref: DeLorme Arizona Atlas and Gazetteer

Crossing State Historic Park, open daily except May through Oct. when it is open Thursday through Sunday.

Fees: There is an entrance fee for both parks.

Closest town: Yuma.

For more information: Yuma Territorial Prison State Historic Park, PO Box 792, Yuma, AZ 85364. Phone (520) 783-4771. Yuma Crossing State Historic Park, 201 N. Fourth Avenue, Yuma, AZ 85366. Phone (520) 329-0471. Web site www.pr.state.az.us.

The Valley of the Sun

[Fig. 44] Within the Valley of the Sun lies the sprawling, vibrant city of Phoenix and its satellite cities of Scottsdale, Mesa, Tempe, Glendale, Sun City, and more. This metro area is one of the largest and fastest growing in the nation—triple the overall U.S. rate—and home to more than 3 million people. But others lived here long before the city founded.

Two thousand years ago the Hohokam people were building canals to divert water from the Salt River to make the desert bloom with crops of corn, beans, squash, and cotton. By 1450, the Hohokam had disappeared. In 1867, Jack Swilling, a former Confederate soldier, formed a company of unemployed miners to dig out the long-abandoned Indian canals. By the next summer, he was harvesting wheat and barley. Other farmers took notice and moved to the desert valley.

There are numerous places to learn about the region's natural and cultural history including the **Phoenix Museum of History**, 105 N. Fifth Street, phone (602) 253-2734; the **Desert Botanical Garden**, 1201 N. Galvin Parkway, phone (602) 941-1225; the **Arizona Science Center**, 600 E. Washington, phone (602) 716-2000; and the **Phoenix Zoo**, within **Papago Park**, phone (602) 273-1341. And, of course, Phoenix has all the other amenities one expects in a modern city.

For more information: Arizona Office of Tourism, 2702 N. Third St., Suite 4015, Phoenix, AZ 85004. Phone (602) 230-7733 or (888) 520-3434. Web site www.arizonaguide.com.

HEARD MUSEUM OF NATIVE CULTURES AND ART

[Fig. 44(14)] One of the best museums in the state for insight into the rich history of Arizona's native people is the Heard. Exhibits include clothing, tools, weapons, an Apache wickiup, and a Navajo hogan. Navajo, Hopi, and Zuni jewelry, baskets, pottery, and weavings are also on display, as well as an extensive kachina doll collection.

The museum's Gallery of Indian Art houses contemporary artwork, and a large gift shop carries many fine pieces for purchase. Docents offer guided tours of the museum daily.

Directions: Located on the east side of Central Avenue between McDowell and Thomas.

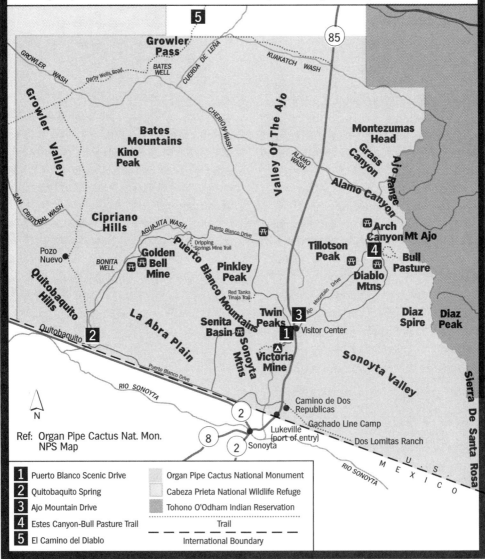

Organ Pipe Cactus National Monument

Organ Pipe Cactus National Monument, established in 1937, protects 516 square miles of the Sonoran desert.

5
Growler Pass
85
Growler Wash
Darby Wells Road
BATES WELL
CUERDA DE LENA
KUAKATCH WASH
Growler Valley
Bates Mountains
Kino Peak
CHERION WASH
Valley Of The Ajo
ALAMO WASH
Montezumas Head
Grass Canyon
Ajo Range
Alamo Canyon
SAN CRISTOBAL WASH
Cipriano Hills
AGUAJITA WASH
Puerto Blanco Drive
Pozo Nuevo
BONITA WELL
Golden Bell Mine
Puerto Blanco
Pinkley Peak
Dripping Springs Mine Trail
Tillotson Peak
Arch Canyon
Mt Ajo
4
Bull Pasture
Diablo Mtns
Quitobaquito Hills
Red Tanks Tinaja Trail
Mountains
Senita Basin
Twin Peaks
3
Ajo Mountain Drive
Diaz Spire
Diaz Peak
Quitobaquito
2
La Abra Plain
Sonoyta Mtns
1
Visitor Center
Puerto Blanco Drive
Victoria Mine
Sonoyta Valley
Sierra De Santa Rosa
RIO SONOYTA
Camino de Dos Republicas
Gachado Line Camp
N
2
Lukeville (port of entry)
Dos Lomitas Ranch
Ref: Organ Pipe Cactus Nat. Mon. NPS Map
8
2
Sonoyta
MEXICO
U. S.
RIO SONOYTA

1	Puerto Blanco Scenic Drive	Organ Pipe Cactus National Monument
2	Quitobaquito Spring	Cabeza Prieta National Wildlife Refuge
3	Ajo Mountain Drive	Tohono O'Odham Indian Reservation
4	Estes Canyon-Bull Pasture Trail	Trail
5	El Camino del Diablo	International Boundary

Activities: Touring museum, special events are often held on weekends.
Facilities: Museum, gift shop, and café.
Dates: Open year-round except major holidays.
Fees: There is an admission charge to museum, but the gift shop and café are free.
Closest town: Phoenix.
For more information: The Heard Museum, 2301 N. Central Avenue, Phoenix, AZ 85004. Phone (602) 252-8840 or 252-8848. Web site www.heard.org.

SOUTH MOUNTAIN PARK

[Fig. 44(15)] The greater Phoenix metro area has a number of city and regional parks—**Papago Park**, Van Buren and Galvin Parkway, phone (602) 256-3220 or 261-8318; **Usery Mountain Recreation Park**, Usery Pass Road, phone (602) 984-0032; **McDowell Mountain Regional Park**, north Fountain Hills Boulevard, phone (602) 471-0173; **Lake Pleasant Regional Park**; Lake Pleasant Road, phone (602) 780-9875; **White Tank Mountain Regional Park**, Olive Road at Dunlap Avenue, phone (602) 935-2505; **Estrella Mountain Regional Park**, Estrella Parkway, phone (602) 932-3811; **Squaw Peak**; Squaw Peak Drive, phone 602) 262-7901; **Echo Canyon Recreation Area**, McDonald Drive at Tatum Boulevard, phone (602) 256-3220; and the **Phoenix Bikeway System**, phone (602) 255-8010.

The largest city park in Phoenix and the nation is South Mountain Park. South Mountain's 17,000 acres protect a rugged desert mountain towering over south Phoenix. More than 50 miles of trail crisscross the park, allowing hikers and equestrians to explore the area. A paved road winds to Dobbin's Lookout, which offers terrific views of the Salt River Valley and the city of Phoenix, provided that the air quality is not too bad.

Directions: The main entrance to the park is located at the southern end of Central Avenue.
Activities: Scenic drives, hiking, horseback riding, biking, and nature study.
Facilities: Horse rentals, picnic grounds, and 18 marked trails.
Dates: Open year-round, but summer is very hot.
Fees: None.
Closest town: Phoenix.
For more information: South Mountain Park, 10919 S. Central Avenue, Phoenix, AZ 85040-8302. Phone (602) 495-0222.

Organ Pipe Cactus National Monument

[Fig. 45] Organ Pipe Cactus National Monument, established in 1937, protects 516 square miles of the most pristine section of the Sonoran desert on either side of the U.S./Mexican border. It is world renowned for its forests of giant cactus, including the northernmost population of organ pipe cactus (*Stenocereus thurberi*) and ancient ironwood trees. After a rare wet winter, the spring wildflower displays can be an extraordinary sight.

Organ pipe cactus ranges south into Mexico as far as Sinaloa. Botanists consider it to be a tropical cactus; that is, more frost sensitive than many of the other columnar cacti, such as saguaro. Therefore, organ pipe cactus is most often found growing on south-facing rocky slopes below 3,000 feet in elevation. Nectar-feeding bats are the primary pollinators and some of the major seed dispersers. Because the flowers close during the day, diurnal animals are not significant pollinators, as they are of saguaro. The juicy, sweet, red fruits are widely regarded as one of the best tasting of all the cacti and are sold in markets in Sonora and Baja California.

Several trails offer close looks at the beauty of the desert. The best hiking months are October through April. The Visitor Center Nature Trail, 0.1-mile round trip, is wheelchair accessible. Guide pamphlets are available at the trailhead. The Campground Perimeter Trail, 1-mile round trip, allows leashed pets. The Desert View Nature Trail, 1.2 miles round trip, is a circular route leading to vistas of Sonoyta Valley and the pink granite of the Cubabi Mountains in Mexico. Trailside signs describe features along the way. Palo Verde Trail, 2.6 miles round trip, goes between the visitor center and the campground. Estes Canyon-Bull Pasture Trail, 4.1 miles round trip, is a strenuous climb with grand views of the surrounding terrain. Victoria Mine Trail, 4.5 miles round trip, goes over rolling terrain to the site of the oldest mine in the area. The rangers at the visitor center have trailhead information.

Directions: The monument is bisected by AZ 85 between Why and Lukeville.

Activities: Hiking, mountain biking, scenic drives, and camping.

Facilities: Visitor center and two campgrounds.

Dates: Open year-round, but summers are very hot.

Fees: There is an entrance fee and campground fee.

Closest town: Lukeville, at southern boundary of monument.

For more information: Organ Pipe Cactus National Monument, Rte. 1, Box 100, Ajo, AZ 85321. Phone (520) 387-6849. Web site www.nps.gov/orpi.

A biker in Organ Pipe Cactus National Monument.

PUERTO BLANCO SCENIC DRIVE

[Fig. 45(1)] This 53-mile scenic, graded dirt loop starts just west of the visitor center. A pamphlet that explains features at numbered stops can be picked up at the visitor center. Drivers should allow at least a half day to do this loop. One section is one-way (counterclockwise) and drivers cannot back up. Picnic tables and three short trails invite further exploration. Mountain bikers are welcome and can ride in either direction.

Directions: Starts immediately west of the visitor center and travels in a counter-clockwise direction. The last third is two-way.

QUITOBAQUITO SPRING

[Fig. 45(2)] One mile off of the Puerto Blanco Scenic Drive is the desert oasis of Quitobaquito. More than 150 birds have been identified here. The chubby, 2-inch-long Quitobaquito pupfish (*Cyprinodon macularis*) is an endemic subspecies to the spring. Pupfish can tolerate water nearly twice as salty as the ocean and temperatures of up to 115 degrees Fahrenheit. Other races of desert pupfish are believed to have been eliminated from Arizona. Stocking efforts have met with mixed results, but pupfish have been reintroduced or are being propagated at a number of locations, including the Hassayampa River Preserve, the Arizona-Sonora Desert Museum, and the Boyce Thompson Arboretum.

Directions: Drive south of the visitor center about 6 miles and turn right onto the two-way section of the Puerto Blanco Scenic Drive. Drive in about 15 miles and take the left turn to the spring.

Activities: Nature study along a short trail.

Facilities: None.

Dates: Open year-round, but summers are very hot.

Fees: There is an entrance fee to the monument.

Closest town: Lukeville, at southern boundary of monument.

For more information: Organ Pipe Cactus National Monument, Rte. 1, Box 100, Ajo, AZ 85321. Phone (520) 387-6849. Web site www.nps.gov/orpi.

AJO MOUNTAIN DRIVE

[Fig. 45(3)] This gravel road climbs into the more rugged eastern part of the monument and skirts the base of 4,808-foot Mount Ajo. Most of the 21-mile loop is one-way, although mountain bikers can ride either direction.

If adequate rains come in early spring, the ground between the cacti is covered with colorful fields of blue lupine (*Lupinus* sp.), golden poppy (*Eschscholtzia mexicana*), pink owl's clover (*Orthocarpus purpurascens*), and other wildflowers.

Directions: Starts immediately east of the visitor center, across AZ 85.

Activities: Sight-seeing, mountain biking, picnicking, and hiking.

Facilities: Picnic tables, hiking trails, and numbered interpretive stops.

Dates: Open year-round, but summers are very hot.

Fees: There is an entrance fee to the monument.

Closest town: Lukeville, at southern boundary of monument.

For more information: Organ Pipe Cactus National Monument, Rte. 1, Box 100, Ajo, AZ 85321. Phone (520) 387-6849. Web site www.nps.gov/orpi.

ESTES CANYON-BULL PASTURE TRAIL

[Fig. 45(4)] This moderately difficult loop leading to an overlook is a great way to see the monument and its namesake, organ pipe cactus.

Directions: About 11.4 miles from the beginning of the Ajo Mountain Drive is the Estes Canyon Picnic Area and trailhead.

Trail: 4.1-mile loop.

Degree of difficulty: Moderate.

Elevation: 2,440 to 3,135 feet at Bull Pasture.

Surface: Rocky.

Cabeza Prieta National Wildlife Refuge

[Fig. 45] One of the last large, fairly pristine sections of the Sonoran desert in North America is the Cabeza Prieta area, stretching from Organ Pipe Cactus National Monument westward toward Yuma. Desert enthusiasts will find plenty of untracked wilderness to hike and explore, but you may be surprised to learn that you are not the first.

This extremely arid, hostile but awesome desert region was home to the Sand Papago and earlier people, but little is known about them. Recorded history begins with Spaniard Melchior Diaz making the first recorded traverse in the winter of 1540. As a member of Coronado's expedition (*see* page 180), Diaz was searching for the lost city of Cibola, a legendary city of fabulous riches.

In 1699, a missionary explorer, Padre Kino, traversed the area looking for Indian souls to save and discovered that California was connected to Arizona; earlier Spanish explorers had assumed that it was an island. In 1744, the Spanish conquistador Captain de Anza is credited with pioneering the route through the area (although he was actually following an ancient Indian trail) that a century later would become known as *El Camino del Diablo*, "the Devil's Highway." The trail received this moniker because hundreds of travelers died of thirst and exposure while trying to reach the California goldfields. These unfortunate souls had been lured into taking the hot, dry desert route to avoid potentially hostile Indians living along the Gila and other Arizona rivers. Today, adventurous souls tackle the old camino in four-wheel-drive vehicles.

Captain D.D. Gaillard, a member of the International Boundary Commission that surveyed the U.S./Mexico border west of the Rio Grande between 1891 and 1896, complained, "It is hard to imagine a more desolate or depressing ride. Mile after mile the journey stretches through this land of 'silence, solitude, and sunshine,' with little to distract the eye from the awful surrounding dreariness and desolation except the

*The pleated stems of the hedgehog cactus (*Echinocereus engelmannii*) expand quickly when water is available and shrink slowly in dry times.*

bleeching [sic] skeletons of horses and the painfully frequent crosses which mark the graves of those who perished of thirst."

In 1939, Cabeza Prieta National Wildlife Refuge was established to protect a portion of the Sonoran desert. Desert bighorn sheep, the lesser long-nosed bat (*Leptonycteris curasoae*), and the endangered Sonoran pronghorn (*Antilocarpa americana sonoriensis*) are among the species that live in the refuge. However, the Sonoran pronghorn are barely surviving. There are only about 140 adults, and in the last three years only two out of almost 100 fawns have survived. An extended drought seems to be the main detrimental factor.

The refuge shares a 56-mile international border with Mexico. Within the 860,000-acre refuge are craggy mountains separated by broad valleys, which are peppered with sand dunes or covered with lava flows. Cabeza Prieta, Spanish for "black head," refers to a lava-capped, granite peak. Most of the refuge was designated wilderness in 1990 to further protect its natural resources. However, there are two four-wheel-drive roads that still allow vehicular access. One of these roads follows the infamous El Camino del Diablo. Cross-country hiking is possible, but there are very few reliable watering holes. Carry plenty of water with you.

Directions: Most of the refuge is within the air space of the Barry M. Goldwater

JOSHUA TREE
(Yucca brevifolia)

Air Force Range; therefore no one may enter the refuge without obtaining a Refuge Entry Permit and signing a Military Hold Harmless Agreement. Both permits are available at the refuge office in Ajo. They can also provide a map showing vehicle access points.

Activities: Scenic four-wheel driving, camping, hiking, limited hunting for desert bighorn sheep, and nature study.

Facilities: Visitor center in Ajo; no facilities on refuge.

Dates: Open year-round except on days when the military is practicing aerial gunnery. Military schedules are known in advance and available at the refuge office. Summers are dangerously hot for humans and their vehicles. Travel is not recommended during the summer.

Fees: None.

Closest town: Ajo, about 12 miles northeast.

For more information: Cabeza Prieta National Wildlife Refuge, 1611 North Second Avenue, Ajo, AZ 85321. Phone (520) 387-6483. Regarding conservation of the area, contact Friends of Cabeza Prieta, PO Box 65940, Tucson, AZ 85728-4940. E-mail FoCabeza@aol.com.

🏵 EL CAMINO DEL DIABLO

[Fig. 45(5)] Despite Captain Gaillard's grim description, for the properly equipped visitor, driving the length of the El Camino del Diablo—as described below, about a 107-mile, 2-day minimum drive—can be an incredible adventure. Take along a copy of *Desert Heart* by William Hartmann to learn more about the intriguing history of this region and some of the enigmatic historic sites along the trail.

A four-wheel-drive vehicle is necessary. Carry at least 2 to 3 gallons of water per person per day, go in the winter, take a shovel and an emergency vehicle survival kit including at least one good spare tire, and obtain a permit from the Cabeza Prieta

National Wildlife Refuge Office. There are no established hiking trails. Be prepared with maps and compass.

From the Cabeza Prieta National Wildlife Refuge Office, drive south on AZ 85 through Ajo about 4 miles to the Darby Wells Road. Turn right (west) and set the odometer to 0.0. At mile 12.7, you enter the remote northwest corner of Organ Pipe Cactus National Monument. Two more miles and you cross Growler Pass between the Growler and Bates mountains.

At mile 26, the road enters Cabeza Prieta National Wildlife Refuge, home to the endangered Sonoran pronghorn antelope and at one time the Sand Papago people. To the north is the first recorded archaeological site in the area, known as the "Lost City." This was an important Hohokam site were they would rest from shell-gathering trips to the Gulf of California, before continuing north to the Gila River. This formidable journey not only crossed this harsh area, but also El Gran Desierto in Mexico, the driest and largest desert in North America.

At mile 44 is O'Neil's Grave. In 1916, prospector Dave O'Neil became the only known person to have drowned in this dry desert. Between mile 53 and 70 are many graves of hapless travelers. At mile 85.4, enter the western half of the Barry M. Goldwater Range, which is administered by the Marine Corps Air Station in Yuma. The Border Patrol maintains the El Camino del Diablo from this point in the Lechuguilla Valley.

At mile 89.2, a left fork goes 2 miles to Tinajas Altas, a series of 10 natural rock tanks that often catch rainwater and were an extremely important water source along the trail. Unfortunately, many early travelers discovered the lower tanks dry; and while trying to climb to the higher ones, they either fell to their death or succumbed to dehydration. Dozens of old graves dot the area. The road now turns north and parallels the Tinajas Altas Mountains. At mile 107, the dirt road returns to pavement at Interstate 8.

There is a citizens' proposal to combine Cabeza Prieta National Wildlife Refuge with the adjacent Goldwater Air Force Range and Organ Pipe Cactus National Monument to create a huge Sonoran Desert National Park. This park, along with the contiguous Pinacate Biosphere Reserve in Mexico, would preserve a significant section of the Sonoran desert.

For more information about this proposal, contact Sonoran Desert National Park Project, The Southwest Center, University of Arizona, 1052 North Highland Avenue, Tucson, AZ 85721-0185. Phone (520) 621-9922. E-mail SonDesNP@U.ARIZONA.EDU.

For more information: Cabeza Prieta National Wildlife Refuge, 1611 North Second Avenue, Ajo, AZ 85321. Phone (520) 387-6483.

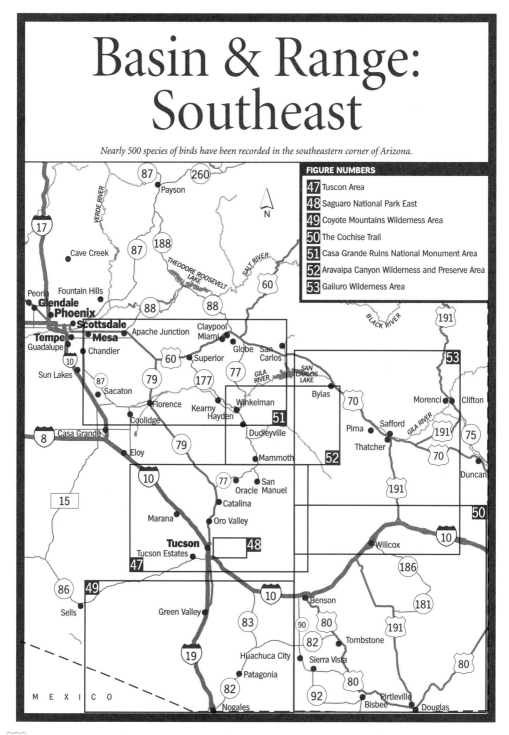

Basin & Range: Southeast

Nearly 500 species of birds have been recorded in the southeastern corner of Arizona.

FIGURE NUMBERS

47 Tuscon Area
48 Saguaro National Park East
49 Coyote Mountains Wilderness Area
50 The Cochise Trail
51 Casa Grande Ruins National Monument Area
52 Aravaipa Canyon Wilderness and Preserve Area
53 Galiuro Wilderness Area

Basin and Range: Southeast

L ike the other Basin and Range areas of the state, the desert floor of southeastern Arizona gives way to isolated mountain ranges. But unlike those other
areas, many of these ranges rise thousands of feet, allowing their summits to be
biological worlds apart from their arid, hot bases; they are forested sky islands adrift
in a desert sea. Populating the desert habitats is curious blend of Sonoran and
Chihuahuan desert species; and higher in elevation, a mix of Rocky Mountain and
Sierra Madrean species can be found. There is also an amazing variety of weather
conditions that can be encountered while visiting these mountains. Travelers need to
be prepared (*see* warning about mountain and desert travel, page IX).

The largest city in this corner of Arizona is Tucson. Like Phoenix, the Tucson area
first attracted Native Americans, then much later came the Spanish. In the 1690s,
Padre Eusebio Francisco Kino visited southern Arizona to convert the Indians to

[*Above:* The extraordinary rock sculptures of Chiricahua National Monument]

Tucson Area

The Santa Catalina Ranger District takes its name from the Santa Catalina Mountains that dominate the northern skyline of Tucson.

Ref: DeLorme Arizona Atlas and Gazetteer

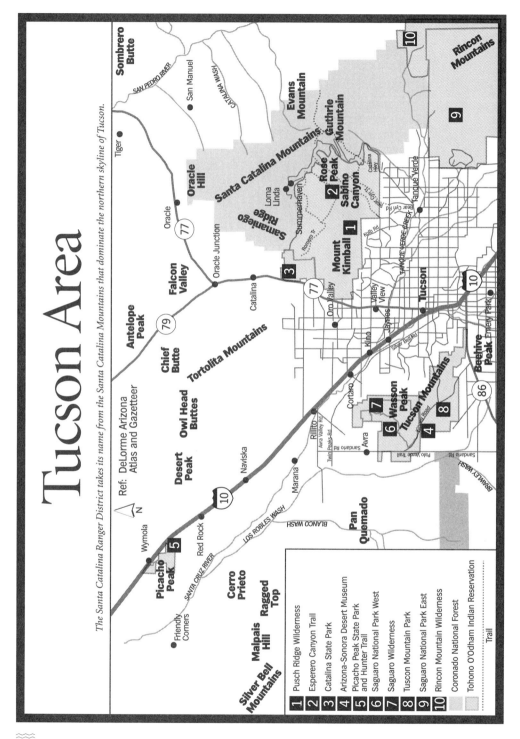

1. Pusch Ridge Wilderness
2. Esperero Canyon Trail
3. Catalina State Park
4. Arizona-Sonora Desert Museum
5. Picacho Peak State Park and Hunter Trail
6. Saguaro National Park West
7. Saguaro Wilderness
8. Tucson Mountain Park
9. Saguaro National Park East
10. Rincon Mountain Wilderness

Coronado National Forest
Tohono O'Odham Indian Reservation
Trail

Christianity, and a few years later work began, using Indian laborers, on what would become the beautiful church San Xavier del Bac. The church is still in use today and visitors are welcome.

By 1775, other Spaniards were constructing the Presidio de San Agustin del Tucson near a Pima Indian village called *Stjuk-shon*, corrupted to Tucson. The ruins of the Presidio were discovered in the 1950s during new construction in the downtown area. Below the Presidio were the ruins of a much older Hohokam pit house. Today, many Tucsonians are descendents of these earlier residents. Modern Tucson has attempted to retain its Spanish and Indian heritage through museums, cultural events, and the preservation of historic sites. Sixty-five miles south of Tucson, at the end of I-19, is Nogales, Arizona's major gateway to old Mexico.

Southeastern Arizona is an internationally renowned birder's paradise. The sky island mountain ranges are a crossroads for Rocky Mountain species and tropical species from the Sierra Madre in Mexico. In addition, the Sonoran and Chihuahuan deserts, each with its own unique bird species, meet in this corner of the state. Eastern U.S. species sometimes migrate through the area. Almost 500 species of birds have been recorded here.

Besides the many excellent specific birding areas described in this chapter, the **Southeastern Arizona Bird Observatory** (phone 520-432-1388), along with a number of private and governmental organizations, is developing a Southeastern Arizona Birding Trail. The trail is a highway route linking the best birding locations. A trail map shows the route and highlights the sites and birding opportunities.

An indispensable guidebook for birders is *Davis and Russell's Finding Birds in Southeastern Arizona* published by the Tucson Audubon Society, 300 E. University #120, Tucson, AZ 85705. Phone (520) 629-0510. Web site www.audubon.org/chapter/az/tucson. Another helpful resource is the Cornell Lab of Ornithology and National Audubon Society sponsored Web site www.birdsource.org.

For more information: Tucson Visitor Center, 130 S. Scott Avenue, Tucson, AZ 85701. Phone (520) 624-1817 or (888) 2-TUCSON.

Coronado National Forest

[Fig. 47] Because of the scattered locations of forested land in southeastern Arizona, the 1,700,000-acre Coronado National Forest is broken into 12 units administered by 5 different ranger districts—Santa Catalina, Nogales, Sierra Vista, Douglas, and Safford. Elevations range from 3,000 feet to over 10,700 feet. Year-round opportunities for outdoor recreation exist.

Fishing can be done at Pena Blanca and Arivaca lakes (both northwest of Nogales), Rose Canyon Lake (in the Santa Catalinas), Riggs Flat Lake (in the Pinaleños), and Parker Canyon Lake (west of the Huachucas). For a recorded message of

Cactus Ferruginous Pygmy-owl

Cactus ferruginous pygmy-owl (*Glaucidium brasilianum*)—its name is almost as long as its body. These owls measure only 7 inches from beak to tail and are the second smallest owl in North America. Only the elf owl (*Micrathene whitneyi*), also native to southern Arizona, is smaller. Pygmy-owls live at desert oases and along washes. They feed on other small birds, lizards, insects, small mammals, and frogs.

In 1998, researchers found only 32 cactus ferruginous pygmy-owls in southern Arizona. The once more common owl was on the verge of extirpation in the state. One major reason for the owls' decline is loss of nesting habitat. They nest in cavities in trees and saguaro cacti and as more and more of the Sonoran Desert is urbanized and developed, these plants disappear. Although some saguaro continue to exist even within sprawling desert cities like Tucson, the little owl often gets out-competed for the remaining nest sites by other cavity nesters, such as Gila woodpeckers (*Melanerpes uropygialis*) and the non-native European starling (*Sturnus vulgaris*).

Now that the owl is federally listed as endangered, permits for new developments around Tucson have been slowed until a regional study is completed to determine the impact of these projects on the owl and 17 other endangered species.

fishing conditions, call the fishing hotline at (602) 789-3701. Anglers can also call the local regional office of the Arizona Game and Fish Department at (520) 628-5376.

For more information: Coronado National Forest, Federal Building, 300 W. Congress, Tucson, AZ 85701. Phone (520) 670-4552. Web site www.fs.fed.us/r3/coronado.

SANTA CATALINA RANGER DISTRICT

The Santa Catalina Ranger District takes its name from the massive Santa Catalina Mountains that dominate the northern skyline of Tucson. The mountains' proximity makes for easy escapes from the busy city. Here visitors will find the Sabino Canyon Recreation Area and visitor information center. A shuttle bus carries visitors under towering cliffs and along a boulder-filled stream crossed by nine bridges. Stops along the way provide opportunities for picnics, nature study, day hikes, and access to the Pusch Ridge Wilderness.

Mount Lemmon (Catalina) Highway is a remarkable 25-mile, one-hour journey that takes one from the desert floor to cool, shady forest. The drive begins in northeast Tucson; head east on Tanque Verde Road and follow the signs. At about milepost 5, a toll fee is collected to continue up the highway. At milepost 19.7, all your recreation and natural history questions can be answered at the Palisades Information Center. Near the summit of the range is Mount Lemmon Ski Valley, the southernmost ski area in the U.S. Ski season usually lasts from mid-December to mid-April. One chairlift takes skiers to 16 different runs. For more ski information, call (520) 576-1400.

Granite cliffs in Sabino Canyon, Windy Point, located part way up the Mount Lemmon Road, and the Wilderness of Rocks, in the north central part of the wilderness area, are all popular climbing spots. Eric Fazio-Rhicard describes the routes in his *Squeezing the Lemmon: A Rock Climber's Guide to the Mount Lemmon Highway*.

Directions: To find the Sabino Canyon Recreation Area, take Tanque Verde Road east to Sabino Canyon Road, then turn north and drive 4.5 miles to the canyon entrance and the visitor center.

Activities: Hiking, skiing, horseback riding, rock climbing, picnicking, camping, and nature study.

Facilities: Visitor center, hiking trails, picnic areas, and campgrounds (*see* campground table, page 348).

Dates: Open year-round.

Fees: There are fees for some campgrounds, to use Mount Lemmon Highway, to enter the Sabino Canyon Recreation Area, and to use the shuttle bus system in Sabino Canyon.

Closest town: Tucson.

For more information: Santa Catalina Ranger District, Sabino Canyon Visitor Center and Shuttle, 5700 North Sabino Canyon Road, Tucson, AZ 85750. Phone (520) 749-8700.

▒ PUSCH RIDGE WILDERNESS

[Fig. 47(1)] Taking in about a third of the Santa Catalina Mountains, the 56,933-acre Pusch Ridge Wilderness extends from the desert floor adjacent to metropolitan Tucson to peaks covered with pine, fir, aspen, and maple. The great variety of vegetation and wildlife found as one ascends from 2,800 to 8,800 feet above sea level is truly remarkable— saguaro cactus to Douglas fir, coatimundis to black bears, cactus wrens to Steller's jays (*Cyanocitta stelleri*). Lower elevations are extremely steep and rugged, with spectacular granite bluffs and pinnacles which attract rock climbers. Water is scarce, but several live streams originate on the highest peaks of the Santa Catalina Mountains within the wilderness.

Over 20 trails allow numerous day hiking and backpacking possibilities. An excellent resource is Pete Cowgill and Eber Glendening's *Trail Guide to the Santa Catalina Mountains*. The wide range in elevations allows trips year-round. The rangers at the Sabino Canyon Visitor Center are very helpful in planning hikes. Note that dogs are not permitted in the Bighorn Sheep Management Area

CACTUS FERRUGINOUS PYGMY-OWL
(*Glaucidium brasilianum*)

Scorpions

Scorpions have changed little in the 350 to 400 million years since they first climbed from the sea and became one of the first terrestrial arthropods. There are more than 30 species found in Arizona, but only the sting of the bark scorpion (*Centruroides exilicauda*) is considered life threatening. Its slender shape and its long, delicate pincers and tail distinguish it from other, more stoutly built species.

Bark scorpions display negative geotaxis; that is, they orient themselves upside down. Pick up a rock, and they will be clinging to the rock's undersurface. Defensive stinging is a series of quick jabs, after which the scorpion makes a hasty retreat.

The giant hairy scorpion (*Hadrurus arizonensis*) can be up to 6 inches long. Its large size allows it to prey upon other scorpions and even lizards. Fortunately, its sting is mild to humans and generally only causes local pain and swelling.

One of the most fascinating things about scorpions is that they fluoresce under ultraviolet light. Taking a black light out to the desert on a warm moonless night will reveal just how amazingly common scorpions are in their natural habitat.

portion of the wilderness. Refer to the Forest Service Pusch Ridge Wilderness Map for more trail information.

Directions: Access can be easily gained from the south at trailheads near the city (Magee Road, Alvernon Way, Kolb Road, Sabino Canyon) or by driving the paved Mount Lemmon (Catalina) Highway to the upper elevations. Access from the west is possible through Catalina State Park (*see* page 280).

Activities: Hiking, rock climbing, hunting, camping, and nature study.

Facilities: None in the wilderness; developed campgrounds outside the wilderness.

Dates: Open year-round.

Fees: There are fees to access various entry points.

Closest town: Tucson.

For more information: Santa Catalina Ranger District, 5700 N. Sabino Canyon Road, Tucson, AZ 85715. Phone (520) 749-8700.

ESPERERO CANYON TRAIL

[Fig. 47(2)] There are many hiking possibilities in the Pusch Ridge Wilderness. This trail climbs steeply through saguaro-studded hills to a ridge. From here, the trail contours along the ridge and some of the desert plants are replaced by manzanita and evergreen oak. The trail then drops down into a wooded area to Esperero Creek. Follow the creek upstream about 1.4 miles to tiny Bridal Veil Falls. The 15-foot waterfall plunges into an idyllic, shady pool.

Directions: From the visitor center in Sabino Canyon, walk or take the shuttle bus about 0.5 mile north to the marked trailhead at the Cactus Picnic Area.

Trail: 6.2 miles to Bridal Veil Falls.

Degree of difficulty: Moderate.

Elevation: 2,600 to 5,300 feet.

Surface: Rocky.

RINCON MOUNTAIN WILDERNESS

[Fig. 47(10)] The sharply rising Rincon Mountains are located just east of Tucson. The 38,590-acre wilderness area embraces three sides of the eastern unit of Saguaro National Park. Like the Santa Catalinas, the Rincon Mountains have tremendous vertical relief. The base of the range is around 3,000 feet in elevation and the higher peaks and ridges extend to over 8,000 feet. Every life zone from Sonoran desert to evergreen forest can be found here. One of the primary functions of this wilderness area is to complement the park and protect as complete an ecosystem as possible.

Several trails cross the area, and hikers can quickly find complete solitude in its canyon bottoms or along the ridgelines leading to the higher elevations of the Rincons. However, access to the area is rather difficult. Only roads suitable for four-wheel-drive vehicles lead to the area, except on the east side in Happy Valley. Happy Valley is served by FR 35 (Mescal Road), which is generally passable to conventional vehicles. The wilderness is also accessible from trailheads within Saguaro National Park (*see* page 287). Many of the trails are difficult on foot and virtually impassable on horseback. Also, the portion of the Miller Creek Trail that enters the park is closed to pack stock.

Directions: To reach the east side of the wilderness, drive east 39 miles from Tucson on I-10 to the Mescal Road Exit (#297). Drive north on Mescal Road (which becomes FR 35)16 miles to the trailheads for Turkey and Miller creeks. To reach the northern part of the wilderness, drive east from Tucson on the Tanque Verde Road until it becomes the Redington Pass Road. Continue another 8 miles, and then turn south on FR 37, a four-wheel-drive road to the Italian Spring trailhead.

Activities: Hiking, rock climbing, hunting, camping, and nature study.

Facilities: None.

Dates: Open year-round, but lower areas are very hot during summer.

Fees: There is a fee to access trailheads within Saguaro National Park.

Closest town: Tucson.

For more information: Santa Catalina Ranger District, Coronado National Forest, 5700 N. Sabino Canyon Road, Tucson, AZ 85715. Phone (520) 749-8700. The six designated wilderness campsites are all within Saguaro National Park and a free camping permit is required from them. Saguaro National Park Headquarters, 3693 S. Old Spanish Trail, Tucson, AZ 85730. Phone (520) 733-5153.

TANQUE VERDE RIDGE TRAIL

[Fig. 48(2)] Seventeen trails crisscross the wilderness area. For directions to three trailheads see Rincon

BARK SCORPION
(*Centruroides exilicauda*)

Mountain Wilderness, page 287. However, one of the most easily accessible trailheads is within Saguaro National Park (eastern unit). From the Javelina Picnic Area, the Tanque Verde Ridge Trail goes south to pick up the lower end of Tanque Verde Ridge. The trail follows the ridge eastward giving hikers excellent views across the low desert and up to the higher peaks. About 7 miles in, the trail reaches Juniper Basin, one of several primitive campgrounds within the park-administrated part of the wilderness. A free camping permit is required.

Longer backpacks can be done by continuing past Juniper Basin, where trails climb to over 8,000 feet. Although you start out in the desert, remember that it can be cold and snowy at those higher elevations during the winter.

Directions: The trail begins at the Javelina Picnic Area on the Cactus Forest Drive (*see* page 287) in Saguaro National Park (eastern unit).

Trail: 7 miles one-way.

Degree of difficulty: Moderate.

Elevation: 2,700 to 5,700 feet.

Surface: Rocky.

DOUGLAS RANGER DISTRICT

For the naturalist, the Douglas Ranger District is one of the most interesting in the state because it includes the Chiricahua Mountains, which are a northern extension of the Sierra Madres in Mexico. Thus, many Mexican species of plants and wildlife are at their northernmost limit here. One of the few perennial streams in the Chiricahuas is Cave Creek, a mecca for birders and others interested in wildlife.

The upper reaches of the creek are bordered by Arizona cypress (*Cupressus arizonica*), Apache pine (*Pinus latifolia*), Chiricahua pine (*Pinus chihuahuana*), and Douglas fir (*Pseudotsuga taxifolia*). Descending in elevation, the vegetation changes to Arizona black walnut, madrone (*Arbutus arizonica*), Gambel oak, silver-leaf oak (*Quercus hypoleucoides*), Emory oak (*Quercus emoryi*), and Mexican pinyon (*Pinus cembroides*). At the lower end of the creek, the banks hold Arizona sycamore, cottonwood, bigtooth maple (*Acer grandidentatum*), willow, and velvet ash (*Fraxinus velutina*).

Besides the huge variety of bird life along Cave Creek, including hepatic tanager (*Piranga flava*), red-faced warbler (*Cardellina rubrifrons*), and elegant trogon, there are many other forms of wildlife. Look for black bear (*Ursus americanus*), white-tailed deer, coatimundi (*Nasua nasua*), ringtail (*Bassariscus astutus*), javelina, mountain lion, coyote, striped skunk, Mexican fox squirrel (*Sciurus nayaritensis*), and wild turkey. The Chiricahuas were once home to grizzly bear (*Ursus arctos*), Mexican gray wolf (*Canis lupus*), and jaguar (*Panthera onca*). By the early 1900s, the grizzly and jaguar were hunted out; by the mid-1900s, the wolf was gone, too. Conservationists hope that these three magnificent species may be re-introduced to the area someday.

The various forks of Cave Creek offer a variety of recreational opportunities from bird-watching to hiking and camping. On the lower stretches of the creek, camping is allowed only at developed sites such as South Fork, Idlewild, Stewart, and Sunny Flat. On the upper main fork of Cave Creek is a slot-like gorge bordered by sheer cliffs with caves, arches, and natural windows. The rock is mostly latite, a volcanic rock which can be colored orange, pink, yellow, and salmon. More than 200 miles of trails can be accessed from the Cave

Coatimundi (Nasua nasua) are more gregarious members of the raccoon family.

Creek area and include South Fork, Burrow, Basin, Greenhouse, and Snowshed, all of which cross the creek at some point. There are picnic areas located at John Hands and Herb Martyr. More information and maps can be obtained from the Cave Creek Visitor Information Center or the Douglas Ranger District office.

The Southwestern Research Station, about 5 miles southwest of Portal on FR 42 and owned by the American Museum of Natural History in New York, is home to biologists studying the region's natural history. Visitors can obtain books, maps, information, and lodging here.

Directions: From Portal, drive southwest on FR 42 to enter the national forest lands along Cave Creek. The visitor center is located about 1 mile from town.

Activities: Camping, picnicking, hiking, horseback riding, and nature study.

Facilities: Campgrounds, picnic areas, hiking trails, and visitor center.

Dates: Open year-round; Cave Creek Visitor Information Center, open Apr. through Oct.

Fees: Some of the campgrounds charge a fee; *see* campground table on page 348.

Closest town: Portal.

For more information: Cave Creek Visitor Information Center, PO Box 126, Portal, AZ 85632. Phone (520) 558-2221. Douglas Ranger District, 3081 North Leslie Canyon Road, Douglas, AZ 85607. Phone (520) 364-3468. Southwestern Research Station, phone (520) 558-2396.

CORONADO NATIONAL FOREST CAMPGROUNDS

Camping at large is generally allowed throughout the Coronado National Forest except in high use areas, designated recreation areas, and ecologically sensitive sites. Fees are charged at most developed campgrounds. Campers may stay a maximum of 14 days in any one location. See Appendix G for a table of information on individual campgrounds.

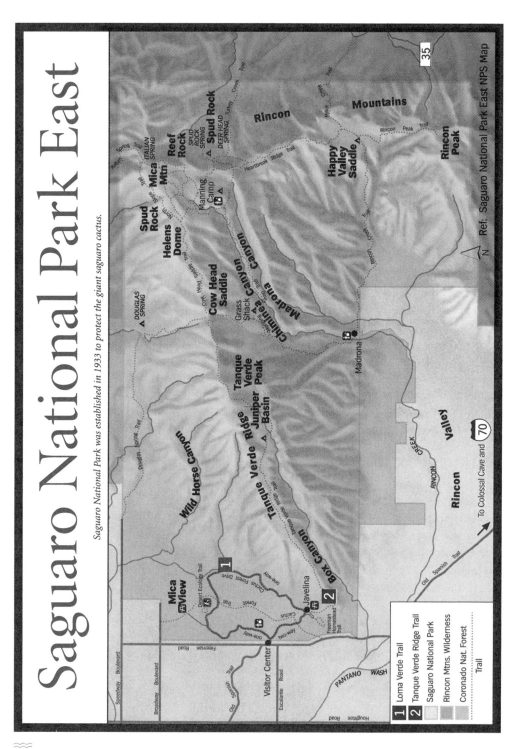

Saguaro National Park East

Saguaro National Park was established in 1933 to protect the giant saguaro cactus.

Ref: Saguaro National Park East NPS Map

1 Loma Verde Trail
2 Tanque Verde Ridge Trail
Saguaro National Park
Rincon Mtns. Wilderness
Coronado Nat. Forest
Trail

Saguaro National Park

[Fig. 48] The signature plant of the Sonoran desert has to be the saguaro cactus. This giant cactus begins life as a shiny black seed no bigger than pinhead. Seeds and young saguaros have the best chance of survival if they grow under sheltering nurse trees such as palo verde or mesquite. The saguaro's growth is extremely slow and occurs in spurts. After the first year, the seedling may measure only 0.25 inch. After 15 years, the cactus may be barely a foot tall. Saguaros that live 150 years or more attain heights of 50 feet and weigh about eight tons.

Saguaro National Park was established in 1933 to protect two major stands of the giant columnar cactus and the surrounding Sonoran Desert. The park consists of two widely separated districts. One is located on the eastern fringe of Tucson. The other unit is 30 miles west. Each unit has a very good visitor center with exhibits that depict how plant and animal communities have adapted to their arid environment.

In Saguaro East, the 8-mile Cactus Forest Drive starts at the visitor center and winds through the heart of an extensive but aging saguaro forest. From this loop road are several short hiking trails and a trailhead for a trail leading into the vast wilderness of the Rincon Mountains and their foothills. Backcountry camping is permitted only at designated sites, and a free permit is required. The park rangers in the visitor center can help in planning a hiking adventure.

Saguaro West also has a scenic drive, the 9-mile Bajada Loop, which features an unusually dense and vigorous stand of saguaro. Several short hiking trails penetrate the desert from the road. Again, rangers in the Red Hills Visitor Center can help you plan your visit.

Adjacent to the western district is **Tucson Mountain County Park**, which contains a campground and hiking and horse trails. For more information, phone (520) 882-2690.

Directions: The eastern district entrance is located near the junction of Old Spanish Trail and Freeman Road in east Tucson. The western district entrance is off Kinney Road, about 1 mile west of the Arizona-Sonora Desert Museum.

Activities: Scenic drives, hiking, horseback riding, picnicking, and camping.

Facilities: Visitor centers, picnic areas, and backcountry campsites.

Dates: Open year-round, but summers are very hot.

Fees: There is an entrance fee.

Closest town: Tucson.

For more information: Saguaro National Park Headquarters, 3693 S. Old Spanish Trail, Tucson, AZ 85730. Phone (520) 733-5153. Red Hills (Saguaro West) Visitor Center, phone (520) 733-5158. Web site www.nps.gov.sagu.

LOMA VERDE TRAIL

[Fig. 48(1)] The Loma Verde Trail begins on the Cactus Forest Drive. The trail starts off in mesquite woodland studded with barrel cactus and saguaros. Crossing Monument Wash twice, the trail climbs a bluff onto the bajada, the gentle slope of gravel at the base of Tanque Verde Ridge. A sign describes the history of the nearby Loma Verde Mine.

The Loma Verde Trail then joins the Pink Hill Trail. Turn right and ascend the iron-stained slope for a panoramic view of the cactus forest and Catalina Mountains. The vivid color of the Sonoran Desert comes from the many evergreen shrubs, the green-barked palo verde tree, and the numerous cacti. Where the trail crosses the wash, torrents of water occasionally come flooding through during the summer monsoon season. Turn right at Squeeze Pen Trail. The name recalls the days when cattle were rounded up on this range. Creosote bush, with its shiny leaves and yellow flowers, lines the trail. Its fuzzy seed capsules are a favorite food of the kangaroo rat (*Dipodomys* sp.). The rocky slopes of the Rincon Mountains are also a prime habitat for ocotillo (*Fouquieria splendens*), teddy bear cholla (*Opuntia bigelovii*), and saguaro. Passing an old cattle fence, the trail turns west toward an outstanding example of the park's namesake—a truly giant saguaro.

Directions: In the eastern unit of Saguaro National Park, take the Cactus Forest Drive about 3.5 miles to the Loma Verde trailhead.

Trail: 3.3-mile loop.

Degree of difficulty: Easy.

Elevation: About 2,700 feet, and the trail only gains about 60 feet.

Surface: Rocky.

Tucson Area

COLOSSAL CAVE MOUNTAIN PARK

[Fig. 49(1)] A few miles south of Saguaro National Park (eastern unit) is Colossal Cave Mountain Park, which contains a dry, limestone cave. A local legend relates how $60,000 worth of gold hidden in the cave by outlaws has not yet been discovered. The 0.5-mile tour of the cave requires negotiating 363 stairsteps.

Directions: From Tucson, take I-10 east to Vail-Wentworth Exit 279, then go 7 miles north. From Saguaro National Park (eastern unit), drive south 12 miles on the Old Spanish Trail.

Activities: Guided tour of cave and nearby trail rides.

Facilities: Museum, snack bar, gift shop, and campground.

Dates: Open year-round; the interior of the cave is a constant 70 degrees Fahrenheit.

Fees: There is an entrance and tour fee.

Closest town: Tucson.

For more information: Colossal Cave, Old Spanish Trail, Tucson, AZ 85747. Phone (520) 647-7275.

CATALINA STATE PARK

[Fig. 47(3)] Catalina State Park encompasses over 5,500 acres at the base of the spectacular northwestern slopes of the Santa Catalina Mountains. The foothills, canyons, and streams of the park contain a vast array of desert plants and animals. Easy trails crisscross the park and also allow access to trails extending into the Coronado National Forest and the Pusch Ridge Wilderness.

Directions: Drive 9 miles north of Tucson on AZ 77.

Activities: Camping, picnicking, hiking, horseback riding, and nature study.

Facilities: Campground, nature trails, picnic area, and drinking water.

Dates: Open year-round.

Fees: There is an entrance fee.

Closest town: Tucson, about 9 miles south.

Saguaro (Carnegiea gigantea) grow to more than 50 feet tall and have 3-inch-long, green fruits containing up to 2,000 seeds embedded in juicy, red pulp.

For more information: Catalina State Park, PO Box 36986, Tucson, AZ 85740. Phone (520) 628-5798.

ARIZONA-SONORA DESERT MUSEUM

[Fig. 47(4)] A visit to the Arizona-Sonora Desert Museum will greatly increase one's enjoyment of exploring the Sonoran Desert. Founded in 1952, the museum is a world-renowned zoo, natural history museum, and botanical garden. More than 1,400 kinds of plants and 300 species of animals native to the Sonoran Desert are displayed in natural-looking habitats. Docents conduct various educational activities throughout the day. Photographers will have a field day shooting native animals in realistic surroundings.

Directions: About 14 miles west of Tucson on Kinney Road within Tucson Mountain County Park.

Activities: Touring the facility.

Facilities: Museum, gardens, art gallery, gift shops, restaurants, and restrooms.

Coyote Mtns. Wilderness Area

The 5,080-acre Coyote Mountains Wilderness is located 40 miles southwest of Tucson.

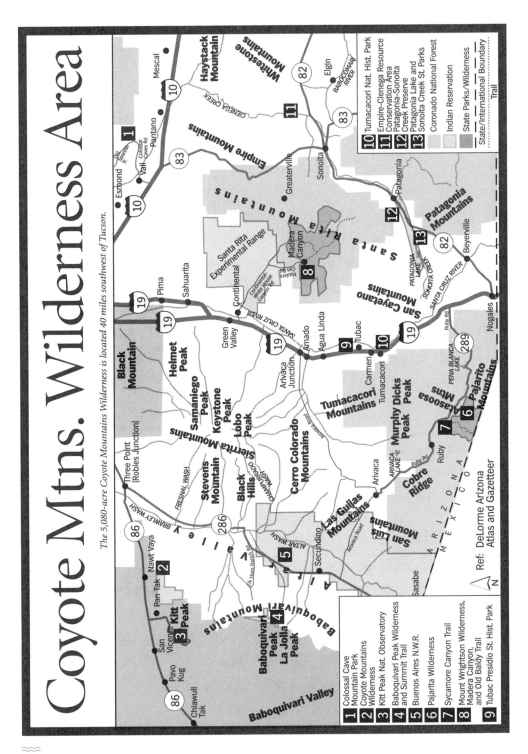

1 Colossal Cave Mountain Park
2 Coyote Mountains Wilderness
3 Kitt Peak Nat. Observatory
4 Baboquivari Peak Wilderness and Summit Trail
5 Buenos Aires N.W.R.
6 Pajarita Wilderness
7 Sycamore Canyon Trail
8 Mount Wrightson Wilderness, Madera Canyon, and Old Baldy Trail
9 Tubac Presidio St. Hist. Park

10 Tumacacori Nat. Hist. Park
11 Empire-Cienega Resource Conservation Area
12 Patagonia-Sonoita Creek Preserve
13 Patagonia Lake and Sonoita Creek St. Parks

Coronado National Forest
Indian Reservation
State Parks/Wilderness
State/International Boundary
Trail

Ref: DeLorme Arizona Atlas and Gazetteer

Dates: Open year-round.
Fees: There is an entrance fee.
Closest town: Tucson.
For more information: Arizona-Sonora Desert Museum, 2021 N. Kinney Road, Tucson, AZ 85743-8918. Phone (520) 883-2702. Web site www.desertmuseum.org.

The Desert Ranges, Grasslands, and Canyons South of Tucson

▓ COYOTE MOUNTAINS WILDERNESS
[Fig. 49(2)] The 5,080-acre Coyote Mountains Wilderness is located 40 miles southwest of Tucson. The wilderness includes the Coyote Mountains with their jagged granite peaks, massive rounded bluffs, sheer cliff faces, and large open canyons. The vegetation found includes palo verde, saguaro, chaparral, and oak woodlands. Big and small game is abundant in the wide range of habitats, from Sonoran desert to interior chaparral to oak woodland to riparian communities. Archaeological remains of prehistoric Indians include petroglyph sites and a classic period Hohokam Indian compound covering many acres.

The wilderness is popular with rock climbers, hikers, hunters, birders, backpackers, botanists, and rock hounds. Artists, photographers, and sightseers are also drawn to the area's scenery.

Directions: From Tucson, take AZ 86 west toward the Kitt Peak Observatory, then go south on AZ 286 for approximately 8 miles. The Coyote Mountains lie 4 miles east of Kitt Peak. Currently there is no legal access to the Coyote Mountains Wilderness. Permission to park and access the wilderness must be obtained from the private landholder or the Tohono O'odham Nation. Call the BLM or tribe for current regulations.

Activities: Hiking, rock climbing, hunting, and camping.
Facilities: None.
Dates: Open year-round.
Fees: None.
Closest town: Robles Junction, about 15 miles northeast.
For more information: BLM, Tucson Field Office, 12661 East Broadway, Tucson, AZ 85748. Phone (520) 722-4289. Web site www.az.blm.gov. Tohono O'odham Nation, PO Box 837, Sells, AZ 85634. Phone (520) 383-2221.

Yucca Moths

There are many remarkable symbiotic relationships between plants and animals. One such relationship in Arizona is the close association between yuccas (*Yucca* sp.) and yucca moths (*Tegiticula* sp. and *Parategitcula* sp.). The yucca blossoms require pollen from another plant in order to produce seed. Additionally, the pollen must be packed into a deep receptacle on the stigma, an event that could not occur by chance. The moth is equally dependent on the yucca. The moth lays its eggs on each pollinated ovary, and the hatched larvae eat some of the developing seeds. Since yuccas may or may not flower every year, some of the moth larvae drop to the ground, burrow in, and emerge at different year intervals. That way some of the emerging moths are assured of finding a yucca in bloom. Biologists have only recently discovered that each species of yucca has its own species of yucca moth; to ensure better reproductive success some yuccas even have two moth species.

KITT PEAK NATIONAL OBSERVATORY

[Fig. 49(3)] Atop the 6,875-foot summit of Kitt Peak are large white domes housing 24 telescopes operated by the Association of Universities for Research in Astronomy. A visitor center shows an introductory video and contains exhibits about telescopes and astronomy. One unique instrument found at Kitt Peak is the McMath-Pierce Solar Telescope that produces a 30-inch image of the sun that visitors can safely view. Nighttime stargazing through one of the telescopes is possible, but a reservation is necessary as well as paying a fee.

Directions: From Tucson, drive 56 miles southwest on AZ 86. Turn onto AZ 386, which winds 12 miles up to the summit.

Activities: Touring facility, reservations are required for nighttime viewing.

Facilities: Visitor center, gift shop, and picnic area.

Dates: Open year-round, except Thanksgiving, Christmas, Christmas Eve, and New Years Day.

Fees: There is a fee for nighttime viewing programs.

Closest town: Robles Junction, about 22 miles east.

For more information: Kitt Peak National Observatory, PO Box 26732, Tucson, AZ 85726. Phone (520) 318-8200 or 318-8726. Web site www.noao.edu.

BABOQUIVARI PEAK WILDERNESS

[Fig. 49(4)] The 2,065-acre Baboquivari Peak Wilderness is located about 50 miles southwest of Tucson. The wilderness includes a small, but spectacular portion of the east side of the Baboquivari Range. The sharp rise of Baboquivari Peak dominates the wilderness area. Elevations range from 4,500 to 7,734 feet. The complexity of terrains and relative abundance of water support a wide variety of plants and animals. Vegetation varies from saguaro, palo verde, and chaparral communities to oak, walnut, and pinyon at the higher elevations. Many birds are attracted to the area, including the rare and unusual thick-billed kingbird (*Tyrannus crassirostris*), five-striped sparrow (*Aimophila quinquestriata*), northern beardless-tyrannulet (*Camptostoma imberbe*), and zone-tailed hawk (*Buteo albonotatus*).

Recreation opportunities such as photography, sight-seeing, and day hikes are enhanced by the dramatic and scenic landscapes. However, Baboquivari Peak is the only major peak in Arizona that requires technical climbing ability to reach its summit.

The first recorded climb was by Dr. R.H. Forbes and Jesus Montoya in 1898 after four previously unsuccessful attempts. On the successful climb, the good doctor had brought along a grappling hook fitted with an extension so that, "…he was able to extend his arm…." Forbes made his sixth and final ascent of Baboquivari in 1949 on his 82nd birthday!

The late Supreme Court Justice William O. Douglas also climbed Baboquivari. After his climb in 1951, he wrote, "It was a mountain wholly detached from the earth—a magic pillar of granite riding high above dark and angry clouds. Lightning briefly played around its base; and then it vanished as quickly as it had appeared—engulfed by black clouds that welled upward in some wind." The distinctive Baboquivari Peak is also a sacred place to the Tohono O'odham. The peak marks the center of the universe and the home of Elder Brother I'itoi, who taught the Tohono O'odham how to live in the desert.

Directions: To reach the east slope of Baboquivari, drive from west Tucson on AZ 86 to its junction with AZ 286. Proceed south on AZ 286 about 30 miles to the entrance road to Thomas Canyon. This road goes about 8 miles toward the mountains and gets progressively worse. The road ends at a gate to Humphrey Ranch. From here, The Nature Conservancy maintains a pedestrian access route across the private property to the wilderness. Please respect the property rights of the private landowners. The original "standard route" up the west slope is on the Tohono O'odham reservation and may be reached by taking Indian Highway 19 south of Sells 12.2 miles to Topawa. At Topawa, a sign directs you to the east on a graded road, Indian Highway 10. It's another 12 miles to Baboquivari Park.

Activities: Hiking, camping, rock climbing, and nature study.

Facilities: Baboquivari Park has a picnic area and primitive campground.

Dates: Open year-round, but summer afternoons can be very hot.

Fees: None on the east side of the peak. There are recreation fees charged by the Tohono O'odham tribe for entry to the west side. Payment can be made to the manager at Baboquivari Park every day except Wednesday and Thursday. On those days obtain permits from the Baboquivari District Office in Topawa.

Closest town: Robles Junction, about 35 miles northeast.

For more information: BLM, Tucson Field Office, 12661 East Broadway, Tucson, AZ 85748. Phone (520) 722-4289. Web site www.az.blm.gov. Tohono O'odham Nation, PO Box 837, Sells, AZ 85634. Phone (520) 383-2221. Baboquivari District Office, phone (520) 383-2366.

SUMMIT TRAIL

[Fig. 49(4)] This trail was constructed by the Civilian Conservation Corps in 1934 and takes hikers to the base of the granite dome called Baboquivari Peak, where the "standard" climbing route begins. Along the way, you first pass saguaros, palo verde trees, mesquite, and Arizona rainbow cactus (*Echinocereus pectinatus* var. *rigidissimus*), an endangered variety of hedgehog cactus. As the trail gains elevation, Mexican pinyon (*Pinus cembroides*) and various oaks replace some of the desert vegetation.

Directions: Starts from Baboquivari Park (*see* Baboquivari Peak Wilderness, page 292).

Trail: About 4 miles.

Degree of difficulty: Moderate.

Elevation: About 3,600 to 6,400 feet.

Surface: Rocky.

BUENOS AIRES NATIONAL WILDLIFE REFUGE

[Fig. 49(5)] This 112,000-acre refuge was established in 1985 to preserve grassland habitat for the endangered masked bobwhite (*Colinus virginianus ridgwayi*). The rolling mesquite-grasslands of the refuge also provide habitat for pronghorn, mule deer, Coues white-tailed deer (*Odocoileus virginianus cousei*), javelina, coatimundi (*Nasua nasua*), badger (*Taxidea taxus*), ringtail (*Bassariscus astutus*), mountain lion, and numerous migratory birds. A 1996 alleged sighting of a jaguar (*Panthera onca*) has excited biologists (*see* page 329). Auto and walking trails allow wildlife observation throughout the area. Nature programs and tours are available to Arivaca Cienega or Brown Canyon, both wonderful places to go birding. Call the refuge for schedule. Hunting is permitted for upland and big game species. Masked bobwhite hunting is prohibited.

Directions: The refuge headquarters is located 38 miles south of Robles Junction (Three Points), off AZ 286. Trailheads are also located near Arivaca, which can be reached from AZ 286 or I-19.

Activities: Camping at designated primitive campsites, mountain biking, horseback riding, and nature study.

Facilities: Refuge headquarters, small visitor center in Arivaca, scenic drives, and hiking trails.

Dates: Open year-round.

Fees: There are fees for some of the nature programs.

Closest town: Sasabe.

For more information: Refuge Manager, Buenos Aires National Wildlife Refuge, PO Box 109, Sasabe, AZ 85633. Phone (520) 823-4251.

PAJARITA WILDERNESS

[Fig. 49(6)] The delightful 9-mile-long Sycamore Canyon cuts through the middle of the 7,420-acre Pajarita Wilderness, which is located about 15 miles west of Nogales. The headwaters of Sycamore Canyon are located in the Atascosa Mountains, and after meandering through the wilderness area, the creek continues on into northern Sonora, Mexico.

Pajarita, Spanish for "little bird," is an appropriate name for the wilderness when one considers the large number of birds that live or pass through the area, including elegant trogons (*Trogon elegans*), green kingfishers (*Chloroceryle americana*), northern beardless-tyrannulet, and Anna's hummingbird (*Calypte anna*).

The canyon is also an important migratory route for other wildlife, an historic route, and used today by people illegally crossing from Mexico into the US. Be sure to contact the ranger district office to learn the latest on this potentially dangerous activity!

Part of the canyon has also been designated as the Goodding Research Natural Area, after biologist Leslie Goodding made extensive plant collections in the area between 1935 and the 1950s. He found 624 species of plants including a rare fern, *Asplenium exiguum*, believed to occur only in the Himalayas and in parts of Mexico.

Directions: From Tucson, drive 55 miles south on I-19 to Exit 12, AZ 289, the Ruby Road. Turn right and drive 19.5 miles on the Ruby Road to the Sycamore Canyon trailhead near Hank and Yank Spring.

Activities: Hiking, camping, and nature study.

Facilities: None.

Dates: Open year-round.

Fees: None.

Closest town: Nogales, about 32 miles east.

For more information: Nogales Ranger District, 303 Old Tucson Road, Nogales, AZ 85621. Phone (520) 281-2296.

SYCAMORE CANYON TRAIL

[Fig. 49(7)] This trail follows enchanting Sycamore Creek. Watch for a troop of coatimundi. Unlike many of Arizona mammals, coatis tend to be more active during the day. These raccoon relatives often travel in groups of six or more while busily searching for food such as invertebrates, lizards, snakes, carrion, rodents, nuts and fruits of native trees, prickly pear, and yucca. The trail ends at the international border with Mexico and is marked by a barbed wire fence.

Directions: The trailhead is located at Hank and Yank Spring.

Trail: Approximately 10.6 miles to the Mexican border and back.

Degree of difficulty: Fairly easy, but avoid during summer monsoon season.

Elevation: 4,000 feet at the trailhead to 3,500 feet at the Mexican border.

Surface: Creek bottom, some wading.

MOUNT WRIGHTSON WILDERNESS AND MADERA CANYON

[Fig. 49(8)] Lying at the core of the Santa Rita Mountains, about 30 miles south of Tucson, is the 25,260-acre Mount Wrightson Wilderness. Surrounded on all sides by semiarid hills and sloping savannah, Mount Wrightson soars to 9,453 feet, a full 7,000 feet above the valley floor. A complex of 13 trails crisscross the area, but the easiest ones to access are in Madera Canyon. A comprehensive guide is Betty Leaven-good and Mike Liebert's *Hiking Guide to the Santa Rita Mountains.*

A developed recreation area for both picnicking and camping in Madera Canyon lies at the foot of the wilderness. Mountain bikers also enjoy the area. The canyon is internationally renowned as a unique habitat for a variety of both common and rare birds. Thirteen species of hummingbirds have been recorded in the canyon.

Mount Wrightson's stream-fed canyons are the source of an exceptional abun-dance of animal and plant life. Ponderosa pine and Douglas fir dominate the higher elevations. Rough hillsides, deep canyons, and lofty ridges and peaks characterize the wilderness.

Directions: To reach Madera Canyon, drive about 36 miles south from Tucson on I-19. Turn east at the Continental Exit and drive 16 miles to the canyon. Here, two trailheads allow access to the most popular trails in the wilderness.

Activities: Hiking, mountain biking, horseback riding, camping, and nature study.

Facilities: Picnic areas, lodging, and campgrounds in Madera Canyon.

Dates: Open year-round, but higher elevations can receive snow in the winter.

Fees: None for wilderness area, but a donation may be requested to enter Madera Canyon Recreation Area. There are fees for the campground.

Closest town: Tucson, about 50 miles north.

For more information: Nogales Ranger District, 303 Old Tucson Road, Nogales, AZ 85621. Phone (520) 281-2296.

OLD BALDY TRAIL

[Fig. 49(8)] There are two trails that climb to the top of Mount Wrightson—the Super and Old Baldy. The Super Trail is 3 miles longer than Old Baldy and is less steep; however, the extra horizontal miles wipe out any advantage you may get from the slightly more gradual grade.

Old Baldy offers great views along the more than 4,000-foot vertical climb to the top of one of the most scenic mountains around Tucson. The first part of the trail is partially shaded by large evergreen oaks. At Josephine Saddle, about 2.5 miles in, there is a memorial to three Boy Scouts who lost their lives here in a snowstorm in 1958, a somber reminder that Mount Wrightson is high enough to experience some fairly severe winter storms.

In another couple of miles, ponderosa pines begin to replace the oaks. Out to the south the astronomical observatory on Mount Hopkins can be seen. To the west, the distinctive dome of Baboquivari Peak is on the horizon.

From the summit, on a clear day, you have 100-mile views in all directions. There is a summit register, interpretive signs, and lots of good places for a well-deserved rest.

Directions: Starts at Roundup Picnic Area at the Madera Canyon Road's end.

Trail: 5.4 miles one-way.

Degree of difficulty: Strenuous.

Elevation: 5,420 to 9,453 feet.
Surface: Rocky.

TUBAC PRESIDIO STATE HISTORIC PARK

[Fig. 49(9)] Founded in 1752, Tubac is the oldest town in Arizona established by people of European descent. The park's visitor center contains exhibits and shows a video that highlight the contributions of Indians, Spaniards, Mexican, and Anglo-Americans to Arizona's development.

Between the state park and Tumacacori National Historical Park runs a 4.5-mile section of the 600-mile-long Juan Bautista de Anza Trail that can be hiked. The trail was used in 1775-76 by Tubac Presidio Captain Juan Bautista de Anza to lead 240 colonists from Culiacan, Mexico north to start a settlement in northern California, the present city of San Francisco.

Directions: From Tucson, drive south 45 miles on I-19 and take Exit 34.
Activities: Living history program on Sunday afternoons from Oct. to Mar.
Facilities: Museum.
Dates: Open year-round.
Fees: There is an entrance fee.
Closest town: Tubac.
For more information: Tubac Presidio State Historic Park, Box 1296, Tubac, AZ 85646. Phone (520) 398-2704 or 398-2252. Web site www.tubacaz.com.

TUMACACORI NATIONAL HISTORICAL PARK

[Fig. 49(10)] This park preserves an early Spanish colonial mission that was established as the result of a visit by Father Kino to the Pima Indians in 1691. Other missionaries continued to convert, teach, and farm at this location; however, construction of an adobe church building didn't begin until 1800. Although never quite finished, the church was used until 1828 when the last resident priest left. For a few decades devout Indians maintained the church and received occasional visits by traveling missionaries, but the church was abandoned in 1848.

The National Park Service acquired the church in 1908. Today, the massive adobe ruin is still in remarkably good condition. A self-guided tour of the church and the grounds is possible. Scheduled tours are offered September through June, as well as weekend demonstrations of Mexican or Indian crafts. A small museum recalls the mission life with a video, exhibits, and artifacts. An annual highlight is the Tumacacori Fiesta held the first weekend of December and features Indian dances, crafts, and food.

Directions: From Tucson, drive 48 miles south on I-19 and take Exit 29.
Activities: Self-guided and guided tours.
Facilities: Museum, picnic area, and patio garden.
Dates: Open year-round.

Fees: There is an entrance fee.

Closest town: Tubac.

For more information: Tumacacori National Historical Park, PO Box 67, Tumacacori, AZ 85640. Phone (520) 398-2341. Web site www.nps.gov/tuma.

EMPIRE-CIENEGA RESOURCE CONSERVATION AREA

[Fig. 49(11)] This is a 45,000-acre land of tall grasses, some as high as 6 feet, and scattered mesquite trees. In some ways it resembles an African veldt; pronghorn stare curiously at a passing vehicle, flocks of horned larks (*Eremophila alpestris*) flash their white outer tail feathers, and a large hawk circles lazily in the flawless blue sky.

Within this resource conservation area is a perennial portion of Cienega Creek, a creek that originates in the Canelo Hills south of Sonoita and meanders north toward the Rincon Mountains before becoming one of the main tributaries to the Santa Cruz River. The wetlands formed by this creek are some of the last *cienegas*, Spanish for "marshy place," in the state, overgrazing having destroyed this once common habitat in southeastern Arizona. The endangered Gila topminnow lives here, as well as native Gila chub and longfin dace. Mexican garter snake (*Thamnophis eques*), lowland leopard frog (*Rana yavapaiensis*), and Chihuahua leopard frog (*Rana chiricahuensis*) are also riparian residents. Ten miles of the creek have been recommended as a National Wild and Scenic River.

One main entrance to the resource conservation area is found by driving north from Sonoita about 10 miles on AZ 83 to a signed dirt road heading east. There are no established hiking trails, but several dirt roads crisscross the resource conservation area, and visitors are free to walk or ride horseback cross-country.

Directions: A few miles from Sonoita, AZ 83 and AZ 82 essentially make up, respectively, the west and south boundaries of the resource conservation area. Dirt roads leading into the resource conservation area take off from the highways at several locations.

Activities: Camping, hiking, horseback riding, mountain biking, and nature study.

Facilities: None.

Dates: Open year-round.

Fees: None.

Closest town: Sonoita, about 10 miles.

For more information: BLM, Tucson Field Office, 12661 East Broadway, Tucson, AZ 85748. Phone (520) 722-4289. Web site www.az.blm.gov.

PATAGONIA-SONOITA CREEK PRESERVE

[Fig. 49(12)] The 750-acre Nature Conservancy's Patagonia-Sonoita Creek Preserve is an extraordinary birding location, with 2.5 miles of trail running along the perennial stream. However, no picnicking, camping, or pets are allowed.

After a morning of birding, mountain bikers can stretch their legs on many miles of pleasant gravel roads around the area. One 25-mile loop takes off southeast from the town of Patagonia and travels by the ghost towns of Harshaw and Mowry.

Directions: The entrance is located on Blue Canyon Road, near Patagonia.

Activities: Birding, nature study, and led nature walks on Saturday mornings.

UTAH JUNIPER
(Juniperus osteosperma)

Facilities: Visitor center.

Dates: Open year-round, Wednesday through Sunday.

Fees: None, but donations are welcomed.

Closest town: Patagonia.

For more information: Patagonia-Sonoita Creek Preserve, PO Box 815, Patagonia, AZ 85624. Phone (520) 394-2400. Web site www.tnc.org.

PATAGONIA LAKE AND SONOITA CREEK STATE PARKS

[Fig. 49(13)] Tucked into the high, rolling grasslands of Sonoita Valley is the 640-acre Patagonia Lake, offering a variety of water sports, including boating and fishing. Anglers hook largemouth bass, crappie, sunfish, bluegill, catfish, and rainbow trout (in winter). Adjacent to the lake is the recently designated Sonoita Creek State Natural Park, a 5,000-acre parcel that preserves important riparian wildlife habitat.

Directions: From Nogales, drive 12 miles north on AZ 82.

Activities: Boating, water skiing, swimming, fishing, and camping.

Facilities: Boat ramp, marina, boat rentals.

Dates: Open year-round.

Fees: There is an entry fee and a camping fee.

Closest town: Patagonia, 7 miles north.

For more information: Patagonia Lake State Park, PO Box 274, Patagonia, AZ 85624. Phone (520) 287-6965. Web site www.pr.state.az.us.

The Cochise Trail

The Cochise Trail is a 200-mile loop from Benson to Bisbee to Douglas to Chiricahua National Monument to Wilcox then back to Benson.

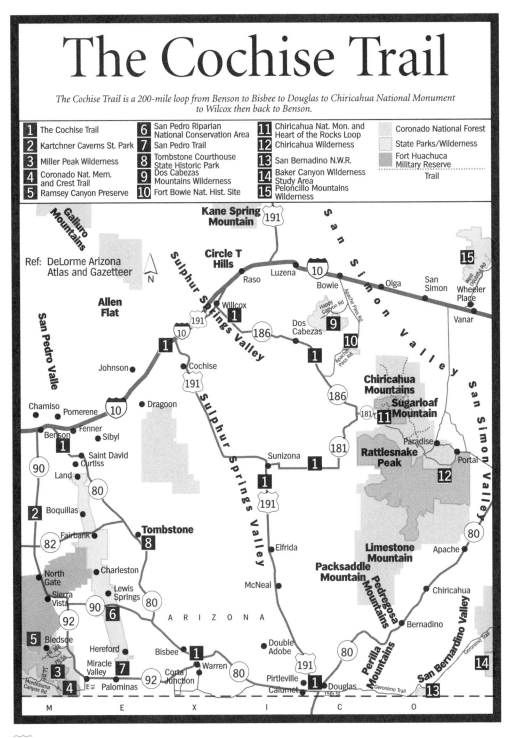

1 The Cochise Trail
2 Kartchner Caverns St. Park
3 Miller Peak Wilderness
4 Coronado Nat. Mem. and Crest Trail
5 Ramsey Canyon Preserve
6 San Pedro Riparian National Conservation Area
7 San Pedro Trail
8 Tombstone Courthouse State Historic Park
9 Dos Cabezas Mountains Wilderness
10 Fort Bowie Nat. Hist. Site
11 Chiricahua Nat. Mon. and Heart of the Rocks Loop
12 Chiricahua Wilderness
13 San Bernadino N.W.R.
14 Baker Canyon Wilderness Study Area
15 Peloncillo Mountains Wilderness

Coronado National Forest
State Parks/Wilderness
Fort Huachuca Military Reserve
Trail

The Cochise Trail

[Fig. 50] The approximately 200-mile loop that can be done by driving south from Benson to Bisbee then east to Douglas then north to Chiricahua National Monument and Willcox and then back to Benson is sometimes referred to as The Cochise Trail. Cochise was a greatly respected chief of the Chiricahua Apaches in the nineteenth century. The loop travels mostly through broad valleys bordered by mountains. Along this route are many historic and natural sites to explore.

Directions: From Benson, take either AZ 90 or AZ 80 to Bisbee. From Bisbee, take AZ 80 to Douglas and then US 191 and AZ 181 to Chiricahua National Monument. From the monument, take AZ 186 to Willcox and then I-10 back to Benson.

For more information: Benson-San Pedro Valley Chamber of Commerce, PO Box 2255, Benson, AZ 85602. Phone (520) 586-2842. Web site www.theriver.com/benson-spvchamber. Douglas Chamber of Commerce, 1125 Pan American Avenue, Douglas, AZ 85607. Phone (520) 364-2477.

KARTCHNER CAVERNS STATE PARK

[Fig. 50(2)] The stunning Kartchner Caverns is one of Arizona's newest state parks. The world-class cave was discovered in 1974, purchased by the Arizona State Park system in 1988, and opened to the public in 1999. It has been surveyed at 2.4 miles in length.

About 330 million years ago, a shallow sea covered most of Arizona. Sediment deposited in this sea eventually became the Escabrosa Limestone. Millions of years later, the limestone layer, along with other rock layers, was uplifted to form the Whetstone Mountains. Groundwater moving through the limestone has slowly dissolved it into a labyrinth of passageways and rooms. Lowering groundwater levels left behind vast, air-filled chambers. For the last 200,000 years, dripping, mineralized water has created a spectacular array of travertine cave decorations called speleothems. The speleothems in Kartchner Caverns include delicate soda straws, stalactites, stalagmites, drapery, shelfstone, spar crystal, turnip shields, helectites, and many other strange and wonderful formations.

The Discovery Center is the best way to begin one's visit. Here you can find displays and exhibits that help you understand the formation and significance of this world-class cave.

Directions: From Benson, drive west on I-10 to Exit 302. Go south on AZ 90 about 9 miles to the park entrance.

Activities: Cave tour, hiking, camping, and nature study.

Facilities: Discovery Center, gift shop, hiking trails, picnic areas, campground, and amphitheater.

Dates: Open year-round, except Christmas Day.

Fees: There is an entrance fee and additional charges for the cave tour and camping.

Closest town: Benson.

For more information: Kartchner Caverns State Park, PO Box 1849, Benson, AZ 85602. Phone (520) 586-4100. For tour reservations, phone (520) 586-CAVE. Web site www.pr.state.az.us.

MILLER PEAK WILDERNESS, RAMSEY CANYON PRESERVE, AND CORONADO NATIONAL MEMORIAL

[Fig. 50(3), Fig. 50(5), Fig. 50(4)] Located just a few miles south of the rapidly growing town of Sierra Vista, in the southern half of the Huachuca Mountains, is the 20,190-acre Miller Peak Wilderness, the Ramsey Canyon Preserve, and the adjacent Coronado National Memorial. Miller Peak, at 9,466 feet, is the highest summit in the range and the highest, southernmost peak in the U.S. Once covered by a pine and Douglas fir forest, a large intense fire has now changed much of the area growth to evergreen oak woodland and grassland.

Miller Peak Wilderness is one of the most rugged, yet best wildlife areas in southern Arizona. The Huachuca Mountains are famous as a haven for birds; more than 170 species have been sighted, including 14 species of hummingbirds and the elegant trogon. More than 60 species of reptiles and 78 species of mammals, including coatimundi, javelina, black bear, and mountain lion, also occur here. Well-maintained trails go to the major points of interest and lead to exceptional panoramas. For hiking information, refer to the *Hiker's Guide to the Huachuca Mountains* by Leonard Taylor.

The area has a rich and colorful gold mining and ranching history. Near the Reef Townsite campground (*see* Coronado National Forest campground table, page 351) is a historic mining camp, which was active from the late 1800s to the early 1900s. Gold, silver, and tungsten were the primary ores. An interpretative 0.5-mile loop trail departing from the campground introduces the visitor to ore processing mill ruins, mining adits and tunnels, geologic features, and the role of past fires in the surrounding forest.

Adjacent to the northeast corner of the wilderness is The Nature Conservancy's Ramsey Canyon Preserve, renowned for its outstanding scenic beauty and the diversity of its plant and animal life. A permanent spring-fed stream, favorable east-west orientation, and high canyon walls provide Ramsey Canyon with a moist, cool, and stable environment unusual in the desert Southwest. Water-loving plants such as Arizona sycamore (*Plantanus wrightii*), maples (*Acer* sp.), and columbines (*Aquilegia* sp.) line the banks of Ramsey Creek. Plant communities ranging from semi-desert grassland to pine-fir forest are found within the canyon and provide habitat for such southwestern rarities as lemon lily (*Lilium parryi*), Tepic flame-flower (*Macranthera* sp.), Ramsey Canyon leopard frog (*Rana subaquavocalis*) (unusual for its habit of croaking underwater), ridge-nosed rattlesnake (*Crotalus willardi*), lesser (Sanborn's) long-nosed bat (*Leptonycteris sanborni*), and blue-throated hummingbird (*Lampornis clemenciae*).

However, birds are still the number one attraction. The best months for birding are April through September. Self-guided walks are possible, and guided tours are available on a seasonal basis. Call the preserve for the schedule.

The preserve headquarters, located by the entrance, contains interpretive exhibits, an outstanding natural history bookstore, information, and hiking permits. Additionally, nestled along the creek, there are six comfortable housekeeping cabins available for rent.

Tucked in between the wilderness area and the U.S./Mexican border is the 4,750-acre Coronado National Memorial. This Park Service-managed area honors Francisco Vásquez de Coronado's march into Arizona in 1540. Coronado and his expedition were in search of the mythical Seven Cities of Cibola (*see* page 180).

The memorial offers hiking, a shallow limestone cave to explore, and a scenic drive into the Huachuca Mountains. The visitor center has exhibits that include authentic sixteenth century armor and weaponry, Spanish cultural items, and a video detailing Coronado's historic trek. The Arizona Trail begins in the southwest corner of the park (*see* page 321).

Directions: Drive about 10 miles south of Sierra Vista on AZ 92. Major access points for the wilderness are at or near the end of FR 368 in upper Carr Canyon; at the end of FR 56 in Miller Canyon; and from FR 61 and FR 771 along the southern and western edge of the Huachucas. To reach the Ramsey Canyon Preserve, drive 6 miles south of Sierra Vista on AZ 92 to the Ramsey Canyon Road turnoff. The preserve is at the end of the road, about 4 miles. Coronado National Memorial is reached by staying on AZ 92 past the Ramsey Canyon Road turnoff another 8 miles. Turn right at the memorial sign. The visitor center is 4 miles in.

Activities: Hiking, horseback riding, mountain biking (outside the wilderness), and camping.

Facilities: Coronado National Memorial Visitor Center and Museum; Ramsey Canyon Preserve headquarters with exhibits, rental cabins; wilderness, none.

Dates: Open year-round. Coronado

COLUMBINE
(*Aquilegia* sp.)

National Memorial Visitor Center closed Thanksgiving and Christmas.

Fees: None for wilderness or memorial; a donation requested for Ramsey Canyon.

Closest town: Sierra Vista.

For more information: Sierra Vista Ranger District, 5990 S. Hwy. 92, Hereford, AZ 85615. Phone (520) 378-0311. Ramsey Canyon Preserve, 27 Ramsey Canyon Road, Hereford, AZ 85615. Phone (520) 378-2785. Web site www.tnc.org. Coronado National Memorial, 4101 East Montezuma Canyon Road, Hereford, AZ 85615. Phone (520) 366-5515. Web site www.nps.gov/coro.

CREST TRAIL

[Fig. 50(4)] Over a dozen trails make the Miller Peak Wilderness relatively easy to explore. One especially good route is the Crest Trail, which goes from Montezuma's Pass in Coronado National Memorial 11.5 miles to a trailhead on the west side of the wilderness within the Fort Huachuca Military Reservation. Fort Huachuca is the home of the Buffalo Soldiers, an Indian name for the black soldiers, and has a free museum devoted to early military life on the Southwest frontier. Along the way the trail passes Miller Peak, which can be climbed via a 0.5-mile side trail.

Directions: To reach Montezuma Pass, take the curvy Montezuma Pass Road from AZ 92 through Coronado National Memorial. The western trailhead can be accessed by picking up a visitor's pass at the entrance station for Fort Huachuca. The military personnel have directions to the trailhead.

Trail: 11.5 miles one-way.

Degree of difficulty: Moderate.

Elevation: 6,575 feet at east trailhead to 9,466 feet at Miller Peak.

Surface: Rocky.

SAN PEDRO RIPARIAN NATIONAL CONSERVATION AREA

[Fig. 50(6)] This area offers opportunities for world-class bird-watching, wildlife viewing and photography, hiking, mountain biking, camping, seasonal hunting, horseback riding, nature study, and environmental education. The San Pedro River has been called one of America's last great places. It's one of the few rivers of any size in the desert Southwest that isn't bone-dry most of the year. Preservation of this riparian habitat was recognized as being so important that in 1988 Congress created the 58,000-acre San Pedro Riparian National Conservation Area, the first such preserve in the nation.

The San Pedro Riparian National Conservation Area is a rare remnant of what was once an extensive network of similar riparian systems throughout the Southwest. The national conservation area stretches from the international border nearly 40 miles north to St. David. The San Pedro River enters Arizona from Sonora, Mexico, flows north between the Huachuca and Mule mountain ranges, and joins the Gila River 140 miles downstream near the town of Winkelman. Sometimes the river flows in only a trickle, but perennial springs keep the ecosystem alive.

Fremont cottonwood and Goodding willow dominate the river corridor. Lesser amounts of Arizona ash (*Fraxinus velutina glabra*), Arizona black walnut (*Juglans major*), netleaf hackberry (*Celtis reticulata*), and soapberry (*Sapindus saponaria*) occur as well. Chihuahuan desert-scrub, typified by thorny species such as tarbush (*Flourensia cernua*), creosote, and acacia, characterize the uplands bordering both sides of the river, while mesquite and sacaton grass (*Sporobolus* sp.) dominate the bottomland adjacent to the riparian corridor.

Wildlife abounds in the national conservation area because of abundant food, water, and cover. The area supports more than 350 species of birds, 80 species of mammals, 2 native and several introduced species of fish, and more than 40 species of amphibians and reptiles.

After dark, birders can call for owls, but those visitors with an interest in the heavens may want to check out the **Skywatcher's Inn** (5655 N. Via Umbrosa, Tucson, AZ 84750. Phone 520-615-3886. Web site www.communiverse.com/skywatcher.), a unique bed and breakfast on the San Pedro River just east of Benson. The inn boasts eight professional-quality telescopes, the most popular being the two Maksutov telescopes. These telescopes use both magnifying lenses and mirrors to increase their depth perception and image quality.

Prehistoric and historic sites are also plentiful. The Clovis Culture, named for a unique type of stone projectile point, were the first human occupants in the upper San Pedro River Valley, dating back approximately 11,000 years. Stone tools and weapons used by these people to butcher large mammals, such as mammoths and bison, were found with the bones of their prey at the Lehner Mammoth Kill Site and the Murray Springs Clovis Site. Directions to these sites can be obtained from the San Pedro Riparian National Conservation Area Office. Remains of other cultures include the Archaic people (6000 B.C.-A.D.1) and the Mogollon and Hohokam (A.D.1-1500).

The historic cultures can be divided into three major periods. First came the Spanish. Francisco Vasquez de Coronado led his 1540 expedition through the San Pedro Valley. Around 1775, Spanish troops led by an Irish mercenary began to build the *Presidio Santa Cruz de Terrenate*, a fortified settlement. It was never completed and was abandoned by 1780 due to continuous Apache raids. Directions to the ruins of the Presidio can be obtained from the San Pedro National Conservation Area Office.

The next invading culture was the Mexican. Upon declaring independence from Spain in 1821, Mexicans moved into the San Pedro Valley to homestead and ranch. However, as with the Spanish occupation, Apache raids kept the Mexican settlers from prospering.

The Mexican period end when the area became United States territory through the Gadsden Purchase of 1853. The latter nineteenth century witnessed more cattle ranching, farming, and the discovery of silver in nearby Tombstone and other locations. Most Apache raiding ended in 1886 with the surrender of Geronimo and his followers. By 1900, large-scale, corporate-financed cattle ranching and farming became the norm, a trend which persisted until the BLM acquired the land in 1986.

Directions: There are six entrance points scattered the length of the areas, but first time visitors should go the San Pedro House on AZ 90 about 7 miles east of Sierra Vista.

Activities: Bird-watching, wildlife viewing and photography, hiking, mountain biking, camping, seasonal hunting, fishing, horseback riding, nature study, and environmental education.

Facilities: San Pedro House visitor center and bookstore.

Dates: Open year-round.

Fees: There is an entrance fee and camping fee.

Closest town: Sierra Vista, 7 miles west; Benson, 6 miles north.

For more information: San Pedro Riparian National Conservation Area Office, BLM, 1763 Paseo San Luis, Sierra Vista, AZ 85635. Phone (520) 458-3559.

SAN PEDRO TRAIL

[Fig. 50(7)] The San Pedro Trail parallels the river through most of the national conservation area. Hiking, mountain biking, and horseback riding are permitted. Along the way you pass old mills, town sites, ranch ruins, and other historic and prehistoric sites. Several highways cross it, as well as several connector trails, allowing users to do shorter sections. The San Pedro National Conservation Area Office has additional trail information.

Directions: The southernmost trailhead is at Palominas, located where AZ 92 crosses the San Pedro River, about 20 miles southeast of Sierra Vista. The northern-most trailhead is at St. David Cienega, about 5 miles southwest of St. David on the Apache Powder Road.

Trail: About 41 miles.

Degree of difficulty: Easy to moderate.

Elevation: 3,650 to 4,225 feet.

Surface: Packed dirt.

TOMBSTONE COURTHOUSE STATE HISTORIC PARK

[Fig. 50(8)] Tombstone, a nineteenth century silver mining boomtown, was known as "the town too tough to die" and the location of the famous shootout between the Earps and the Clantons at the OK Corral (which is reenacted daily). An excellent place to learn about the area's authentic and fascinating history is the Tombstone Courthouse State Historic Park. The courthouse, a Victorian building completed in 1882, features exhibits recalling the turbulent history.

Directions: Located on the corner of Third and Toughnut in Tombstone.

Activities: History study.

Facilities: Historic courthouse with exhibits, historic archives, and gift shop.

Dates: Open year-round.

Fees: There is an entrance fee.

Closest town: Tombstone.

For more information: Tombstone Courthouse State Historic Park, Third and Toughnut Streets, Tombstone, AZ 85638. Phone (520) 457-3311. Visitor Information Center, PO Box 280, Tombstone, AZ 85638. Phone (520) 457-3929. Web site www.cityoftombstone.com.

BISBEE

[Fig. 50] About 23 miles south of Tombstone, nestled in the Mule Mountains, is the historic mining town of Bisbee. This pleasant mile-high town features European charm and turn-of-the-nineteenth century architecture. The downtown area is a National Historic District. In its heyday, Bisbee was known as the "Queen of the Copper Camps." Aboveground and underground tours of the old Queen Mine reveals how copper ore was wrestled from the earth. Historic hotels, quaint bed and breakfasts, antique shops, art galleries, and fine restaurants take care of visitors' needs.

For more information: Bisbee Chamber of Commerce, PO Drawer BA, Bisbee, AZ 85603. Phone (520) 432-5421. Web site www.azguide.com/bisbee.

DOS CABEZAS MOUNTAINS WILDERNESS

[Fig. 50(9)] The 11,700-acre Dos Cabezas Mountains Wilderness lies 20 miles east of Willcox and 7 miles south of Bowie. The twin-headed 8,300-foot summit of the Dos Cabezas Mountains is visible for many miles around. The range lies between the Sulphur Springs and San Simon valleys. This remote wilderness provides outstanding opportunities for hiking, backpacking, camping, rock scrambling, and sight-seeing.

The Dos Cabezas look down on slopes of juniper and scrub oak that blend into desert scrub and mesquite. Broad-leaved trees grow along canyon bottoms and around springs.

White-tailed and mule deer, mountain lion, golden eagle, and many other species occur here. Reportedly, there is a large population of handsome collared lizards (*Crotaphytus collaris*) living in the upper part of Buckeye Canyon.

Directions: From Bowie on I-10, travel 4.5 miles south along Apache Pass Road. Then turn right (west) on the Happy Canyon Road and go 3 miles to the Indian Bread Rocks Picnic Area. There are no established trails, but you can walk up Happy Canyon into the wilderness. Some lands adjacent to the wilderness are not federally administered. Please respect the property rights of the owners and do not cross or use these lands without their permission.

Activities: Hiking, camping, and nature study.

Facilities: None.

Dates: Open year-round, but spring and fall have the best temperatures for hiking.

Fees: None.

Closest town: Bowie, about 8 miles north.

For more information: BLM, Safford Field Office, 711-14th Avenue, Safford, AZ 85546. Phone (520) 348-4400. Web site www.az.blm.gov.

🏜 FORT BOWIE NATIONAL HISTORIC SITE

[Fig. 50(10)] Fort Bowie was built in 1862 to guard the Butterfield Overland Stageline Route and protect settlers. This site became the center of many battles between the Chiricahua Apaches and the U.S. Cavalry until the surrender of Geronimo in 1886. Today only a few crumbling adobe walls remain, but the short walk to the fort takes you back in time.

Directions: From Willcox, drive 22 miles south on AZ 186 to the graded dirt road leading east toward Apache Pass. Drive 7 miles to the visitor center. From there it is an easy 1.5-mile walk to the fort's remains and a Butterfield Stage Station.

Activities: Self-guided walking tour of a historic site.

Facilities: Small ranger station with exhibits and picnic area.

Dates: Open daily, except Christmas.

Fees: None.

Closest town: Willcox, about 29 miles.

For more information: Fort Bowie National Historic Site, c/o Chiricahua National Monument, Dos Cabezas Route, Box 6500, Willcox, AZ 85643. Phone (520) 847-2500.

🏜 CHIRICAHUA NATIONAL MONUMENT

[Fig. 50(11)] Chiricahua National Monument is a fantasy world of extraordinary rock sculptures. To the Chiricahua Apaches it is the "land of the standing-up rocks." This monument in the northeast corner of the Chiricahua Mountains harbors towering rock spires, massive stone columns, and balance rocks weighing hundreds of tons perched on tiny pedestals. *Chiricahua* may be a corruption of an Apache word for "great mountain" or an Opata word meaning "mountain of the wild turkeys."

Nearly 20 miles of trail beckon the visitor to explore this monument. The trails pass the unusual rock formations and traverse the park's forest. One trail leads to a small natural bridge and another to a ledge of volcanic "hailstones." Trails range from 0.25-mile to 9-mile day trips. Ask for a hiking brochure at the visitor center.

The story behind this fantastic collection of rocks is not completely understood, but geologists believe that about 27 million years ago violent volcanic eruptions spewed red-hot pumice and ash over a 1,200-square-mile area. The hot particles became "welded" together to form an 800-foot-thick layer of tuff with a composition of rhyolite. As cooling took place, the tuff contracted and vertical cracks (joints) formed. The extent and thickness of this deposit indicates eruptions substantially greater than the 1980 Mount St. Helens eruption in Washington.

From 25 to 5 million years ago, tectonic plate movement caused the earth's crust in this area to stretch and brake into large fault-bounded blocks. One uplifted block created the Chiricahua Mountains, and the masters of erosion—water, wind, and ice—began to sculpt the rock into odd formations. The horizontal bedding planes and joints provided weak places for erosion to act upon. Fanciful names such as Organ Pipe, Sea Captain, China Boy, Punch and Judy, and Duck on a Rock describe some of the strange rock shapes. Although many pinnacles and rocks appear to be precariously balanced, they were sufficiently stable to withstand the magnitude 7.2 earthquake that shook southeastern Arizona in 1887.

The Chiricahua Mountains were the home of the Chiricahua Apaches. From these mountains, the Apaches, led by Cochise and Geronimo, launched attacks against the tide of pioneers for more than 25 years. Their resistance slowed but did not stop settlement. When Geronimo's band surrendered in 1886 and was removed to a distant reservation, ranches and farms replaced the traditional Apache culture.

Among the first pioneers to settle in the area were Neil and Emma Erickson. One of their daughters, Lillian, and her husband, Ed Riggs, turned the homestead into a guest ranch in the 1920s. Strong-willed Lillian, whose nickname was "Lady Boss," named their place Faraway Ranch since it was so "god-awful far away from every-thing." Together she and Ed explored the Chiricahuas, built trails, and took guests on horseback rides to see the "Wonderland of Rocks." The Riggses promoted the idea of preserving the strange rocks and, in 1924, Chiricahua National Monument was established by President Calvin Coolidge. Today their ranch is abandoned, but the Park Service conducts tours of the main house daily.

Bonita Canyon Scenic Drive leads from the Visitor Center and slowly climbs through oak-juniper and pine forests. The road winds 8 miles to the mountain's crest and Massai point. The overlook gives a commanding view of the park, the landmark peaks of Sugarloaf Mountain and Cochise Head, and desert valleys beyond.

Near the visitor center is a campground providing first-come, first-serve camping with tables, grills, restrooms, and drinking water.

Directions: From Willcox, drive southeast on AZ 186 about 31 miles to the entrance road to the monument.

Activities: Scenic driving, hiking, camping, and picnicking.

Facilities: Visitor center, campground, picnic areas, scenic drive, and more than 20 miles of hiking trails.

Dates: Open year-round.

Fees: There is an entrance fee and campground fee.

Closest town: Willcox, about 31 miles northwest.

For more information: Superintendent, Chiricahua National Monument, Dos Cabezas Route, Box 6500, Willcox, AZ 85643. Phone (520) 824-3560. Web site www.nps.gov/chir.

HEART OF ROCKS LOOP

[Fig. 50(11)] There are about 17 miles of maintained day-use trails in Chiricahua National Monument. Most are 1 mile or less in length. Heart of Rocks Loop is one of the longer day hikes, but it features the most massive balanced rock in the monument and many rock caricatures of people and animals. There are also wonderful sweeping views of the Sulphur Springs Valley, Cochise Head, and the Chiricahua Mountains along this trail. A side trip to Inspiration Point provides a spectacular view of Rhyolite Canyon.

Directions: It is easiest to start at Massai Point at the top end of the Bonita Canyon Scenic Drive (*see* Chiricahua National Monument, page 308).

Trail: 7.5-mile loop via Ed Riggs Trail, Mushroom Rock Trail, and Big Balanced Rock Trail. Add another mile for the side trip to Inspiration Point.

Degree of difficulty: Moderate.

Elevation: 6,840 feet at Massai Point to a low of about 6,200 feet along the loop.

Surface: Maintained packed dirt and rock.

CHIRICAHUA WILDERNESS

The 87,700-acre Chiricahua Wilderness in the Coronado National Forest is a few miles south of Chiricahua National Monument, which for the most part is also managed as wilderness. There is a wide variation in elevation, exposure, slope, moisture, and plant and animal life. Many species that live here are unusual in the U.S.—such as Mexican chickadees (*Poecile sclateri*), sulphur-bellied flycatchers (*Myiodynastes luteiventris*), and elegant trogons—but common in Mexico.

Because of the dense brush and timber, steep slopes, precipitous canyons, and uncertain sources of water, travel is difficult except on trails. Unfortunately a 27,000-acre wildfire in 1994 caused severe destruction of many of the trails in the wilderness. Contact the ranger district for the latest update on trail conditions. Forest Service campgrounds outside the wilderness provide good access for day hikes into the wilderness (*see* Cave Creek, page 284).

Directions: The wilderness can be approached from the west side via AZ 186 or AZ 181. The communities of Paradise and Portal are the main east side entrance points into the national forest and wilderness.

Activities: Hiking, horseback riding, hunting, camping, and nature study.

Facilities: None in wilderness (*see* Coronado National Forest campground table, page 351, for campgrounds outside but near the wilderness area).

Dates: Open year-round, although winter snows may close the higher areas.

Fees: None for the wilderness, but there are fees to use campgrounds.

Closest town: Willcox, about 40 miles northwest.

For more information: Douglas Ranger District, 3081 N. Leslie Canyon Road, Douglas, AZ 85607. Phone (520) 364-3468.

SAN BERNARDINO NATIONAL WILDLIFE REFUGE

[Fig. 50(13)] The 2,330-acre San Bernardino National Wildlife Refuge is located on the U.S./Mexico border in extreme southeastern Arizona. The refuge terrain varies from rolling uplands to flat bottomland. Springs and ponds attract more than 240 species of birds and harbor endangered fish—Yaqui topminnow (*Poeciliopsis occidentalis sonoriensis*), Yaqui chub (*Gila purpurea*), and Yaqui catfish (*Ictalurus pricei*).

The area has a colorful history. Much of the refuge land once belonged to the John Slaughter Ranch. In 1884, former Texas Ranger and soon-to-be sheriff of Cochise County John Slaughter began what became the quintessential Southwestern cattle ranch. The ranch has been meticulously restored to give a feeling of what ranch life was like and is open for tours.

Directions: To reach the Slaughter Ranch, drive east on 15th Street from Douglas. It turns into Geronimo Trail. Continue 16 miles to the white Slaughter Ranch gate with the large "Z" representing his cattle brand. The national wildlife refuge headquarters is 11 miles north of Douglas on US 191, but the national wildlife refuge is located about 0.75 mile past the Slaughter Ranch turnoff.

Activities: Hiking, hunting, and nature study.

Facilities: Slaughter Ranch has a visitor center. No facilities in national wildlife refuge.

Dates: San Bernardino National Wildlife Refuge open year-round, headquarters open Monday through Friday. Slaughter Ranch open Wednesday through Sunday year-round, except Christmas and New Year's Day.

Fees: Slaughter Ranch charges for admission; the national wildlife refuge does not.

Closest town: Douglas, about 16 miles west.

For more information: San Bernardino National Wildlife Refuge, PO Box 3509, Douglas, AZ 85607. Phone (520) 364-2104. Slaughter Ranch, Box 438, Douglas, AZ 85608. Phone (520) 558-2474. Web site www.vtc.net/~sranch.

▨ BAKER CANYON WILDERNESS STUDY AREA

[Fig. 50(14)] The 4,812-acre Baker Canyon Wilderness Study Area is 30 miles east of Douglas. The Wilderness Study Area is unusually rich in wildlife and is part of a wildlife corridor connecting ecosystems in Arizona, New Mexico, and Mexico. Bird life is extraordinary, with unusual species of hummingbirds, trogons, and wild turkey (*Meleagris gallopavo*) among others. The Wilderness Study Area is also home to a variety of animal species including bats, coatimundi, Coues white-tailed deer, bobcat, and mountain lion. Interesting plant species, including Chihuahua pine, Mexican pinyon, and Arizona rosewood (a federal candidate for threatened and endangered species status), have been identified. Public access is not available across private lands adjacent to the Wilderness Study Area. Check with the BLM for current accessibility.

For more information: BLM, Safford Field Office, 711-14th Avenue, Safford, AZ 85546. Phone (520) 348-4400. Web site www.az.blm.gov.

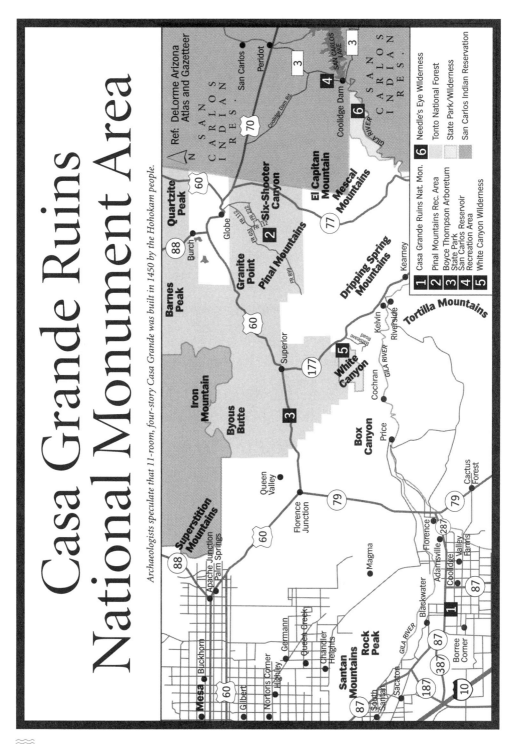

Casa Grande Ruins National Monument Area

Archaeologists speculate that 11-room, four-story Casa Grande was built in 1450 by the Hohokam people.

Ref: DeLorme Arizona Atlas and Gazetteer

1 Casa Grande Ruins Nat. Mon.
2 Pinal Mountains Rec. Area
3 Boyce Thompson Arboretum State Park
4 San Carlos Reservoir Recreation Area
5 White Canyon Wilderness

6 Needle's Eye Wilderness
Tonto National Forest
State Park/Wilderness
San Carlos Indian Reservation

The Desert Ranges North and East of Tucson

▨ CASA GRANDE RUINS NATIONAL MONUMENT

[Fig. 51(1)] One of Arizona's tallest and most mysterious prehistoric buildings is 11-room, four-story Casa Grande. The rectangular mud structure sits on an earthen platform surrounded by smaller rooms and a wall. The purpose of this building is unknown. Archaeologists speculate that it may have been used for ceremonies or astronomical observations. Small holes in its walls seem to line up with certain celestial events like solstices and lunar phases.

The visitor center has exhibits on the Hohokam, who are most likely the people who built this great house around 1450. Rangers lead tours or visitors can take the self-guided trail.

Directions: The monument is 1 mile north of Coolidge just off AZ 87.

Activities: Visiting the ruin.

Facilities: Visitor center.

Dates: Open year-round.

Fees: There is an entrance fee.

Closest town: Coolidge, about 1 miles south.

For more information: Casa Grande Ruins National Monument, PO Box 518, Coolidge, AZ 85228. Phone (520) 723-3172. Web site www.nps.gov/cagr.

▨ PICACHO PEAK STATE PARK

[Fig. 47(5)] Rising 1,500 vertical feet above the surrounding desert floor, 3,374-foot Picacho Peak is an isolated, 22 million-year-old volcanic mountain situated midway between the Gila River and Tucson. This is the site of Arizona's only Civil War battle. The "Battle of Picacho Pass" took place on April 15, 1862, lasted about an hour and a half, and cost the lives of four "Johnny Rebs" and three "Yanks."

Petroglyphs abound in the area, testifying that the Hohokam were here long before the white man. In 1933, the CCC built a trail to the summit that now sees 10,000 or more hikers a year.

Directions: Take I-10 approximately 41 miles northwest of Tucson to the well-marked Exit 219 for the state park.

Activities: Hiking, nature study, picnicking, and camping.

Facilities: Picnic areas and campgrounds.

Dates: Open year-round, but very hot during summer.

Fees: There are entrance and camping fees.

Closest town: Eloy, about 10 miles northwest.

For more information: Picacho Peak State Park, PO Box 275, Picacho, AZ 85241.

Phone (520) 466-3183. Web site www.pr.state.az.us.

HUNTER TRAIL

[Fig. 47(5)] In the early 1970s, an Explorer Scout Troop constructed a new trail to replace the lower half of the original CCC trail. Frequent trail signs and steel-cable handrails show the way over the eastern headwall to the main saddle. From the saddle, railroad-tie wooden steps, steel cables, wire-mesh-enclosed catwalks, and gangplanks lead to the summit. On a clear day, there are 100-mile views in all directions. Unfortunately, with each passing year there is less of the desert landscape and more urban development.

Directions: The trailhead is located in the southwest corner of the park's Barrett Loop, near the Saguaro Ramada.

Trail: 2 miles one-way.

Degree of difficulty: Moderate.

Elevation: 1,900 to 3,374 feet.

Surface: Rocky.

PINAL MOUNTAINS RECREATION AREA

[Fig. 51(2)] Rising a few miles south of the historic copper mining town of Globe are the Pinal Mountains. The mountains are a popular Forest Service recreation area, especially during the summer when the higher elevation allows escape from the hot surrounding desert. A number of Forest Service roads make for good access to nine hiking trails and three developed campsites (*see* the Tonto National Forest campground table, page 350). The Forest Service has a Recreation Guide to help campers and hikers enjoy the recreation area.

Directions: To access most of the trailheads and campgrounds, take Jess Hayes Road southeast of Globe to its junction with Icehouse Canyon Road (FR 112) and Six-shooter Canyon Road (FR 222). The two Forest Service roads lead into the mountains and other Forest Service roads.

Activities: Camping, picnicking, and hiking.

Facilities: Campgrounds and picnic areas.

Dates: Open year-round.

Fees: None.

Closest town: Globe.

For more information: Globe Ranger District, Rt. 1, Box 33, Globe, AZ 88501. Phone (502) 402-6200.

BOYCE THOMPSON ARBORETUM STATE PARK

[Fig. 51(3)] The Boyce Thompson Arboretum is the state's oldest botanical garden, founded in 1924 by mining magnate William Boyce Thompson. There are desert plants from all over the world, a streamside woodland, mountain cliffs, panoramic vistas, miles of easy nature trails, and specialty gardens.

Directions: Drive 3 miles west of Superior on US 60.

Activities: Nature study, self-guided tours, desert gardening workshops, and informative lectures.

Facilities: Visitor center, arboretum store, plant sale greenhouse, interpretive center, historic greenhouses, and picnic area.

Dates: Open year-round, except Christmas Day.

Fees: There is an entrance fee.

Closest town: Superior.

For more information: Boyce Thompson Arboretum, 37615 Hwy. 60, Superior, AZ 85273-5100. Phone (520) 689-2811. Web site http://arboretum.ag.arizona.edu.

SAN CARLOS RESERVOIR RECREATION AREA

[Fig. 51(4)] The 23-mile-long San Carlos Lake is the largest body of water on the San Carlos Apache Reservation (*see* page 323). The reservoir was created in 1930 when the 880-foot-high Coolidge Dam was built on the Gila River not far down-stream from its confluence with the San Carlos River. The lake is a popular destination for boaters and campers. Record-size black crappie and flathead catfish (*Pylodictis olivaris*) have been caught in San Carlos Lake. Anglers also go after largemouth bass, channel catfish, and bluegill.

Directions: From Peridot on US 70, drive about 10 miles south on Tribal Route 3 to Coolidge Dam.

Activities: Camping, fishing, and other water sports.

Facilities: Store, gas, showers, boat ramps, picnic area, and campgrounds.

Dates: Open year-round.

Fees: There are fees for camping and fishing.

Closest town: San Carlos, about 12 miles north.

For more information: San Carlos Recreation and Wildlife Department, PO Box 97, San Carlos, AZ 85550. Phone (520) 475-2343 or (888) 275-2653.

WHITE CANYON WILDERNESS

[Fig. 51(5)] Hikers and rock climbers are drawn to this 5,800-acre wilderness that takes in White Canyon, a deep, colorful gorge that cuts south toward the Gila River through layers of volcanic ash flows and welded tuffs. The canyon bottom holds a lively stream that seasonally presents a series of delightful oases with cascades, swimming holes, and dense riparian vegetation. There is no well-defined rim to the canyon but rather a series of weirdly eroded ridgelines, benches, and terraces, many composed of naked brown and buff-colored rock.

The wilderness also includes the southeast portion of the Mineral Mountains. A major topographical feature is the Rincon, a large escarpment which towers above the White Canyon.

The area is primarily covered with Sonoran desert vegetation and harbors typical desert animals. One exception is black bear (*Ursus americanus*), a definite rarity for the Sonoran desert. Other extraordinary features of the wilderness are a large bat cave filled with guano, a huge 50-foot tall saguaro with more than 20 arms growing in White Canyon, as well as a pinyon tree thought to be one of the largest in Arizona.

Directions: From Superior, travel 9.5 miles south on AZ 177. At about 0.5 mile south of milepost 159, turn west onto a dirt road (Battle Ax Road) toward Walnut Canyon and White Canyon. High-clearance or four-wheel-drive vehicles are recommended. At Walnut Canyon, periodic flooding has damaged the road. Proceed with caution. Some lands around the wilderness are not federally administered. Please respect the property rights of the owners and do not cross or use these lands without their permission. For additional access information, contact the BLM.

Activities: Hiking, rock climbing, camping, and nature study.

Facilities: None.

Dates: Open year-round, but very hot during the summer.

Fees: None.

Closest town: Superior, about 10 miles north.

For more information: BLM, Tucson Field Office, 12661 East Broadway, Tucson, AZ 85748. Phone (520) 722-4289. Web site www.az.blm.gov.

NEEDLE'S EYE WILDERNESS

[Fig. 51(6)] The Needle's Eye is a beautiful canyon with 1,000-foot walls cut through the Mescal Mountains by the Gila River. Numerous side canyons feed into the river, slicing up the surrounding countryside. Within the 8,760-acre wilderness, elevations range from 2,300 feet to 4,300 feet. Riparian vegetation borders the river, while Sonoran desert plants clothe the rest of the area. Recreational opportunities include birding, hiking, backpacking, hunting, and photography. This area offers a high level of solitude to hardy adventurers.

The cliffs provide good nesting sites for raptors. At least one pair of bald eagles makes their home along the river. Swifts and swallows dart along the escarpment. A host of other birds nest in the riparian area.

Directions: Currently there is no public access to the Needle's Eye Wilderness unless you obtain a recreation permit from the San Carlos Apache Indian Tribe in advance. You must also obtain permission to cross State Trust lands and private lands in advance. Contact the tribe through their recreation and wildlife department and/or the BLM office.

Activities: Hiking, hunting, camping, and nature study.

Facilities: None.

Dates: Open year-round, but summer is very hot.

Fees: None.

Closest town: Globe, about 30 miles north.

For more information: BLM, Tucson Field Office, 12661 East Broadway, Tucson,

AZ 85748. Phone (520) 722-4289. Web site www.az.blm.gov. San Carlos Recreation and Wildlife Department, PO Box 97, San Carlos, AZ 85550. Phone (520) 475-2343 or (888) 275-2653. Arizona State Land Department, Phoenix Office, 1616 W. Adams, Phoenix, AZ 85007. Phone (602) 542-2119.

ARAVAIPA CANYON WILDERNESS AND PRESERVE

[Fig. 52(1)] Aravaipa Canyon, which cuts through the northern part of the Galiuro Mountains, has long been recognized for its spectacular scenery and important wildlife habitat. Thousand-foot cliffs rise above a green ribbon of rich riparian habitat found along the 11-mile segment of Aravaipa Creek, which flows through the wilderness. The 19,410-acre wilderness area consists of Aravaipa Canyon as well as surrounding tablelands and nine side canyons. More than 200 species of birds live among shady cottonwoods and willows growing along the perennial waters of Aravaipa Creek. During late spring and summer, birders can expect to encounter yellow-billed cuckoos, vermilion flycatchers, northern beardless tyrannulets, yellow warblers, yellow-breasted chats, and summer tanagers.

Two federally listed threatened fish occur in the creek, spikedace (*Meda fulgida*) and loach minnow (*Tiaroga cobitis*). There are an additional five species of native fish, making Aravaipa Creek one of the best native fisheries remaining in Arizona. The stream has been recommended to be named a National Wild and Scenic River.

There is no established trail through Aravaipa Canyon, but there is a "trailhead" and parking area at each end of the canyon. Stream wading and numerous crossings (up to knee deep), as well as hiking through dense riparian brush, can slow travel time. It takes a strong hiker about 10 hours to hike the length of the canyon. Topographic maps are handy in keeping track of your progress.

The Bureau of Land Management manages the wilderness and a permit is required in advance to enter the area. Use is limited to 50 people per day, 30 from the west end and 20 from the east end. Maximum length of stay is three days/two nights, and party size is limited to 10 people. Equestrians can have only five stock/pack animals per party and may not have animals overnight in the canyon. These regulations help ensure a desirable level of solitude for visitors and reduce the potential for impacts to the environment. An in-depth Aravaipa Canyon Wilderness brochure is available to explain permit requirements. Payment of a fee is required to enter the wilderness. Contact the Safford Field Office for additional permit and fee information.

Adjacent to the east boundary of the wilderness area is The Nature Conservancy's Aravaipa Canyon Preserve. About 6.4 miles northwest of Klondyke, where the road goes down to cross the creek for the second crossing, is the preserve manager's house. To go off the public road, a permit is required from the preserve manager. No permit is needed if you are going straight to the wilderness boundary. A guest house on the preserve can be rented, but the nearest food is in Safford or Willcox. For those who want to camp, the BLM does operate a fee campground 1 mile west of Klondyke.

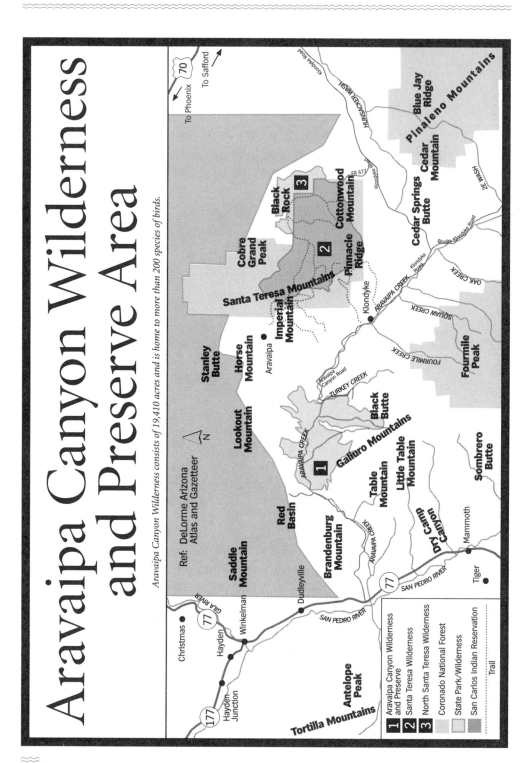

Aravaipa Canyon Wilderness and Preserve Area

Aravaipa Canyon Wilderness consists of 19,410 acres and is home to more than 200 species of birds.

Ref: DeLorme Arizona Atlas and Gazetteer

N

To Phoenix
To Safford
70

Klondyke Road

HUNSACKER WASH

Pinaleno Mountains

Blue Jay Ridge

Cedar Mountain

2E WASH

FR 677

Cottonwood Mountain

Black Rock
3

Cobre Grand Peak

Cedar Springs Butte

Klondyke Road

Pinnacle Ridge
2

Santa Teresa Mountains

Bonita Klondyke Road

ARAVAIPA CREEK

Klondyke

OAK CREEK

SQUAW CREEK

Imperial Mountain

Aravaipa

Horse Mountain

Stanley Butte

FOURMILE CREEK

Fourmile Peak

Aravaipa Canyon Road

TURKEY CREEK

Black Butte

Lookout Mountain

ARAVAIPA CREEK

1

Galiuro Mountains

Little Table Mountain

Sombrero Butte

Red Basin

Table Mountain

Saddle Mountain

Brandenburg Mountain

ARAVAIPA CREEK

Dry Camp Canyon

Mammoth

77

SAN PEDRO RIVER

Tiger

Dudleyville

GILA RIVER

Christmas

77

Hayden

Winkelman

SAN PEDRO RIVER

Hayden Junction

177

Antelope Peak

Tortilla Mountains

1 Aravaipa Canyon Wilderness and Preserve

2 Santa Teresa Wilderness

3 North Santa Teresa Wilderness

Coronado National Forest

State Park/Wilderness

San Carlos Indian Reservation

Trail

Directions: From Winkelman, take AZ 77 south for 11 miles to the Aravaipa Road. Follow the Aravaipa Road 12 miles east to the trailhead for the wilderness. Access to the east end of the wilderness is 10 miles northwest of Klondyke on the Aravaipa Canyon Road, which requires a high-clearance vehicle. Most of the land from AZ 77 to the wilderness boundary is private. Please stay on the Aravaipa Road.

Activities: Hiking, horseback riding, camping, and nature study.

Facilities: None in the wilderness; BLM campground near Klondyke; Aravaipa Canyon Preserve guest house.

Dates: Open year-round, but the access roads may be closed after thunderstorms.

Fees: There is a fee for hiking and camping in the wilderness.

Closest town: Winkelman, about 23 miles northwest of the west wilderness boundary; Safford and Willcox, about 75 miles east and southeast, respectively, of the preserve.

For more information: BLM, Safford Field Office, 711-14th Avenue, Safford, AZ 85546. Phone (520) 348-4400. Web site www.az.blm.gov/aravaipa.html. Aravaipa Canyon Preserve, phone (520) 828-3443.

GALIURO WILDERNESS

[Fig. 53(1)] The 7,633-foot-high Galiuro Mountains are two 25-mile-long, parallel chains of northwest-trending mountains cleaved lengthwise by Redfield Canyon on the south and Rattlesnake Canyon on the north. This 76,317-acre Forest Service wilderness is so difficult to reach that few hikers explore the area—great if you are seeking solitude. Most of the trails are poorly marked and infrequently maintained. Maps and compass are necessary. There are few dependable water sources, so go properly prepared.

One of the earliest recorded traverses of the range was by trapper James Ohio Pattie in the spring of 1824. He and his party ran out of food and water, but upon "...descending from these icy mountains...I killed an antelope, of which we drank the warm blood...."

Directions: To reach the northern end of the wilderness, drive north from Willcox on Fort Grant Road 33 miles to Bonita. Take Aravaipa Road 27 miles to the junction with Rattlesnake Canyon Road, FR 96; turn left and follow FR 96 11 miles to the Rattlesnake Canyon trailhead at the top of Power's Hill.

Activities: Hiking, camping, and nature study.

Facilities: None.

Dates: Open year-round, but very hot in the summer and winter snows may block higher terrain.

Fees: None.

Closest town: Willcox, about 71 miles.

For more information: USFS, Safford Ranger District, PO Box 709, Safford, AZ 85548-0709. Phone (520) 428-4150.

Galiuro Wilderness Area

The 7,633-foot-high Galiuro Mountains are two 25-mile-long, parallel chains of northwest-trending mountains.

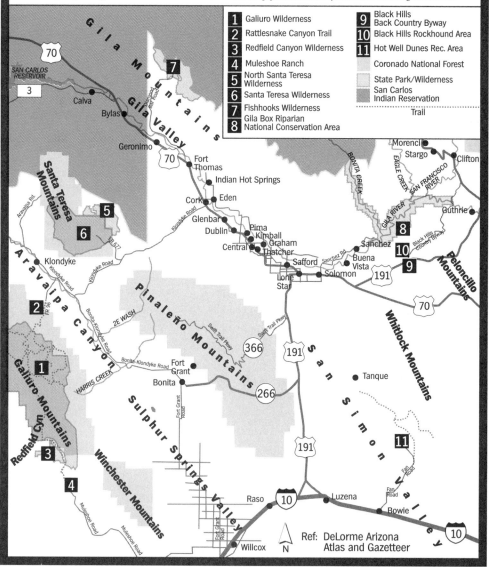

Legend:

1. Galiuro Wilderness
2. Rattlesnake Canyon Trail
3. Redfield Canyon Wilderness
4. Muleshoe Ranch
5. North Santa Teresa Wilderness
6. Santa Teresa Wilderness
7. Fishhooks Wilderness
8. Gila Box Riparian National Conservation Area
9. Black Hills Back Country Byway
10. Black Hills Rockhound Area
11. Hot Well Dunes Rec. Area

- Coronado National Forest
- State Park/Wilderness
- San Carlos Indian Reservation
- .... Trail

Ref: DeLorme Arizona Atlas and Gazetteer

RATTLESNAKE CANYON TRAIL

[Fig. 53(2)] This trail is a good introduction to canyoneering in the rugged Galiuros. It leads to Powers Garden, where an old cabin, corral, and shed still stand in a grassy meadow surrounded by ponderosa pine. The idyllic setting belies the tragic shootout that took place here in 1918. A warrant had been issued for the arrest of Tom and John Powers for draft dodging. The sheriff's posse rode into the heart of the range to serve the warrant. Shots rang out and within a few minutes the sheriff, an undersheriff, and a deputy lay dead and the Powers boys' father was mortally wounded. Tom, John, and an accomplice were eventually arrested in Mexico. The brothers were paroled in 1961.

Don't expect outlaws today but rather keep an eye out for troops of coatimundis, bighorn sheep, Gila monsters, and the Arizona black rattlesnake (*Crotalus viridis cerberus*). Birders should note peregrine falcons, bald eagles, Scott's oriole, black-tailed gnatcatcher, Gila woodpecker, wild turkey, scrub jay, brown-crested flycatcher, Gambel's quail, western tanager, and cactus wren.

Directions: See Galiuro Wilderness, page 319.

Trail: 5 miles one-way to Powers Garden.

Degree of difficulty: Strenuous.

Elevation: About 5,000 feet at trailhead, 4,600 feet at bottom of Rattlesnake Canyon to 4,920 feet at Powers Garden.

Surface: Rocky.

REDFIELD CANYON WILDERNESS AND MULESHOE RANCH

[Fig. 53(3)] Adjacent to the southern boundary of the Galiuro Wilderness is the 6,600-acre BLM Redfield Canyon Wilderness, a topographically spectacular area of steep, plunging escarpments, dike swarms, volcanic outcrops, and canyons. Elevations range from 3,500 feet in the bottom of Redfield Canyon to over 6,200 feet along the rim. Significant acreage of oak and alder (*Alnus* sp.) woodland occurs along the canyon bottoms. South-facing slopes support one-seed juniper (*Juniperus monosperma*) and Mexican blue oak (*Quercus oblongifolia*), whereas north-facing slopes have a mixture of oak, skunkbush (*Rhus trilobata*), yucca, chaparral, and many Sierra Madrean species from Mexico at the northern limit of their range

Wildlife includes desert tortoise, nesting peregrine falcons and golden eagles, common black-hawk, zone-tailed hawk, an expanding herd of desert bighorn sheep, black bear, javelina, white-tailed and mule deer, and mountain lion. The waters of Redfield Canyon contain one of the largest intact populations of the rare desert fish Gila chub (*Gila intermedia*); there are no known introduced species of fish, a rarity these days.

Other small canyons containing perennial streams can be found in the area where photographers can capture hidden cascades and casual visitors may occasionally find deep pools to enjoy. Located in the eastern part of the wilderness is the impressive

Galiuro escarpment, an example of the fault-block development of the Basin and Range Province.

The Muleshoe Ranch Cooperative Management Area is adjacent to this and the Galiuro wilderness areas. It is jointly owned and managed by The Nature Conservancy, the Forest Service, and the Bureau of Land Management. This 55,000-acre area of trackless beauty is the watershed for seven permanently flowing streams, representing some of the best remaining aquatic habitat in Arizona. About 80 percent of the region's wildlife depends upon these streamside communities at some point in their life cycle. Some of the birds that live here or migrate through include green-tailed towhee (*Pipilo chlorurus*), yellow-eyed junco (*Junco phaeonotus*), white-crowned sparrow (*Zonotrichia leucophrys*), hooded oriole (*Icterus cucullatus*), zone-tailed hawk, common black hawk, golden eagle, Cooper's hawk, Gambel's and Montezuma quail (*Callipepla gambelii* and *Cyrtonyx montezumae*), northern pygmy and great horned owl (*Glaucidium gnoma* and *Tyto alba*), and sharp-shinned hawk (*Accipiter striatus*).

At the Muleshoe Ranch headquarters, previously a nineteenth century resort, is a nature trail, visitor center, hot springs, housekeeping cabins, and a campground. All visitors should register at the visitor center. Reservations for overnight accommodations should be made in advance by calling (520) 586-7072.

From the headquarters, a rough 14-mile, four-wheel-drive track continues north, along the eastern boundary of the Redfield Canyon Wilderness and the southern boundary of the Galiuro Wilderness, to Jackson Cabin, a good jumping off place to explore the area on foot. From here, it's possible to hike up- or downstream in Redfield Canyon.

Directions: The best access to the wilderness areas is by going to Muleshoe Ranch. In Willcox, take Exit 340 off of I-10 and proceed 32 miles northwest to the Muleshoe Ranch. From the ranch, follow the four-wheel-drive Jackson Cabin Road (FR 691) north to the wilderness boundary. At the Muleshoe Ranch, please sign in at The Nature Conservancy registration area before continuing along Jackson Cabin Road.

Activities: Hiking, horseback riding, camping, and nature study.

Facilities: None in wilderness; Muleshoe Ranch has a nature trail, visitor center, cabins, and a campground.

Dates: Open year-round.

Fees: None for wilderness; Muleshoe Ranch asks for a donation and there are fees to use their facilities.

Closest town: Willcox, about 32 miles.

For more information: BLM, Safford Field Office, 711-14th Avenue, Safford, AZ 85546. Phone (520) 348-4400. Web site www.az.blm.gov. USFS, Safford Ranger District, PO Box 709, Safford, AZ 85548. Phone (520) 428-4150. Muleshoe Ranch Headquarters, R.R. 1, Box 1542, Willcox, AZ 85643. Phone (520) 586-7072.

▨ NORTH SANTA TERESA AND SANTA TERESA WILDERNESSES

[Fig. 53(5)] The BLM's 5,800-acre North Santa Teresa Wilderness abuts the Santa Teresa Wilderness in the Coronado National Forest. Golden eagles and peregrine falcons nest here. Arizona sycamores and Arizona black walnuts grow along the larger drainages. Several threatened plant species are known to live here—Leding hedgehog cactus (*Echinocereus ledingii*), echeveria (*Graptopetalum rusbyi*), and plummera (*Plummera ambigens*).

Black Rock, a volcanic rhyolitic plug rising 1,000 feet above the surrounding plain, attracts rock climbers. To this day the rock holds spiritual significance for local Native Americans, as well as mystique for visitors. Jackson Mountain rises to 5,890 feet southeast of the rock and is dissected by several canyons. The majority of this sister to the boulder-strewn Forest Service Santa Teresa Wilderness consists of desert and mountain shrub, grassland and riparian vegetation.

The Forest Service portion of the wilderness varies in elevation from less than 4,000 feet to nearly 7,500 feet at the summit of Cottonwood Peak. This 26,780-acre wilderness is dominated by chaparral vegetation with stands of ponderosa pine and Douglas fir along the north flank and crest of Cottonwood Peak. A wide variety of wildlife is present, including black bear and peregrine falcon.

Holdout and Mud Spring mesas dominate the central part of the wilderness. Holdout Canyon typifies the Santa Teresa Mountains because its extreme ruggedness provides extraordinary solitude. Trails are hard to follow due to their remoteness and lack of maintenance. There are few trail signs. Bring topographic maps and a compass and know how to use them. Water is available seasonally at a few isolated springs.

The San Carlos Apache Reservation runs along the North Santa Teresa Wilderness's north side, and permission must be obtained from the tribe to cross their land. A more practical way is to come through the Santa Teresa Wilderness.

Directions: From Safford, drive northwest 13.5 miles on US 70 to the Klondyke Road. Turn left and go 18 miles to FR 677. Turn right and go 4 miles to the end of the road and the Cottonwood Mountain trailhead.

Activities: Hiking, rock climbing, camping, and nature study.

Facilities: None.

Dates: Open year-round, but summers are hot.

Fees: None.

Closest town: Bylas, about 25 miles north.

For more information: BLM, Safford Field Office, 711-14th Avenue, Safford, AZ 85546. Phone (520) 348-4400. Web site www.az.blm.gov. San Carlos Recreation and Wildlife Department, PO Box 97, San Carlos, AZ 85550. Phone (520) 475-2343 or (888) 275-2653.

🌂 PINALEÑO MOUNTAINS

[Fig. 52] The Pinaleño Mountains, just southwest of Safford, are the third highest range in Arizona and encompass a 300-square-mile area. These Precambrian granite and gneiss mountains also have the greatest vertical relief of any range in the state—more than 7,000 vertical feet. According to the Maricopa Audubon Society, these high peaks harbor the southernmost true subalpine forest of spruce and fir in North America. In 1999, dendrochronologists were surprised to find a dead white pine tree near Solder Creek Trail that lived 1,220 years ago. Previously, the reliable tree-ring record for the region stopped at 1250 (750 years ago).

One resident of the upper coniferous forest is the Mount Graham red squirrel (*Tamiasciurus hudsonicus grahamensis*). This endemic subspecies of squirrel apparently evolved when their ancestors became stranded in these mountains at the end of the last Ice Age, when coniferous forests disappeared from the surrounding plains. Scientists thought the race was extinct, but small numbers of the squirrel were discovered here in the 1970s. The squirrels are 12 to 14 inches in length, with dark gray fur tinged with red and white underparts. A narrow black stripe runs down each side where the gray and white fur meet. Although their population is small, visitors may hear them chattering their warning call from the canopy of the forest.

Atop Emerald Peak is the **Mount Graham International Observatory** (520-428-2739, or for tours, phone 520-428-6260). This facility contains the Vatican Advanced Technology Telescope; the Heinrich Hertz Submillimeter Telescope, the world's most accurate radio telescope; and the Large Binocular Telescope, which, when completed in 2003, will be the world's most powerful telescope. Weekly tours are given mid-May through mid-November, weather permitting.

Initially, biologists worried that construction of the observatory would have a detrimental effect upon the squirrels. So far, the squirrels seem to be doing fine. Still, 1,800 acres atop Mount Graham are closed to all sightseers, hikers, and tourists to protect squirrel habitat.

First Lieutenant George M. Wheeler, of the U.S. Army Corps of Engineers, most likely made the first recorded ascent of 10,713-foot Mount Graham in 1872, the highest summit in the Pinaleño Mountains. It was, no doubt, a long, arduous, trailless journey. Today, visitors can ascend the mountain easily via the Swift Trail Parkway (Forest Highway 366), which starts 7 miles south of Safford, off US 191. In the way the vegetation and animal communities change with elevation, the road trip is like going from Mexican desert to Canadian boreal forest.

This parkway ascends the mountain in 35 spectacular miles; the first 23 miles are paved, the rest graded dirt. A number of campgrounds and trailheads are located long the road. At about mile 29 is the Columbine Visitor Information Station, open on weekends from Memorial Day through Labor Day and occasionally during the week. The road is open April 15 to November 15, snow permitting. A detailed guide including mileage is available from the Safford Ranger District.

The best views along the parkway are from two fire lookouts. Heliograph Peak, 10,028 feet, is reached by either walking a 2.2-mile gated road or 2 miles via the Arcadia and Heliograph trails from the Shannon Campground. The lookout on Webb Peak, at 10,086 feet, can be reached by taking the 1-mile-long Web Peak Trail beginning at the corrals at Columbine.

Near the northeast base of the range, 5 miles south of Pima, is the **Cluff Ranch Wildlife Area**, which is owned and managed by the Arizona Game and Fish Department. The ranch has been a popular hunting and fishing spot for over a century. For more information, contact the Arizona Game and Fish Department, Cluff Ranch Wildlife Area, Pima, AZ 85543. Phone (520) 485-9430.

Also not far from the northeast base of the Pinaleños is the 30-acre cattail-edged **Roper Lake**, which has a swimming beach and attractive stone tubs fed by natural hot springs. Anglers try for trout (in winter), catfish, bass, bluegill, and crappie. This state park is located 5 miles south of Safford along US 191. It is open year-round. There are fees for admission and camping. **For more information:** Roper Lake State Park, Route 2, Box 712, Safford, AZ 85638. Phone (520) 428-6760. Web site www.pr.state.az.us.

Directions: The best access to the Pinaleño Mountains is 7 miles south of Safford on US 191 and then turning right onto the Swift Trail Parkway.

Activities: Scenic drives, hiking, fishing, horseback riding, picnicking, and camping.

Facilities: Visitor center, campgrounds, and scenic drive.

Dates: Open year-round, except higher elevations closed by winter snows.

Fees: There are fees for camping.

Closest town: Safford, 7 miles north.

For more information: Safford Ranger Station, PO Box 709, Safford, AZ 85548-0709. Phone (520) 428-4150.

FISHHOOKS WILDERNESS

[Fig. 53(7)] This 10,500-acre mountainous and canyon-carved wilderness area is tucked between the San Carlos Indian Reservation to the north and west and the Gila River to the south. The Fishhooks offer the explorer austere scenery, solitude, and wildlife. It is a very important corridor for wildlife moving between the Gila Mountains and the lower Sonoran desert in the Gila River Valley. The canyon bottoms are also about the only practical hiking access to this trailless wilderness.

Upper and Lower Fishhook canyons contain what is probably the largest continuous stand of Lowell ash (*Fraxinus lowellii*) in Arizona. This ash, named after astronomer Percival Lowell who discovered them in Oak Creek Canyon, is a central Arizona endemic and is being considered for threatened status under the Endangered Species Act. Other plant communities range from pinyon-juniper woodlands to oak-juniper-mountain mahogany woodlands to Sonoran desert.

The area also has a high concentration of prehistoric cultural sites, including lithic scatters, rock shelters, and rock art. Remember to take only photographs and memories; these archaeological treasures are irreplaceable.

Directions: The edge of the wilderness can be reached by turning off US 70 at Fort Thomas and following the unimproved Diamond Bar Road toward the mountains and the wilderness boundary. Further access information can be obtained from the BLM.

Activities: Hiking, camping, and nature study.

Facilities: None.

Dates: Open year-round.

Fees: None.

Closest town: Safford, about 30 miles southeast.

For more information: BLM, Safford Field Office, 711-14th Avenue, Safford, AZ 85546. Phone (520) 348-4400. Web site www.az.blm.gov.

GILA BOX RIPARIAN NATIONAL CONSERVATION AREA

[Fig. 53(8)] The Gila River originates in the mountains of New Mexico and enters Arizona near Duncan. As the river traverses Arizona, it links with the Salt River southwest of Phoenix then merges with the Colorado River north of Yuma. Of the 400 miles of Gila River in Arizona, only the upper 40 miles remain free flowing and unaffected by dams.

The Gila Box segment is located southwest of Clifton and includes 23 miles of the Gila River, which has been recommended as a National Wild and Scenic River. The Gila Box Riparian National Conservation Area was designated by Congress to include this section of the Gila and 15 miles of the tributary Bonita Creek. Both streams are lined with large Fremont cottonwoods, Arizona sycamores, willows, and mesquite. Cliff dwellings, historic homesteads, bighorn sheep, and more than 200 species of birds attract hikers and campers. Look for black-bellied whistling ducks (*Dendrocygna autumnalis*), osprey (*Pandion haliaetus*), and black-crowned night-heron (*Nycticorax nycticorax*).

Kayak, canoe, and rafting enthusiasts take advantage of the variable water flows through a 500-foot deep canyon carved through basalt and andesite and enjoy an easy to moderate floating, fishing, and camping adventure on the Gila River. The main river running season is March through April, and occasionally into May. The BLM can supply information regarding flow levels and recommended watercraft.

Furthermore, a 10-mile section of the Gila River upstream of Winkelman is also floated. There are only gentle rapids and canoes, kayaks, and small rafts run this river section in two or three hours. The flow is controlled by releases from San Carlos Reservoir and the boating season usually lasts from March to August. Contact the BLM for more information. For a commercial river trip, contact either Desert Voyagers (602) 998-RAFT or (800) 222-RAFT or Chandelle River Tours (520) 577-1824.

Directions: To reach the east end of the Gila Box Riparian National Conservation Area, drive 4 miles south from Clifton on US 191 and take the Black Hills Back Country Byway 4 miles to the Gila River and the Old Safford Bridge. For river runners, the best river put in is on the south side of the bridge. To reach the west end of the Gila Box Riparian National Conservation Area from Safford, go 5 miles east on US 70 to Solomon and turn left onto Sanchez Road. Go north about 5 miles and cross Gila River bridge. Drive 7 more miles until reaching the Bonita Creek BLM sign and then turn left onto the dirt road. Drive 2.5 miles to the West Entry sign. For boaters, the river take out is 0.5 mile beyond the sign. Park at the Dry Canyon parking area. Additional primitive roads provide access to other points within the national conservation area.

Activities: River floating, fishing, hiking, camping, picnicking, hunting, and nature study.

Facilities: Picnic areas and two campgrounds.

Dates: Open year-round.

Fees: There is a campground fee.

Closest town: Safford, about 17 miles; Clifton, about 8 miles.

For more information: BLM, Safford Field Office, 711-14th Avenue, Safford, AZ 85546. Phone (520) 348-4400. Web site www.az.blm.gov.

🌊 BLACK HILLS BACK COUNTRY BYWAY

[Fig. 53(9)] The BLM maintains the old route between Clifton and Safford. The Black Hills Back Country Byway offers sweeping vistas of the Black Hills, Mount

OSPREY
(Pandion haliaetus)

Graham, Gila Box, and the Phelps Dodge Morenci copper mine. Along the 21-mile improved dirt road, travelers may view wildlife and historic sites, or they can venture off onto one of the many primitive side roads, many of which are perfect for mountain biking adventures. The Byway also provides access to the eastern portion of the Gila Box National Conservation Area.

Directions: Begins 18 miles northeast of Safford, near milepost 139 on US 191. Joins US 191 again 4 miles south of Clifton.

Activities: Scenic driving.

Facilities: Interpretive kiosks and two BLM campgrounds.

Dates: Open year-round.

Fees: There is a fee for campground use.

Closest town: Clifton, 4 miles.

For more information: BLM, Safford Field Office, 711-14th Avenue, Safford, AZ 85546. Phone (520) 348-4400. Web site www.az.blm.gov.

BLACK HILLS ROCKHOUND AREA

[Fig. 53(10)] The Black Hills Rockhound Area is a good place to collect fire agate, a form of silica formed by volcanic activity. The multitude of shapes and colors is caused by mineral impurities in the silica. Fire agate is considered a gemstone because of the play of colors beneath its surface. Other minerals found near here include turquoise, Apache tears, chryscola, and peridot. There are no established trails, but several poor dirt roads cross the area.

Directions: To reach the Black Hills, drive 18 miles east of Safford on US 70. Then turn left on the signed Black Hills Road. About 2 miles in along this rough road is the collecting area.

Activities: Mineral collecting, hiking, and nature study.

Facilities: None.

Dates: Open year-round.

Fees: None.

Closest town: Safford, about 18 miles west.

For more information: BLM, Safford Field Office, 711-14th Avenue, Safford, AZ 85546. Phone (520) 348-4400. Web site www.az.blm.gov.

HOT WELL DUNES RECREATION AREA

[Fig. 53(11)] When 1928 oil drillers broke into a pocket of hot water at a depth of 1,920 feet, Hot Well sprang into existence. The artesian well produces more than 250 gallons of 106-degree-Fahrenheit water per minute. The hot water is piped into a couple of whirlpool-style basins separated by a shallow wading area for children. The remains of the early drilling equipment lay 100 yards west of the well.

The 2,000 acres of sand dunes around the well are popular with the off-road vehicle crowd, so don't expect much peace and quiet, especially on holiday weekends. However, the dunes are a wonderful place for a stroll and to look for animal tracks, everything from the tractorlike tread of a beetle to coyote paw prints.

Directions: From Bowie, go north 2 miles on Central Avenue. Then turn right onto Fan Road and continue 8 miles. Turn left onto Haekel Road and proceed 9 miles to the area.

Activities: Soaking in the hot tubs and driving over the dunes.

Facilities: Tubs, picnic tables, restrooms, and campground.

Dates: Open year-round.

Fees: There is an entrance fee.

Closest town: Bowie, about 19 miles south.

For more information: BLM, Safford Field Office, 711-14th Avenue, Safford, AZ 85546. Phone (520) 348-4400. Web site www.az.blm.gov.

PELONCILLO MOUNTAINS WILDERNESS

[Fig. 50(15)] The corrugated Peloncillo Mountains stretch from New Mexico to the Gila River. A particularly rough 19,440-acre section northeast of San Simon has been designated wilderness. Vegetation ranges from desert shrub grasslands in the surrounding flatlands to oak juniper woodlands on the higher slopes. Desert bighorn sheep have been recently reintroduced to the region and share their new home with peregrine falcons and other sensitive animal species. In the spring of 1996, a jaguar was photographed in the mountains. This former resident of Arizona's desert grass-lands and lower mountains had not been definitely seen in the state since the early 1900s. Some biologists think that the cat is expanding its range from Mexico back into its historic home.

This remote and primitive area shows little signs of human activity. There are no established trails; therefore, the wilderness area offers outstanding opportunities for primitive recreation, including hiking, backpacking, rock scrambling, hunting, and sight-seeing. A section of the historic Butterfield Overland Stageline Route forms the southern boundary of the wilderness (*see* page 308).

Directions: Access to the southern portion of the wilderness area can be gained by traveling about 12 miles northeast of San Simon on either the West Doubtful Road or the road leading to McKenzie Peak. High-clearance or four-wheel-drive vehicles are recommended for access to the wilderness boundary. Some lands adjacent to the wilderness are not federally administered. They are fenced off. Please respect the property rights of the owners and do not cross or use these lands without permission.

Activities: Hiking, camping, hunting, and nature study.

Facilities: None.

Dates: Open year-round, but spring and fall are the best times to visit.

Fees: None.

Closest town: San Simon, 12 miles southwest.

For more information: BLM, Safford Field Office, 711-14th Avenue, Safford, AZ 85546. Phone (520) 348-4400. Web site www.az.blm.gov.

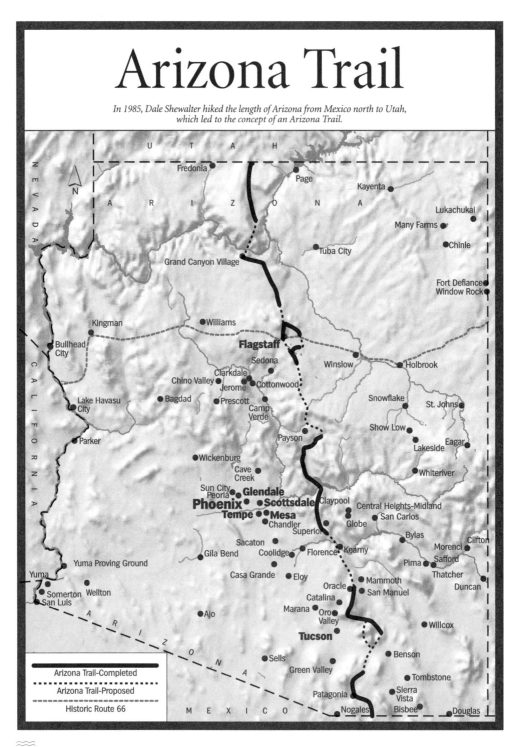

Arizona Trail

In 1985, Dale Shewalter hiked the length of Arizona from Mexico north to Utah,
which led to the concept of an Arizona Trail.

U T A H

NEVADA

A R I Z O N A

Fredonia

Page

Kayenta

Lukachukai

Many Farms

Chinle

Tuba City

Grand Canyon Village

Fort Defiance
Window Rock

NEVADA

Kingman

Williams

Flagstaff

Bullhead
City

CALIFORNIA

Sedona

Winslow

Holbrook

Clarkdale

Chino Valley

Jerome

Cottonwood

Snowflake

St. Johns

Lake Havasu
City

Bagdad

Prescott

Camp
Verde

Show Low

Parker

Payson

Lakeside

Eagar

Wickenburg

Whiteriver

Cave
Creek

Sun City

Peoria

Glendale

Claypool

Central Heights-Midland

Phoenix

Scottsdale

San Carlos

Tempe

Mesa

Chandler

Globe

Bylas

Clifton

Superior

Morenci

Sacaton

Florence

Kearny

Safford

Gila Bend

Coolidge

Pima

Yuma Proving Ground

Casa Grande

Eloy

Mammoth

Thatcher

Duncan

Oracle

San Manuel

Yuma

Catalina

Somerton

Wellton

Marana

Oro
Valley

San Luis

Ajo

Willcox

A R I Z O N A

Tucson

Benson

Sells

Green Valley

Tombstone

Patagonia

Sierra
Vista

M E X I C O

Nogales

Bisbee

Douglas

| Arizona Trail-Completed |
| Arizona Trail-Proposed |
| Historic Route 66 |

The Arizona Trail, Route 66, And Other Historic Trails

A trail traversing Arizona from Mexico north to Utah has been the dream of many trail users through the years. However, one individual did more than dream. In 1985, Dale Shewalter, a Flagstaff schoolteacher, spent his summer vacation hiking from Nogales to Utah. He mapped out a route through some of Arizona's finest natural landscapes and developed the concept of the Arizona Trail, offering opportunities for hikers, equestrians, mountain bikers (where allowed), and cross-country skiers to experience the state's wild places.

Over the next few years, Shewalter promoted his vision to state and federal agencies, service groups, corporations, and individuals. The Arizona State Parks Board took notice, as well as their Arizona Hiking and Equestrian Trails Committee. They have been helping to coordinate the project ever since.

In 1988, Shewalter became the first Arizona Trail Steward Coordinator under the

[*Above:* Hikers enjoy traversing the Arizona Trail from Utah to Mexico]

sponsorship of the Kaibab National Forest, and 7 miles of the proposed Kaibab Plateau portion of the trail were dedicated and opened to the public. Thus began a cooperative effort between many governmental agencies and individuals to identify existing trails and the need for new trail construction to complete a border-to-border trail. Alternate routes are planned to allow mountain bikers to pass around designated wilderness areas. By the end of 1999, about 575 miles of the 790-mile long Arizona Trail were completed and signed.

The southern terminus for the Arizona Trail is in the Coronado National Memorial. From there, the Arizona Trail travels north through the Miller Peak Wilderness of the Huachuca Mountains before descending the ponderosa- and sycamore-lined Sunnyside Canyon and heading toward Parker Canyon Lake.

After leaving the Huachuca Mountains, the trail crosses the lush rolling grass and woodlands of the Canelo Hills, which is where the musical *Oklahoma!* was filmed. Near the town of Patagonia, the trail briefly leaves national forest land to follow public roads before entering the foothills of the Santa Rita Mountains. Here the trail ascends into ponderosa pine and Douglas fir forest within the Mount Wrightson Wilderness. After passing around Mount Wrightson, the trail reaches an old mining area called Kentucky Camp.

The trail leaves the Santa Ritas and crosses the BLM's Empire-Cienega Resource Conservation Area. The trail goes under I-10 and then divides and offers hikers two possibilities. One route goes to Saguaro National Park, offering an "urban" trail experience. The second choice traverses the southeastern slopes of the Rincons for a more wilderness-type adventure.

North of Saguaro National Park, the two trails merge and the Arizona Trail enters the Santa Catalina Mountains following forest and public roads and then trails. The Arizona Trail climbs into the Pusch Ridge Wilderness and ascends Mount Lemmon. From here, the trail drops toward Oracle and exits the Coronado National Forest.

The trail continues northward through the Black Hills and Tortilla Mountains on its way to the Tonto National Forest and the cactus-studded Superstition Wilderness. Eventually, the trail passes near the Salado Indian ruins in Tonto National Monument before crossing the Salt River at Roosevelt Dam and then heading west into the rugged Mazatzal Wilderness.

At the north end of the Mazatzal Mountains, the Arizona Trail follows the Highline Trail along the base of the Mogollon Rim for almost 20 miles before climbing to the top of the Mogollon Plateau. Now in the Coconino National Forest, the trail continues through forest and canyons, and across meadows to Anderson Mesa, a broad, grassy upland. As the trail nears Flagstaff, there are great views of the San Francisco Peaks. The trail crosses Walnut Canyon and then offers hikers two options: (1), to hook into Flagstaff's Urban Trails System, or (2), to bypass the city on an eastern route. The trails reconnect near Schultz Pass before traversing the San Francisco Peaks.

From the Peaks, the trail heads to the Grand Canyon, where it overlaps the Bright Angel and North Kaibab trails to cross the great gorge. Once on the Kaibab Plateau, the Arizona Trail winds through spruce, fir, pine, and aspen forest interspersed with meadows. Several viewpoints afford spectacular views across House Rock Valley to the Vermillion Cliffs and Marble Canyon. The trail descends off the north end of the Kaibab and finishes at the Utah border.

For more information: Arizona Trail Association, PO Box 36736, Phoenix, AZ 85067-6736. Phone (602) 252-4794. Web site www.aztrail.org.

Historic Route 66

The famous Route 66, America's Main Street, roughly followed the old Beale Wagon Road across northern Arizona. In the fall of 1857, during the first great westward migration, Lieutenant Edward Fitzgerald Beale was ordered to lay out a wagon road from Fort Defiance to the eastern frontier of California. As a grand experiment, Beale used 22 camels during his explorations, but most of the soldiers considered the beasts foul smelling, evil tempered, and ugly. Beale's Wagon Road was later followed by the railroad. In the early 1920s, the Old Trails Highway was built along the tracks. This unpaved road, designated Route 66 in 1926, was rough, narrow, twisting, and steep, but it opened the door to the American Southwest. In 1938, Route 66 became the first completely paved cross-country highway in the United States, connecting Chicago with Los Angeles. In his 1939 novel *The Grapes of Wrath*, John Steinbeck christened the route the "Mother Road," and described the migration of thousands of people to California to escape the Dust Bowl of Oklahoma. Route 66 has been immortalized in songs, movies, and a long-running television show. Then during the 1960s, I-40 began to replace the old highway. Route 66 was decommissioned and abandoned by the federal highway department in 1985. However, there has been renewed interest in preserving the remaining parts of Route 66 and documenting its colorful history. State and city governments, along with the forest service, continue to maintain certain sections of the route.

From east to west, Arizona drivers can follow parts of the original highway or take I-40. Along the way, there are a number of historic towns and fascinating natural features. Here is a list of some of them:

From the New Mexico/Arizona state line to Sanders, the route crosses the southern edge of the **Navajo Reservation** (*see* page 97). West of Chambers, drivers enter the **Painted Desert**, a land of barren clay hills colored in a palette of muted pastels.

Preserving part of the vast Painted Desert and straddling the old route is the **Petrified Forest National Park** (*see* page 123).

About 26 miles farther west is **Holbrook**, where there is a visitor center housed in the handsome 1898 courthouse. The center displays on local history and geology, including examples of petrified wood and dinosaur remains.

In the 1970s, Jackson Browne's lyric "...I'm a-standin' on the corner in Winslow, Arizona..." helped make this town famous, but its notoriety goes back much farther. Celebrated Grand Canyon architect and designer Mary Colter built the **La Posada Hotel** and train depot in Winslow in 1930 to be the jumping off point for tours into the Indian country, Painted Desert, Petrified Forest, and Grand Canyon. La Posada was the last great resort hotel built and managed by Fred Harvey and the Santa Fe Railway. The hotel was done in the grand hacienda style. Unable to find appropriate furniture, Colter had it made onsite by carpenter E.V. Birt and his Mexican and Indian crew. The hotel grounds had an orchard and beautiful gardens. Regrettably, the Great Depression, which had begun the year before, made the venture unprofitable. The Santa Fe Railroad turned the hotel into its division headquarters and auctioned off all the handmade furniture and fixtures. Neglected for decades, this National Historic Landmark hotel has now been refurbished and is open for guests. Phone (520) 289-4366. Web site www.laposada.org.

John Lorenzo Hubbell, the trader of Ganado fame (*see* page 117), also owned a large wholesale trading post and warehouse in Winslow on Hicks and First streets. This location provided access to the railroad. The building is now owned by the Arizona Historical Society and the Affiliation of Native American Groups, and has been renovated into an office building.

Homolovi Ruins State Park is a few minutes north of Winslow (*see* page 129).

Just a few miles west of **Meteor Crater** (*see* page 131), the highway bridges **Canyon Diablo**. Speeding along the interstate, it is easy to miss this canyon that is only a few hundred feet deep. But so precipitous is this small gorge that in 1857, Beale and his expedition had to make a 40-mile detour to get around it.

This lyric, "...and don't forget **Winona**," from the tune *Get Your Kicks on Route 66* is referring to a place east of Flagstaff that was one of the first tourist camps built in the 1920s along the highway. The largest city along old Route 66 is **Flagstaff** (*see* page 155).

Between Flagstaff and Williams, **Kaibab National Forest** has listed 22 miles of Route 66 on the National Register of Historic Places. Heading west from Flagstaff, exit I-40 at the Bellemont Exit 185. Go west along the frontage road, which becomes Forest Road 146. This road follows various alignments of the historic highway. The road passes through **Brannigan Park** where you will see historic residences. The road leaves the residential area and ascends to 7,300 feet, the highest point on Route 66. Continue west on the gravel road, which was paved from 1931 until it was bypassed in 1941. Soon you arrive at the **Parks Country Store**, which has been in operation since 1910. A couple of miles beyond the store is the **Garland Prairie Vista**, which affords spectacular views of the San Francisco Peaks and surrounding countryside. Another couple of miles west, you come to the **Oak Hill Snowplay Area** (Williams's original 1940s ski area) and the trail to **Keyhole Sink**, a short trail to a petroglyph site. From here to the Pittman Valley Exit 171 on I-40, the concrete pavement dates to 1939. The interstate replaced this section in 1964.

Williams is the location of the railway to the South Rim of the Grand Canyon. In 1995, a replica of the **Fray Marcos Hotel**, an elegant structure that once graced the Williams's train station, was constructed. To obtain tickets for the train or hotel room reservations, phone (520) 635-4010 or (800) THE TRAIN. Web site www.thetrain.com.

Between Williams and Ashfork, there are two stretches of Route 66 that are popular with mountain bikers. The **Devil Dog Bike Tour** is about a 5-mile loop covering part of the 1922 roadway and a section of 1932 roadway. It begins at the I-40 Exit 157. The **Ash Fork Hill Bike Tour** begins at I-40 Exit 151 and loops about 6 miles also following pieces of the 1922 and 1932 roadways. A free map is available from the Williams Ranger District, phone (520) 635-2633.

Near **Ashfork**, the lovely cross-bedded Permian Coconino Sandstone is mined for use as flagstone.

A trip across Arizona on Route 66 would not be complete without a stop in Seligman at the world famous **Delgadillo's Snow Cap** for a malt or burger and fries. Not far from Seligman is the **Aubrey Valley Black-footed Ferret Reintroduction Area**. The reintroduction program started in 1996 after a 65-year absence of black-footed ferrets in Arizona. The ferrets were released in a large Gunnison's prairie dog town, the vernacular for one of their colonies. Prairie dogs are one of the ferrets' favorite food items. For more information about the endangered ferrets, contact the Arizona Game and Fish Department, Nongame Branch, 2221 West Greenway Road, Phoenix, AZ 85023-4399. Phone (602) 789-3290.

Between Seligman and Kingman, one of the longest sections of Route 66 still in use, passes by **Grand Canyon Caverns**, through the **Hualapai Reservation** (*see* page 91), and by the tiny settlements of **Truxton**, **Valentine**, and **Hackberry**.

At Grand Canyon Caverns, an elevator descends 210 feet to well-lit, paved paths and a 45-minute guided tour of the caverns. You will see a replica of a giant ground sloth, an animal that roamed the Grand Canyon region during the last Ice Age. For more information, contact Grand Canyon Caverns, PO Box 180, Historic Route 66, Peach Springs, AZ 86434. Phone (520) 422-3223.

Kingman is where actor Andy Devine grew up. The **Mohave Museum of History and Arts** preserves the heritage of northwestern Arizona and presents that history through dioramas, murals, displays, and exhibits. The **Bonelli House** was built in 1915 and gives visitors a taste of what life was like for an early prominent family (430 East Spring Street, phone 520-753-1413).

The 42 miles of historic Route 66 from Kingman to Topock has been designated a National Back Country Byway by the Bureau of Land Management. A descriptive brochure is available from the BLM Kingman Field Office, phone (520) 757-3161. Along the way is **Oatman**, which began shortly after 1900 when gold was discovered lying free upon the ground. By the early 1900s more than 8,000 people had flocked to

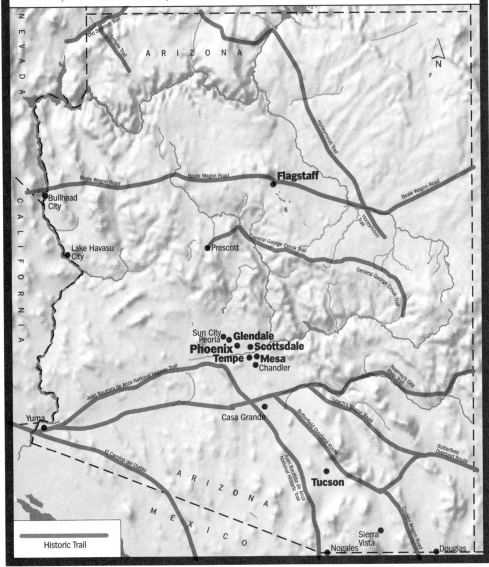

Historic Trails in Arizona

The Butterfield Overland Route was the first reliable transcontinental trail developed for mail, freight, and passenger service.

Historic Trail

the town, but in 1942, Congress declared that gold mining was no longer essential to the war effort and Oatman almost became a ghost town. The town was the last stop before Route 66 entered the dreaded Mohave Desert in California.

Today, tourists come to Oatman to see the old buildings including the hotel where movie stars Clark Gable and Carol Lombard spent their wedding night, marvel at the towering mountains, photograph the wild burros that wander in the streets, participate in the annual International Burro Biscuit Toss, and browse the unique shops.

For more information: Historic Route 66 Association of Arizona, PO Box 66, Kingman, AZ 86402. Diehard Route 66 fans, shouldn't miss the new Route 66 National Museum in Elk City, Oklahoma, phone (580) 225-2207.

Other Historic Trails in Arizona

[Fig. 54] Arizona has many other historic trails. Some followed prehistoric routes, while others were blazed through virgin territory. Following and learning about these old trails can help bring Arizona's colorful history alive.

For more information: Arizona State Parks, 1300 West Washington, Phoenix, AZ 85007. Phone (602) 542-4174. Web site www.pr.state.az.us.

OLD SPANISH TRAIL

This trail was first mentioned in 1833 and connected settlements in northern New Mexico with southern California. The name is a misnomer since Mexicans and later Americans used it, not the Spanish. In Arizona, I-15 follows some of the old route.

HONEYMOON TRAIL

This wagon road led from Mormon settlements in northern Arizona to St. George, Utah. It was completed in the 1870s and used extensively by newly married couples journeying to Utah to have their marriages consecrated in the Mormon Temple in St. George. Parts of US 89 and US 89A follow this old trail.

TEMPLE TRAIL

The Temple Trail (*see* page 25) was built to allow wagons to carry timber from the forests around Mount Trumbull on the Arizona Strip to the St. George, Utah area. Parts of the original trail have been marked by the BLM and can be followed by foot or four-wheel-drive vehicle.

GENERAL GEORGE CROOK TRAIL

In August 1871, General George Crook and a small group of soldiers left Fort Apache seeking the best route for supply wagons and patrol soldiers to Fort Verde (now Camp Verde) and Fort Whipple (present-day Prescott). The trail was used for

22 years by the army and then another 24 years by the public until completion of highways between those towns. Many miles of the original trail have been marked with rock cairns and white and yellow V-shaped chevrons placed on trees and can be followed by foot, horseback, or vehicle (*see* page 171).

▓ CORONADO TRAIL

The first definite invasion of Arizona by Europeans was the Coronado Expedition in 1540 (*see* page 180). Various roads and hiking trails trace parts of his route.

▓ JUAN BAUTISTA DE ANZA NATIONAL HISTORIC TRAIL

During 1775-1776, Lieutenant Colonel Juan Bautista de Anza led about 240 people, including a Catholic priest, 30 families, and a dozen soldiers, and more than 1,000 head of cattle, sheep, horses, and mules from Mexico to San Francisco Bay, California (*see* page 272). The expedition took three months to reach the Pacific coast and then another three months to work their way north to the bay. Part of their route parallels I-8 between Gila Bend and Yuma.

▓ SOUTHERN TRAILS TO CALIFORNIA

Between 1846 and 1856, more than 2,000 hopeful "forty-niners" trod across southern Arizona to reach California. Some followed the Gila River Trail surveyed by General Stephan Watts Kearney and his Army of the West in 1846. Other variations included Leach's Wagon Road and Cooke's Wagon Road (a.k.a. The Mormon Battalion Trail).

The Butterfield Overland Stageline Route (*see* page 308), constructed in 1858, was the first reliable transcontinental trail developed for mail, freight, and passenger service. The stage traveled the 2,700 miles in less than 25 days. John Butterfield's famous instructions to his drivers were: "Remember boys, nothing must stop the Overland mail!" In its three-year history, the stage was late only three times. I-10 and I-8 follow segments of the southern trails today.

▓ EL CAMINO DEL DIABLO

The Devil's Highway (El Camino Del Diablo [*see* page 272]) across the Sonoran desert in southwestern Arizona was an alternate route for pioneers and prospectors who hoped to avoid the Indians who lived along the Gila River (*see* page 326). Unfortunately, the hostile desert environment possibly took more lives than any confrontations with Indians would have.

Appendices

A. Books and References

A Field Guide to Western Reptiles and Amphibians by Robert Stebbins. Houghton Mifflin Company, Boston, MA 1985.

A Floater's Guide to the Verde River by Bob Williams. Graphic Center, Prescott, AZ 1996.

A Guide to Contemporary Southwest Indians by Bernard L. Fontana. Southwest Parks and Monuments Association, Tucson, AZ 1999.

A Guide to Exploring Oak Creek and the Sedona Area by Stewart Aitchison. RNM Press, SaltLake City, UT 1989.

A Guide to Salt River Canyon Natural History and River Running by Glenn Rink. Worldwide Exploration, Flagstaff, AZ 1990.

A Guide to the Beale Wagon Road by Jack Beale Smith. Tales of the Beale Road Publishing, Flagstaff, AZ 1991.

A Guide to the General Crook Trail by Eldon Bowman. Museum of Northern Arizona Press, Flagstaff, AZ 1978.

A Little War of Our Own: The Pleasant Valley Feud Revisited by Don Dedera. Northland Press, Flagstaff, AZ 1988.

A Natural History of the Sonoran Desert edited by Steven Phillips and Patricia Comus. Arizona-Sonora Desert Museum Press and University of California Press, Tucson, AZ 2000.

A Naturalist's Guide to Hiking the Grand Canyon by Stewart Aitchison. Prentice-Hall, Inc., Englewood Cliffs, NJ 1985.

An Introduction to Grand Canyon Ecology by Rose Houk. Grand Canyon Association, Grand Canyon, AZ 1996.

An Introduction to Grand Canyon Geology by L. Greer Price. Grand Canyon Association, Grand Canyon, AZ 1999.

An Introduction to Grand Canyon Prehistory by Christopher Coder. Grand Canyon Association, Grand Canyon, AZ 2000.

Arizona: A History by Thomas Sheridan. University of Arizona Press, Tucson, AZ 1995.

Arizona Ghost Towns and Mining Camps by Philip Varney. Arizona Highways, Phoenix, AZ 1995.

Arizona's 144 Best Campgrounds by James Tallon. Arizona Highways, Phoenix, AZ 1996.

Arizona Trout Streams and Their Hatches by Charles Mech and John Rohmer. Backcountry Publications, Woodstock, VT 1998.

A Sand County Almanac by Aldo Leopold. Ballantine Books, New York, NY 1966.

A Traveler's Guide to Monument Valley by Stewart Aitchison. Voyageur Press, Stillwater, MN 1993.

A View of Saguaro National Monument and the Tucson Basin by Gary Paul Nabhan. Southwest Parks and Monuments Association, Tucson, AZ 1986.

A Wilderness Called Grand Canyon by Stewart Aitchison. Voyageur Press, Stillwater, MN 1991.

Bibliography of the Grand Canyon and Lower Colorado River compiled by Earle Spamer. Grand Canyon Association, Grand Canyon, AZ 2000. Online version www.grandcanyonbiblio.org.

Bike Tours in Southern Arizona by Mort Solot and Philip Varney. Breakaway Press, Tucson, AZ 1991.

Birding Sedona and the Verde Valley by Virginia Gilmore. Northern Arizona Audubon Society, Sedona, AZ 1999.

Birds of Phoenix and Maricopa County, Arizona by Janet Witzeman, Salome Demaree, and Eleanor Radhe. Maricopa Audubon Society, Phoenix, AZ 2000.

Call of the Canyon by Zane Grey. Harper and Brothers, New York, NY 1924.

Canyoneering by John Annerino. Stackpole Books, Mechanicsburg, PA 1999.

Davis and Russell's Finding Birds in Southeast Arizona by Tucson Audubon Society. Tucson Audubon Society, Tucson, AZ 1999.

Desert Heart by William Hartmann. Fisher Books, Tucson, AZ 1989.

Down the Blue edited by the Blue River Cowbelles. Cartman's Valley West, Goodyear, AZ 1987.

Exploring Arizona's Wild Areas: A Guide for Hikers, Backpackers, Climbers, X-C Skiers, and Paddlers by Scott Warren. The Mountaineers, Seattle, WA 1996.

Fat Tire Tales and Trails by Cosmic Ray. Privately published, Flagstaff, AZ 1998.

Fieldguide to the Geology of Chiricahua National Monument by John Bezy. Arizona Geological Survey, Tucson, AZ 1998.

Fishes of Arizona by W.L. Minckley. Arizona Game and Fish Department, Phoenix, AZ 1973.

Flagstaff Hikes by Richard and Sherry Mangum. Hexagon Press, Flagstaff, AZ 1998.

Flagstaff Historic Walk: A Stroll Through Old Downtown by Richard and Sherry Mangum. Hexagon Press, Flagstaff, AZ 1993.

Geologic Landscapes of the Southwest by Stephen Reynolds. Grand Canyon Association, Grand Canyon, AZ 2000.

Geology of Arizona by Dale Nations and Edward Stump. Kendall/Hunt Publishing Company, Dubuque, IA 1997.

Grand Canyon Birds by Bryan Brown, Steven Carothers, and Roy Johnson. University of Arizona Press, Tucson, AZ 1987.

Grand Canyon-Flagstaff Stagecoach Line: A History and Exploration Guide by Richard and Sherry Mangum. Hexagon Press, Inc., Flagstaff, AZ 1999.

Grand Canyon Treks: 12,000 Miles Through the Grand Canyon by Harvey Butchart. Spotted Dog Press, Bishop, CA 1998.

Grand Canyon: Window of Time by Stewart Aitchison. Sierra Press, Mariposa, CA 1999.

Guide to Arizona's Wilderness Areas by Tom Dollar. Westcliffe Publishers, Inc., Englewood, CO 1998.

Hiker's Guide to the Huachuca Mountains by Leonard Taylor. Thunder Peak Productions, Sierra Vista, AZ 1991.

Hiker's Guide to the Santa Rita Mountains by Betty Levengood and Mike Liebert. Pruett Publishing, Boulder, CO 1994.

Hiker's Guide to the Superstitions by Jack Carlson and Elizabeth Stewart. Clear Creek Publishing, Tempe, AZ 1995.

Hiking and Exploring the Paria River by Michael Kelsey. Kelsey Publishing, Provo, UT 1987.

Hiking Arizona by Stewart Aitchison and Bruce Grubbs. Falcon Press, Helena, MT 1992.

Historic Atlas of Arizona by Henry P. Walker and Don Bufkin. University of Oklahoma Press, Norman, OK 1986.

Horse Trails in Arizona by Jan Hancock. Golden West Publishers, Inc., Phoenix, AZ 1994.

Lake Mead National Recreation Area Guide to Boating: Places to Go and Things to See by Geoffery Schneider and Rose Houk. Southwest Parks and Monuments Association, Tucson, AZ 1997.

Lee's Ferry: From Mormon Crossing to National Park by P.T. Reilly. Utah State University Press, Logan, UT 1999.

Life in a Narrow Place by Stephen Hirst. D. McKay Co., New York, NY 1976.

Mammals of Arizona by Donald F. Hoffmeister. University of Arizona Press and Arizona Game and Fish Department, Tucson, AZ 1986.

Mountain Biking Arizona by Sarah Bennett. Falcon Press, Helena, MT 1996.

Native Roads: The Complete Motoring Guide to the Navajo and Hopi Nations by Fran Kosik. Creative Solutions Publishing, Flagstaff, AZ 1996.

Natural History of the Colorado Plateau and Great Basin edited by Kimball Harper, Larry St. Clair, Kaye Thorne, and Wilford Hess. University Press of Colorado, Niwot, CO 1994.

Official Guide to Hiking the Grand Canyon by Scott Thybony. Grand Canyon Association, Grand Canyon, AZ 1996.

On the Arizona Trail: A Guide for Hikers, Cyclists, and Equestrians by Kelly Tighe and Susan Moran. Pruett Publishing, Boulder, CO 1998.

Organ Pipe Cactus National Monument: Where the Edges Meet by Bill Broyles. Southwest Parks and Monuments Association, Tucson, AZ 1996.

Plants of Arizona by Anne Orth Epple. LewAnn Publishing Company, Mesa, AZ 1995.

Poisonous Dwellers of the Desert by Trevor Hare. Southwest Parks and Monuments Association, Tucson, AZ 1995.

Quest for the Dutchman's Gold by Robert Sikorsky. Golden West, San Marino, CA 1991.

Recollections of Phantom Ranch by Elizabeth Simpson. Grand Canyon Association, Grand Canyon, AZ.

Recreational Opportunity Guide: North Kaibab Ranger District by Kaibab National Forest. Southwest Natural and Cultural Heritage Association, Albuquerque, NM.

Recreation Guide to Barrier-Free Facilities, Southwest National Forests by U.S. Forest Service. U.S. Department of Agriculture, Washington, DC 1993.

Recreation Sites in Southwestern National Forests and Grasslands by U.S. Forest Service. U.S. Department of Agriculture, Washington, DC 1998.

Red Rock-Sacred Mountain: The Canyon and Peaks from Sedona to Flagstaff by Stewart Aitchison. Voyageur Press, Stillwater, MN 1992.

Roadside Geology of Arizona by Halka Chronic. Mountain Press Publishing Company, Missoula, MT 1983.

Roadside History of Arizona by Marshall Trimble. Mountain Press Publishing Company, Missoula, MT 1986.

Rock Climbing Arizona by Stewart Green. Falcon Press, Helena, MT 1999.

Rockhounding Arizona by Gerry Blair. Falcon Press, Helena, MT 1998.

Route 66: The Mother Road by Michael Wallis. St. Martins Press, Inc., New York, NY 1990.

Scenic Driving Arizona by Stewart Green. Falcon Press, Helena, MT 1997.

Sedona Hikes by Richard and Sherry Mangum. Hexagon Press, Flagstaff, AZ 1998.

Ski Touring Arizona by Dugald Bremner. Northland Press, Flagstaff, AZ 1987.

Southern Apache County Nature Areas by R.P. Robertsen. Red GK, St. Johns, AZ 1999.

Squeezing the Lemmon: A Rock Climber's Guide to the Mount Lemmon Highway by Eric Fazio-Rhicard. Privately published, Tucson, AZ 1991.

Stone Landmarks: Flagstaff's Geology and Historic Building Stones by Marie Jackson. Piedra Azul Press, Flagstaff, AZ 1999.

Tales of Lonely Trails by Zane Grey. Harper and Brothers, New York, NY 1922.

Tertiary History of the Grand Cañon District by Clarence E. Dutton. Peregrine Smith, Santa Barbara, CA 1977.

The Colorado in Grand Canyon: A Comprehensive Guide to its Natural and Human History by Larry Stevens. Red Lake Books, Flagstaff, AZ 1998.

The Domínguez-Escalante Journal: Their Expedition through Colorado, Utah, Arizona, and New Mexico in 1776 edited by Ted Warner. University of Utah Press, Salt Lake City, UT 1995.

The Man Who Walked Through Time by Colin Fletcher. Alfred A. Knopf, New York, NY 1967.

Those Who Came Before: Southwestern Archaeology in the National Park System by Robert and Florence Lister. University of New Mexico Press, Albuquerque, NM 1994.

Trading Post Guidebook by Patrick Eddington and Susan Makov. Northland Publishing, Flagstaff, AZ 1995.

Trail Guide to the Santa Catalina Mountains by Pete Cowgill and Eber Glendening. Rainbow Expeditions, Tucson, AZ 1997.

Travel Arizona II by Leo Banks, Tom Dollar, Rose Houk, Sam Negri, and Joe Stocker. Arizona Highways, Phoenix, AZ 1998.

Travel Arizona: The Back Roads by James Cook. Arizona Highways, Phoenix, AZ 1989.

Travel Arizona: The Scenic Byways by Paula Searcy. Arizona Highways, Phoenix, AZ 1997

Tucson Hiking Guide by Betty Levengood. Pruett Publishing, Boulder, CO 1997.

Verde River Recreation Guide by Jim Slingluff. Golden West Publishing, San Marino, CA 1990.

Volcanoes of Northern Arizona: Sleeping Giants of the Grand Canyon Region by Wendell Duffield. Grand Canyon Association, Grand Canyon, AZ 1997.

Wilderness and Primitive Areas in Southwestern National Forests by U.S. Forest Service. U.S. Department of Agriculture, Washington, DC 1997.

Williams Guidebook by Richard and Sherry Mangum. Hexagon Press, Flagstaff, AZ 1998.

B. Conservation Organizations

Arizona Archaeological and Historical Society, Arizona State Museum, University of Arizona, Tucson, AZ 85721-0026. Phone (520) 621-6302. Promotes the study and protection of cultural resources.

Arizona Native Plant Society, Box 41206, Sun Station, Tucson, AZ 85717. Dedicated to the appreciation and protection of Arizona's native plants.

National Audubon Society. Phone (480) 829-8209. Promotes conservation of natural resources, with an emphasis on birds.

    Huachuca Chapter, PO Box 63, Sierra Vista, AZ 85636. Phone (520) 432-4634.

    Maricopa Chapter, 3340 West Maricopa Avenue, Phoenix, AZ 85017.

    Northern Arizona Chapter, PO Box 1496, Sedona, AZ 86339.

    Tucson Chapter, 300 E. University Boulevard, Suite 120, Tucson, AZ 85705. Phone (520) 629-0510.

    Yuma Chapter, PO Box 6395, Yuma, AZ 85366. Phone (520) 782-3552.

Friends of Cabeza Prieta, PO Box 65940, Tucson, AZ 85728-4940. Promotes the protection of Cabeza Prieta and the surrounding Sonoran desert.

Glen Canyon Institute, PO Box 1925, Flagstaff, AZ 86002. Phone (520) 556-9311. Web site www.glencanyon.org. Examines the feasibility and desirability of re-establishing a free flowing Colorado River.

Grand Canyon Trust, 2601 N. Fort Valley Road, Flagstaff, AZ 86001. Phone (520) 774-7488. Web site www.grandcanyontrust.org. Dedicated to protecting and restoring the canyon country of the Colorado Plateau.

Southwest Center for Biological Diversity, PO Box 710, Tucson, AZ 85702-0710. Phone (520) 623-5252. Promotes the protection of natural ecosystems and imperiled species through science, education, policy, and environmental law.

The Arizona Nature Conservancy, 300 E. University Boulevard, Suite 230, Tucson, AZ 85705. Phone (520) 622-3861. Devoted to the purchase and preservation of critical wildlife habitat.

The Sky Island Alliance, phone (505) 243-5319. Strives to link parks and isolated protected areas throughout New Mexico, Arizona, and northern Mexico to help re-establish and/or maintain wildlife-migration corridors.

C. Selected Outfitters and Guides

There are many tour operators in Arizona that offer one- to multi-day vehicle tours. A list of these can be secured from the Arizona Department of Tourism, 1100 W. Washington Avenue, Phoenix, AZ 85007. Phone (602) 542-TOUR. The following list includes some of the smaller and/or unique outfitters and guide services available. Additionally many of the local conservation organizations offer tours and programs.

Arizona Ed-Venture Tours. Specializes in ecological, cultural, and historical tourism. PO Box 4317, Prescott, AZ 86302-4137. Phone (520) 541-0734. Web site www.gorp.com/azedventure.

Arizona Raft Adventures. Offers a wide variety of river trips through the Grand Canyon. 4050 E. Huntington Drive, Flagstaff, AZ 86004. Phone (520) 526-8200 or (800) 786-7238. Web site www.azraft.com.

Arizona River Runners. Grand Canyon river trips. PO Box 47788, Phoenix, AZ 85068-7788. Phone (602) 867-4866 or (800) 477- 7238. Web site www.raftarizona.com.

Arizona-Sonora Desert Museum. Offers educational trips and workshops, mostly in southern Arizona. 2021 N. Kinney Road, Tucson, AZ 85743-8918. Phone (520) 883-2702. Web site www.desertmuseum.org.

Buckhorn Llama Company. Offers naturalist-led, llama-supported hikes into various wilderness areas of Arizona. PO Box 343, Bluff, UT 84512. Phone (435) 672-2466.

Canyon Explorations. Grand Canyon river trips. PO Box 310, Flagstaff, AZ 86002. Phone (520) 774-4559 or (800) 654-0723. Web site www.canyonx.com.

Canyoneers, Inc. Grand Canyon river trips. 7195 N. Hwy 89, Flagstaff, AZ 86004. Phone (520) 526-0924.

Chandelle River Tours. Gila River trips. Phone (520) 577-1824 or (800) 242-6335.

Coyote Pass Hospitality. *See* listing under Selected Guest Ranches.

Desert Voyagers. Gila River trips. Phone (602) 998-RAFT or (800) 222-RAFT.

Diamond River Adventures. Grand Canyon river trips. PO Box 1316, Page, AZ 86040. Phone (520) 645-8866 or (800) 343-3121. Web site www.diamondriver.com.

Dolly's Steamboat Tours. Offers 90-minute boat tours on Canyon Lake in the Superstition country. PO Box 977, Apache Junction, AZ 85217. Phone (602) 827-9144.

Don Donnelly Horseback Vacations. *See* listing under Selected Guest Ranches.

Far Flung Adventures. Salt River trips. PO Box 2804, Globe, AZ 85502. Phone (800) 231-7238.

Left-Handed Hunter Tour Company. Cultural tours in Hopiland. PO Box 434, Second Mesa, AZ 86043. Phone (520) 734-2567.

Grand Canyon Dories. Features river trips in wooden dories through the Grand Canyon. PO Box 67, Angels Camp, CA 95222. Phone ((209) 736-0805 or (800) 877-3679. Web site www.oars.com.

Grand Canyon Field Institute. Offers educational hikes, backpacks, llama treks, and other tours in and around the Grand Canyon. PO Box 399, Grand Canyon, AZ 86023. Phone (520) 638-2485. Web site www.thecanyon.com/fieldinstitute.

Hualapai River Runners. Offers Colorado River trips from Diamond Creek to Lake Mead. PO Box 246, Peach Springs, AZ 86434. Phone (520) 769-2210 or (888) 255-9550 or (800) 622-4409. Web site www.arizonaguide.com/grandcanyonwest.

Museum of Northern Arizona. Offers educational trips primarily on the Colorado Plateau. 3101 North Fort Valley Road, Flagstaff, AZ 86001. Phone (520) 774-5211.

Pink Jeep Tours. Informative tours of the Sedona area. PO Box 1447, Sedona, AZ 86339. Phone (520) 282-5000 or (800) 8 SEDONA. Web site www.pinkjeep.com.

Rivers and Oceans. Acts as a booking agent for various Grand Canyon river companies. Phone (520) 526-4575 or (800) 473-4576. Web site www.grand-canyon.az.us/R7O.

Ross Joseyesva. Hopi Reservation tour guide. PO Box 686, Second Mesa, AZ 86043. Phone (520) 734-9565.

Thunderbird Lodge Tours. Offers scheduled half- and full-day jeep tours into Canyon de Chelly. PO Box 548, Chinle, AZ 86503. Phone (520) 674-5443.

Touch the Southwest Tours. Luxury wilderness experiences. 11320 N. Crestview Street, Flagstaff, AZ 86004. Phone (520) 527-0499 or (888) CHILAKO.

Wilderness River Adventures. Offers a one-day flatwater float from Glen Canyon Dam to Lees Ferry at the head of the Grand Canyon. PO Box 717, Page, AZ 86040. Phone (520) 645-3296 or (800) 992-8022. Web site www.riveradventures.com.

D. Map Sources

Arizona Atlas and Gazetteer, DeLorme Mapping, PO Box 298, Freeport, ME 04032. Phone (207) 865-4171. Web site www.delorme.com.

Arizona Geological Survey, 416 West Congress Street, Suite 100, Tucson, AZ 85701. Phone (520) 770-3500. Web site www.azgs.state.az.us.

Arizona Public Lands Information Center, 222 North Central Avenue, Suite 101, Phoenix, AZ 85004-2203. Phone (602) 417-9300. Web site www.publiclands-usa.com. Probably the single best source for all types of Arizona maps. They also carry books and can issue hunting and fishing licenses and national and state park permits.

Bureau of Land Management, State Office, PO Box 16563, Phoenix, AZ 85011. Phone (602) 417-9200.

GTR Mapping, PO Box 1984, Cañon City, CO 81215-1984. Phone (719) 275-8948.

National Geographic Trails Illustrated, phone (800) 962-1643. Web site www.trailillustrated.com.

U.S. Forest Service Southwestern Region, Public Affairs Office, 517 Gold Avenue, SW, Albuquerque, NM 87102. Phone (505) 842-3292.

U.S. Geological Survey, Denver Federal Center, PO Box 25268, Lakewood, CO 80225. Phone (303) 202-4700.

E. Selected Special Events, Fairs, and Festivals

GENERAL

Arizona Office of Tourism, phone (602) 230-7733. Web site www.arizonaguide.com.

JANUARY

New Millennium First People's World's Fair and Powwow. This is a large powwow and craft market held in Tucson. 1st week. Phone (520) 622-4900 or (800) 638-8350.

Quartzsite Gem and Mineral Show. This month-long event attracts about 1 million visitors to Quartzsite. Look for the camel and ostrich races, too. Phone (520) 927-5600.

Sandhill Crane Celebration. Bird-watching, seminars, workshops, and field trips in the Willcox area. 3rd weekend. Phone (520) 384-2272 or (800) 200-2272.

FEBRUARY

Arizona Renaissance Festival. A celebration of medieval theater, crafts, games, food, and costumed performers held near Apache Junction. Month-long. Phone (520) 463-2700.

Flagstaff Winterfest. A month of skiing, sled-dog races, clinics, games, and entertainment in the Flagstaff area. Phone (520) 774-9541 or (800) 842-7293.

O'odham Tash Indian Festival. A large gathering of people from the Tohono O'odham, Gila River, Salt River, Fort McDowell, and Ak Chin reservations. This festival held in Casa Grande includes a parade, powwow, juried arts and crafts exhibits and sales, and traditional foods. 3rd weekend. Phone (520) 836-4723.

Tucson Gem and Mineral Show. Billed as the world's biggest mineral show. 1st and 2nd weeks. Phone (520) 624-1817 or (800) 638-8350.

Yuma Crossing Day. Pioneer craft demonstrations, Indian dances, art exhibits, and music mark this event in Yuma. February 25. Phone (520) 782-0071.

MARCH

National Archaeology Expo. Held at the Arizona State Museum in Tucson, this event features archaeologists who share information about their research and volunteer opportunities. 3rd weekend. Phone (520) 621-6302.

Heard Museum Guild Indian Fair and Market. Southwestern Indian art, crafts, food, and dances at the Heard Museum in Phoenix. 1st weekend. Phone (602) 252-5588.

APRIL

Route 66 Road Rally. Classic and antique cars are gathered in Kingman to celebrate the Mother Road. Phone (520) 753-6106.

Tucson International Mariachi Conference. Concerts, a parade, an art exhibit, and a golf tournament highlight this event. 4th weekend. Phone (520) 884-9920, ext. 243, or (800) 638-8350.

Yaqui Indian Easter Celebration. From Ash Wednesday to Easter Sunday, dancers re-enact the story of the crucifixion. The nearly 300-year-old ceremonies are held in Guadalupe. Phone (602) 252-5588.

MAY

Cinco de Mayo. The Hispanic community of Tucson celebrates May 5, the anniversary of Mexico's 1862 expulsion of the French, through art, music, dances, and food. Phone (520) 624-1817 or (800) 638-8350.

Lake Havasu Striper Derby. Anglers try to catch the big one. Phone (520) 453-3444.

JUNE

Flagstaff's Route 66 Festival. Classic and antique cars are gathered for this celebration of historic Route 66. 3rd and 4th weeks. Phone (520) 779-5300 or (800) 842-7293.

June Bug Blues Festival. Enjoy blues music at this event held in Payson. Phone (520) 474-4515 or (800) 6-PAYSON.

Pine Country Rodeo. A parade, horse racing, and rodeo are the highlights of this event in Flagstaff. 3rd weekend. Phone (520) 774-9541 or (800) 842-7293.

Sharlot Hall Folk Art Fair. This fair in Prescott celebrates pioneer skills with costumed participants demonstrating blacksmithing, woodworking, spinning, weaving, and cowboy cooking. 1st weekend. Phone (520) 445-2000 or (800) 266-7534.

JULY

Frontier Days. Held during the July 4 holiday, this Prescott event is host to the world's oldest rodeo, a parade, a Western art show, entertainment, dances, and fireworks. Phone (520) 445-2000 or (800) 266-7534.

Square Dance Festival. Break out your dancing shoes for this annual event in Show Low. 2nd weekend. Phone (520) 537-2326 or (888) SHOW LOW.

AUGUST

Arizona Cowboy Poets Gathering. Poetry readings, yodeling, and old-time cowboy singing highlight this event held at the Sharlot Hall Museum in Prescott. 2nd week. Phone (520) 445-3122.

Fiesta de San Agustin. Tucson's patron saint is honored through music, dancing, and food. Phone (520) 624-1817 or (800) 638-8350.

Southwest Wings Birding Festival. Field trips, presentations, animal exhibits, and arts and crafts highlight this event in Sierra Vista. Mid-month. Phone (520) 378-0233 or (800) 946-4777.

SEPTEMBER

Flagstaff Festival of Science. Field trips, hands-on exhibits, museum open houses, and lectures. From the last weekend through 1st week of October. Phone (800) 842-7293.

Mexican Independence Day Celebration. A traditional Mexican fiesta held in Tucson with folkloric dancers, music, arts, and food on or near September 17. Phone (520) 624-1817 or (800) 638-8350.

Santa Cruz County Fair. This fair held in Nogales boasts a cowchip-chucking contest, fiddlers' competition, rooster-crowing contest, as well as the usual fair agricultural products. Phone (520) 287-3685.

OCTOBER

Arizona State Fair. Held in Phoenix, this fair features the state's best in agriculture, livestock, and home crafts, along with concerts and carnival rides. 2nd, 3rd, and 4th weeks. Phone (602) 252-6771.

Cowboy Artists of America Exhibition. The Phoenix Art Museum displays the best in cowboy art. Phone (602) 252-5588.

La Fiesta de los Chiles. This fiesta celebrates the chili pepper with entertainment, food, and crafts at the Tucson Botanical Gardens. 4th weekend. Phone (520) 326-9686 or (800) 638-8350.

Sedona Arts Festival. Native American and western art are highlighted. Phone (520) 445-2000 or (800) 266-7534.

NOVEMBER

Hot Air Balloon Race. Held near Phoenix. Phone (602) 252-5588.

Western Music Festival. Western musicians from around the country gather in Tucson to make music and hold workshops. 3rd week. Phone (520) 743-9794 or (800) 638-8350.

DECEMBER

Fall Festival of the Arts. This Tempe event is the largest arts and crafts exhibition held in the Southwest. 1st weekend. Phone (480) 967-4871.

Tumacacori Fiesta. Indian dances, crafts, and food mark this celebration held at Tumacacori National Historic Park. 1st weekend. Phone (520) 398-2341.

Wahweap Festival of Lights Parade. Boats decorated for the holidays float across Lake Powell. Phone (520) 645-2741.

F. Selected Guest Ranches and Other Unique Accommodations

For more information on unique accommodations, contact one of these groups: Arizona Dude Ranch Association, PO Box 603, Cortaro, AZ 85652. Arizona Association of Bed and Breakfast Inns, PO Box 7186, Phoenix, AZ 85011-7186. Phone (800) 284-2589. Mi Casa, Su Casa Bed and Breakfast Reservation Service, PO Box 950, Tempe, AZ 85280-0950. Phone (602) 990-0682 or (800) 456-0682.

Bar 10 Ranch. This is the only guest ranch in the new Grand Canyon-Parashant Canyon National Monument. The ranch caters mainly to those river rafters who end their Colorado River trip through the Grand Canyon at Whitmore Wash, but the ranch is open to anyone. Open April through November, but off-season dates may also be arranged. PO Box 1465, St. George, UT 84771. Phone (435) 628-4010 or (800) 582-4139.

Circle Z Ranch. A guest ranch since 1926, Circle Z Ranch is situated at 4,000 feet in the Santa Rita Mountains. Equestrians follow trails in the foothills or along Sonoita Creek. There are excellent birding opportunities and overnight pack trips are available. Open November to mid-May. PO Box 194AZ, Patagonia, AZ 85624. Phone (888) 854-2525. Web site www.circlez.com.

Coyote Pass Hospitality. Minutes from Canyon de Chelly National Monument is this unique hogan bed and breakfast run by Navajo cultural consultant William Tsosie. Guests stay in a traditional hogan, eat typical Navajo foods, and learn about the Navajo culture through storytelling and custom tours of the area. PO Box 91-B, Tsaile, AZ 86556. Phone (520) 724-3383.

Don Donnelly's Horseback Vacations. This outfit differs from the usual guest ranch experience in that it is mobile. A first-class tented camp with sturdy cots, walk-in tents, hot showers, and incredible meals is set up in various locations across Arizona. Monument Valley, the Superstition Wilderness, the Chiricahuas, the San Rafael Valley, and White Mountains are some this company's favorite areas to ride. 6010 S. Kings Ranch Road, Gold Canyon, AZ 85219. Phone (480) 982-7822 or (800) 346-4403. Web site www.dondonnelly.com.

Elk Horn Ranch. Located just north of the Mexico border, 51 miles southwest of Tucson, not far from Baboquivari Peak. This 10,000-acre guest ranch has been in operation by the Miller family since 1945. The ranch can accommodate 32 guests, has a swimming pool and tennis courts, and emphasizes trail rides. Open mid-November through April. HC1 Box 97, Tucson, AZ 85736. Phone (520) 822-1040. Web site www.guestranches.com/Elkhorn.

Flying E Ranch. This guest ranch, set in the desert hills of the Hassayampa Valley, is not far from famed Vulture Peak, where Henry Wickenburg discovered gold in 1863. Thirty-four guests can enjoy home-style cooking, a heated swimming pool, an exercise room, a sauna, tennis courts, and, of course trail riding. Open November to May. 2801 W. Wickenburg Way, Wickenburg, AZ 85390-1087. Phone (520) 684-2690 or (888) 684-2650. Web site www.flyingeranch.com.

Grapevine Canyon Ranch. Nestled in the rugged Dragoon Mountains, about 80 miles southeast of Tucson, is the Grapevine Canyon Ranch. The ranch owners, Eve and Gerry Searle, aim to make each guest's vacation a special occasion. The ranch boasts first-class accommodations, three tasty, country-style meals a day, and a riding program tailored to all experience levels. Guests can occasionally participate in cattle work and horsemanship clinics. Open year-round. PO Box 302, Pearce, AZ 85625. Phone (520) 826-3185 or (800) 245-9202. Web site www.gcranch.com.

Horseshoe Ranch. Saddle up and do cowboy chores: Search, gather, drive, brand, and doctor cattle the way it has been done for more than 100 years on the Horseshoe Ranch. Over 1,600 head of cattle graze on 100 square miles of mountains, mesas, and canyons near Cordes Junction. Open September to November and March to May. HCR 34, Box 5005, Mayer, AZ 86333. Phone (520) 632-8813 or (520) 713- 4219. Web site www.horseshoeranch.net.

Ironhorse Ranch. Ironhorse Ranch, located in the San Pedro River valley, is a working cattle ranch. The ranch is open year-round and within easy driving distance of many attractions such as Tombstone, the Chiricahua Mountains, Cochise Stronghold, Saguaro National Park, and Kartchner Caverns State Park. PO Box 536, Tombstone, AZ 85638. Phone (520) 457-9361. Web site www.ironhorseranch.com.

Kay El Bar Ranch. This small ranch is on the National Register of Historic Places and has been welcoming guests since 1926. Professional wranglers guide guests through thousands of acres of open desert not far from Wickenburg. Open mid-October to May. PO Box 2480, Wickenburg, AZ 85358. Phone (520) 684-7593 or (800) 684-7583. Web site www.kayelbar.com.

Lazy K Bar Ranch. Located near Tucson, this small, intimate guest ranch has been in operation since 1936. The ranch offers trails rides in desert and mountain plus weekly picnic rides into the Saguaro National Park. Amenities include a swimming pool, spa, tennis courts, mountain bikes, and trap shooting. Open mid-September to mid-June. 8401 N. Scenic Drive, Tucson, AZ 85743. Phone (520) 744-3050 or (800) 321-7018. Web site www. lazykbar.com.

Merv Griffin's Wickenburg Inn & Dude Ranch. Located an hour northwest of Phoenix, not far outside of Wickenburg is this popular guest ranch. Besides swimming pools and spas, it offers an arts and crafts studio, mountain biking, jeep tours, and a resident naturalist. 34801 North Hwy 89, Wickenburg, AZ 85390. Phone (520) 684-7811 or (800) 942-5362. Web site www.merv.com.

Price Canyon Ranch. The 100-year-old ranch headquarters are at an elevation of 5,600 feet in the Chiricahua Mountains, offering four moderate seasons for riding or relaxing by the pool. Open year-round. PO Box 1065, Douglas, AZ 85608. Phone (520) 558-2383.

Rancho de la Osa. A trading post built in 1725 by Franciscan padres is now part of this guest ranch bordering the state of Sonora, Mexico. The nearby Baboquivari Mountains and Buenos Aires National Wildlife Refuge invite exploration by foot, horseback, or mountain bike. Guests stay in territorial-style adobe rooms, each with a fireplace and furnished with Mexican antiques. Open year-round. PO Box 1, Sasabe, AZ 85633. Phone (520) 823-4257 or (800) 872-6240. Web site www.guestranches.com/ranchodelosa.

Rancho de los Caballeros. This guest ranch has it all, including a guest rodeo, a resident tennis pro, a trap and skeet area, and even a golf course. Open October to May. 1551 Vulture Mine Road, Wickenburg, AZ 85390. Phone (520) 684-5484 or (800) 684-5030. Web site www.SunC.com.

Sprucedale Ranch. Unlike most of Arizona's guest ranches, which are located in desert country, Sprucedale Ranch is nestled in the pine country of the White Mountains. Horseback riding is the main activity at the ranch. The Wiltbank family raises and trains its own horses and will choose the right mount for you. The guest cabins are rustic with modern conveniences. Open end of May to October. Summer address: HC 61, Box 10, Alpine, AZ 85920. Winter address: PO Box 880, Eager, AZ 85925. Phone (520) 333-4984. Web site www.sprucedaleranch.com.

Tanque Verde Ranch. This historic working ranch is in the foothills of the Rincon Mountains and borders Saguaro National Park and Coronado National Forest. Your hosts combine the adventurous lifestyle of the Old West with all the comfort and amenities of a world-class resort. Open year-round. 14301 E. Speedway, Tucson, AZ 85748. Phone (520) 296-6275 or (800) 234-DUDE. Web site www.tvgr.com.

The White Stallion Ranch. This working ranch borders Saguaro National Park and offers fast and slow rides along miles of scenic trails. Ranch facilities include a swimming pool, hot tub, tennis courts, shuffleboard, horseshoes, and pocket billiards. Open September through May. 9251 W. Twin Peaks Road, Tucson, AZ 85743. Phone (520) 297-0252 or (888) WSRANCH. Web site www.wsranch.com.

G. Campgrounds

Coconino National Forest Campgrounds

Name	Location	Phone (520)	Elevation	Season	Fee	Campsites	Drinking Water	Boating	Fishing
Bonito	18 mi NE of Flagstaff, US 89 & FR 545	526-0866	6,900	Mar-Oct	Y	44	Y	N	N
Little Elden Springs	5 mi NE of Flagstaff, US 89 & FR 556	526-0866	7,200	May-Sept	Y	16	Y	N	N
Lakeview	16 mi SE of Flagstaff, FH 3	774-1147	6,900	May-Oct	Y	30	Y	Y	Y
Pine Grove	19 mi SE of Flagstaff, FH 3	774-1147	7,000	May-Oct	Y	46	Y	Y	Y
Ashurst Lake	20 mi SE of Flagstaff, FH 3 & FR 82E	774-1147	7,000	May-Sept	Y	40	Y	Y	Y
Forked Pine	20 mi SE of Flagstaff, FH 3 & FR 82E	774-1147	7,100	May-Sept	Y	25	Y	Y	Y
Dairy Springs	28 mi SE of Flagstaff, FR 90	774-1147	7,000	May-Sept	Y	27	Y	Y	Y
Double Springs	29 mi SE of Flagstaff, FR 90	774-1147	7,000	May-Sept	Y	16	Y	Y	Y
Kinnikinick	33 mi SE of Flagstaff, FH 3 & FR 82	774-1147	7,000	May-Sept	N	18	N	N	Y
Clint's Well	15 mi S of Happy Jack, AZ 87 & FH 3	477-2255	7,000	May-Nov	N	12	N	N	N
Kehl Springs	29 mi S of Happy Jack, AZ 87 & FR 300	477-2255	7,500	May-Sept	N	8	N	N	N
Blue Ridge	1 mi W of Blue Ridge off of AZ 87	477-2255	7,300	May-Sept	Y	10	Y	N	Y
Rock Crossing	3 mi W of Blue Ridge, 2 mi S on FR 751	477-2255	7,500	May-Sept	Y	35	Y	Y	Y
Knoll Lake	23 mi S of Blue Ridge, FR 295	477-2255	7,400	May-Sept	Y	33	Y	Y	Y
Manzanita	6.3 mi N of Sedona, AZ 89A in Oak Creek Canyon	282-4119	4,800	Jan-Dec	Y	19	Y	N	Y
Banjo Bill	8.2 mi N of Sedona, AZ 89A in Oak Creek Canyon	282-4119	5,100	Mar-Oct	Y	8	Y	N	Y
Bootlegger	8.9 mi N of Sedona, AZ 89A in Oak Creek Canyon	282-4119	5,200	Mar-Oct	Y	10	N	N	Y
Cave Springs	11.6 mi N of Sedona, AZ 89A in Oak Creek Canyon	282-4119	5,400	Apr-Sept	Y	78	Y	N	Y
Pine Flat	12.6 mi N of Sedona, AZ 89A in Oak Creek Canyon	282-4119	5,500	Mar-Nov	Y	58	Y	N	Y
Beaver Creek	3 mi SE of junction of AZ 179 & I 17	282-4119	3,800	All Year	Y	13	Y	N	Y
Clear Creek	6 mi SE of Camp Verde, AZ 260 & FR 626	282-4119	3,200	All Year	Y	18	Y	N	N

Kaibab National Forest Campgrounds

Name	Location	Phone (520)	Elevation	Season	Fee	Campsites	Drinking Water	Boating	Fishing
White Horse Lake	19 mi S of Williams	635-2633	6,600	May-Oct	Y	94	Y	Y	Y
Cataract Canyon	1 mi W of Williams	635-2633	6,800	May-Oct	N	18	Y	N	Y
Kaibab Lake	4 mi NE of Williams	635-2633	6,800	May-Oct	Y	72	Y	Y	Y
Dogtown Lake	8 mi SW of Williams	635-2633	7,000	Apr-Nov	Y	51	Y	Y	Y

Apache-Sitgreaves National Forests Campgrounds

Name	Location	Phone (520)	Elevation	Season	Fee	Campsites	Drinking Water	Boating	Fishing
Alpine Divide	4 mi N of Alpine, US 191	339-4384	8,500	May-Oct	Y	12	Y	N	Y
Blue Crossing	22 mi SE of Alpine, US 180, FR 281	339-4384	5,800	May-Oct	N	4	N	N	Y
Buffalo Crossing	24 mi SW of Alpine, US 191, FR 26, FR 24	339-4384	7,600	May-Oct	N	16	N	N	Y
West Fork	29 mi SW of Alpine, US 191, FR 26, FR 24, FR 25, FR 89	339-4384	7,740	May-Oct	N	60	N	N	Y
Aspen	19 mi SW of Alpine, US 191, FR 249, FR 276	339-4384	7,780	May-Oct	N	6	N	N	Y
Deer Creek	20 mi SW of Alpine, US 191, FR 249, FR 276	339-4384	7,645	May-Oct	N	6	N	N	Y
Raccoon	20 mi SW of Alpine, US 191, FFR 249, FR 276	339-4384	7,600	May-Oct	N	10	N	N	Y
Diamond Rock	17 mi SW of Alpine, US 191, FR 249, FR 276	339-4384	7,900	May-Oct	N	12	Y	N	Y
Hannagan	23 mi SW of Alpine, US 191	339-4384	9,100	May-Oct	N	8	Y	N	N
KP Cienega	29 mi SW of Alpine, US 191, FR 155	339-4384	9,000	May-Sept	N	5	Y	N	Y
Luna Lake	6 mi SE of Alpine, US 180, FR 570	339-4384	8,000	May-Sept	Y	51	Y	Y	Y

Apache-Sitgreaves National Forests Campgrounds (cont.)

Name	Location	Elevation	Phone (520)	Season	Fee	Campsites	Drinking Water	Boating	Fishing
Upper Blue	17 mi SE of Alpine, US 180, FR 281	6,200	339-4384	May-Oct	N	3	Y	N	Y
Horse Springs	22 mi SW of Alpine, US 191, FR 249, FR 276	7,600	339-4384	May-Oct	N	27	Y	N	Y
Granville	16 mi N of Clifton, US 191	6,600	687-1301	May-Sept	N	11	Y	N	N
Honeymoon	50 mi NW of Clifton, US 191, FR 217	5,400	687-1301	May-Dec	N	5	N	N	Y
Lower & Upper Juan Miller	27 mi N of Clifton, US 191, FR 475	5,700	687-1301	All Year	N	8	N	N	N
Stray Horse	26 mi S of Alpine, US 191	7,800	687-1301	May-Nov	N	7	Y	N	N
Coal Creek	19 mi SE of Clifton, US 191, AZ 78	5,900	687-1301	All Year	N	5	N	N	N
Black Jack	14 mi SE of Clifton, US 191, AZ 78	6,300	687-1301	All Year	N	10	N	N	N
Chevelon Crossing	18 mi NW of Heber, AZ 260, FR 504	6,300	535-4481	All Year	N	6	N	N	Y
Aspen	27 mi SW of Heber, AZ 260, FR 300, FR 105	7,600	535-4481	May-Oct	Y	136	Y	Y	Y
Spillway	27 mi SW of Heber, AZ 260, FR 300, FR 105	7,500	535-4481	May-Oct	Y	26	Y	Y	Y
Crook	27 mi SW of Heber, AZ 260, FR 300, FR 105	7,500	535-4481	May-Oct	Y	26	Y	Y	Y
Mogollon	27 mi SW of Heber, AZ 260, FR 300	7,600	535-4481	May-Oct	Y	26	Y	Y	Y
Black Canyon Rim	15 mi SW of Heber, AZ 260, FR 300	7,600	535-4481	May-Oct	Y	21	Y	Y	Y
Canyon Point	17 mi SW of Heber, AZ 260	7,600	535-4481	May-Oct	Y	118	Y	N	N
Gentry	17 mi SW of Heber, AZ 260, FR 300	7,700	535-4481	May-Oct	N	6	N	N	N
Sink Hole	22 mi SW of Heber, AZ 260, FR 149	7,500	535-4481	May-Oct	Y	26	Y	Y	Y
Rim	26 mi SW of Heber, AZ 260, FR 300	7,500	535-4481	May-Oct	Y	26	Y	N	Y
Benney Creek	2 mi N of Greer, AZ 373	8,300	333-4372	Mar-Dec	Y	24	Y	Y	Y
Brook Char	27 mi SW of Springerville, AZ 260, AZ 273, FR 113, FR 115	9,100	333-4372	May-Oct	Y	12	Y	Y	Y
Cutthroat	27 mi SW of Springerville, AZ 260, AZ 273, FR 113, FR 115	9,100	333-4372	May-Oct	Y	18	Y	Y	Y
Grayling	27 mi SW of Springerville, AZ 260, AZ 273, FR 113, FR 115	9,200	333-4372	May-Oct	Y	23	Y	Y	Y
Rainbow	27 mi SW of Springerville, AZ 260, AZ 273, FR 113, FR 115	9,200	333-4372	May-Oct	Y	152	Y	Y	Y
Gabaldon	12 mi SW of Greer, AZ 373, FR 87, AZ 273	9,400	333-4372	Apr-Nov	N	5	N	N	Y
Rolfe C. Hoyer	1 mi N of Greer, AZ 373	8,300	333-4372	May-Oct	Y	100	Y	N	Y
South Fork	8 mi W of Eagar, AZ 260, FR 560	7,600	333-4372	All Year	Y	12	N	N	Y
Winn	12 mi SW of Greer, AZ 373, FR 87, AZ 273, FR 554	9,300	333-4372	Apr-Nov	Y	63	Y	N	N
Fool Hollow Lake	1 mi NW Show Low, FR 137	6,300	368-5111	All Year	Y	125	Y	Y	Y
Lakeside	In Lakeside	7,000	368-5111	May-Sept	Y	82	Y	Y	Y
Los Burros	7 mi N of McNary, FR 224	7,900	368-5111	May-Oct	N	10	N	N	N
Scott Reservoir	In Lakeside	7,000	368-5111	Apr-Oct	N	15	N	Y	Y
Granite Campground	5 mi NW of Prescott on CR 10, 3 mi N on FR 374	5,600	445-7253	All Year	Y	14	Y	Y	Y
Groom Cr. Horse Camp	7 mi S of Prescott on CR 56 (Senator Hwy)	6,000	445-7253	Seasonal	Y	37	Y	N	N
Hazlett Hollow	7 mi SE of Crown King on FR 52 (Horsethief RD)	6,000	445-7253	Seasonal	Y	15	Y	N	N
Hilltop	5 mi E of Prescott on AZ 69, 4 mi S on CR 57	5,700	445-7253	Seasonal	Y	38	Y	N	N
Indian Creek	4.5 mi SW of Prescott on AZ 89, .5 mi SE on CR 102	5,800	445-7253	Seasonal	Y	27	Y	Y	Y
Kentuck Springs	8 mi SE of Crown King on FR 52	6,000	445-7253	Seasonal	N	15	N	N	N
Lower Wolf Creek	7.5 mi S of Prescott on CR 56, 1.5 mi W on CR 101	6,000	445-7253	Seasonal	N	20	N	N	N
Lynx Lake	5 mi E of Prescott on AZ 69, 3 mi S on CR 57	5,600	445-7253	Seasonal	Y	39	Y	Y	Y

Name	Location	Elevation	Phone (520)	Season	Fee	Campsites	Drinking Water	Boating	Fishing
Prescott National Forest Campgrounds									
White Spar	2 mi S of Prescott on AZ 89	5,700	445-7253	Seasonal	Y	61	Y	N	N
Yavapai	5 mi NW of Prescott on CR 10, 2 mi N on FR 374	5,600	445-7253	All Year	Y	25	Y	N	N
Mingus Mountain	9 mi SW of Jerome on AZ 89A, 3 mi SE on FR 104	7,600	567-4121	Seasonal	N	24	N	N	N
Potato Patch	7 mi SW of Jerome on AZ 89A, .5 mi NW on FR 106	7,000	567-4121	Seasonal	Y	30	Y	N	N
Powell Springs	13 mi NE of Dewey on AZ 169, 4 mi N on CR 75	5,300	567-4121	All Year	N	10	N	N	N
Tonto National Forest Campgrounds									
Seven Springs	18 mi NE of Carefree, FR 24	3,300	595-3300	All Year	N	23	N	N	N
CCC	18.5 mi NE of Carefree, FR 24	3,300	595-3300	All Year	N	16	N	N	N
Horseshoe	23 mi. E of Carefree, 7 mi FR 24, 6 mi FR 19, 10 mi FR 205, .5 mi FR 205A	1,900	595-3300	All Year	Y	12	N	Y	Y
Riverside	22 mi E of Carefree, 7 mi FR 24, 16 mi FR 19	1,600	595-3300	All Year	Y	12	N	Y	Y
Mesquite	22 mi E of Carefree, 7 mi FR 24, 6 mi FR 19, 9 mi FR 205	1,900	595-3300	All Year	Y	12	N	Y	Y
Needle Rock	24 mi SE of Carefree, 6 mi Scottsdale Rd, 15 mi Dynamite Rd/Rio Verde Dr, 3 mi FR 20	1,550	595-3300	All Year	Y	10	N	Y	Y
Oak Flat	4 mi E of Superior, US 60	4,200	520-402-6200	All Year	N	16	N	N	N
Devil's Canyon	6 mi E of Superior, US 60	4,000	402-6200	All Year	N	5	N	N	N
Sulphide del Rey	10 mi SW of Globe, 2.5 mi FR 112, 651, 2.5 mi FR 55, 5.5 mi FR	6,000	402-6200	Apr-Nov	N	10	N	N	N
Pinal & Upper Pinal	15 mi SW of Globe, 2.5 mi FR 112, 651, 2.5 mi FR 55, 10 mi FR	7,500	402-6200	May-Nov	N	19	Y	N	N
Pioneer Pass	9 mi S of Globe, FR 112	6,000	402-6200	May-Nov	N	25	N	N	N
Kellner	6 mi SW of Globe, 2.4 mi FR 112, 2.7 mi FR 55	4,500	402-6200	All Year	N	4	N	N	N
Jones Water	17 mi NE of Globe, US 60	4,500	402-6200	All Year	N	12	N	N	N
Bagley Flat	35 mi NE of Mesa, 27 mi AZ 87, 4 mi FR 204, 4 mi by boat	1,500	379-6446	All Year	N	30	N	Y	Y
The Point	17 mi NE of Apache Jct, 14 mi AZ 88, 3 mi by boat	1,700	379-6446	All Year	N	3	N	Y	Y
Tortilla	18 mi NE of Apache Jct, AZ 88	1,800	379-6446	Oct-Apr	Y	77	Y	Y	Y
Houston Mesa	N edge of Payson, FR 199	5,100	474-7900	All Year	Y	105	Y	N	N
Christopher Creek	19 mi NE of Payson, 20.8 mi AZ 260, .2 mi FR 159	5,800	474-7900	May-Oct	Y	43	Y	N	Y
Lower Tonto Creek	15 mi NE of Payson, AZ 260	5,600	474-7900	Apr-Nov	Y	17	Y	N	Y
Upper Tonto Creek	16 mi NE of Payson, 16 mi AZ 260, 1 mi FR 289	5,600	474-7900	Apr-Nov	Y	9	Y	N	Y
Ponderosa	12 mi NE of Payson, AZ 260	5,600	474-7900	All Year	Y	61	Y	N	N
Rose Creek	40 mi NE of Globe, 15 mi AZ 88, 25 mi AZ 288, .5 mi FR 152	5,400	462-4300	Apr-Nov	N	5	Y	N	N
Valentine Ridge	41 mi E of Payson, 33 mi AZ 260, 6 mi FR 512, 2 mi FR 188	6,700	462-4300	Apr-Nov	N	9	N	N	N
Burnt Corral	6 mi SW of Roosevelt, AZ 88	1,900	467-3200	All Year	Y	79	N	Y	Y
Indian Point	8 mi SE of Punkin Center, 4 mi AZ 188, 2 mi FR 60, 2 mi FR 661	2,200	467-3200	All Year	Y	90	Y	Y	Y
Cholla	7 mi NW of Roosevelt, 2 mi AZ 88, 5 mi AZ 188	2,100	467-3200	All Year	Y	200	Y	Y	Y
Lakeview Trailer Park	At Roosevelt, AZ 88	2,100	467-3200	All Year	Y	10	Y	Y	Y
Windy Hill	6 mi E of Roosevelt, 3 mi AZ 88, 3 mi FR 82	2,100	467-3200	All Year	Y	346	Y	Y	Y
Schoolhouse	11 mi E of Roosevelt, 7 mi AZ 88, 4 mi FR 447	2,100	467-3200	Year Round	Y	200	Y	Y	Y

Coronado National Forest Campgrounds

Name	Location	Elevation	Phone (520)	Season	Fee	Campsites	Drinking Water	Boating	Fishing
Pinery Canyon	18 mi W of Portal, FR 42	7,000	364-3468	Apr-Nov	N	4	N	N	N
Rustler Park	18 mi W of Portal, FR 42	8,500	364-3468	Apr-Nov	Y	22	Y	N	N
Herb Martyr	6 mi SW of Portal, FR 42	5,800	364-3468	Jan-Dec	N	5	N	N	N
John Hands	5 mi SW of Portal, FR 42	5,600	364-3468	Jan-Dec	N	5	Y	N	N
Sunny Flat	3 mi SW of Portal, FR 42	5,200	364-3468	Jan-Dec	Y	11	Y	N	N
Stewart	2 mi SW of Portal, FR 42	5,100	364-3468	Mar-Oct	Y	6	Y	N	N
Idlewilde	2 mi SW of Portal, FR 42	5,000	364-3468	Mar-Oct	Y	10	Y	N	N
Cochise Stronghold	7 mi W of Sunsites, US 191 & FR 84	5,000	364-3468	Jan-Dec	Y	18	Y	N	N
Bathtub	24 mi E of Elfrida, US 191 & FR 74	6,300	364-3468	Mar-Oct	Y	11	Y	N	N
Rucker Forest Camp	24 mi E of Elfrida, US 191 & FR 74	6,500	364-3468	Mar-Oct	Y	14	Y	N	N
Rucker Lake	24 mi E of Elfrida, US 191 & FR 74	6,300	364-3468	Mar-Oct	N	8	N	N	N
Cypress Park	24 mi E of Elfrida, US 191 & FR 74	6,000	364-3468	Mar-Oct	Y	7	Y	N	N
Sycamore	23 mi SE of Willcox, AZ 186 & 181, FR 41	6,200	364-3468	Jan-Dec	N	5	N	N	N
West Turkey Creek	23 mi SE of Willcox, AZ 186 & 181, FR 41	5,900	364-3468	Jan-Dec	N	4	N	N	N
White Rock	16 mi NW of Nogales, I-19 & AZ 289	4,000	281-2296	Jan-Dec	Y	15	Y	N	N
Calabasas	16 mi NW of Nogales, I-19 & AZ 289	4,000	281-2296	Jan-Dec	Y	12	N	N	N
Bog Springs	16 mi SE of Green Valley, I-19, FR 62, FR 70	5,600	281-2296	Jan-Dec	Y	13	Y	N	N
Lakeview	28 mi SE of Sonoita, AZ 83	5,400	378-0311	Jan-Dec	Y	65	Y	Y	Y
Reef Townsite	14 mi SW of Sierra Vista, AZ 92, FR 368	7,200	378-0311	Jan-Dec	Y	14	Y	N	N
Ramsey Vista	14 mi SW of Sierra Vista, AZ 92, FR 368	7,200	378-0311	Jan-Dec	Y	8	N	N	N
Arcadia	19 mi SW of Safford, US 191 & AZ 366	6,700	428-4150	Jan-Dec	Y	19	Y	N	N
Shannon	30 mi SW of Safford, US 191 & AZ 366	9,100	428-4150	May-Oct	Y	11	Y	N	N
Hospital Flat	31 mi SW of Safford, US 191 & AZ 366	9,000	428-4150	May-Sept	Y	10	Y	N	N
Cunningham	33 mi SW of Safford, US 191 & AZ 366	9,000	428-4150	May-Oct	Y	10	Y	N	N
Columbine Corrals	36 mi SW of Safford, US 191 & AZ 366	9,600	428-4150	May-Oct	Y	6	Y	N	N
Soldier Creek	37 mi SW of Safford, US 191 & AZ 366	9,300	428-4150	May-Sept	Y	12	Y	N	N
Riggs Flat	41 mi SW of Safford, US 191 & AZ 366	8,500	428-4150	May-Oct	Y	26	Y	Y	Y
Molino	18 mi NE of Tucson, Catalina Hwy, MP 6	4,500	749-8700	Oct-Apr	Y	37	N	N	N
Prison Camp	19 mi NE of Tucson, Catalina Hwy, MP 7	4,900	749-8700	Jan-Dec	N	8	N	N	N
General Hitchcock	25 mi NE of Tucson, Catalina Hwy, MP 12	6,000	749-8700	Apr-Oct	Y	12	N	N	N
Rose Canyon	29 mi NE of Tucson, Catalina Hwy, MP 17	7,000	749-8700	Apr-Oct	Y	74	Y	N	Y
Spencer Canyon	39 mi NE of Tucson, Catalina Hwy, MP 22	7,800	749-8700	Apr-Oct	Y	62	Y	N	N
Catalina State Park	10 mi N of Tucson, Oracle Road	2,700	749-8700	Jan-Dec	Y	48	Y	Y	N
Peppersauce	15 SE of Oracle, FR 382	4,700	749-8700	Jan-Dec	Y	17	Y	N	N

G. Glossary

Alluvial fan—The cone-shaped deposit of gravel and finer sediments at the base of a mountain range where a stream runs out onto a level plain.

Atlatl—A spear throwing device; a short stick that is held in the hand to make one's arm longer and give one a better mechanical advantage in throwing the spear.

Bajada—The nearly flat surface created by confluent alluvial fans along the base of a mountain range.

Basalt—Any fine-grained, dark-colored igneous rock.

Cinder cone—A conical-shaped volcano composed of volcanic ash and clinkerlike material.

Coniferous—A plant that bears cones.

Deciduous—A plant that sheds its leaves in a specific season, usually autumn.

Endemic—An organism that is native or confined to a restricted area.

Evergreen—A plant with foliage that is green throughout the year.

Hogan—A traditional one-room house, usually made of juniper logs and clay, built by Navajos.

Igneous rock—Rock formed by the cooling and hardening of magma within the earth's crust or on the surface.

Life zones—Vertically arranged, major communities of plant and animal life, especially seen in western North America landscapes.

Metamorphic rock—Rock that has been changed by heat and pressure, but not melted.

Monocline—A bend in rock strata that is usually flat-lying except in the flexure itself.

Mutualistic—A close relationship between two or more organisms where all benefit from the relationship.

National monument—An area of historic, scenic, and/or natural significance set aside by presidential proclamation.

National park—An area of historic, scenic, and/or natural significance designated by the U.S. Congress.

Peneplain—A land surface worn down by erosion to a nearly flat plain.

Pit house—A partially subterranean house, made of logs, sticks, brush, and mud, built by prehistoric Indians.

Pueblo—A community dwelling, usually of several stories, made of stone and adobe and lived in by Southwestern Indians.

Pyroclasts—Fragments of volcanic rock that are explosively ejected from a volcano.

Relict—A plant or animal from an earlier time surviving in an environment that has undergone considerable change.

Sedimentary rock—Rock formed by the cementing together of sediments (e.g., sandstone made of quartz grains) or by chemical precipitation from solution (e.g., travertine formed at a spring).

Stratovolcano—A volcano composed of alternating layers of pyroclastic materials and lava.

Symbiotic—The close relationship between two or more organisms, which may be but is not necessarily of benefit to each.

Travertine—A mineral composed of calcium carbonate (limestone) that is formed from solution in ground and surface waters.

Tuff—An igneous rock formed from compacted small volcanic fragments, generally less than 4 millimeters in diameter.

Index